CHURCH DO

KARL BARTH

CHURCH DOGMATICS

VOLUME I

THE DOCTRINE
OF THE WORD OF GOD

§ 16–18

THE REVELATION OF GOD: THE OUTPOURING
OF THE HOLY SPIRIT

EDITED BY
G. W. BROMILEY
T. F. TORRANCE

t&t clark

Published by T&T Clark

A Continuum Imprint

The Tower Building, 11 York Road, London, SE1 7NX

80 Maiden Lane, Suite 704, New York, NY 10038

www.continuumbooks.com

Translated by G. W. Bromiley, G. T. Thomson, Harold Knight

British Library Cataloguing-in-Publication Data
A catalogue record for this book is available from the British Library

ISBN13: 978-0-567-18081-0

Typeset by Interactive Sciences Ltd, Gloucester, and Newgen Imaging Systems Pvt Ltd, Chennai
Printed and bound in Great Britain by CPI Antony Rowe, Chippenham, Wiltshire

PUBLISHER'S PREFACE TO
THE STUDY EDITION

Since the publication of the first English translation of *Church Dogmatics I.1* by Professor Thomson in 1936, T&T Clark has been closely linked with Karl Barth. An authorised translation of the whole of the *Kirchliche Dogmatik* was begun in the 1950s under the editorship of G. W. Bromiley and T. F. Torrance, a work which eventually replaced Professor Thomson's initial translation of *CD I.1*.

T&T Clark is now happy to present to the academic community this new *Study Edition* of the *Church Dogmatics*. Its aim is mainly to make this major work available to a generation of students and scholars with less familiarity with Latin, Greek, and French. For the first time this edition therefore presents the classic text of the translation edited by G. W. Bromiley and T. F. Torrance incorporating translations of the foreign language passages in Editorial Notes on each page.

The main body of the text remains unchanged. Only minor corrections with regard to grammar or spelling have been introduced. The text is presented in a new reader friendly format. We hope that the breakdown of the *Church Dogmatics* into 31 shorter fascicles will make this edition easier to use than its predecessors.

Completely new indexes of names, subjects and scriptural indexes have been created for the individual volumes of the *Study Edition*.

The publishers would like to thank the Center for Barth Studies at Princeton Theological Seminary for supplying a digital edition of the text of the *Church Dogmatics* and translations of the Greek and Latin quotations in the original T&T Clark edition made by Simon Gathercole and Ian McFarland.

London, April 2010

HOW TO USE THIS
STUDY EDITION

The *Study Edition* follows Barth's original volume structure. Individual paragraphs and sections should be easy to locate. A synopsis of the old and new edition can be found on the back cover of each fascicle.

All secondary literature on the *Church Dogmatics* currently refers to the classic 14-volume set (e.g. II.2 p. 520). In order to avoid confusion, we recommend that this practice should be kept for references to this *Study Edition*. The page numbers of the old edition can be found in the margins of this edition.

CONTENTS

§ 16–18

THE FREEDOM OF MAN FOR GOD

According to Holy Scripture God's revelation occurs in our enlightenment by the Holy Spirit of God to a knowledge of His Word. The outpouring of the Holy Spirit is God's revelation. In the reality of this event consists our freedom to be the children of God and to know and love and praise Him in His revelation.

1. THE HOLY SPIRIT THE SUBJECTIVE REALITY OF REVELATION

We have now to take the third and last step in our development of the concept of revelation as the necessary basis of a Church doctrine of the Word of God and to that extent as the basis of a Church dogmatics, in accordance with the rule of Holy Scripture and with due regard to Church dogma. When we put the question about the self-revealing God, we could not raise it in a vacuum, or in the light of revelation generally, but only in the light of the revelation attested in the Bible. Necessarily, therefore, two other questions forced themselves upon us: the question of the event in which God is revealed as God; and the question of that aspect of the event which is, as it were, turned towards us, the revealedness of God for us. Hence the answer to that first question, the question of the Subject in revelation, developed into a threefold knowledge of the God who is Himself the Revealer, Himself the act of His revelation, and Himself His revealedness, in the doctrine of Father, Son and Holy Spirit in their oneness and threeness, threeness and oneness. But in the light of the very doctrine of the Trinity the second question, the question of the reality of revelation from God's side, had also to be put and answered independently. We did this in the christological section which is now behind us, the doctrine of the incarnation of the Word. What we have now to do is to give the third question a central place in our deliberations, and, in the closest connexion, of course, with both our trinitarian and our christological inquiries, to give it an independent answer.

Let us again think of its particular meaning, especially in relation to the [204] second question. From the doctrine of the Trinity we know that to the question, how the state of revealedness is achieved for us men, there can be only one answer. The one true God and Lord Himself, in the "person" of the Holy Spirit, is His own state of revealedness for us. The answer is, therefore, the same as we had also to give to the question, what was the event in revelation, except that then its special content was the indication of the Son or Word.

1

Over and above the identifying in essence of God the Son and God the Father, the question of the How of revelation is quite a legitimate one because it is in fact answered quite definitely by the biblical witness to revelation. In the same way we ought not and cannot be satisfied with finding, important in itself, that the Holy Spirit in His essential identity with the Father and the Son, in His divinity, is therefore once more God Himself, is also His own revealed state for us. We ought not to be satisfied with this finding, because from the standpoint of Scripture there has been prescribed for us a definite declaration of the aim or end of revelation, we might also say, a definite declaration of the How of God's actual state of revealedness for us. In the light of this declaration the further question is not only legitimate and meaningful, but imperative and necessary. For where definite answers are prescribed for us by Scripture, we not only ought, we should and must ask them in order to achieve the imperative knowledge and understanding of the biblical answers and therefore the proper knowledge of them by the Church, which is the task of dogmatics. But the imperative question here is this. What is the meaning of revelation as the presence of God Himself, so far as it is not only an event proceeding from God but also an event that reaches man. To what extent, in the occurrence of revelation, are we men free for God, so that He can be revealed to us? To what extent is there in this occurrence a revealed state of God for man, and to that extent a human receptivity for God's revelation? The object of this question we call "the subjective reality of revelation." By this is meant no less than the answer prescribed in Holy Scripture, namely, the outpouring of the Holy Spirit.

At the corresponding point in § 13, I asked how in the freedom of God it was real that His revelation reached man. Our question now is: In what freedom of man's is it real that God's revelation reaches him?

By our first answer, the doctrine of the Trinity, and ultimately and decisively by Holy Scripture as the source and norm of all our present answers, our whole investigation of the concept of revelation is directed to a very definite area which we cannot quit without abandoning objectivity. If we remain objective and so pursue our thinking in this area, one thing can and must be regarded as fixed *a priori*[EN1]. This freedom of man's can only be a freedom created by God in the act of His revelation and given to man. In the last resort it can only be God's own freedom. The question of a freedom originally proper to man, the question how it is real from man's side that God's revelation reaches him, does not tally with any answer prescribed by Holy Scripture. In this regard the Bible nowhere speaks of anything that is real from man's side. It does speak of God and His action as an action for man and on man. But it speaks of God's action and man's action only so far as they have their possibility in God. Even the fact that God's revelation reaches man, and therefore man's freedom for God, cannot be explained from man's side if we mean to hold fast to the answer pre-

[205]

EN1 at the outset

2

scribed in the Bible. What we have to explain is how there is such a thing as faith and obedience, i.e., in the Bible sense, God's work and gift in man's freedom to believe in Him and to obey Him. It is in this sense, which we must, of course, consider in detail, that we have to regard the concept of "the subjective," when we speak of the "subjective reality of revelation."

And so our first question is this: How does this freedom in man become real? It is not: How does it become possible? The latter question will also have to be raised and answered, but *secundum ordinem*[EN2], and therefore not first. Only when raised second is it the genuine question of our attitude to God's revelation. If raised first it again leads to lack of objectivity. It means that we are first trying to lay down the conditions upon which we can regard the way from God to man as traversable. And it is in the framework or through the spectacles of these conditions that we later have to realise how far God in the reality of His revelation has actually trodden a traversible way to man. We are thus putting ourselves in a place where we have no right. For what do we know of the traversibility of this way? We cannot imagine that we even know ourselves, man, so well, that we can make clear from our side which way from God to man is a traversible one! And we cannot presume to think of understanding the way which God has actually trodden in the light of conditions which we ourselves have discovered and set up. If we do, then on either side our claim is an immediate denial of revelation, whatever our results. Therefore the claim must be dropped at once, i.e., in this context the question of the reality of revelation must come first, the question of its possibility follows. The former is the question of fact, the latter the question of our attitude to it.

At this point, too, our exposition in the first draft of this book (§ 17, 284 ff.) involved a parlous obscuration at least in form. Even at that time I was aware that in this case too a "renewed recourse to the reality of God" is obviously the only possible answer (p. 285). I knew that in all inquiries into the possibility of God's revelation we had first to reckon with the reality of it (p. 291). I was aware that I had to express this if only in the form of numerous "reservations." But I did it only in the form of "reservations" within an investigation, in which, by pointing to grace confirmed by baptism, I aimed to advance from a description of the subjective possibility of revelation to the description and valuation of its reality, or, as it were, from the problems raised by this concept to their solution. No "reservations" could be of any avail against the uncertainty of this method, although I might appropriately have raised a good many more. It was most instructive that in spite of all the reservations Karl Heim (*Glaube und Denken*, 1st edn., 1931, 417 ff.) claimed to find in this exposition the question of the certainty of faith, the question of "man in despair about himself," and an attempt to answer it. In other words, Heim saw an answer to a question of his own, and as such he certainly and very rightly found it highly unsatisfactory. I suppose I must have seemed to be on the way from possibility to reality, from the riddle of man in despair about himself to the solution of the riddle in the certainty of faith. And if I was, it must have looked like an illegitimate palliation, when after rejecting all other attempts at solution, "in a manner almost Roman and sacramental," I pointed to baptism as the basis of the knowledge of grace, as Heim reproached me with doing, instead of speaking like an ordinary Reformed

[206]

[EN2] second in order

3

theologian about the certainty of election on the basis of being sealed by the Holy Spirit. How painfully I felt that I had been misunderstood on this point! When I pointed to baptism my intention was to say the strongest thing I could think of about the utterly supreme truth of grace and the Holy Spirit, and therefore about real "sealing," as compared with any immanent certainty in the soul. But I was myself to blame if this was not patent. Within a line of thought which Heim could so easily confuse with his own—in fact in one place (p. 301) I spoke specifically of "sacramental self-knowledge"—it could so easily not be patent. We can end with baptism only if we have begun with baptism. And this I had not done; I had begun "by inquiring *in abstracto*EN3 into the conditions of the subjective possibility of revelation." But this possibility necessarily remains in the air, so long as it is not regarded strictly as the possibility already realised in revelation, and therefore so long as the question is not in terms of its realisation, and the answer to this question is not regarded. For, when we talk obscurely about the possibility of revelation, what perhaps we say quite seriously about its possibility is bound to revert to obscurity, and therefore leave the impression that even the indication of baptism, the ultimate and strongest point which we can produce here, is perhaps no more than a palliation on the part of self-despairing man, and not a very attractive one at that. Heim has really done me a great service by his criticism. He has forced me still further from his own way, the way of reflection upon the possibility of certainty in faith. The right way— which makes the very reservations superfluous—can only be the reverse of that way which I then thought it necessary to take in Heim's company, in spite of all the reservations. Certainty of faith, i.e., a grounded awareness that God's revelation reaches man and how it does so, has first to be regarded simply in its reality, and only then, and on that basis, in its possibility, and in the various conditions of that possibility. Even in theology we can end in certainty of faith only if we have already started in certainty of faith.

First of all, then, we have to speak of the reality of God's revealedness for man. This must be our exclusive starting-point. But if that is the case, then first we have to make one thing clear. The existence of men who render faith and obedience to the Word of God; the fact that there is such a thing among men as faith and obedience to the Word of God; the entire correspondence on man's side to the divine act of revelation: all this is just as seriously the content of the biblical witness to revelation as is the objective reality of revelation, i.e., Jesus Christ as the incarnate Word of God. Scripture did not attest for us the existence and work, the deeds and words of God in Jesus Christ, and yet leave open the question of the result of it all on the men whom it is supposed to reach. As distinct from objective proclamation we are not here abandoned to quite a different field of inquiry. We are not left to our own field of inquiry. We do not have to raise such questions as "Where do I begin?" or "What has this to do with me?" or "How did I get here?" simply from a standpoint which we have discovered or selected for ourselves, and then answer them with a corresponding self-possession and arbitrariness. Quite the contrary. The fact and form of the coming of God's Word to man so that man becomes a hearer and doer of it, the fact that Jesus Christ the Son of God acquires many brothers and His eternal Father many children, the fact of the fulfilment of grace: these very facts constitute an integral part of the biblical testimony to revelation and of

[207]

EN3 in the abstract

4

revelation itself, and that part belongs directly and indispensably to the substance of the record. We can say, not only that "*God* with us" is a fact, but also, and included in the former statement, that "God with *us*" is a fact. We cannot say this of ourselves—the latter statement any more than the former. God's revealedness among us and in us really comes to us in revelation. It is part of revelation. We cannot meditate upon it *in abstracto*EN4. No arbitrary decisions can be reached in relation to it. But if it does exist for us, then we have to listen to it and acknowledge it very much in the form in which Scripture tells us of that occurrence from God's side which is its objective presupposition. Not God alone, but God and man together constitute the content of the Word of God attested in Scripture. Yet the relation between the two is not an indifferent one. It is not reversible. It is not a relation in which man can be, as it were, the partner and workmate of God. It is not of such a kind as to permit us to intrude ourselves in place of biblical man with our own reflections and meditations upon ourselves, and with the view-points and principles by which we usually make up our minds. God and biblical man confront one another as the Lord confronts the servant, the Creator the creature, the Reconciler the pardoned sinner, the Redeemer the one who never ceases to expect His redemption, the Holy Spirit the Virgin Mary. It is this man who together with God (this God) constitutes the content of the Word of God attested in Scripture. And it is as the witness to this man that Scripture is meant to win our ear, having something to tell us about man in the sight of God and therefore about God's revealedness for us. But in this sense and with this restriction Scripture does in fact have something quite definite to say not only about God but also about man, and with a like seriousness also about man. The Holy Spirit acting upon man is also God. Hence his work upon us is also revelation, and knowledge of him is knowledge of revelation, and therefore rests upon knowledge of the witness to revelation. We have no right, then, to expect to import into the reality of God's process of revelation to and among men any contribution learned from a source of knowledge different from Holy Scripture. In this [208] respect also, we must realise the adequacy of Holy Scripture as the source of our knowledge. We must submit to our bondage to Scripture. We must submit to be content with it. We must do so no less because man is in the very presence of God. Indeed, because of the special parlousness of this point, we have to say, *just* because man is in the very presence of God. Actually Scripture does not abandon us even on this its subjective side. We are not left to our own guess-work or to the findings of a religious anthropology—not even to those of a Christian anthropology, which claims to assert something different from what it has previously been told.

That the Bible is not dumb on this side is revealed clearly by the contrast between Law and prophets in the Old Testament, and in the New Testament by the corresponding contrast between Gospels and Epistles. In the Old Testament particularly the subjective element

---

EN4 in the abstract

which is represented in the first instance by the prophets is further strengthened by the third section of the Canon, the *ketubim*[EN5]. In this section the community which adopts the revelation, and the individual within it who is moved by the needs and hopes of Israel, express themselves in the most varied literary forms. With sublime naturalness both Synagogue and Church took account of this subjective element as well when constructing the Canon. It was regarded as an integral part of the witness to revelation and of revelation itself. On principle, therefore, we must not think of speaking about its subordination to the objective element, because any subordination in principle would indirectly call in question the *homoousia*[EN6] of the Holy Spirit, compared with the Father and the Son; *qui cum Patre et Filio simul adoratur et conglorificatur*[EN7]. From this standpoint the emphatic insistence upon Gospel before Epistle in the first part of the Roman Mass carries with it an awkward reminder of subordinationist trains of thought. And the dispute about "Jesus and Paul," or "Jesus or Paul," which has preoccupied Protestant theology since the 18th century, is incontestably painful. There is an element of tragicomedy in the development of Neo-Protestantism. Its desire was to enforce the problem of man in his relation to God. But in its polemic, it unwittingly rejected the only branch on which it might have sat with honour. The desire was and is no doubt a legitimate one. In relative distinction from the aim of the trinitarian and christological dogmas of the early Church, it wished to see and to understand not only God in His relation to man but also man in his relation to God. We may say that even in the early days this was always the special desire of the Western Church and it found its active representative especially in Augustine. At the peak of mediaeval Scholasticism, in the *Summa* of Thomas Aquinas, it was enforced on a broad front over against the objective dogma, which for its part was not neglected. At the Reformation it came to the very forefront: so much so that unreflecting historians of a later date could believe that the objective dogma had now become a *caput mortuum*[EN8]. It was no accident that the favourite and best exploited books were the Psalms and Romans, not the Law and the Gospels. Luther orients his whole theology by the reality of the justification of the sinner, Calvin by the reality of the sanctification of the same sinner. Their interest is as one-sided as that of Athanasius, who had formerly oriented his whole theology by the reality of the incarnation. There was both an inner and an outer necessity for this one-sidedness of interest on the part of the Reformers, and the danger involved in it never came to anything as long as the divinity of the Holy Spirit was the self-evident presupposition upon which they prosecuted their interest. It is this which in the same sense con-

[209] verts both Luther's doctrine of justification and Calvin's doctrine of sanctification into proclamation of the mystery of revelation, as had formerly been the case with the Christology of Athanasius. If we are to call the special dogmas of the Reformation subjective dogmas, we can do so only in the sense—and this is what turns them into genuine Church dogmas—that they treat particularly, not so much of God's freedom for man become an event in Christ, as man's freedom for God actualised in the Holy Spirit. And it was at this point that Neo-Protestantism failed. It claimed to be fostering the particular interest of the Reformers. Indeed, it appeared to do so. But it was so interested in man's freedom that it forgot the divinity of the Holy Spirit. At the outset the "freedom from man's side" was still problematically confronted with a freedom from God's side. But logically the latter freedom was drawn in and sucked up by its opposite pole. Man came to be understood quite apart from all mystery or revelation. And the final result was that God's freedom became simply a more precise establishing of the all-dominating "freedom from man's side." This being the

---

[EN5] writings
[EN6] one being
[EN7] who with the Father and the Son together He is worshipped and glorified
[EN8] outdated teaching

case, it was only logical that they should be compelled to read the Gospels with critical spectacles, the necessary result being a Christology emptied of all mystery. And not only that, but
they were completely baffled when confronted with the epistolary part of the New Testament, with the "apostle." They thought that either in part or as a whole they could invalidate
the apostle as a witness to revelation in favour of what was left of the Gospel when all critical
deductions had been made, i.e., of the "historical Jesus." It was inevitable that this theology
should come into conflict with the specific witness of biblical man represented by the apostle
as distinct from the Evangelist. For at its heart this theology was not concerned as the Reformers were with the creature man, the pardoned sinner, the mortal who, together with the
God who acts upon him, constitutes the content of the biblical witness to revelation. It was
concerned with man in himself, the man who understands himself because he controls himself. The very conflict makes it plain that they accepted the Bible as witness to revelation only
conditionally, conditionally, that is to say, upon the parallel presupposition that there is
another and primary witness in respect of a revelation in man *per se*[EN9], a witness which is
self-given, and in the light of which the former witness has now to be understood. But if such
a primary witness to revelation is presupposed, the second is already rejected, however seriously we protest our continued acceptance of it. For the claim of the alleged second witness
is this: that we men cannot witness to ourselves of a revelation of God within us, so that no
such primary witness to revelation is possible. If we refuse to acknowledge this, we obviously
cease in any real sense to confront Scripture as a witness to revelation, and we can no longer
understand it as a single whole, either according to the objective or to the subjective content
of its witness. Not even according to its subjective content, where we might have found the
legitimate answer to the question about man as the Reformers did, but quite a different
answer, of course, from the one which we think we ourselves can give in that alienation from
Scripture to which we have fallen victim.

Now if we ask Scripture about its witness to man as he stands before God and
receives His revelation, at the very outset the following point is basic. By God's
election and calling, by his hearing of the Word, by the witness of the Holy
Spirit, this man is distinguished not only invisibly and inwardly, but also and in
spite of all that remains invisible and inward in the reality of the revelation
which comes to him, very visibly and outwardly. He stands at a definite place in
history, which not by accident, but by a most definite necessity, is this particular place and not another. Revelation does not encounter man in any general
way, as though it were the eternal definition or eternal meaning of all time, or [210]
the general solution of the riddle of temporal occurrence. As we saw in an
earlier context, revelation has its own time, which is just this one and not
another, which can reach men of all times only as the revelation which has
entered this time. To this objective particularity in revelation there corresponds a subjective. The men who receive it are quite special men. They are
special men not only invisibly and inwardly, but in their very existence, in their
visible outward position. In the Old Testament they belong to the nation with
which God has made His covenant, which He has put under His judgment and
His promise, to the nation of Israel. In the New Testament they belong to the
Church in which Jesus Christ is present as the real acting subject, as the head

---

[EN9] in and of himself

7

of all the members gathered in the Church with their definite tasks and functions. Certainly it cannot be said that this membership of the nation or Church turns these men into recipients of revelation. God turns them into that. And God is not forced to turn them into that because of this membership: at the given place in the Old Testament as well as the New Testament we always find men who appear not to be recipients of revelation at all. And God is not bound to this membership; in the Old Testament, at all events, figures are constantly turning up, who, quite away from the given place, outside the nation Israel, seem nevertheless to have become genuine recipients of God's revelation. But this last possibility appears more and more to have the significance of a corrective. Those who perhaps boast of their membership instead of boasting in God must be checked and shamed. Those who within this membership do not become recipients of revelation must be given a sign of judgment. The freedom of grace which is so easily forgotten and so lightly treasured must be made manifest. And to do this, every now and then there turns up, at least in the given place in the Old Testament, a heathen who standing in his own quite different place has nevertheless heard God and obeyed God. When such heathen turn up in the New Testament as unexpected confessors of the Messiahship of Jesus, it occurs as a continuation of the Old Testament corrective for Israel, not as a corrective for the Church. The Church is not limited by the addition of the heathen, but confirmed and revealed as the body of Him before whom every knee shall bow. So indeed Israel itself, so far as it points to and prophesies the Church, is not limited but confirmed and manifested by the corrective, against a confusion of the Israelite community and the Israelite nationality. The exception, therefore, proves the rule. God Himself and God alone turns man into a recipient of His revelation—but He does so in a definite area, and this area, if we may now combine the Old Testament and the New Testament, is the area of the Church. The Old Testament corrective retains its validity for those who are in the Church. It indicates the separation between good and bad, the judgment of God to which they are subject. But it does not

[211] call in question the reality and clarity, the finality and exclusiveness with which the Church is the place in which God turns men into recipients of His revelation. That the world contains such a place created and indicated by God is declared to be true and not untrue by the development of the universal Church from the national community of Israel. This truth cannot be ignored. Put pointedly and to be taken *cum grano salis*[EN10], there exist over against Jesus Christ, not in the first instance believers, and then, composed of them, the Church; but first of all the Church and then, through it and in it, believers. While God is as little bound to the Church as to the Synagogue, the recipients of His revelation are. They are what they are because the Church is what it is, and because they are in the Church, not apart from the Church and. not outside the Church. And when we say "Church", we do not mean merely the

---

[EN10] with a pinch of salt

8

inward and invisible coherence of those whom God in Christ calls His own, but also the outward and visible coherence of those who have heard in time, and have confessed to their hearing, that in Christ they are God's. The reception of revelation occurs within, not without, this twofold coherence.

This significance of the Church for the subjective reality of revelation is not a Roman Catholic but a biblical and therefore of necessity a universally Christian doctrine. As in the Old Testament the individual as such who fears Yahweh and walks before Yahweh only exists so far as the people of the covenant exists and Himself as one of this people, so according to the Gospels Jesus by no means addresses men in any abstract individuality of their existence, but *a priori*[EN11] as members of the community which, now that the time is fulfilled, is to be summoned forth and called together by His word out of the relative darkness of the nation-community as its completed form. The real function of the Messiah is to save His people from their sins (Mt. 1²¹); He is the ἡγούμενος[EN12], who shall feed my people Israel (Mt. 2⁶). In order that this saving and feeding may come true, it is to this people Israel that the call of Jesus is directed: "Repent ye; for the kingdom of heaven is at hand" (Mt. 3²). And how are we to understand either the introduction to the Sermon on the Mount (Mt. 5²ᶠ·). or from that standpoint its whole content, if we do not consider that it is not this or that individual with his definite religious and moral possibilities, but again the people that is called blessed, summoned forth, and called together, namely the spiritually poor, the mourners, the meek, etc., in short the nation of those who with Simeon (Lk. 2²⁵) wait for the "consolation of Israel" and are as such the true Israel. Thus it is that from the very first the result of Jesus' call is not the existence of a medley of more or less convinced and reliable adherents, but, in the company of the Twelve who suddenly shoot up as it were out of the ground (in whom the twelve tribes of Israel reappear), the existence of the foundation, the rock upon which He will build His ἐκκλησία[EN13] (Mt. 16¹⁸). To them the Lord promises that He will be with them alway even unto the end of the world (Mt. 28²⁰). To them He gives ἐξουσία[EN14] (Mt. 10¹). Whoso receiveth them receiveth Him (Mt. 10⁴⁰). He that heareth them heareth Him (Lk. 10¹⁶). He is in the midst of them, even if only two or three of them should be gathered together in His name (Mt. 18²⁰). To them the Holy Spirit is promised (Ac. 1⁴ᶠ·) and upon them—note that already beforehand they were "all with one accord in one place"—He is actually poured out at Pentecost, with the result that they receive the gift of speech and that men of every nation can understand them: "we do hear them speak in our tongues τὰ μεγαλεῖα τοῦ θεοῦ[EN15]." And then there were "added unto them" the same day about three thousand souls (Ac. 2¹ᶠ·). For "neither pray I for these alone, but for them also which shall believe on me through their word; that they all may be one" (Jn. 17²⁰ᶠ). If this is what we find already in the first part of the New Testament, how much more is it the case in the second part, the Epistles, where we cannot understand a single word in relation to either writers or recipients, unless we discern the tightly closed circle within which the speaking and hearing takes place. I will refer to only one decisive point, Paul's account of his conversion in Gal. 1¹⁵ᶠ·. Who had this Paul been till then? Someone *in vacuo*[EN16]? No, but one set apart and called by God's grace from his mother's womb, like the prophet Jeremiah. And what does he become now that God reveals His Son in him? A Christian? Amongst other things, yes: and yet no mention is made of it, but there is immediate mention of his duty to proclaim Christ

[212]

[EN11] at the outset
[EN12] leader
[EN13] church
[EN14] authority
[EN15] the wonders of God
[EN16] in a vacuum

among the Gentiles. Therefore he did not and he will not exist except in his function in the life of the Church. And it is on the same assumption that he now addresses his congregation, quite irrespective of whether he is dealing with former Jews or Gentiles. It is upon their being κλητοὶ ἅγιοι EN17 (Rom. 1⁷; 1 Cor. 1²) that everything that is real between him and them is based. The very fact that it is comparatively rare for such explicit mention to be made of the Church as such, as in Rom. 12³ᶠ, 1 Cor. 12⁴ᶠ, Eph. 4¹ᶠ, 1 Pet. 2⁵ᶠ, shows how naturally existence in Christ and existence in the Church are seen and understood as an actual unity, although the difference between them is as great as that between existence in heaven and existence on earth.

From this standpoint we ought at least to understand what was the intention in the utterances of the fathers on this matter; though to a certain extent they are already overshadowed by the developing Roman Catholic conception of the Church. Ὅσοι ἂν μετανοήσαντες ἔλθωσιν ἐπὶ τὴν ἑνότητα τῆς ἐκκλησίας, καὶ οὗτοι Θεοῦ ἔσονται, ἵνα ὦσιν κατὰ Ἰησοῦν Χριστὸν ζῶντες EN18 (Ignatius of Antioch, *Ad. Philad.* 3, 2). *Ubi enim ecclesia, ibi et Spiritus Dei et ubi Spiritus Dei illic ecclesia et omnis gratia; Spiritus autem veritas* EN19 (Irenaeus, *C.o.h.* III, 24, 1). *Si de illo populo vult aliquis salvari, ad hanc domun veniat, et salutem consequi possit* …. *Extra hanc domum, id est extra ecclesiam, nemo salvatur* EN20 (Origen, *In Jesu Nave hom.* 3, 5). *Habere non potest Deum patrem, qui ecclesiam non habet matrem. Si potuit evadere quisque extra arcam Noe, et qui extra ecclesiam forts fuerit, evadit* …. *Hanc unitatem qui non tenet; non tenet Dei legem, non tenet Patris et Filii fidem, vitam non tenet et salutem* EN21 (Cyprian, *De cath. eccl. un.* 6). *Hic est fons veritatis, hoc domicilium fidei, hoc templum Dei quo quis non intraverit vel a quo si quis exierit, a spe vitae ac salutis alienus est* EN22 (Lactantius, *Div. inst.* IV, 30, 11). *Nec deputabo te inter Christianos, nisi in ecclesia Christi te videro* EN23 (Augustine, *Conf.* VIII, 2, 4). It is obvious what points of interrogation and exclamation have to be affixed to such statements. In any case it is good to be alive to the fact that Luther related very closely to the Church the sentence in the *Smaller Catechism*: "The Holy Ghost hath called me by the Gospel, illumined me by His gifts, sanctified and sustained me in the true faith," for he immediately continued: "like as He calleth, gathereth, illumineth, sanctifieth and by Jesus Christ sustaineth the whole of Christendom on earth in the one true faith," and then concluded quite unmistakably: "in which Christendom He daily forgiveth me and all believers all their sins and shall at the last day raise me and all the dead and to me together with all believers in Christ shall give an eternal life." And in the *Larger Catechism*, to the question how and wherewith the Holy Spirit makes us holy, the answer is: "By the Christian Church …. For firstly He hath a special community in the world, which is the mother that begetteth and supporteth every Christian by the Word of God which He revealeth and plieth, lightening and kindling hearts that they

---

EN17 called saints

EN18 Whoever has repented has come to the unity of the church, and they will belong to God, so that they might live according to Jesus Christ

EN19 For where there is the Church, there is the Spirit of God; and where there is the Spirit of God, there is the church and all grace. And the Spirit is the Truth

EN20 If anyone of that people wants to be saved, let him come to this house, and he could be saved … Outside of that house, that is, outside the church, no one can be saved

EN21 No one can have God as Father, who does not have the Church as mother. If everyone could have escaped outside Noah's ark, they who are outside the doors of the church will also escape … Whoever does not hold this unity, does not hold to the Law of God and does not hold to faith in the Father and the Son and does not hold to life and salvation

EN22 Here is the fountain of truth, this is the household of faith, this is the Temple of God in which anyone who does not enter or from which anyone who departs is a stranger to the hope of life and salvation

EN23 I will not think of you as among the number of Christians, unless I see you in the Church of Christ

grasp it, adopt it, cling thereto and abide thereby" (*W.A.* 30¹, 188, 22). And at the corresponding point in one of the sermons which precede and are the basis of the *Larger Catechism*, we read expressly, and with the same exclusivism as that of the patristic citations: *Et in hac*[EN24] *ecclesia*[EN25] thou too art, that the *Spiritus sanctus*[EN26] leadeth thee thereinto, *per* [213] *praedicationem Evangelii. Prius nihil nosti de Christo, sed Christiana ecclesia annuntiat tibi Christam .... Per ... officium eius sanctificaris ... alioqui nunquam Christum agnosceres et audires*[EN27], (*ib.* 92, 13)." Therefore whoso would find Christ must first find the Churches. How would we know where Christ and His faith were, if we wot not where His faithful are? And whoso would know somewhat of Christ must not trust himself nor build a bridge to heaven by his own understanding, but go to the Churches, visit and question the same. For outwith the Christian Church is no truth, no Christ, no blessedness" (*Pred. üb.* Luc. 2¹⁵ᶠ·, *Kirchenpost*, 1522, *W.A.* 10¹, 140, 8). Similarly, Calvin heads his chapter *Instit.* IV, 1: *De vera ecclesia cum qua nobis colenda est unitas, quia piorum omnium mater est*[EN28], and in clear reminiscence of the quotation from Cyprian, he says: *Haec enim quae Deus coniunxit separari fas non est, ut quibus ipse est pater, ecclesia etiam mater sit*[EN29] (*ib.*, IV, 1, 1). Whoever separates himself from the *communio ecclesiae*[EN30] must be held *pro transfuga et desertore religionis*[EN31]. He renders himself guilty of an *abnegatio Dei et Christi*[EN32] (*ib.*, IV, 1, 10). We must, of course, make many reservations in face of the Roman Catholic interpretation of the necessity of the Church to salvation. But the necessity itself it would be unwise either to reject or to avoid. Indeed, it is necessarily prescribed for us, when we ask concerning the subjective reality of revelation.

To understand this we must above all try to see that over against Jesus Christ the Church is not a chance, i.e., an arbitrary construction. It is not created, formed and introduced by individual men on their own initiative, authority and insight. It is not the outcome of a free undertaking to analyse and come to terms with the self-revealing God by gathering together a community which confesses Him, by setting up a doctrine which expounds and proclaims His truth in the way that seems most appropriate to these men. Applied to such a church, the *extra ecclesiam nulla salus*[EN33] would in fact be an enormity. In face of such a church we should all have not only the right but the duty, a duty to faith, to appeal to the free grace of God to be made blessed outside of it. In face of such a church we should have to insist at least upon civil toleration, not only in the name of humanity but in the name of God. A church of that kind has nothing to do with the subjective reality of revelation. We can say quite simply that a church of that description is not the Church but the work of sin,

---

[EN24] And in that

[EN25] church

[EN26] Holy Spirit

[EN27] through the preaching of the Gospel. Before you knew nothing of Christ, but the Christian church announces Christ to you ... Through its office, you will be sanctified ... otherwise you will never know or hear Christ

[EN28] On the true church with which we must pursue unity, because it is the mother of all the pious

[EN29] For those things which God has joined together, must not be put asunder, since those whose Father He is, have the church also as mother.

[EN30] communion of the church

[EN31] as a fugitive and as a deserter from the church

[EN32] denial of God and of Christ

[EN33] outside the church there is no salvation

of apostasy in the Church. Naturally none of the fathers whom we mentioned could possibly be thinking of that kind of church. We can and must say, of course, that where the Church is, there also we have always this church which is not the Church, i.e., that in the Church the work of sin and apostasy is always going on as well. There is no time at which to a greater or less degree the Church does not also have the appearance of such a church. There is no time at which to a greater or lesser degree it is not actually a church in this sense. There is no time at which it is quite inappropriate to remember that Jesus Christ is the Lord of the Church, and not the Church the Lord of Jesus Christ. There is no time at which the Church is not compelled by the arbitrary human action which constantly arises at its very heart to remind itself through Holy

[214] Scripture of its origin, and to let itself be ruled and therefore corrected from the standpoint of this origin against upstart arbitrarinesses. But the nature of the Church cannot be gathered from man's upstart arbitrarinesses in it. Just as, similarly, Jesus Christ cannot be understood from the standpoint of man's nature and kind, which He assumed and adopted, and which are only too familiar to us. What we men apprehend is ultimately and at bottom an accidental or arbitrary search after God, in which we can see only sin against God and a falling away from Him—never the unity between God and man, in which our nature and kind are in Jesus Christ genuinely and finally liberated from such strivings. That there took place in Him revelation and reconciliation between God and man we can comprehend only when we see and understand that the eternal divine Word was here made flesh. It is that which at this point brings light into our darkness. It is that which signifies liberation and purification. It is that which effects revelation and reconciliation. It is that which is the unique reality of the person of Jesus Christ. And the same is true of the Church of Christ. Because it is true of Jesus Christ, it is also true of His Church. The place or area in history at which—and at which alone—reception of revelation is achieved, the visible and invisible coherence of those whom God in Christ calls His own and who confess Him in Christ as their God, in other words the Church, has no reality independent of or apart from Jesus Christ. It is not that because of the sovereignty of their reason, will or feeling men have concluded for Christ or have become "Christians," i.e., subjects of the predicate Christ. Where that occurs you have sin or falling away. And where any church is only the Christian Church in this sense, namely the church in which Christ is the predicate and not himself the subject, it has itself become the church of sin and apostasy, a heretical church. But the Church of Christ, which really is what it is called, does not exist in this independent reality. Although there is in it no lack of man's upstart arbitrariness, it exists in dependence on Jesus Christ. And it is because it lives by Jesus Christ, not because it is constantly involved in upstart and arbitrary action, that it is the true Church.

Cf. for what follows K. L. Schmidt, *Die Kirche des Urchristentums* (in *Festgabe für A. Deissmann*, 1927, 258 ff.); E. Thurneysen, *Christus und die Kirche*, Z.d.Z., 1930, 177 ff.; E. Fuchs, Die

1. The Holy Spirit the Subjective Reality of Revelation

Auferstehung Jesu Christi und der Anfang der Kirche, *Z.f. Kgsch.*, Vol. 51, pt. 1–2, 1932, p. 1 ff.

That the Church has its origin in Christ means four things.

1. It derives from the Word that became flesh. That the Word was made flesh was not without meaning for the world of flesh. It was not a superfluous occurrence which might have happened anywhere and at any time. The fact of the occurrence has not passed unnoticed by the world and it has not left it unaffected. This was the Word by which all things were created. It was the Word by which God supports all things. It was the Word which only came to its own when it came into the world. Above all it was the omnipotent Word of God   [215] which cannot return void, the Word which when it is spoken always has the result that what is declared in it occurs. And one thing at least is declared in it (by the very fact that the eternal Word of God is spoken in our world), and that is that it should be heard in this world of ours. And so the result of its being spoken is that it is now heard in this world of ours. In Jesus Christ our human nature and kind were adopted and assumed into unity of being with the Son of God. And this was no futile or superfluous occurrence. Necessarily, therefore, there are among the men whose nature and kind were met by this occurrence in Jesus Christ those who live in this adoption and assumption. They are the children of God because, in spite of the sinfulness of their nature and kind, they are justified and sanctified by that which meets their nature and kind in Jesus Christ. This life of the children of God for Jesus Christ's sake is the reality of the Church, the subjective reality of revelation. In virtue of the omnipotence of the Word of grace, there is this meeting, this life of the children of God. And for that reason and to that extent, the saying *extra ecclesiam nulla salus*[EN34] holds good. There is no reality of revelation outside the circumference described by this meeting.

In New Testament passages like Rom. 12[4f.]; 1 Cor. 10[16f.], 12[12f.]; Col. 1[18. 24]; Eph. 1[22f.], 4[12], 5[23 29f.], etc., the Church is described as the body of Christ. One meaning of this description is undoubtedly this: that the existence of the Church involves a repetition of the incarnation of the Word of God in the person of Jesus Christ in that area of the rest of humanity which is distinct from the person of Jesus Christ. The repetition is quite heterogeneous. Yet for all its heterogeneity it is homogeneous too (although the uniqueness of the objective revelation forbids us to call it a continuation, prolongation, extension or the like). The fulness of the Godhead dwelt in Him "bodily" (Col. 2[9]). In Him God immediately (but also, of course, externally and visibly) delimited, touched and determined human history. In this particular history one man or person (for that is at least one meaning of σῶμα[EN35]) delimited, touched and determined another and all others, so that now they are no longer what they are without this One who delimits them. And all this is proved to be real in the history of the Church, in the historical, the externally and visibly actual form of the totality of those who are delimited, touched and determined by Him as the Son of God. *Verbum Patri coaeternum in utero virginali domum sibi aedificavit corpus humanum et huic tanquam capiti membra, ecclesiam,*

[EN34] outside the Church there is no salvation
[EN35] body

adiunxit[EN36] (Augustine, *De civ. Dei* XVII, 20, 2). "He was by his sufferings buried in the earth and, like a root unset, hidden in the world, and there grew from it that fair tree, the Christian Church, outspread over all the world" (Luther, *Pred. üb.* Röm. 15, 4 f., *Adu. Post.*, 1522, W.A. 10¹², 91, 10). "He will not be content that the story occurred and he fulfilled it for his person, but he mingleth it with us and maketh thereof a brotherhood, that he might be a common good and heirship for us all; he setteth it not in a *praedicamento absoluto*[EN37], but *relationis*[EN38], to say that he hath done so not for his own person or sake, but as our brother and for our sole good; and will not be otherwise regarded and known of us, save as he who with all this is ours and we in turn his and so we belong together most intimately, so that we cannot be more closely tied, like those who alike have one father and are set in the like common and undivided inheritance and can assume, glory and take comfort in all his power, glory and goodness as in our own" (*Pred. üb. Mc.* 16¹ᶠ; *E.A.* 11, 208).

[216]   2. But this life of the children of God is always a life for Christ's sake. The foundation of the Church is also its law and its limit. We might say that it corresponds to the *anhypostasis* of Christ's human nature. By its inmost nature the Church is forbidden to want independence of Jesus Christ, or sovereignty in thought or action. If it did, it would relapse into the unjustified and unsanctified nature from which it is withdrawn in Christ. This will always find plenty of means to assert itself in its life. But it cannot want to relapse into it. It is born of the omnipotent Word of grace; it would only die if it were to become or to be anything but the fulfilment of that Word. Grace holds good only where grace rules. The rule of grace which is unfailing where men are God's children for Christ's sake, the dependence of these men upon the Word of which they are reborn—this is the reality of the Church, the subjective reality of revelation. And in the light of it, it is and must be true that *extra ecclesiam nulla salus*[EN39]. There is no reality of revelation apart from this dependence on the Word.

A second meaning of the description of the Church as Christ's body is undoubtedly this: that the repetition of the incarnation of the Word of God in the historical existence of the Church excludes at once any possible autonomy in that existence. The Church lives with Christ as the body with its head. This means that the Church is what it is, because in consequence of what human nature and kind became in Jesus Christ, human nature and kind are made obedient to the eternal Word of the Father and are upheld by that Word. "The cup of blessing which we bless, is it not the communion (κοινωνία) of the blood of Christ? The bread which we break, is it not the communion of the body of Christ" (1 Cor. 10¹⁶ᶠ)? In and by this participation the Church lives. It lives by the fact that within it as the circumference nothing happens except a real repetition of what has happened in its midst, in Jesus Christ, to men and for men. It lives by growing up to him who is the head, Christ (Eph. 4¹⁵), i.e., by receiving its whole existence, comfort and direction from Him and only from Him. He is always the subject of the Church. "What believest thou concerning the holy, universal, Christian Church? That the Son of God out of the whole human race gathereth, guardeth and sustaineth for himself an unworldly Church unto eternal life, by his spirit and word in unity with true faith, from the beginning of the world unto the end, and that I am and shall

---

[EN36] The co-eternal Word of God built in the womb of the virgin His house, a human body, and joined to it the church, as members to a head
[EN37] absolute context
[EN38] context of relation
[EN39] outside the church there is no salvation

eternally remain a living member of the same" (*Heid. Cat. qu.* 54). *Nostre Seigneur Jesus Christ ne nous donne pas quelques instructions, comme si on enseignoit l'A B C à un enfant, et puts qu'on le baillast à un maistre plus excellent: nostre Seigneur donc ne parle pas ainsi à demi à nous: mais en toute perfection. tellement qut et en la vie et en la mart il nous fait tousiours persister à ce que nous tenons de luy et renoncer à ce qui viendra du costé des hommes: car tout meslinge ne sera sinon corruption .... Il faut que l'Eglise se bastisse tellement que Jésus Christ nostre chef ait tousiours la preeminence. Car si on vouloit tellement exalter les hommes que Jésus, Christ fust obscurci au milieu, voilà un bastiment espouvantable. et qui n'emporte que ruine et confusion. Et de faict, si un homme devenoit gros comme un pilier de ce temple, et que ca teste fust comme un poing et qu'elle fust cachee dedans ces espaules, ce seroit un monstre: il vaudroit beaucoup mieux qu'il retinst sa mesure commune*EN40 (Calvin, *Serm. on Gal.* 1*11f.*, 1557; *C.R. Calv.* 50, 329 f.). "Askest thou what the Christian Church is, or where the Christian Church is to be found? I will tell thee. The Christian Church thou must seek, not that it lie at Rome or at St. James or at Nuremberg or at Wittenberg or among countryfolk, townsfolk or nobility, but it saith, 'the government shall be upon His shoulders' ... that a [217] right Christian and true member of the Churches is he who believeth that he sitteth upon Christ's shoulders, that is, that all his sins are hung on Christ's neck, so that his heart saith, I know no other comfort save that all my sins and misdeeds are laid upon His shoulders. Therefore those who lie on Christ's shoulders and let themselves be carried by Him, are called and are the Church and proper Christians" (Luther, *Pred. üb. Jes.* 9. 1 f., 1532, *E.A.* 6, 59 f.). *Rectus itaque confessionis ordo poscebat, ut trinitati subiungeretur ecclesia, tanquam habitatori domus sua et Deo templum suum et conditori civitas sua .... Unde nec tola, nec ulla pars eius vult se colt pro Deo, nec cuiquam esse Deus pertinenti ad templum Dei, quod aedificatur ex diis, quos facit non factus Deus*EN41 (Augustine, *Enchir.* 56).

3. Seeing then that the life of the children of God is a dependence upon the incarnate Word, it is a common life. Not secondarily, but primarily and radically, it is the life of a community. A Church community or congregation, as distinguished from all mere association, is grounded in the essential being of those who are united within it. But they are what they are from and by the Word. Their existence is none other than that of the Word. Therefore they are one, and originally one, as surely as the Word in which they exist is one. They could only be disunited without the Word—but they are not without the Word, for they would not yet be, or would have ceased to be what they are, if they were disunited. Thus the Church as a collection, coherence, or unity of many

---

EN40 N.B. shouldn't it be 'sa teste', not 'ca'? Our Lord Jesus Christ does not give us some instructions, like some-one teaching the alphabet to a child, and then gives him to a more excellent teacher. Our Lord does not speak to us in half-measures, but in complete perfection, such that both in life and death, he makes us persist in that which we have from Him, and to renounce that which comes from men. For there is no mixing without corruption ... It is necessary that the Church be fortified that Jesus Christ our head always has preeminence. For one wished so to exalt men that Jesus Christ was thereby obscured, that would be a fearful construction, and which would bring only ruin and confusion. And in fact, if a man were to become as large as a pillar in this temple, and his head was like a fist, and it was concealed within his shoulders, that would be a monster. It would be much better that he keep the measure common to all

EN41 Therefore, the right order of confession requires that the Church be subordinated to the Trinity, just as a house is to its dweller and the temple to God and state to its founder ... Therefore neither the whole, nor any part of it should wish to be worshipped instead of God, nor should anything be God which belongs to the temple of God which was built by the gods, which the unmade God made

does not rest upon the sense of association in any love or brotherliness with which the many might be filled. In this respect also it rests directly upon Christ, in whom the many are what they are. And it is only on the basis of this existence that brotherliness and love are possible and necessary, even though they do not constitute the Church as such. Those who are in the Church are brothers and sisters. They are simply confirming their own existence and in it the Church's basis, when this becomes visible in their attitudes and modes of action; and they are denying the Church's basis and nothing less than their own existence, if this remains invisible in their attitudes and modes of action. But the unity of the Church is grounded upon the one Christ. And whatever the case with the attitudes and actions of the men who participate in it, the Church is the congregation; subjective reality is the congregation. And *extra ecclesiam nulla salus*[EN42] necessarily means: that by belonging to Christ we belong to all who belong to Him—not secondarily but *a priori*[EN43], not by the exercise of Christian virtue, but according to our nature, i.e., for Christ's sake, and therefore not by accident or disposition or choice, but in the strictest possible sense, by necessity.

The third meaning of the description of the Church as the body of Christ now becomes clear. Those who live within the circumference of which Christ is the centre do not constitute, but they are as such a single and indivisible whole. Each in his own place—as a member, is drawn into the identity of the body with its head. If the members are not equal but unequal, they are still not different but one. They are just as much one as they are one with Jesus Christ by participating in the justification and sanctification of His human nature and kind. This connexion between justification and the congregation is well seen in the Epistle of Barnabas (4¹⁰): Μὴ καθ᾽ ἑαυτοὺς ἐνδύνοντες μονάζετε ὡς ἤδη δεδικαιωμένοι, ἀλλ᾽ ἐπὶ τὸ αὐτὸ συνερχόμενοι συνζητεῖτε περὶ τοῦ κοινῇ συμφέροντος[EN44].

"By the Word Christ goeth up into the heart and illumineth it. All hearts behold one kind of light, have one faith and one knowledge. This is the day He hath made here, and hath so made as it departeth not therefrom. As the sun abideth during the day and uplifteth the day, so too the sun Christ maketh day of Himself and from Him goeth radiance into every believing heart, and He is at once in all. And as so many eyes all together see the sun perfectly and entirely, nor doth it give but one ray of itself but everyone hath radiance and all have it in common, so too here is one Christ, all have Him in common and yet each hath Him wholly in his heart. When He cometh, He so illumineth us and ruleth us all by one faith. So the false view departeth and the heart beholdeth God's word and work aright, so there is a new world, a new people and a new light" (Luther, *Pred. üb. Luc.* 24¹³ᶠ, 1521, W.A. 9, 669, 6). "Christ then sayeth not that they have one will or mind, however true it is that all Christians are of one faith, love, mind and thought, as those that have one Christ, spirit and faith, notwithstanding all the differences between individuals in respect of their external function and works. But here He speaketh not of the unity which we call an equality, but the Word layeth it down *ut sint unum*[EN45], that they be one thing, just as 'the Father and I' are one thing; so that it is said concerning the essence and meaneth much more than to be one in heart and mind.

[218]

[EN42] outside the church there is no salvation

[EN43] at the outset

[EN44] Do not remain alone, staying in with yourselves since you have already been justified, but coming together in common pursue together what is for the common good

[EN45] so that they may be one

1. The Holy Spirit the Subjective Reality of Revelation

But what the one or one sort of thing is, we shall never see or grasp, we have to believe ... Therefore as the body is one thing and is called one, so the whole of Christendom is called one body or one cake, not simply because of a oneness or similarity in outlook but rather because of a oneness in essence. Now there is a much greater unity between the member and the body than between thine and another's thoughts. For His thoughts are in His body and also thine in thine and it cannot be said that my and thy thoughts are one thing, in the way that all members are together one thing, i.e., one body, so that if a member is away from or out of the body, it is not one thing or essence with the body, but a body or essence of its own; but so long as they are all together, it remaineth one cake, without any difference or separation of essence. So then here also Christ meaneth that His Christians must depend on each other, so that they are altogether a single thing and useparated body and continue so, like as He and the Father are one .... There standeth therein a mighty great comfort for all who believe in Christ and hold to His word, namely, that we are all members of one body as one flesh and blood. And have the advantage that all that befalls a member befalls the whole body, which doth not occur in the likeness or harmony alleged. For although many have one heart and will, one doth not partake of another as in a body .... For it belongeth to such unity that there is no bit or part that liveth and feeleth for itself alone and hath not the life and feeling of every other, that is, of the whole body. Where then the meanest member of Christendom suffereth, the whole body soon feeleth it and is aroused so that they all at once begin to run and cry and shriek. For so our head Christ heareth it and feeleth it. And although He holdeth in a little, yet when He beginneth to smell trouble and to wrinkle the nostrils, He maketh not light of it. For so it saith in the prophet Zechariah: 'he that toucheth you toucheth the apple of mine eye.' Lo! there thou hast a precious promise of exquisite comfort and courage to Christians .... But in none other wise can we attain it but by this, that God (as He hath said) sustain us in His name, that is, if we abide in the word which we have received from Christ. For the word holdeth us together, that we all remain under one head and depend on Him, see none other holiness or aught that should hold for God save in Him .... By the word are we incorporated in Christ, all that He hath is ours and we can take to ourselves what is His as of our own body, furthermore He too must take to Himself all that befalleth us, which neither world, devil nor any ill chance can spoil or overpower. There is no power on earth so great that it has any effect upon this unity. But the devil goeth about to break this bond and by his cunning and craft to snatch us from the word. Where that hath happened, he hath already won. For apart from the word there is no more unity, but futile fission, unhallowed sects and schisms, which he casteth amongst us by his nets and snares, that is, by men's teaching" (*ib.*, *Pred. üb. Jn.* 17[11f.], 1528–9, *W.A.* 28. 147–52).

[219]

4. The life of the children of God, and therefore the Church, the subjective reality of revelation, is divine and human, eternal and temporal, and therefore invisible and visible. It is also human, also temporal, also visible. Always in its entire hiddenness in God it is also a historical reality. How can it be otherwise, seeing it has its origin, its ground, its centre in the incarnation of the Word? According to His human nature Jesus Christ was also a historical reality. Otherwise revelation would not be revelation, reconciliation would not be reconciliation. Otherwise even after the incarnation God would continue to live and be only on high and in Himself, far from man. He is on high. But He is also with them that are of a broken and contrite heart. In eternity He is God in Himself and God with us. But if He is God with us, then He is so in historical reality; for we live and have our being in historical reality. And if this revelation of His in historical reality did not take place in vain, if to the time which He had for us

17

there corresponds a time which we ought to have for Him, then that which corresponds to His incarnation, the life of the children of God, the Church, is also visible. Invisible, too, of course. Even in the incarnation, it still cannot be seen that it is the eternal Word that there became man. At that point, too, temptation and offence are still possible. It is only through God that God can become manifest even in the flesh. Yet when He does become manifest, He becomes manifest in the flesh, visibly. In the same way the Church is not only invisible in virtue of divine election, calling, illumination, justification and sanctification, which turn the children of God into what they are. It is not only invisible in virtue of the invisible grace of the invisible Lord who rules it. It is not only invisible in virtue of the Word invisibly spoken to it, in which they all are one. But in all these things it is also visible. The children of God are visible men. A visible event brings them together. A visible unity holds them to each other. The fact that they have received God's revelation is invisible, but they themselves are visible as those who have to remember that fact, and are glad to do so. That the event is the call of God is invisible; but the event of their being brought together is visible. That their unity is the Word heard is invisible; but that they belong together and keep together is visible. The problem of their existence as the Church can be perceived with a perspicacity which is pro-portionate to our constant perception of the problem of the God-manhood of

[220] Jesus Christ. But at the very least the problem of their existence as the Church is set in a complete visibility, and as a problem at least it cannot be denied. Therefore we have always to look for the Church on the plane of temporal things, of things which can be seen and thought and experienced. And so *extra ecclesiam nulla salus*[EN46] is always an assertion that for every man, at every time and place, the subjective reality of revelation is fulfilled in a temporal encoun-ter and decision, an encounter and decision which can be seen and thought and experienced.

If from this standpoint we again reach back to the description of the Church as Christ's body, we shall now have to insist upon a fourth meaning. The Church has a further point in common with the incarnate Word of God. As distinguished from the eternal nature of God, it has a spatio-temporal form and extension. It is therefore visible in the same way as any other σῶμα[EN47]. It has this form and extension only from the incarnate Word of God, i.e., only by the free gracious will of the Son of God, who gives it this visible reality of existence by assuming it into communion with His own existence in space and time. Apart from Him there would be no visibility of the Church, because apart from Him there would be no Church at all. Apart from Him that which is visible as the Church will never really be the visibility of the Church. But in Him and through Him there is not only the invisible reality of the spiritual life of the Church proceeding from His Word. In Him and through Him there is also its bodily life, without which it could not be a gathering of real men and the permanent setting of witness to Him amid human history. In Him and through Him the Church is the wholly concrete area of the subjective reality of revelation. Within this area the justification

---

[EN46] outside the church there is no salvation
[EN47] body

and sanctification of men may become an event. At the gates and borders of this area concrete encounters and decisions may be reached. By the existence of this area revelation is concretely recognised and attested by men. By this area the question of faith is concretely put to men. In his *De Fide rerum quae non videntur* (4, 7 f.) Augustine has expounded the thought in this way. The Church, he says, by its visibility stands security to outsiders for the reality of the invisible, which it proclaims as happening at God's instance and as coming from God. *Me attendite, vobis dicit Ecclesia, me attendite quam videtis etiamsi videre nolitis .... Haec aspicite, in haec attendite, haec, quae cernitis cogitate, quae vobis non praeterita narrantur, nec futura praenuntiantur, sed praesentia demonstrantur*EN48. In expounding Gal. 4²⁶ Luther declared most emphatically that by the words "Jerusalem which is above, the free" we are not to think of the *ecclesia triumphans*EN49 but of the *ecclesia in hoc tempore*EN50. It is upon earth the Church must be, *ut sit omnium nostrum mater ex qua nos sumus generati et quotidie generamur. Ergo necesse est hanc matrem nostram, ut et eius generationem. esse in terris inter homines. Genera. tamen in Spiritu*EN51 (*Komm. zu Gal.*, 1535, *W.A.* 40¹, 663, 18). And Melanchthon, in rebutting a misunderstanding on the part of Counter-reformation polemics, made it clear that *neque vero somniamus nos Platonicam civitatem, ut quidam impie cavillantur, sed dicimus existere hanc ecclesiam, videlicet vere credentes ac iustos sparsos per totum orbem. Et addimus notas: Puram doctrinam evangelii et sacramenta. Et haec ecclesia propria est columna veritatis*EN52 (*Apol.* VII, 20).

Thus reception of revelation, into the reality of which we are now inquiring, occurs in the Church, namely, in the twofold coherence of those whom God confesses in Christ and who in Christ confess God. We have insisted (1) that it involves the coherence of those who are raised by the omnipotent grace of the incarnate Word from the world of the flesh to the life of the children of God; (2) that in this coherence it involves the lordship of the grace of the incarnate Word; (3) that it involves a coherence which from the standpoint of the cre- [221] ative and ruling Word is a unity of those who cohere in it; (4) that it at least also involves, once more from the standpoint of the creative and ruling Word, the fact that this coherence may, as well or as ill as any other historical reality, be seen, experienced, thought and recognised by man. It is this coherence which is meant when we describe the Church as the area by which the subjective reality of revelation is invariably enveloped. In our description of this area we have used the most general term, which is yet the most concrete and indeed decisive that could be used in a statement about this reality, if we are to say anything about it from the standpoint of Holy Scripture. On our human

---

EN48 Listen to me, the Church says to you. Listen to me whom you see, even if you do not want to see me ... Look at these things, listen to these things, and consider these things which you see, which are not overlooked, but are told to you, which are not foretold as things to come, but which are shown as present

EN49 church triumphant

EN50 church at the present time

EN51 such that it is the mother of us all, from whom we were all born, and are every day begotten. Therefore it is necessary that this mother of ours – and her offspring – be among men in all lands. But she gives birth in the Spirit.

EN52 we do not dream that we are Plato's Republic, as some impiously accuse us; rather we say that this church exists, evidently as those who truly believe and are righteous, scattered throughout the earth. And add to this, the pure teaching of the Gospel, and the sacraments. It is this church which is a pure pillar of truth

side, on the world's side, that which corresponds to the objective reality of revelation in Jesus Christ is the existence of the coherence which arises, consists and is articulated in the way which we described, the existence of the Church. According to what we have just said, this corresponding factor, the Church, even though it is a human gathering and institution, cannot therefore be regarded as a human production. Although it is in the world, it cannot be thought of as owing its existence to this world. Although we are in the Church, are indeed ourselves the Church, the Church cannot be thought of otherwise than as the reality of God's revelation for us, i.e., it is in strict relation to the revelation of God to us, it is in complete subordination to it, yet in that relation and subordination it is equally revelation, it is equally God's own act. If we tried to say anything else, we should have grievously misunderstood the biblical image which so far has served as our main statement, that the Church is the body of Christ.

In our concrete description of the subjective reality of the revelation of God, we have made a fundamental statement, which we must now make clear to be such, if the description is to possess the character of a genuine recognition of reality. Strictly speaking, the indication of the Church, with which we had to begin, was in the first instance a demarcation of the area of the reality, although we could not speak of the area without at the same time speaking of the reality itself. But what fills this area? What happens in it? What is the Church? We shall have to extend our inquiries much further afield, with an inquisitiveness for definitions of content. The decisive answer and therefore the expression of what is fundamental in the description must certainly be to the effect that it involves the outpouring of the Holy Spirit, i.e., it involves the fact that, after He has become man in Christ for us, God also adopts us, in such a way that He Himself makes us ready to listen to the Word, that He Himself intercedes with us for Himself, that He Himself makes the speaking and hearing of His Word possible among us. Therefore the decisive answer to the question of the existence of the Church must certainly be to indicate the mystery of Pentecost, the gift which men who themselves are not Christ now receive in [222] their entire humanity for Christ's sake, the gift of existing from Christ's standpoint for Christ and unto Christ, "the power to become the sons of God" (Jn. 1¹²).

But in order to understand this decisive answer we must distinguish between what has to be said about the divine giving and what has to be said about man's being endowed. The problem of the subjective, the question how man becomes a recipient of revelation, breaks up, as it were (in a way corresponding to the two-sidedness of the christological question), once again into an objective and a subjective question, (1) How does revelation come from Christ to man? and (2) How, as such, does it come into man? And clearly even the first of these questions has not yet been answered by the doctrine of the incarnation of the Word. This first question, too, must obviously be answered in the doctrine of the outpouring of the Holy Spirit.

1. The Holy Spirit the Subjective Reality of Revelation

The distinction which we have to make at this point does not rest upon a logical abstraction. Ac. 2 cannot be understood without Ac. 1. In Ac. 1 we are told that those upon whom the Holy Spirit subsequently came were men. He had already been promised to them, promised by the risen Christ Himself. And they were already προσκαρτεροῦντες ὁμοθυμαδὸν τῇ προσευχῇ[EN53] (1¹⁴). The gift of the Holy Spirit is thus imparted to men who expect it with a quite definite awareness and by a quite definite method. They are already on Christ's side, since their existence is to be given them from Christ's side. Here, of course, we can and must at once think of some similar two-sided statements in the Old Testament. For instance, Ps. 51¹⁰: "Create in me a clean heart, O God, and renew a right spirit within me." Or Ezek. 36²⁵ᶠ: "I will sprinkle clean water upon you and ye shall be clean .... A new heart also will I give you, and a new spirit will I put within you ... and will make of you people that walk in my statutes and keep my judgments to do them." Or the relation between Jer. 1⁴ᶠ, where his election and calling is imparted to the prophet, and Jer. 1⁹ᶠ, where we find expressed his equipment and institution as a prophet. The stylistic form of *parallelismus membrorum*[EN54] in this particular passage does not explain everything. On the contrary, this is the very place at which we may ask whether the style itself does not point to situations like that which we are now considering. And we must also remember that passage in the Nicodemus dialogue which is always so startling when we read it (Jn. 3⁵): ἐὰν μή τις γεννεθῇ ἐξ ὕδατος καὶ πνεύματος, οὐ δύναται εἰσελθεῖν εἰς τὴν βασιλείαν τοῦ θεοῦ[EN55]. Again Eph. 5²⁶ᶠ: Χριστὸς ἠγάπησεν τὴν ἐκκλησίαν καὶ ἑαυτὸν παρέδωκεν ὑπὲρ αὐτῆς, ἵνα αὐτὴν ἁγιάσῃ καθαρίσας τῷ λουτρῷ τοῦ ὕδατος ἐν ῥήματι, ἵνα παραστήσῃ αὐτὸς ἑαυτῷ ἔνδοξον τὴν ἐκκλησίαν[EN56]. Again Tit. 3⁵: κατὰ τὸ αὐτοῦ ἔλεος ἔσωσεν ἡμᾶς διὰ λουτροῦ παλιγγενεσίας καὶ ἀνακαινώσεως πνεύματος ἁγίου[EN57]. Above all we have to think at this point of the fact which is expressly recalled in Ac. 1⁵. Christ baptises us with the Holy Spirit. But according to the account given in all the four Gospels, most emphatically in John, He had a predecessor in His activity. According to Mt. 3², cf. 4¹⁷ this predecessor preaches nothing but Jesus Himself. According to Jn. 1⁶ᶠ· ¹⁵ᶠ, etc., he has no other function except only to point to Jesus. According to Mt. 3¹¹ he is distinguished from Jesus because he baptised "with water unto repentance." In him all the Evangelists see the obviously necessary fulfilment of Is. 40³: "It is the voice of one preaching in the wilderness, Prepare ye the way of the Lord !" So necessary is this fulfilment that Jesus Himself, before entering on His own activity, has Himself baptised by him in order "to fulfil all righteousness." What does it all mean? Simply this. Let us suppose that God's revelation is real on God's side, that the Word has become flesh, that Christ exists. Then two things are still required for revelation to be revealed to men, for Christ to become the Saviour of men. First something which is again objective, if you like, a special presentation of revelation on man's behalf, so that it may find and reach him, so that his heart may be pure, open, ready for it—and only then something subjective, in the narrower sense that he now really receives and possesses the Holy Spirit and with it receptivity for Christ, the actual power to listen to the Word spoken to him.

[223]

1. The first point we have to make is that in its subjective reality God's revelation consists of definite signs of its objective reality which are given by God.

EN53 with one accord continued steadfastly in prayer

EN54 parallelism

EN55 If anyone has not been born of water and Spirit, he cannot enter the Kingdom of God

EN56 Christ loved the Church and gave himself for her, so that he might sanctify her, having purified her by the washing of water with the Word, so that He might present her to Himself as a glorious church

EN57 According to His mercy, He saved us through the washing of regeneration and renewal by the Holy Spirit

Among the signs of the objective reality of revelation we have to understand certain definite events and relations and orders within the world in which revelation is an objective reality, and therefore within the world which is also our world, the world of our nature and history. The special determination of these events and relations and orders is that along with what they are and mean within this world, in themselves, and from the standpoint of immanence, they also have another nature and meaning from the side of the objective reality of revelation, i.e., from the side of the incarnation or the Word. Their nature and meaning from this transcendent standpoint is that by them the Word which entered the world objectively in revelation, which was spoken once for all into the world, now wills to speak further in the world, i.e., to be received and heard in further areas and ages of this world. By them it will have "free course" in this world. They are the instruments by which it aims at becoming a Word which is apprehended by men and therefore a Word which justifies and sanctifies men, by which it aims at executing upon men the grace of God which is its content. And their instrumental function is to veil the objective of revelation under a creaturely reality; and yet to unveil it, i.e., in the actual form of such creaturely reality to bring it close to men, who are themselves also a creaturely reality. They point to revelation. They attest it. No, the Word of God made flesh attests by them that it was not made flesh in vain, that it was spoken once for all, that it is the valid and effective Word. All the formulations just attempted point at once to what we must now state directly: that it cannot depend upon our caprice whether we see or do not see that these events and relations and orders are signs; not only from the standpoint of immanence but also from that of transcendence. There is no world view which can prevent us from doing so. Even ontically, the fact that these events and relations and orders are signs in the sense indicated does not rest upon a determination proper to them in their creatureliness, but upon a determination acquired by them in addition to what they are and signify in their creatureliness, because the Word of God actually avails itself of them. They are not instruments in the sense in which a hammer or shears are instruments in the hand of a workman who avails himself of these instruments because, prepared by another workman, they now possess the qualities required for the purpose for which he handles them. The instruments of the Word of God become what in its service

[224]   they ought to be, solely because of the Word of God itself, which makes it possible for men to see them from the transcendent standpoint that lies beyond the immanent, that is, to meet the signs and to understand them. Their nature as signs does not rest upon a capacity resident in these particular creaturely realities as such, either to be or to become testimonies to revelation. Nor does it rest upon any *analogia entis*[EN58]. It rests upon the divine foundation and institution. It is in virtue of this that, as distinct from the host of other creaturely realities, they become what once they were not and could not

---

[EN58] analogy of being

become, yet now do become and are. They do so by the omnipotence of the divine will to manifest itself to the world, to reconcile the world to itself. That is, they do so by the omnipotence of the same gracious will which in Christ adopted the human nature which in itself is incapable of revelation, and by its own agency made it capable thereof. But, again, even the actual manifestation of the sign, even the fact that it is now seen and understood as that which it is and signifies, is not its own work. God has not, as it were, handed over His own work to it and departed. His foundation and institution does not mean that it now contains grace, as a vessel contains a liquid with which it has been filled. The activity of the sign is, directly, the activity of God Himself. The manifestation of the sign is God's manifestation, even though it is always a creaturely reality. Again, therefore, it takes place by the omnipotence and yet also the freedom of God's gracious will. God has bound us, but not Himself, to the signs of His revelation. They are testimonies, but they are not limitations to His majesty and glory.

It is because these signs have been given, and by way of them, that men may receive direction and promise from the side of the objective reality of revelation, of the incarnation of the Word. The fact that God's revelation is also a sign-giving is one side, the objective side, as it were, of its subjective reality. We are saying the same thing when we say that this giving of signs is the objective side of the Church as the sphere in which God's revelation is subjectively real.

To make this point, the biblical material with which we must begin is as follows. According to the Holy Scripture of the Old Testament and New Testament, God's revelation always comes to man both immediately and mediately. Immediately, for whatever mediators or media God makes use of, in order to speak to man and to act on him, He always remains Himself the subject of this speaking and acting. Immediately, for the fact that He does make use of particular mediators and media never means a withdrawal by God Himself, or a transfer of His properties and activities to the creatures concerned. But God's revelation comes mediately to man in that it actually never does come without creaturely mediators or media, and it always occurs in a creaturely area and framework which is fixed in outline and unvarying in appearance. For according to His man-ness—which we always have to recall in this connexion—Jesus Christ was one particular man and not another, with all the spatio-temporal contingency which that involved. Similarly, that which corresponds to Jesus Christ in the world is one specific thing which cannot be confused with any other. There is no accidental or uncontrolled occurrence of this, that, and the other thing which in themselves might quite well be a divine sign-giving—and why not? According to Holy Scripture even the divine sign-giving in the world has the character of contingence, of factuality, and therefore a quite definite character. Definite signs are as such chosen and set up. They constantly recur. They stand in definite relations to each other. They are, and signify with a certain regularity, what they are supposed to be and signify as such signs.

Let us think of a sign which is the most visible and in a certain sense includes all the rest, the sign of the election of the people of Israel. It is not identical with objective revelation, the incarnation. Yet in an extremely comprehensive way it obviously corresponds to it. It belongs to objective revelation, to the extent that that revelation does not remain objective, but reaches man, and for that very reason, on its subjective side it has a place in history. We

[225]

23

might as well eliminate the whole of the biblical witness and its object, the incarnation, or replace it by some other witness and its object by another, if we ever thought of eliminating the election of the people of Israel or substituting another sign. The manifestation of Jesus Christ has this to correspond to it, or it is not the manifestation of Jesus Christ; for in its utter concreteness it points to this sign and this very sign points back to it, in the sense that He is the seed promised to Abraham. But why this sign in particular? Why particularly the election of Abraham? Why the particular confirmation of it in Jacob? Why the deliverance of these particular tribes from Egypt? Why God's dwelling on Sinai and later in Jerusalem amidst this particular people? Why the judgments of God which indicate the close of their particular place and function in history? Why finally Jesus Christ as the Messiah of the Jews in particular? Why indeed? We can only give a negative answer. It was certainly not because the people of Israel was specially adapted for such a sign-giving, or because the achievement of the sign-giving required that it should be led in this particular way. Of course, everything might equally well have been quite different. There might have been no election of a particular people, or the election of quite a different people from this one, or the election of this people, but with quite different circumstances and results. But the weighing of such possibilities is a matter which clearly never entered the minds of the biblical witnesses in the Old Testament and New Testament. For that reason we must put it right out of our minds when we read their testimonies. It is just because they escape all positive proof that the contingency and factuality constitute the election of Israel a genuine sign. This is the way in which the Son of God elects and calls and justifies and sanctifies His own people in and from the midst of the world.

It is exactly the same with other relevant factors in the biblical testimony. In itself, what has it to do with Christ that this people was set apart and separated from other peoples by the sign of circumcision? It only helps to clarify our understanding that to-day we know that other Near Eastern peoples were also familiar with the same rite. In itself nothing depends upon the rite; but everything depends upon its founding and institution. Everything depends upon the Lord of the covenant, who among this people promises by this rite the judgment which is to be fulfilled and His grace which is to come in Christ. And therefore because of the Lord of the covenant who has so willed and done, once again everything depends upon this rite. It is a genuine sign, not because it is this rite, but because it is the sign of the divine command and promise.

But the main sign-giving, in the sense of a manifestation of the covenant between God and man concluded in Christ, is the existence and activity of the prophets in Israel. These are men of God who again are specially elected from among the elect people. They speak the Word of God to meet special situations among that people. They always do it by proclaiming to them the salvation and condemnation, the condemnation and salvation which come from God. Their existence and their word as such are something quite different from the objective reality of revelation in the incarnation of the Word. We see nothing but what is human. Men speak to men because they have a specific human understanding of a human situation. They are human, too, in their depiction of the coming of salvation and condemnation. Only as the intangible margin of the whole, i.e., in the shape of the unheard-of claim and emphasis with which they speak, and only in the equally intangible form of the divine source of the salvation and condemnation announced, is there any sign here that God's Word is central. That it really is central here we can only affirm from our awareness of the incarnation of the Word of God in Christ. For what we see here is obviously only a sign, only something that corresponds to the Word of God. But what is meant here by "only"? The fulness of revelation in the Old Testament word of the prophets is just this. Here amid the world of men the Word of God Himself is inconceivably laid upon the lips of these men. It is inconceivably uttered to meet this or that situation in human history. It is just as inconceiv-

24

ably heard by the men of that time. And in the whole process it possesses this sign, this thing that corresponds to it. The Old Testament attests that the existence and activity of the prophets is the Word of God. In so doing it plainly and comprehensively declares that there is a human way of uttering this Word and a human way of hearing it; and that inconceivably but in fact this utterance and hearing are so related to God's own Word, that God's own Word can be heard in it. There is a "Thus saith the Lord" on human lips, which the Lord not only acknowledges subsequently but which He has already acknowledged before it was spoken, because what is here said by men is actually His commission, because He Himself has willed and constituted this creaturely correspondence to His own Word. The same is true of the other form-concepts of the Old Testament which we have already touched upon in an earlier context. The king, the priest, the Law, sacrifice, the tabernacle, the temple, the holy land: all of them have to be assessed as a coherent group of signs pointing to a common centre.

But, of course, we have also to see a sign—the sign, as it were, of the superiority and freedom of the thing signified as compared with any of the signs—in the fact that this whole world of Old Testament signs disappears, so to speak, in a flash at the manifestation of Christ. Or rather, it is recognised as the "shadow of good things to come" (Heb. 10^1). And it is prolonged in the New Testament Church by only a small number of new signs, which merely indicate, as it were, the indispensability of the signs and also their continuity with the ancient sign-world. Into the place of the whole ancient sign-world steps the Church with its apostles and its *kerygma*^{EN59}, with baptism and the Lord's Supper; for that is really all there is to be said about the Church and its visibility. Obviously, the change and reduction in the signs and the things corresponding is conditioned by the transition from the age of Messiah expected to that of Messiah come. The substance remains the same, but the *oeconomia*^{EN60}, the *dispensatio*^{EN61}, the *exhibitio*^{EN62}, the *manifestatio*^{EN63} of revelation has been changed (Calvin, *Instit.* II, 9–11). *Christum aliis signis et absentem figurari et venturum praenuntiari oportuit; aliis nunc exhibitum repraesentari decet*^{EN64} (II, 11, 14). It should be noted, however, that this does not amount to the removal or abolition of sign-giving as such. Even the manifestation of Christ Himself can be seen and understood to be what it is only in the form of sign-giving. The sayings of Jesus in this world rang in human ears, and His acts in this world took place before human eyes: they are the language of the incarnate Word. Even the Church after the manifestation of Christ is in the world and consists of men who as such continue to require sign-giving. The Church is not Christ. The Church does not possess His incomparable authority, that of the eternal Word itself. Neither has it authority to do His deeds. According to Acts, prophecy and miracles were at first still active among His disciples. But obviously they were only a reflection of the manifestation of Christ Himself, a reflection which was bound to cease. What does not cease is the calling, commissioning and sending forth of the [227] twelve apostles by the crucified and risen One. What does not cease is the extension of the Church's work on the basis of its witness to Christ: the proclamation of Christ by the preaching of Christ, the institution of baptism, and the festival of the Lord's Supper; and the gathering of the people out of all nations by this proclamation. That is the new and simplified and concentrated sign-world of the New Testament. In a further derivative sense requiring

---

^{EN59} proclamation
^{EN60} economy
^{EN61} dispensation
^{EN62} exhibition
^{EN63} manifestation
^{EN64} It was right that Christ be symbolised in some signs, though He was absent, and that it be foretold that He was to come. Now it is right that, since He has been shown, He be represented in others

careful demarcation, it can also be said that the whole existence and history of the Christian Church, so far as it actually has an existence and history of its own, belong to this sign-world of the New Testament. But as such they must submit to continual measurement by the original sign-giving at the calling, commissioning and sending forth of the twelve apostles, and they must be justified at that tribunal. Even the sign-world of the New Testament, whether in the former and narrower or in the latter and broader sense, is dependent upon the reservation "till he come" (1 Cor. 11²⁶). Measured by the reality of the coming of God's Kingdom at the end of our time, it is certainly also the "shadow of good things to come." But with this reservation, that is, within our time, it stands and holds good. It cannot be separated from the objective revelation in Christ. It belongs to it just as strictly as the earlier sign-world of the Old Testament. The Church, the body of Christ, and therefore Christ Himself exists and exists only where there are the signs of the New Testament, that is, preaching, baptism and the Lord's Supper, in accordance with their institution fulfilled at the inauguration of the apostolate. We can conclude our biblical deliberations quite simply at this point with the declaration from the *Conf. Aug. art. 7: Item docent, quod una sancta ecclesia perpetuo mansura sit. Est autem ecclesia congregatio sanctorum, in qua evangelium pure docetur et recte administrantur sacramenta*ᴱᴺ⁶⁵. Even less than in the case of the Old Testament signs do we either expect or desire to have to prove or demonstrate the necessity and the utility of these particular signs except by pointing to their contingent, factual given-ness. We are not asked whether a quite different sign-giving from this particular one might not have been possible for the objective revelation of God in Jesus Christ. Nor are we asked whether we could think of or would prefer a quite different sign-giving from this particular one. With God all things are possible, and with us at least very many. But in the revelation of God in Jesus Christ one possibility is selected and thereby set up and finally confirmed as God's reality. And so, too, it is with the sign-giving which attests this revelation. Our reflection upon it can start only with what it actually is.

Since this sign-giving stands in the closest possible connexion with objective revelation, like that revelation it must be regarded as a divine act. It is the moving of an instrument in the hand of God. God is still the Lord over it and therefore free. In the mystery of His mercy He does not suffer any diminution because He avails Himself of this instrument. The given-ness of these signs does not mean that God manifest has Himself as it were become a bit of the world. It does not mean that He has passed into the hands or been put at the disposal of men gathered together to form the Church. On the contrary, what it does mean is that in Christ the world and man have fallen into the hands of God. It means the setting-up of God's lordship, not of a sacral human lordship. We stand here at the point at which the Evangelical conception of the Church diverges abruptly from the Roman Catholic and also the Modernist Protestant (whose innermost tendencies have recently been unmasked). But the act of [228] the objective revelation of God is an act in the existence of Jesus Christ as very God who is also very man. So, too, the act of sign-giving by which the objective revelation comes to us is an act in the existence of these signs as they were given us once and for all at the inauguration of the apostolate. And since it is a

---

ᴱᴺ⁶⁵ Augsburg Confession, They teach that the one holy church will remain in perpetuity. And the church is the congregation of the saints, in which the Gospel is purely taught, and the sacraments rightly administered

sign-giving which awaits the seeing eyes and hearing ears of ever new men, this sign-giving must receive an ever new recognition and understanding in the Church with each succeeding generation. And it must do so in such a way that never even in part can the Church believe that it has mastered it, that it has learned what Christ really wants of us in the message of the apostles, what preaching and sacrament ought really to be in our midst. It must do so in such a way that at any time in the Church, naturally with respectful consideration for what the fathers apprehended and taught, there exists a challenge to render an account *ab ovo*[EN66] and to discharge one's own responsibility thoroughly, whether it stands with this sign-giving as it was primarily intended to stand. In this respect, too, the Evangelical concept of the Church and that of the Roman Catholic Church, as well as that of a Protestantism which knows only of an "intact" confession, are widely divergent. Yet at every fresh recognition of revelation, an act which devolves upon the Church in every age, it must always be strictly a matter of interpreting the sign-giving which belongs inseparably to revelation. There cannot be in the Church any valid recognition which is really new, i.e., a real recognition of revelation at some new date and under some new conditions, which bypasses the institution of the apostolate, and that means concretely, Holy Scripture, which is concerned with something other than the exercise *pure* and *recte*[EN67], i.e., in accordance with Scripture, of preaching and the administration of the sacraments. No matter what arguments may be adduced in their favour, innovations which have their norm in a different *pure* and *recte*[EN68] are achieved only outside the Church and *eo ipso*[EN69] apart from Jesus Christ, as He has really made Himself known to us. To summarise: we shall see to it that with revelation itself the signs of it are always made new, as much because they are God's act as because they extend to the Church that lives in time. But we shall also see to it that as there is no new revelation, there are likewise no new signs. We need none of them. There is no way in which we could have any knowledge of them. So we have no need to inquire about them. We shall have all our work cut out to apprehend and understand both revelation itself and its one and only sign-giving. The Church as the sphere in which God's revelation is subjectively real does have this strictly objective side.

It is of more than historical value for us to remember at this point that originally the concept *sacramentum*[EN70] (the translation of μυστήριον[EN71]) had a far more comprehensive sense than was later given to it (as is particularly clear from the usage of Tertullian and Cyprian). It formerly denoted the mysteries of the faith as such, as they were offered to humanity in the Church—the very thing we have just been describing as sign-giving. And in

---

[EN66] from the beginning [lit. from the egg]
[EN67] purely and rightly
[EN68] purely and rightly
[EN69] in and of themselves
[EN70] sacrament
[EN71] mystery

fact, even in the later special sense, no general definition of a sacrament can be given which does not unintentionally coincide with the definition of a sign in the comprehensive sense just described. *Sacramcntum est signum rei sacrae in quantum est sanctificans homines*[EN72] (Thomas Aquinas, *S. th.* III, *qu.* 60 *a.* 2*c*). *Sacramenta instituta sunt … ut sint signa et testimonia voluntatis Dei erga nos ad excitandam et confirmandam fidem in his, qui utuntur, proposita*[EN73] (*Conf. Aug. art.* XIII). *Sacramentum … externum esse symbolum, quo benevolentiae erga nos suae promissiones conscientiis nostris Dominus obsignat*[EN74] (Calvin, *Instit.* IV, 14, 1). *Sacramentum est sacra et solemnis actio divinitus instituta qua Deus mediante hominis ministerio sub visibili et externo elemento per verbum certum bona coelestia dispensat ad offerendum singulis utentibus et credentibus applicandam atque obsignandam promissionem de gratuita remissione peccatorum Evangelii propriam*[EN75] (J. Gerhard, *Loci theol.* 1610 L. XVIII, 109). *Sacramentum est actio sacra divinitus instituta, in qua gratia per Christum foederatis promissa a Deo, visibilibus signis obsignatur atque hi vicissim in ipsius obsequium adiguntur*[EN76] (J. Wolleb, *Chr. Theol. Comp.*, 1626, I, *c.* 22, § 1). "Sacraments are the regular means of grace given by Christ to the Church which He founded, by which the gracious fruits of the redemption once effected by Him on the cross are applied to man" (J. Braun, *Handlex. d. kath. Dogm.*, 1926, 249). Obviously the whole objective side of the Church could be intended in all these definitions just as well as the sacraments in the special and narrower sense of the word. Note the metaphors with which Calvin, for example (*Instit.* IV, 14, 5 f.), seeks to represent the general meaning of sacraments. They are, so to speak, seal-impressions, or paintings, or reflections of the divine promise of grace; they are supporting pillars of faith, or exercises (*exercitia*) to develop certainty about the Word of God. These figures are just as suited to the more comprehensive concept of sign-giving, which belongs to revelation and mediates objectively to the human subject. And this is not an accidental but a necessary coincidence. This may be shown in two ways.

1. The concept of sacrament in the later and narrower sense has obviously a special meaning within the concept of sacrament in the older ard wider sense and so, too, within the general concept of divine sign-giving which is occupying us here. In the definitions quoted, the concepts emphasised were *externum symbolum, elementum, signum visibile, actio sacra*[EN77]. Now, of course, these do indicate baptism and the Lord's Supper in particular. But they also emphasise marks which are proper to divine sign-giving as such. Think in particular of the concept of *signum*[EN78], which has been so decisive for Western sacramental doctrine since the time of Augustine. Of course in the narrower sense the sacrament is called *signum visibile*[EN79], since it is a matter of symbols and actions which are visually apprehensible. And at first glance it might be thought that in this way we exclude the element of man's word which is generally so important for divine sign-giving. But Augustine himself counted man's spoken or written word among the signs. *Nihil aliud sunt verba quam signa*[EN80] (*In Joann. tract.*

[EN72] A sacrament is a sign of a holy thing in as much as it makes men holy

[EN73] The sacraments were instituted … so that they might be signs and witnesses of the will of God set before us, to stir up and confirm faith among those who make use of them.

[EN74] A sacrament is an outward sign, by which the Lord seals on our consciences His the promises of His goodness towards us

[EN75] A sacrament is a holy and solemn act, instituted by God, by which God through the mediation of man's ministry dispenses heavenly blessings through His certain word with the visible and external element

[EN76] This is to be offered to those to each person who makes use of them and believes the true promise of the free forgiveness of sins which is to be applied to them and sealed upon them

[EN77] external symbol, element, visible sign, holy action

[EN78] sign

[EN79] visible sign

[EN80] Words are nothing other than signs.

45, 9). What is decisive is not the concept of the *visibile* as such, but the superior one of the *sensibile*, under which the *audibile* also falls. And without a *visibile*, i.e., without man speaking or without Scripture, there is no *signum audibile*[EN81] either. "The Word is also an external thing, which can be grasped with the ears or read with the eyes" (Luther, *Pred. üb. Luc.* 11[14f.], *Hauspost.*, 1544, *W.A.* 52, 185, 17). *Visibile* declares (pretty much as in the concept *ecclesia visibilis*[EN82]) that the sign belongs by nature to our world as well, to the sphere of our observation and experience. It may be met, as other realities are met. As such a *signum visibile*[EN83] the sacrament is a *symbolum*[EN84], and an *externum symbolum*[EN85], i.e., an inalienable sign of the coherence, indeed the unity of the Church, on the basis of the objective revelation in Christ to which it owes its origin. This unity of the Church is, of course, hidden and invisible. Yet it is also public and visible. It is so from Christ Himself; and to that extent the Church contains the *symbola*[EN86] instituted by Him as *symbola externa*[EN87]. No doubt the things involved in the sacrament in its narrower sense are *elementa*[EN88], i.e., elements of a spatially extended, corporeal nature, water, bread and wine. And this fact seems to assert an out-and-out distinction of the sacrament from all other elements in the divine sign-giving in general. But only in appearance. For the spiritual, historical and moral being of man is also steeped in the elemental sphere, in the cosmos of corporeality, in an ultimately inextricable unity with his natural being, of which it is the counterpart. Finally, the sacrament is emphatically described as an *actio sacra*[EN89]. And we naturally think of the nature of baptism and the Lord's Supper as being the Church's action as opposed to the Church's word in preaching. But we have to note that while not all the Church's speaking is a completed act, at least it is an action. The same is true of all the other elements in our definitions. For example, the sacrament has been instituted by Christ as a sign of the *res sacra*[EN90], namely, the divine grace in Christ. Its purpose is the *sanctificatio or iustificatio*[EN91] of man. Its function is that of applying, *obsignare*[EN92] (confirming a superscription by a seal fixed beneath it), the reconciliation that occurred and was expressed objectively, by the ministry of certain men. But these features obviously do not belong to anything distinctive in a sacrament as compared with preaching. They merely underline the general context to which a sacrament also belongs. It is simply that a sacrament gives prominence to something special within the general context. As a *signum visibile*[EN93], a *symbolum externum*[EN94], a sign in the *elementum*[EN95] and in an *actio*[EN96], a sacrament asserts clearly, and with relatively greater eloquence than the word in the narrower sense can ever do, that the *iustificatio*[EN97] or *sanctificatio hominis*[EN98], which is the meaning of all divine sign-giving, does not rest upon an idea but upon reality, upon an event.

[230]

[EN81] audible sign
[EN82] visible church
[EN83] visible sign
[EN84] symbol
[EN85] external symbol
[EN86] symbols
[EN87] external symbols
[EN88] elements
[EN89] holy acts
[EN90] sacred thing
[EN91] sanctification, Justification
[EN92] sealing
[EN93] visible sign
[EN94] external symbol
[EN95] element
[EN96] action
[EN97] justification
[EN98] sanctification of man

And the event upon which it rests is of such a kind that it does not merely possess the relevance which a powerfully disseminated philosophical doctrine or a popular conviction may have. It is the event which has shown itself to be both spiritual and corporeal, the act of a Creator who is above the antithesis between the corporeal and the spiritual, the event of the entry of this Creator into our history, the event of the rolling up of our history by His presence. That is why *iustificatio or sanctificatio hominis*[EN99], which is the meaning of all divine sign-giving, cannot be treated as a problem and isolated, as we can always do with an idea or a doctrine or a conviction. It can no more be dealt with like this than can the Rhine or Mont Blanc; indeed far less so. For while we can at least interpret nature in any way we like without, of course, having any hold upon it, there is absolutely nothing to interpret when it comes to the presence of God in Christ, the action of God Almighty, Maker of heaven and earth. God is and God exists, exactly as nature uninterpreted is and exists. He is and exists with a necessity beside which all the imperturbability with which nature is and exists can only be regarded as fortuitous. Ὁ λόγος σάρξ ἐγένετο[EN100] (Jn. 1¹⁴)—preaching, too, can and must say this. But in a way which preaching can never do, the sacrament underlines the words σάρξ[EN101] and ἐγένετο[EN102] (cf. Heinrich Vogel, *Das Wort und die Sakramente*, 1936, 6 f.). And we have to think of these words as underlined if we are to understand and treat the divine sign-giving as the objective side of the Church, that is to say, in its given-ness, indeed in its pre-given-ness, comprehensive, undiscernible from any angle, unassailable from any angle. The sacrament's insistence upon this quality in divine sign-giving is its special feature as compared with preaching and its special feature in the whole life of God's people assembled to form the Church. We will not be always noting about a theology whether it has any knowledge of baptism and the Lord's Supper, or whether these things are at bottom an embarrassment to it, which it must pester itself to say anything sensible about. If this is indeed the case, it will surely be revealed at some quite different (though only apparently different) point. We shall perceive that it has no proper knowledge of the distinct validity of the prophetic and apostolic word in the Church, or of the value of dogma, or of the theo-
[231] logical relevance of the decision of Nicaea or the decision of the Reformation. And certainly it will not be able to value preaching as the central part of the Church's liturgy. And we shall have to ask whether a theology of this kind can have any awareness of the comprehensive and unassailable givenness of revelation itself. On the other hand, it may well be that a theology allows itself to learn from the very simple fact that in the Church baptism must always be administered and the Lord's Supper celebrated. By this fact it is reminded that, since it is the reality of revelation, the subjective reality of revelation necessarily has an objective side. It is from this objective side that our thinking must invariably derive. It is in this way (this way and not another) that it becomes thinking with a definite content, thinking which is really connected with the object here set before us. It is from the standpoint of baptism and the Lord's Supper that the prophets and apostles, and in their turn the fathers and Reformers, are really fixed: and fixed in such a way that we cannot evade them. And it is when regarded in the light of baptism and the Lord's Supper that, parallel to every temporal movement in time in which it must occur, preaching too must and will always acquire that peculiar element of fixity, of unchanging similarity to itself, without which it ceases in any really effective way to bear witness by the mouth of man. *Et incarnatus est*[EN103].

2. The inter-relationship to which we have just pointed can also be approached from the

---

[EN] 99 justification, sanctification of man
[EN100] The Word became flesh
[EN101] flesh
[EN102] became
[EN103] And He was made flesh

opposite angle. At every point, the divine sign-giving in which revelation comes to us has itself something of the nature of a sacrament. For in its totality it is always a *signum visibile*[EN104], a *symbolum externum*[EN105], a sign both in the realm of nature and also in an action executed by men. John the Baptist is the prototype of all sign-giving, of all attestation, in the biblical sense. And John says everything that can be said about himself in distinction from and in relation to Christ when he describes himself as him that baptises with water. And so it is quite right that in Jn. 3^4, Eph. $5^{26f.}$, Tit. 3^5. the "laver of baptism" should be set plainly and directly against the inner work of the Holy Spirit. It is quite right that we should learn from Jn. 6^{52-58} that to our eating and drinking unto eternal life there necessarily corresponds a perfectly definite corporeal eating and drinking. We can never understand these and similar passages too realistically. And in so doing, we will not be guilty of any serious blunder, so long as we remember, as we certainly ought to remember, that in the isolation in which it is manifested as the sign, as the objective witness which man must receive, a sacrament has naturally to be conceived as *pars pro toto*[EN106]. It is in this living and concrete way, as a creative event in history, that revelation comes to us and seeks to be received and adopted. It comes in exactly the same way as in a sacrament, stressing the objective quality of grace which it possesses. It is no mere matter of the water in baptism or of the bread and wine in the Lord's Supper. For we have also to remember Jn. 6^{63}: "It is the spirit that quickeneth; the flesh profiteth nothing." To ask whether there are not times when the divine revelation and salvation can be received without the necessity of baptism is a childish question. Neither in salvation nor in revelation can we speak of an absolute and, as it were, automatic necessity for the administration of the sacraments. The possibility has never seriously been discussed in the Church, for to tie us to the divine sign-giving would also be to tie God. But again this does not in any way alter the fact that baptism is once for all enjoined upon us. And, of course, what is involved in the water of baptism and in the bread and wine of the Lord's Supper is the establishment and recognition of the sign of the concrete, living, creatively active lordship of God. And, of course, what is involved in our understanding of the whole divine sign-giving—and to that extent *pars pro toto*[EN107] is true of the passages quoted—is exactly the same as what is involved in the water of baptism and in the bread and wine of the Lord's Supper. The authority of the prophets and apostles and through it the grace of the incarnate Word of God is set at the beginning of the Christian Church and therefore at the beginning of our existence as the children of God, just as baptism is put at the beginning of [232] our Christian life as an objective testimony pronounced upon us. And we live by the word of the prophets and apostles, i.e.. by the proclamation based upon their testimony and again by the grace of God's Word through this proclamation, just as we are fed with bread and given wine to drink in the Lord's Supper. We are bound to baptism and the Lord's Supper in token of this ordering and maintenance of life by the Word mediated through the prophetic and apostolic word. For this ordering, this maintenance of life is inseparable from this life, the life of the children of God. It is this life only because and in so far as it is life by the grace of our Lord Jesus Christ, that is to say, only when it is ordered and maintained in the way indicated by the sacraments. For that reason and in that sense we have to say in all serious-ness that sacraments are an indispensable "means of grace." (In this concept, we have only to stress the word "grace" to understand it correctly!) And no complaints about "Roman sacra-mentalism" will prevent us from declaring that on its objective side the Church is sacramen-tal; that is to say, it has to be understood on the analogy of baptism and the Lord's Supper. In

---

[EN104] visible sign
[EN105] external symbol
[EN106] part for the whole
[EN107] part for the whole

other words: The sphere of subjective reality in revelation is the sphere of sacrament. This has nothing to do with the Roman *opus operatum*[EN108] or with heathen "magic." The sphere of sacrament means the sphere in which man has to think of himself as on the way from the baptism already poured out upon him to the Lord's Supper yet to be dispensed to him, the sphere in which he begins with faith in order to reach faith, ἐκ πίστεως εἰς πίστιν[EN109] (Rom. 1¹⁷). On this way our perception will certainly be a true one if we think of ourselves as the recipients of revelation. And it is in this sphere that theology has to seek both its beginning and its goal, and by the law of this sphere that it must direct its methods.

To balance this first finding we have now to frame a second. The revelation of God in its subjective reality consists in the existence of men who have been led by God Himself to a certain conviction. They believe that objective reality in revelation exists for them. They believe that it exists for them in such a way that they can no longer understand their own existence by itself, but only in the light of that reality: not apart from it, therefore, but only in relation to it. They cannot, therefore, understand themselves except as the brethren of the Son, as hearers and doers of the Word of God.

It will be noted at once that we have taken a leap in thought. We had been speaking of the divine sign-giving by whose mediation revelation, or Jesus Christ, reaches man. We had previously intended to go on to speak of the way in which revelation comes to man. And now we are suddenly speaking of men who are already convinced, who by divine conviction have already discovered that they are brethren of the Son, hearers and doers of the Word of God. Obviously we have not said a single word about the decisive thing, namely, about the way in which it comes about that, when the signs have been given, a man encounters and receives them as the signs of revelation, and therefore in and with them encounters and receives revelation itself. It is quite true that we have not said a single word about this: we have simply taken a leap at this point. But this was not due either to forgetfulness or embarrassment. For that is exactly what has to take place at this point: it is the positive side of that which has to take place. God's revelation in its subjective reality is the person and work of the Holy Spirit, i.e., the person and work of God Himself. This does not mean that we cannot say anything about it, that we have to be silent. How can it possibly mean that? In this matter we have to follow Holy Scripture, which testifies that the person and work of God are manifest. Silence about the person and work of God means only that we reject the witness of Holy Scripture, and ultimately that we deny God's revelation. But we do not deny it. We acknowledge it. Therefore we must be clear that just because the person and work of God are concerned in it, our acknowledgment necessarily means that we start from the fact of it. That is our presupposition. And we really start from it. We get out into that world in the midst of which and for which revelation takes place, and the person of God comes, and the work of God becomes an event—into that world which is not itself the person and the work of God. It is

[233]

[EN108] automatic effect
[EN109] from faith to faith

only by starting at this point, by getting away from revelation and out into this sphere, that we can make definite assertions about revelation, though revelation itself, to the extent that it is identical with the person and the work of God, can never be the object of specific assertions. We see this in the case of Christology. Christology can proceed only from the fact of Jesus Christ. On the basis of that fact, and with a proper awe for the mystery of Christmas, its function is to denote in this world the one specific point in the world: that the Word became flesh. And even as it does this, it can never add the decisive thing, that is, how it all happened, how revelation became objectively real within this world. It is exactly the same with the outpouring of the Holy Spirit by which the objective reality of revelation becomes a subjective reality. We have to respect the mystery of the given-ness of this fact as such, i.e., as the inconceivable and therefore the unspeakable mystery of the person and the work of God. We show this respect by following the example of Holy Scripture and taking it as our starting-point. Again, this means two things: first, that we do accept and use it as our presupposition even on the subjective side; and second, that we are content to accept and use it as our presupposition, without making any rash or subversive attempt to understand its How. And that means in practice that when we are asked how objective revelation reaches man, we can and must reply that it takes place by means of the divine sign-giving. In this sign-giving objective revelation is repeated in such a way that it can come to man in genuinely human form. But the presupposition still remains a mystery. All that we know is that God Himself does really avail Himself of this medium, and that therefore objective revelation is actually shown to man by the signs. To the question how revelation reaches man, our first finding enables us to give only a penultimate and not an ultimate answer. It is always by the free grace of God that objective revelation is really shown to man so that he really sees it. We have no insight into the exercise of this grace, and therefore we can never say the last word on this matter. When we have described the objective [234] side of the Church we are still faced with the need for a leap in thought. We cannot penetrate the possibility of this need, and therefore there is nothing special to say about it. Similarly, to the question how objective revelation reaches men, we cannot give a first but only, as it were, a second and consequent answer. We can answer it only by pointing to man on the far side of that necessary leap, where the subjective reality of revelation in the strict sense of the concept, where the person and work of God, where the event of the free grace of God in the same sense, are already behind him; just as they were still before him according to our first finding, i.e., from the standpoint of the divine sign-giving. In this before and behind God wills to be loved and praised. What lies between them we can never express or state, because it is not revealed to us. And it is not revealed to us because it is revelation itself. Any attempt to state or express anything concerning what lies between would be foolhardy, because it could consist only in arbitrary speculation, based on the presupposition that we can actually bypass God. But it would also be fatal, because it would reveal that we regard the leap not as the divine necessity but as a necessity which we can penetrate, that with the mystery of revelation we do not acknowledge but deny revelation at the critical point. Acknowledgment of revelation necessarily means that we presuppose revelation and therefore look away from that holy centre to what precedes and follows it. It means that we look away to the Old Testament and the New Testament. To be more explicit, it means that we look away to the human form in which revelation does encounter man *Deo bene volente*EN110, i.e., to the existence of sign-giving. But again that means that we look away to the human form in which revelation has penetrated to man *Deo bene volente*EN111, i.e., to the existence of men who are already convicted by God by means of the sign-giving, who have therefore already discovered that they are the children of God. We have to allow full weight to the leap which does in fact intervene, with all its inferences. We have to maintain complete silence in relation to it. We have not to try to incorporate it into our system of knowledge as a kind of paradoxical bridgework. We have to lay down our weapons with an indication of Scripture, preaching and sacrament on the one side, and on the other the indication of man, who by the goodness of God can discover that he is the child of God. When we do these things we declare that the leap is not a *salto mortale*EN112 which, if need be, can always be learned and explained and taught and recommended to others. There can be absolutely no question here of anyone either making a leap or challenging others to make it. All that we have to consider is that here the leap has already been made, the unheard-of and to us impossible leap from God to man. In that fact revelation is already a reality. And it can and must call for our consideration that at this point in our exposition we make a leap in thought, in order to draw attention to the proper object of our discussion both on the one side and on the other, both before the leap and after.

[235]

> This leap in thought will necessarily look like theological forgetfulness or embarrassment. It will fall under suspicion as such. But we must not allow that fact to tempt us. A genuinely forgetful or embarrassed theology will not make a leap at this point. It will offer a synthesis instead. For the same reason we must strenuously resist even the slightest suggestion that this leap involves theological "irrationalism." On the contrary, it takes place precisely in view of the obvious reasonableness of God in His revelation. A genuinely irrationalistic theology, not being aware of its true character—and of the fact that it is very rationalistic as such—is usually very talkative at this point.

If it is now clear that at this point a *silentium altissimum*EN113 is far more eloquent than any attempted demonstration, it is also clear that at this point only a *silentium altissimum*EN114 can say positively what has to be said without

---

EN110 in God's good will
EN111 in God's good will
EN112 deathly jump
EN113 most deep silence
EN114 most deep silence

demonstration. Therefore we can look back and calmly make our second point concerning the subjective reality of revelation.

We began by stating that the subjective reality of revelation consists in the existence of particular men. We recall what was said at the beginning of this section. There is no question of something in the divine act in revelation which emanates "from man's side," but only of something which is "directed towards man." The fact that man's existence is involved does not mean that we can ascribe to man, or to these particular men, the role of autonomous partners or workmates with God co-operating in the work of revelation. Man's existence is involved only as the humanity of Christ is necessarily involved in the doctrine of the incarnation, or the *virgo Maria*[EN115] in the doctrine of the mystery of the incarnation. We are concerned with the existence of man or of definite men only as an existence posited from God's side, and posited afresh in the act of His revelation. For neither of the existence of man as posited by himself, nor of his existence posited by God as his Creator, can we posit the assertion which we have to make at this point, the decisive assertion that he can discover himself to be the child of God. In our creaturely existence we are always the kind of people who think that they can posit themselves, and as such we can never discover, at least never legitimately, that we are the children of God. Therefore from God's side, and from God's side in a new way, which transcends their obscure creaturely being, on the basis of the revelation which comes from God, there exist men who in their existence are the subjective reality of revelation. The basis of it all is the divine movement towards man in revelation. It is the divine condescension in virtue of which the Word assumed humanity. That is what makes these men what they are. That is what incorporates them in revelation from their own side. That is why they themselves not only have but are the revelation in their existence. Of course, it is only as recipients that they are the revelation. It is only in subjective reality. We cannot, therefore, confuse them with Jesus Christ. They are never anything except from Him. And yet they are themselves the revelation. But this is revelation as it is "directed towards man." Revelation now is not only Jesus Christ. "In Jesus Christ" it is also the existence of these men. If it were not, how could it ever attain its goal? How could it really be revelation? If it really is revelation, if it does attain its goal, if there is in fact a revealedness of revelation, then necessarily it must be revealed—and previously it was not revealed—both in the being and, in fact, as the being, of men. But the incorporation of these men in revelation means that they are convinced by God Himself. It means that the objective reality of revelation, i.e., Jesus Christ, exists just for them. What it all amounts to is this. In this work of conviction, materially they do not think of anything but the work of divine sign-giving, the work of the prophetic and apostolic word in Holy Scripture, the work of preaching and sacrament. The conviction about which we are thinking means simply that this work attains its

[236]

[EN115] virgin Mary

goal. We may be tempted to think that it means something else as well. By the testimony of the Holy Spirit we may be tempted—as happens often enough—to understand some hidden communication of revelational content in addition to and beyond the divine sign-giving. We may be tempted to find in this material addition of an immediate spiritual inspiration the very essence of the divine conviction. But if we are, then it can only mean that we are again casting eager side-glances away from objective revelation as it objectively reaches us in the divine sign-giving. We are trying to find a something better which God might have told us, instead of looking at the supposedly less good which He has actually told us. We may later harmonise this something extra with the divine sign-giving. We may re-express it in biblical and confessional terms. But if our starting-point is the material addition which comes from immediate spiritual inspiration, we are not convinced by God Himself. Whatever starts in that way is a concealed or open sectarianism. It forgets that the Holy Spirit is not only the Spirit of the Father but also the Spirit of the Word. It forgets that the Holy Spirit certainly comes to us, not by an independent road which bypasses the Word and its testimonies, but by the Word and its testimonies. We remember that the Word is not bound to the sign-giving. But we also remember that we are bound to the sign-giving. We cannot know anything or say anything about any other Word or Spirit except that which comes to us through the divine sign-giving. If God wishes by immediate spiritual inspiration to create new prophets and apostles of the Word—as of course He can—that is His affair. If He does, they will prove themselves to be such, just as the old prophets and apostles did, through whom the Word of God comes to us not as a possibil-

[237] ity but as an actuality. The divine conviction, the witness of the Holy Spirit, can, as it were, be checked by our relationship to the divine sign-giving. For that reason we do really know them and can say something about them. We can say that they attest the Word of God to us. They do not attest a kind of spiritism. They do not consist in the transmission of a material addition, of a new revelational content. They consist in the attestation to us of the one revelation which has taken place for us. "For us," of course, does not mean the selfish desire for salvation of those who will accept Jesus Christ as a good man because they think that they find in Him the satisfaction of the private religious needs of man, and are therefore bound to honour Him. Real revelation puts man in God's presence. It is quite different from a mere answering of questions raised by the sublime egoism of man, who, in addition to all his other requirements, also wants to go to heaven. Pietism is quite right. We speak of real revelation only when we speak of the revelation which is real for us. It is the revelation which is attested to ourselves. It is the revelation which we ourselves adopt when it is attested. It is the revelation which reaches us. An objective revelation as such, a revelation which consists statically only in its sign-giving, in the objectivity of Scripture, preaching and sacrament, a revelation which does not penetrate to man: a revelation of this kind is an idol like all the rest, and perhaps the worst of all idols. But it is not by our arrangement or contrivance that

it is not an idol, that it is the real objective revelation which therefore penetrates to man, that it is objective revelation which becomes subjective in man himself. On the contrary, the fact that this takes place is something which we must accept as quite beyond our understanding. It was not we who have introduced revelation even in its objectivity. Of ourselves we cannot find any arguments to convince us of its credibility and validity. We do not stand at the summit of some moral or religious undertaking, which has enabled us to manipulate revelation in such a way that it has now become subjectively real as well. In this event, by His objective revelation (i.e., by Himself), God Himself has spoken to us on behalf of His objective revelation (i.e., on behalf of Himself). Therefore He Himself has interceded with us on His own behalf. Objective revelation exists for us because God exists. And it exists in the way that God exists. But, of course, it also exists for us, and because we exist and in the way that we exist. For if God really exists for us, we also exist for Him. And this inconceivable event means no more and no less than that we are caught up together into the event of His revelation, not as co-workers but as recipients, not alongside God but by God and in God—and yet really caught up. Our own existence is revealed to us not as a divine but as a very human existence. Yet it is also revealed as an existence which God in His graciousness had adopted and assumed as such, as the existence of the children of God. This taking up of man into the event of revelation, on the basis of which he is revealed to himself [238] as the child of God, is the work of the Holy Spirit or the subjective reality of revelation.

Let us try to clear this up in detail. We described the inconceivable event in which objective revelation exists for man as his being convinced by God. And indeed what takes place at this point does involve a conviction, an opening up, an uncovering of the truth of objective revelation before the eyes and ears and in the heart of man. It means that he himself recognises it to be true and therefore regards it as true and valid for himself. It means that his reason apprehends it, that he himself is entirely in the truth, i.e., he regards himself entirely from the standpoint of the truth. The truth itself does not undergo any addition. It is the truth, even if man is not in the truth. It is true that God is with us in Christ and that we are His children, even if we ourselves do not perceive it. It is true from all eternity, for Jesus Christ who assumed our nature is the eternal Son of God. And it is always true in time, even before we perceive it to be true. It is still true even if we never perceive it to be true, except that in this case it is true to our eternal destruction. "God was in Christ reconciling the world unto Himself" (2 Cor. 5¹⁹). "It is finished" (Jn. 19³⁰). To this "perfect" of the truth of revelation nothing either need be added or can be added. It is not that there are, as it were, two different points: at the one the Son of God assumes humanity; and then, at quite a different point, the question of our destiny is necessarily raised and answered. In the one reality of revelation He is, in His assumed humanity, the Son of God from eternity, and we, for His sake, are by grace the children of God from eternity. Therefore the "perfect" of the truth of revelation already includes the conception of its existence for us. In objective revelation as such (if we may for a moment speak of such an abstraction) the only thing which is not included is that we also exist for it, that our eyes, ears and hearts are as open to it as it is to us, i.e., that we actually adopt the truth as truth and so are in the truth. To that extent the distinction between objective and subjective revelation is unavoidable. But on neither side need this distinction mean that we are speaking of a revelation which exists apart. Subjective revelation is not the addition of a second revelation to object-ive revelation.

If we think of the subjective as something which has later to be added, then necessarily we have thought of the objective as an idol, and it is hardly likely that the added subjective will not also be portrayed as an idol. There have always been fateful moments in ecclesiastical and theological history when men have had to be arrested in the very act of treating abstractly of objective Christian truth as sign-giving, e.g., in the form of what is supposed (but only supposed) to be a correct dogmatics. That is to say, they have treated of it without asking about their own existence in the truth. And they have then imagined that they can make good the undeniable damage by putting objective truth aside for a while as something which has already been adequately confessed and expounded. And in order to escape the

[239] obvious "danger of intellectualism" they give themselves temporarily to the theme of its appropriation by man. The illusion induced by that abstraction drove them away from a dead orthodoxy straight into the arms of pietism and rationalism. And the same mystifi-cation seems to be exercising a not inconsiderable influence on some modern theological contemporaries. We have only to consider the high value which they place on the "Oxford Group Movement." The illusion in this abstraction consists in the fact that they cannot answer the very justifiable question of their own existence in the truth by taking the question of the truth itself less seriously (because it is suspected of being too intellectual), but only by taking it more seriously, which obviously they do not do when they believe that they have found a great lacuna (as we always must) in respect of man's existence in the truth. There has simply never been a really correct dogmatics which expounded objective revelation as such and *in abstracto*[EN116]. Revelation is objective only in its irruption into the subjective, in its redemptive objective assault upon man. We have to follow objective revelation through its whole unified movement from God to man. It is no use confronting an incorrect dogmatics with an equally incorrect ethics, biology, or pastoral theology. This is simply to fight one error with another.

Subjective revelation can consist only in the fact that objective revelation, the one truth which cannot be added to or bypassed, comes to man and is recognised and acknowledged by man. And that is the work of the Holy Spirit. About that work there is nothing specific that we can say. We can speak about it only by sheer repetition, that is, by repeating what is told us objectively, that "God was in Christ reconciling the world unto himself." The work of the Holy Spirit is that our blind eyes are opened and that thankfully and in thankful self-surrender we recognise and acknowledge that it is so: Amen. Therefore we cannot say anything else about this work, we cannot speak about it in any other way than by repeating over and over the Amen which has been put into our

---

[EN116] in the abstract

mouths by this work. Here, too, we must remember that the Holy Spirit is the Spirit of the Father and also of the Son. He is not a Spirit side by side with the Word. He is the Spirit of the Word itself who brings to our ears the Word and nothing but the Word. Subjective revelation can be only the repetition, the impress, the sealing of objective revelation upon us; or, from our point of view, our own discovery, acknowledgment and affirmation of it. Any subjective revelation or discussion of subjective revelation which claims that it is more than repetition, which claims our interest in any way except as a repetition, which claims that it ought to be considered independently, like ethics or biology or pastoral theology, which claims even for a moment that it is distinct from proclamation, the proclamation of objective revelation: any such revelation involves and necessarily involves an immediate and radical break with revelation of any kind. If we are investigating existence in truth—as we always must—we have to investigate truth. For it is upon truth itself that our existence in truth rests, and it is in truth that we have to look for it. It is in Jesus Christ as the objective reality of revelation, and nowhere else in all the world except in Him, that we are the children of God, and nowhere else in all the world except [240] in Him that we come to recognise ourselves to be such. On principle, we literally cannot assign any other definition of content to the new existence of men convinced by God Himself than that they know, and that they cannot and do not want to know, anything else except that they are in Christ by Christ. That is how we must now expound the phrase "in God by God." "In Christ" means that in Him we are reconciled to God, in Him we are elect from eternity, in Him we are called, in Him we are justified and sanctified, in Him our sin is carried to the grave, in His resurrection our death is overcome, with Him our life is hid in God, in Him everything that has to be done for us, to us, and by us, has already been done, has previously been removed and put in its place, in Him we are children in the Father's house, just as He is by nature. All that has to be said about us can be said only by describing and explaining our existence in Him; not by describing and explaining it as an existence which we might have in and for itself. That is why the subjective reality of revelation as such can never be made an independent theme. It is enclosed in its objective reality. If we try to assert anything but that we are really and finally helped in Christ, that we have to cast all our care upon Him—"for he careth for you" (1 Pet. 5⁷)—then what we say is no longer said about God's revelation. For by Christ we will never be anything else than just what we are in Christ. And when the Holy Spirit draws and takes us right into the reality of revelation by doing what we cannot do, by opening our eyes and ears and hearts, He does not tell us anything except that we are in Christ by Christ. Therefore we have to say, and in principle it is all that we can say, that we are brethren of the Son of God, hearers and doers of the Word of God. We are invited and challenged to understand ourselves from this and not from any other standpoint. When we do say this, we are men convinced by God. His revelation exists for us in such a way that we also exist for it. And are free for it. In fact, we ourselves are revelation, that is, to the extent that there takes place in us the revealedness of God, the life of the children of God which is hid with Christ in God, existence in grace. It is men convinced by God in this sense who constitute the subjective aspect of the reality of the Church.

For the biblical background and the historical context of this exposition, the wealth of adducible material is so great that we must confine ourselves to only one classical document, the foundation which Calvin prefixed to his great exposition of the *modus percipiendae Christi gratiae*[EN117] (*Instit.* III, 1). As the chapter heading reveals, the point at issue is the recognition that *quae de Christo dicta sunt, nobis prodesse*[EN118], i.e., that what is proclaimed to us by Christ as very God and very man belongs to us, helps us and is made our own. This takes place *arcana operatione Spiritus*[EN119], i.e., by that work of the Spirit which is done in secret.

1. *Non in privatum usum*[EN120], not for a divine in-Himselfness, did the eternal Father give to His Son the life of which He was the bearer when He appeared [241] among us, but *ut inopes egenosque locupletaret*[EN121], i.e., with one final determination and direction from all eternity, to be wealth to our poverty and need. And the first thing which we have to say about our receiving the grace of Jesus Christ is necessarily that it concerns this *locuplelalio*[EN122], the occupation by Him of the empty space which is ourselves. As long as He is *extranos*[EN123] and we *ab eo separati*[EN124], He there and we here, this *prodesse* is not actual, the divine will in Christ's presence in the world is unfulfilled, and His presence is without significance for us, *inutile nulliusque momenti. Communicatio*[EN125], impartation of the grace manifested in Him, demands that He be not only there but here. He has to become our own. He has to dwell in us, *nostrum fieri et in nobis habitare*[EN126]: in us, in the sense in which Eph. 4[15] tells us that He is our Head, Rom. 8[29] that He is the firstborn among many brethren, Rom. 11[17] that we on our side are grafted into Him like a shoot into a tree, and Gal. 3[27] that we put Him on as a man puts on a garment. *Communicatio*[EN127] of grace is *communicatio*[EN128] of Christ Himself. It consists, therefore, in this, that He and we are no longer two but one, i.e., that we *cum ipso in unum coalescimus*[EN129]. This is what occurs when we believe the Gospel. But the Gospel is proclaimed to many people and they do not believe it, and so that does not occur. When it does, it is just the secret of the activity of the Spirit, the *arcana Spiritus*

[EN117] means of receiving the grace of Christ
[EN118] the things which are said to be of Christ avail for us
[EN119] by the secret operation of the Spirit
[EN120] Not for His own use
[EN121] but to enrich the impoverished and the needy
[EN122] enriching
[EN123] outside us
[EN124] separated from Him
[EN125] useless and of no consequence, Communication
[EN126] to become ours and to dwell in us
[EN127] Communication
[EN128] communication
[EN129] join with Him into one

*efficacia*EN130. This is what leads to *frui*EN131, participation in Christ and His grace. The Christ "that came by water and blood" became identified with us and died for us (1 Jn.5 6 cf. Jn. 19³⁴; the early Church was quite right to connect these passages with baptism and the Lord's Supper). And the Spirit is His witness. The same Spirit is the eternal Spirit of the Father and of the Son, and His testimony in our hearts is therefore the analogue, the seal-impress of the grace of Father and Son applied to us in Christ in water and blood. Receiving this testimony, man has a right to participate in that grace which is simply the *abltutio* (purification) of human nature accomplished in Christ and the sacrifice offered by Christ for all men, and therefore Christ Himself. It becomes His very own. As we are told in 1 Pet. 1². God's elect are those in whom this *sanctificatio Spiritus*EN132 takes place, i.e., those for whom the decision of God in Christ avails, so that they are put into *oboedientiam et aspersionem sanguinis*EN133 Christi, i.e., into the position of the obedience of faith and of the forgiveness of sins accomplished in the death of Christ. It is in this position that these men exist. But the position has reality for them only in the *arcana irrigatio Spiritus*EN134, in the testimony of the Spirit and therefore in Christ of whom the Spirit testifies. Of this position we must also say, with 1 Cor. 6¹¹, that its basis and power are in "the name of the Lord Jesus Christ" and "the Spirit of our God." In short, the Holy Spirit is the bond of peace (Eph. 4³), by which Christ has bound us to Himself and united us to Himself, just as already and on high He is *vinculum pacis*EN135 in which the Father and the Son are united.

2. Therefore the work of the Spirit is nothing other than the work of Jesus Christ. The Spirit is present in His own as the seed of *coelestis vita*EN136, pointing them away from every here and now. By the Spirit He separates them out from the world and gathers them to the hope of their eternal inheritance. In this way He creates His Church. By the Spirit He calls to Himself prophets, i.e., pupils and teachers of revelation. By the Spirit all men go in the body of death to meet resurrection. As the Spirit of Jesus Christ who, proceeding from Him, unites men closely to Him *ut secum unum sint*EN137. He distinguishes Himself from the Spirit of God who lives as *vita animalis*EN138 in creation, nature and history, and to that extent in the godless as well. And just because He is Christ's Spirit, the work of Christ is never done without Him. Nor is it done except by Him. The grace of our Lord Jesus Christ does not exist except in the fellowship of the Holy Spirit (2 Cor. 13¹⁴), and the love of God is not poured out into our hearts except by the Holy Spirit (Rom. 5⁵).

EN130 secret work of the Spirit
EN131 enjoyment
EN132 sanctification by the Spirit
EN133 obedience, and the sprinkling of the blood of Christ
EN134 secret flow of the Spirit
EN135 bond of peace
EN136 heavenly life
EN137 so that they might be one with Him
EN138 animal life

[242] 3. Scripture speaks about Him in many ways. It calls Him (Rom. 8¹⁵; Gal. 4⁶) the *Spiritus adoptionis*EN139: the One who attests the kindness revealed in the only-begotten Son of God, of Him who wills that we too should call Him Father. It calls Him the secret and earnest of the hope which constantly gives life and confidence to us who are *peregrinantes in mundo et mortuis similes*EN140 (2 Cor. 1²²). It calls Him the water that makes the unfruitful field fruitful (Is. 44³, 55¹), or that gives drink to the thirsty (Jn. 7³⁷), or that cleanses their filthiness (Ezek. 36²⁵). It calls Him the unction that strengthens and quickens (1 Jn. 2²⁰), or the fire which destroys yet is also beneficial (Lk. 3¹⁶ᶠ). And all this in the sense that He imparts to us a life consisting in the fact *ut non iam agamus ipsi a nobis sed eius actione ac motu regamur, ut si qua sunt in nobis bona, fructus sint gratiae ipsius, nostae vero sine ipso dotes, mentis sint tenebrae cordisque perversitas*EN141. If, therefore, we do not think of this life by the Spirit when we speak about Christ, but of a sort of ineffective Christ confronting us somewhere at a distance, we are only speculating. It is only in the *coniunctio*EN142, only in the *coniugium*EN143 which Eph. 5³⁰ describes as a mystery, only in the fact that we are flesh of His flesh, spirit of His Spirit, *adeoque unum cum ipso*EN144, members in Him as the Head, only therefore by the Holy Spirit—for *solo Spiritu unit se nobiscum*EN145—that Christ is the One who has come to us as Saviour.

4. The work of the Holy Spirit within us, by which He effects decisively and comprehensively our oneness with Christ, is faith. And faith as the work of the Holy Spirit is not a magical transformation. It is not a higher endowment with divine powers. It is simply that we acquire what we so much need—an *internus doctor*EN146, a teacher of the truth within ourselves, *cuius opera in mentes nostras penetrat salutis promissio, quae alioqui aerem duntaxat vel aures nostras feriret*EN147. From 1 Jn. 3²⁴, cf. 4¹³, we know that we are not only approached and reached by the promise or external Word, and in the Word Christ Himself. By the Holy Spirit whom He has given us, we know that the Word, that is Christ, abides with us, and so becomes ours and we His. All other teachers would exert themselves to no purpose, all other light would be offered to the blind in vain, if Christ had not constituted Himself our *interior magister*EN148 by the Spirit, if He Himself had not opened our eyes to Him, and drawn us to Himself, as those who

---

EN139 Spirit of adoption

EN140 strangers in this world and like those who are dead

EN141 that we no longer live of ourselves, but we are ruled by His action and movement, so that if thereby there be any good things in us, they be fruits of His grace, without Him our gifts would simply be the darkness and perversity of our minds

EN142 conjunction

EN143 marriage

EN144 therefore one with Him

EN145 only by the Spirit does He unite Himself to us

EN146 inward teacher

EN147 by whose work in our minds the promise of salvation penetrates, that promise which otherwise would only hit against the air, or our ears

EN148 inward teacher

were given Him by the Father (Jn. 6⁴⁴). He and He alone is *perfecta salus*ᴱᴺ¹⁴⁹. Yet to make us participant in the salvation accomplished by Him He Himself must baptise us with the Holy Spirit. In other words, He Himself must give us light to believe the Gospel, which is to make us new creatures, the temples of God.

2. THE HOLY SPIRIT THE SUBJECTIVE POSSIBILITY OF REVELATION

The subjective reality of revelation consists in the fact that we have our being through Christ and in the Church, that we are the recipients of the divine testimonies, and, as the real recipients of them, the children of God. But the fact that we have this being is the work of the Holy Spirit. Therefore the Holy Spirit is the subjective reality of revelation.

And now we must investigate its subjective possibility. This means simply that we must try to understand what we are told about this reality as an answer to the question to which the reality itself challenges, which is so to speak forced upon us by the reality. Our concern cannot be merely with a general question, with any undisciplined "How is this possible?" which might be hurled at us. Nor can we treat of it merely from the standpoint of a general concept of [243] possibility and impossibility which may perhaps illuminate us. In this respect, too, the reality of revelation is in no sense an answer to all kinds of questions originating elsewhere than in itself. They may be thought to be the most essential, or at all events the most relevant questions, and with the best claim to be raised. But that does not make the slightest difference. The reality insists upon being understood in its own light, on its own merits, and therefore with the help only of the questions to which it challenges us itself. And indeed it does challenge us to questions, and it does will to be understood. Again, we must make it clear that whatever we say, we say personally to ourselves, as something said to ourselves. Otherwise we cannot seriously commit ourselves to the statement. Obedience to revelation consists in following it, which means that at the very least we wish to understand it. But the question of understanding cannot precede the question of fact. It must invariably follow it.

We will formulate the question of understanding as we did our first question. It will then run as follows: How in the freedom of man is it possible for God's revelation to reach man? Man is free for God by the Holy Spirit of the Father and the Son. In that consists the reality of revelation. But how can he be free? To what extent is he so? To what extent is the work of the Holy Spirit the reality of revelation, i.e., the adequate ground of man's freedom for God, and therefore of his receiving what God offers him? To what extent has the Holy

---

ᴱᴺ¹⁴⁹ perfect salvation

Spirit the possibility or power to do this work? We are not asking whether He has it. We cannot do that without calling in question His reality. And to call it in question would already be to deny it. Our question is: In what consists the possibility and power already recognised and acknowledged in reality? In that reality, how far do we find a problem solved, a question answered, a condition fulfilled, a need met? We are not putting the question independently of the question of fact. As we face and answer it, we are not withdrawing to an independent point of consideration, where we know from the first what problem has to be solved, what question answered, what condition fulfilled, what need met. On the contrary, we confine ourselves to the problem which this reality has solved, to the question which it has answered, to the condition which it has fulfilled, to the need which it has met.

We must start very much as we did in the christological investigation of the concept of revelation. We have to show that the reality of the Holy Spirit in His work on man has also a strictly negative meaning. It is real in the Holy Spirit that we are free for God. And this settles the fact that we are not free for God except in the Holy Spirit. The work of the Holy Spirit itself cuts away from us the thought of any other possibility of our freedom for God. It encloses this [244] possibility within itself. How could it be otherwise? As God, the Holy Spirit is a unique person. But He is not an independent divinity side by side with the unique Word of God. He is simply the Teacher of the Word: of that Word which is never without its Teacher. When it is a matter of instructing and instruction by the Word, that instructing and instruction are the work of the Holy Spirit. Without that work there is no instruction, for the Word is never apart from the Holy Spirit. And it is by this very work of the Holy Spirit, and because in the Holy Spirit we recognise that God's Word is the truth, that we are convinced of the futility of the only remaining possibility, i.e., that in some sense we already have the Holy Spirit, in other words, that we have a prior knowledge of the Word of God, that we have been instructed in it from the very first, that we are even in a position to instruct ourselves in it. It is God Himself who opens our eyes and ears for Himself. And in so doing He tells us that we could not do it of ourselves, that of ourselves we are blind and deaf. To receive the Holy Spirit means an exposure of our spiritual helplessness, a recognition that we do not possess the Holy Spirit. For that reason the subjective reality of revelation has the distinctive character of a miracle, i.e., it is a reality to be grounded only in itself. In the actual subjective reality of revelation it is finally decided that apart from it there is no other possibility of being free for God.

It should, of course, be noted that when we say that man is not free for God apart from the reality of the Holy Spirit, we are not making a generally self-evident statement after the manner of philosophical agnosticism. Indeed, no agnostic statement can even remotely attain to what is intended by this theological statement. The agnostic informs us that the upward view is blocked. He calls the man a fool who blinkingly turns his eyes in that direction. The incapacity of which he speaks is dreadful enough, but it is certainly not the radical incapacity which is involved when we state theologically that man is not free for God. Again, when the agnostic speaks about the above to which our view is barred, he does not mean God (who, fundamentally, is the only possibility of our life here, and therefore of our upward view to that which is Himself). It is an above of which there is unfortunately no actual view, although, of course, there could be. If there were, it would be at our disposal. And renunciation of it is also at our disposal. It is upon the certainty of our disposing that the agnostic ultimately depends. That is why he dare make his renunciation so absolutely, and therefore proclaim the very system of agnosticism. Because he makes his renunciation so absolutely he cannot possibly mean God when he speaks of the above which is barred to us. If he did mean God, he would have to allow the renunciation he makes so absolutely to be bracketed and relativised by the reality of the Holy Spirit. But what relation could there be between the upward view which this reality opens up and the upward view of which agnosticism speaks, or between the fact that man is not free for God and his ceasing to peer in the direction in which agnosticism looks for the beyond? There can be no doubt that acknowledgment of the reality of the Holy Spirit would necessarily compel the agnostic to speak quite differently. Instead of an absolute claim to renunciation, he would have to forego all claims and speak about the humility enjoined upon us. Instead of eyes which blink (and blink continually), he would have to speak about our blindness and the healing of the blind. In fact, he would have to surrender his agnosticism all along the line.

This incidental note has nothing to do with apologetics. The only reason for it is to make it clear that when we say that apart from the reality of the Holy Spirit we are not free for God, this has nothing whatever to do with the above philosophical theory. The agnostic does not know what he is saying when perhaps he agrees with us that man is not free for God. As an agnostic he knows nothing about it. For this is something which can be known only by revelation, only by the Holy Spirit. [245]

It is exactly the same here as it is with the objective reality of revelation. For only by the knowledge of that revelation, the knowledge of Jesus Christ, do we learn that God is a hidden God. Similarly, it is by the same Holy Spirit by whom God takes up His abode in us and makes us His temple, that God and man are separated with such power and finality, that their unity can no longer be understood except as the unity of the free grace of God with His unconditional adoration by man. We have only to look at it strictly to see that there is not the slightest contradiction between the offices of the Holy Spirit as Comforter and as Judge, between the unity and the distance which He creates. For necessarily as the Teacher of the Word who reconciles us to God, He informs us both about God and also about ourselves. God He sets before us as the almighty Lord, and His kindness as infinite, just because it is so unmerited, so absolutely unconditioned by our encounter with it. But ourselves in the first instance He does not reveal as petty finite creatures of little account in His presence (for this contrast would still not signify that we are not free for Him; the infinite needs the finite just as the finite needs the infinite). In the first instance we are revealed as rebels against this Lord, as unthankful for His kindness, as resisters of His call. Only then and from that standpoint are we shown to be creatures who, not only in their finitude, but as men created by Him out of nothing, are really dust before Him, whose existence is forfeit and would be lost, were it not that we might wait for Him. The Holy Spirit puts God on the one side and man on the other. And then He calls this God our Father and man the child of this Father. He brings God straight to those eyes and ears and hearts of ours which are so utterly unfitted for Him. And He takes us straight to the reality of God's action, the God who so utterly does not need us. Therefore the line is really drawn about which the agnostic wisdom of this world can never even dream, let alone perceive. And this line is not expunged or removed in the Holy Spirit. It remains drawn. The miracle does not cease to be a miracle. It will remain a miracle to all eternity of completed redemption. The children of God are those in whom the miracle of their sonship persists, and with it free grace, and unconditional adoration, and the line, and the knowledge that man is not free to step beyond that line of his own accord. There is no other knowledge apart from this. We cannot pull down God from His throne and set man over against Him in a kind of fore-heaven. There is no other synthesis than that which is [246] achieved solely in the Word of God and in His Holy Spirit. If we suppose that there is, it is simply a product of that theological dilettantism which is no sooner recalled from speculation by a glance of the real subject than it reverts at once to fresh speculation, i.e., to unfettered thought and language about that subject, and all because it does not know the meaning of consistency even at this point. In the Holy Spirit we know the real togetherness of God and man. We do not need to deny what agnosticism denies without even knowing what it is denying. In the Holy Spirit we are confronted by what we cannot deny even if we willed to do so. We know, therefore, that we cannot ascribe to man any freedom of his own for God, any possibility of his own to become the recipient of revelation. And we know it in a way which does not admit of any question. For the Holy Spirit is not a dialectician. And the negation is not our own discovery. Unlike our own positive or negative discoveries, it is not open to revision.

But once we have established that there is no other freedom of man for God, the question arises all the more imperiously, how far the possibility really does exist in that miracle which is the work of the Holy Spirit. Almost everything that we can say about man from the standpoint of revelation tells against the possibility that God can be revealed to us. But the work of the Holy Spirit is in favour of that possibility. Now we cannot make either statement except from the standpoint of revelation. Therefore we cannot mean the same thing when on the one side we say God cannot, and on the other we say God can. "God cannot" means that He cannot do it on the basis of a human possibility. "God can" means, of course, that He can on the basis of His own possibility. It is the possibility which is proper to God in the work of the Holy Spirit which we now have to consider. Let us see to it that we do not look for it anywhere but in the work of the Holy Spirit Himself. There is no independent standpoint from which we can survey and either approve or disapprove the ways of God (as though we could suggest other ways to God). We can only keep God's actual ways before us. We can only try to understand both the fact and the extent that they are actual ways. In so doing we shall not even dream that we can know

46

what actual ways are except from our consideration of the actual ways of God. We can give only one basic answer to the question how in the freedom of man it is possible for God's revelation to reach him. This is that it is possible, as it is real, only in the outpouring of the Holy Spirit. We have now to develop this statement.

1. By the outpouring of the Holy Spirit it is possible for God's revelation to reach man in his freedom, because in it the Word of God is brought to his hearing.

In expounding the subjective reality of revelation we everywhere insisted that it is not only strictly bound to its objective reality, but that it is simply the process by which that objective reality becomes subjective. The Holy Spirit is [247] the Spirit of the Father and of the Son, of the Father who reveals Himself in His Son and only in His Son. But that means that He is the Spirit of Jesus Christ. That is why we insisted at the very outset that to speak about the Holy Spirit and His work we must expound the biblical testimony to the revelation in Jesus Christ. Even on the subjective side this testimony does not let us down, but is perfectly adequate. Again, that is why we had to point so explicitly to the Church. The Church is the one particular spot which corresponds to the particularity of the incarnation. It is there that revelation is really subjective, for there Jesus Christ the Head has in His own people His body, there the only-begotten Son of God has in them His brethren. Again, that is why in the concept of the Church we had to insist so strongly upon the objective sacramental element, and only in the last instance and in relation to it could we speak of man as the recipient of revelation, i.e., of man won by Christ for Christ. That is the reality of revelation as it reaches man from God's side. And at the outset we can only repeat and underline the fact that that and that alone is its possibility. The reason, and the only reason, why man can receive revelation in the Holy Spirit is that God's Word is brought to his hearing in the Holy Spirit. For the capacity of man to do this depends upon the fact, and only upon the fact, that it is God's Word which is brought to his hearing in revelation. God's Word, i.e., God's revealed, incarnate Word spoken to all other men in the man Jesus of Nazareth. According to Scripture, everything which can be, everything which is either objectively or subjectively possible in relation to revelation, is enclosed in the being and will and action of the triune God. All capacity in this respect is His capacity, and we can read it from His working. Again according to Scripture, His working is the working of His Word, the work of His Son. Everything distinct from that is directly or indirectly our working, and it must first receive revelation, it must first be reconciled to God by the divine working and work. Therefore in relation to revelation all capacity is concretely the capacity of the Word, the capacity of Jesus Christ. There is no alternative: when we ask how a man comes to hear the Word of God, to believe in Christ, to be a member of His body and as His brother to be God's child, at once we must turn and point away to the inconceivable, whose conceivability is obviously in question; and we must say that it depends upon the inconceivable itself and as

47

such, that it can become conceivable to men. The Word creates the fact that we hear the Word. Jesus Christ creates the fact that we believe in Jesus Christ. Up there with Him it is possible for it to be possible down here with me. All the other possibilities which I have and of which I may think are perhaps very fine and significant possibilities in another direction. The fact that we have them means, perhaps, that we are free and open and ready in every conceivable direction: but not in this direction. For the thing for which we have to be free and open and ready at this point does not itself derive from our reality. It does not belong to it. It has only assumed our reality. Therefore it confronts us as a new reality. In the whole range of our possibilities there is nothing to correspond to it or to explain it. And if this is true of the thing itself, it is also true of the reality and the possibility of our communion with it. There is such a thing "because the love of God is shed abroad in our hearts by the Holy Ghost which is given unto us" (Rom. 5⁵). But if it is possible for it to exist, the possibility is not in our hearts but in the love of God. Similarly, the "through the Holy Ghost which is given unto us" cannot have its possibility except in the love of God. In other words, the work of the Holy Spirit means that there is an adequate basis for our hearing of the Word, since it brings us nothing but the Word for our hearing. It means that there is an adequate basis for our faith in Christ and our communion with Him, because He is no other Spirit than the Spirit of Jesus Christ. It is, therefore, the subjective possibility of revelation because it is the process by which its objective reality is made subjective, namely, the life of the body of Christ, the operation of the prophetic and apostolic testimony, the hearing of preaching, the seeing of that to which the sacraments point. Of course for us, in our knowledge of revelation, it is something quite new, and strange, and not at all self-evident, that there should be this process of making subjective, this life, this work, this hearing and seeing: that an event in our life should really correspond to the event of Jesus Christ, that a here below should correspond to a there above. Easter and Whitsunday are—and not merely within our knowledge—two different things. So, too, are the objective state and subjective process, Word and Spirit, divine command and human reception. But when we inquire into the possibility of the second, we can only reach back to the first and say that it is there that its whole possibility is to be found. The Holy Spirit is the Spirit of God, because He is the Spirit of the Word. And that is the very reason and the only reason why we acquire eyes and ears for God in the Holy Spirit. If, then, we want truly and properly to understand the Holy Spirit and His work upon us, we can never try to understand them abstractly and in themselves.

Supposing we do look at the work in itself, at the occurrence as it becomes an actual event in our lives. And from it we try to discover how far in this occurrence Christ can be an event in our lives. The result will certainly be either that we merely find something extremely human, in which Christ is unrecognisable, and we completely misunderstand the work of the Holy Spirit, or that we most inappropriately confuse and equate the occurrence which we know, and therefore our human something, with Christ Himself, which means that we

[248]

will seek Christ anywhere and everywhere and expose ourselves to every possible heresy. And either way we can never more mistake the work of the Holy Spirit, and discredit it either in our own eyes or others', than by making it the object of an independent investigation. For when we do that, the result may be disillusionment or gratification, but the possibilities which we will certainly consider have nothing whatever to do with the great possibility that we might receive revelation. There can be no doubt that our feet are already on the road either to scepticism or to a mild or even a violent fanaticism.

[249]

If we want truly and properly to investigate the subjective possibility of revelation, and therefore to understand the Holy Spirit and His work, we must never look at subjective realities in which he might presumably or actually be seen and experienced. We must look rather at the place from which He comes and at what He brings. We must look at the contents of God's hand stretched out to us in Him. We must look at the love of God shed abroad in our hearts by Him. We must look to the objective possibility of our communion with Christ. In other words, we must look at Christ Himself.

It is only when we look in this direction that we can answer the very relevant question: Have I the Holy Spirit? Certainly, "if any man have not the Spirit of Christ, he is none of his" (Rom. 8⁹). But just because He is the Spirit of Christ, this question of "having" is not decided by what we can never do more than think we "have," but only by Christ. For it is only from Christ that we can have it, and therefore we can have it for ourselves only by continually turning to Him. And He says always: "Him that cometh to me I will in no wise cast out" (Jn. 6³⁷). The Church and Holy Scripture and preaching and the sacrament are therefore again the only possible criteria in any practical investigation.

And true and proper proclamation of the subjective possibility of revelation, true preaching from the Holy Spirit of Pentecost, will not consist in pointing to our own or other men's seizure, but in pointing to the divine seizing, and therefore once again to Christ Himself.

Consciously or unconsciously, every hearer is necessarily faced with the question whether and how he can be a real hearer and doer of the Word. And true preaching will direct him rather "rigidly" to something written, or to his baptism or to the Lord's Supper, instead of pointing him in the very slightest to his own or the preacher's or other people's experience. It will confront him with no other faith than faith in Christ, who died for him and rose again. But if we claim even for a moment that experiences are valid and can be passed on, we find that they are marshy ground upon which neither the preacher nor the hearer can stand or walk. Therefore they are not the object of Christian proclamation. If it is really applied to man in a thoroughly practical way, Christian proclamation does not lead the listener to experiences. All the experiences to which it might lead are at best ambiguous. It leads them right back through all experiences to the source of all true and proper experience, i.e., to Jesus Christ.

To sum up: It is Christ, the Word of God, brought to the hearing of man by the outpouring of the Holy Spirit, who is man's possibility of being the recipient of divine revelation. Therefore this receiving, this revealedness of God for us, is really itself revelation. In no less a sense than the incarnation of the Word in Christ, it is the divine act of lordship, the mystery and the miracle of the existence of God among us, the triumph of free grace. The more important

49

[250] the idea and proclamation of this receiving is for a man, and the more seriously he takes his problem, and the more definitely he can speak to it, the more emphatically he must again and again insist upon this fact.

We hardly need any specific evidence to show that this statement and finding has not been spun out of the void, but derives from the New Testament and therefore, implicitly and explicitly, from the Old. Not only in the message of the New Testament Gospels, but also of the Epistles and Apocalypse, it is one of the most self-evident themes that the Holy Spirit, and with the Holy Spirit all that makes the Church the Church, and Christians Christians, does not come from any place but only from Christ. And that means that grace—it may be pardoning grace or sanctifying and enabling grace—is always His grace. It means that faith is always faith in Him. Only as it is awakened and imparted by Him is it faith in God. It means that the gifts of the Spirit in the community are literally subordinated to Him and measured by Him as the Lord of the community. It means that the apostles are His servants. It means that the Word is His commission. It is constantly applied in new ways, but in content it is always an indication of Him and of Him alone. There may be many detours, but they are genuine detours. They may appear to lead us to a subjective whose interest is only abstract. But they always return to what the New Testament has to say, namely to the objective. They return to it as it has to be the objective for the sake of the subjective. It is the one unique thing, the centre. We may draw a circle around that centre, but it can never be anything more than a circle: Διὸ ἀναζωσάμενοι τὰς ὀσφύας τῆς διανοίας ὑμῶν, νήφοντες, τελείως ἐλπίσατε ἐπὶ τὴν φερομένην ὑμῖν χάριν ἐν ἀποκαλύψει Ἰησοῦ Χριστοῦ[EN150] (1 Pet. 1[13]).

We have here the root of that recognition on whose basis the Western Church assumed into the creed, in relation to the eternal procession of the Holy Spirit, the *Filioque*[EN151] as well as the *ex Patre*[EN152] (cf. Vol. 1, 1, 500–511). Its intention was to recognise the fact that in God's revelation the Holy Spirit is the Spirit of Jesus Christ, that He cannot be separated from Him, that He is only the Spirit of Jesus Christ. And it did it with such definiteness that it found it necessary to confess that He is the Spirit of the Father and of the Son not only here and now and for us, but also from all eternity, in the hidden triune being of God which is revealed to us in revelation. It is because the Holy Spirit is from all eternity the communion between the Father and the Son, and therefore not only the Spirit of the Father but also the Spirit of the Son, that in God's revelation He can be the communion between the Father and those whom His Son has called to be His brethren. It is grounded from all eternity in God that no man cometh to the Father except by the Son, because the Spirit by whom the Father draws His children to Himself is also from all eternity the Spirit of the Son, because by His Spirit the Father does not call anyone except to His Son. In respect of revelation the Western Church did not recognise any Spirit to be the Holy Spirit except the Spirit of Christ. But it also spoke of the God who meets us in His revelation as the eternal God. If it was right in this, then we must stand firmly with it on this particular question of the *Filioque*[EN153].

The same recognition will also help us to understand the later development in the medieval West of that objectivism in the concepts of both sacrament and the Church, which was upheld successfully and with stern consistency by the Popes, e.g., against the spiritual kingdom of the Franciscans. The doctrine of the third kingdom of the Spirit first arose with Francis of Assisi and it was added to by his spiritual successors. To understand the struggle we

---

[EN150] Therefore, prepare your minds for action, be self-controlled, set your hope completely on the grace that will come to you at the revelation of Jesus Christ
[EN151] 'and from the Son'
[EN152] 'from the Father'
[EN153] 'and from the Son'

have to remember that with its emphasising and practice of life and love in the discipleship of Christ the Franciscan Christianity of the Spirit obviously claimed to represent a subjectivisation of objective revelation. It imagined that the historical Christ could now be left behind as something antiquated. The disciple would now replace Him as the vehicle of His Spirit. In effect, this meant a dissolution of the recognition stated in the *Filioque*[EN154], and therefore of the recognition of the New Testament unity of Christ and Spirit. Where the Holy Spirit is sundered from Christ, sooner or later He is always transmuted into quite a different spirit, the spirit of the religious man, and finally the human spirit in general. The threads are visible which lead from Franciscan Pneumatology to the anthropology of the humanistic Renaissance. To that extent the Papacy had the better case theologically in this controversy.

[251]

In the 16th century the same position was maintained by the Reformers, headed by Luther. "In these words St. Peter assigneth to this person called Jesus of Nazareth the divine work of pouring forth the Holy Ghost. For to pour forth the Holy Ghost belongeth not to any creature, though he were an angel from heaven, but to God alone" (*Pred. üb. Act.* 2[14f.], 1534, *E.A.* 4, 100). "And mark well this text, how here Christ bindeth the Holy Ghost to His mouth and setteth Him His goal and measure that He go not beyond His own word: 'All things whatsoever have proceeded from my mouth He shall call to your remembrance and transmit by you.' Therewith he sheweth that henceforth in Christianity naught else must be taught by the Holy Ghost than what they, the apostles, heard from Christ (but did not yet understand) and were taught and reminded of by the Holy Ghost, that therefore it always pass out of Christ's mouth from one mouth to the other yet remain Christ's mouth, and the Holy Ghost is the schoolmaster, to teach and recall such" (*Pred. üb. Joh.* 14[23f.]. *Cruz. Somm. Post. W.A.* 21, 468, 35). To the question, why the Holy Spirit is called a "witness," Luther replied: "Because He witnesseth of Christ and otherwise of none other; apart from this testimony of the Holy Ghost to Christ there is no certain, lasting comfort. So all dependeth upon this text being surely grasped and retained; so say thou: 'I believe in Jesus Christ who died for me and know that the Holy Ghost who is called and is a witness and comforter, preacheth or testifieth of none other in Christendom to comfort and strengthen the afflicted, than of Christ. I will also abide thereby and otherwise hold to no other comfort.' For should there be a better or surer comfort than this, the Holy Ghost would bring it also: but He is not to do more than witness to Christ. The comfort shall not fail, if we but hold fast thereto and gladly believe that it is true and the Holy Ghost's witness" (*W.A. Ti.* 6, 6654). Of course, in contrast to the earliest controversy Luther directs all these statements not only against the fanaticism of his time but also and supremely against the Papacy. He lays against the Papacy exactly the same charge as the Papacy itself had formerly made, that it presupposed and asserted a presence and operation of the Holy Spirit apart from and side by side with Christ. There are many contexts in Luther in which on the one front or the other he concretely and uncompromisingly expounds this unity of Christ and the Spirit. He lays it down that the work of the Holy Spirit on our behalf is tied down to Scripture, preaching and the sacraments. He Himself is the measure of its operation, and we can never regard it in any way as the work of an absolutely "subjective" illumination, inspiration or enthusiasm. In the case of Luther the problem of the subjective, of man receiving divine revelation and reconciliation, was, we might almost say, *the* theological problem. There is no doubt, therefore, as to the meaning of the relentlessness with which, when he speaks of the Spirit, he points away from the Spirit and to Christ and therefore to all the objective side of the Church. His aim was to reveal and constantly to recall the descent in virtue of which the subjective reality of revelation is not any reality, but the one reality of the breaking in of God to man, the breaking in of objective

---

[EN154] 'and from the Son'

revelation into our subjective realm. *Observa autem quaenam sint illa omnia, quorum doctorem fore spiritum promittit: Suggeret, inquit, vel reducet in memoriam "quaecunque dixi." Unde sequitur non fore novarum revelationum architectum. Hoc uno verbo refutare licet quaecunque sub praetextu spiritus in ecclesiam figmenta ab initio hucusque Satan invexit. Mahometes et papa commune habent religionis principium, non contineri in scriptura perfectionem doctrinae, sed quiddam altius revelatum esse a spiritu. Ex eadem lacuna nostro tempore Anabaptistae et Libertini sua deliria hauserunt. Atqui impostor est Spiritus, non Christi, qui extraneum aliquod ab evangelio commentum ingerit. Spiritum enim Christus promittit, qui evangelii doctrinam quasi subscriptor confirmct*[EN155] (Calvin, *Comm.* Jn. 14²⁶, *C.R.* 47, 335). It is not a *novum regnum*[EN156] which the Holy Spirit sets up amongst us, but the glory which was given the Son by the Father. *Simul ac spiritus a Christi sermone divellitur, quibuslibet deliriis et imposturis aperta est ianua .... Quorsum igitur spiritus doctrina? Non ut nos abducat a schola Christi, sed potius ut rata sit vox illa qua iubemur ipsum audire*[EN157] (Jn. 16¹⁴ *ib.*, p. 363). To understand what it was that Protestant orthodoxy of the 17th century was trying to safeguard at all costs, it is necessary to bring out the content and bearing of this particular aspect of Reformation thinking—and that quite irrespective for the moment of whether orthodoxy played its part well or badly.

[252]

The case is far otherwise with Neo-Protestantism. This has its forerunners in the *Anabaptistae et Libertini*[EN158] of the Reformation period. Even in its best and purest form it rests upon a declension from the height of this insight. It did not at first instal the human factor in its many forms as a second divine revelation side by side with the revelation in Christ. It did not at first allow this second revelation to evolve into the real revelation. But long before, and even where it still did not appear to do this, or concealed the fact that it did, it separated itself from the New Testament Church by setting over against the knowledge and life of faith in Christ an autonomous knowledge and faith deriving from the Holy Ghost. In the first instance, of course, it claimed, and still claims, only to represent the interests of the subjectivisation of objective revelation as against an objectivism which is actually or apparently dead. Neo-Protestantism in its noblest and earliest form was in every sense a godly and serious piety. It was godly and serious in all the important forms of its second or Enlightenment stage. Even to-day we shall miss the mark if we accuse it of a lack of seriousness or godliness. On the contrary, it must be soberly admitted that as far as seriousness and godliness go it has often enough had the advantage over the representatives of the official teaching. The one reproach we can and must bring against it is that it abandoned an insight which was unambiguously indicated in the New Testament, not so unambiguously asserted in the Middle Ages, and unforgettably renewed in the Reformation theology of justification

---

[EN155] So then, see all those things of which the Spirit promises to be teacher: that He will make mention of, it says, or He will bring back to memory 'everything which I have said'. From this it follows that he would not be the architect of new revelations. With this one statement, one can refute whatever inventions Satan has brought into the church from its beginning [Typo in KD and ET: Hucusque should be huiusque] under the pretext of the Spirit. Mohammed and the Pope have a common religious principle: that the perfection of doctrine is not contained in Scripture but that something higher has been revealed by the Spirit. From this same lack in our time, the Anabaptists and the Radicals have created their delusions. But it is a false spirit, not the Spirit of Christ, which introduces some addition which does not come from the Gospel. For Christ promises a Spirit who will confirm the teaching of the Gospel, like a signatory

[EN156] new kingdom

[EN157] When the Spirit is separated from the word of Christ, the door is opened to any and every delusion and deception ... To what end therefore is the teaching of the Spirit? Not to lead us away from the school of Christ, but rather so that that voice, by which we are commanded to hear Him, might be considered by the mind

[EN158] Anabaptists and Radicals

and sanctification. This was the insight that the Holy Spirit is none other than the Spirit of Jesus Christ. By abandoning it, it opened the doors with only too much seriousness and godliness *quibuslibet deliriis et imposturis*[EN159], i.e., to a recognition of all possible idols, including those with which we have to do to-day.

The clearest monument, accessible to everyone, of this development and of these open doors is the collection of church hymn-books current in Evangelical quarters (cf. for what follows Lukas Christ, *Das evangelische Kirchenlied*, Z.d.Z. 1925, 358 ff.).

It is no accident that in the Evangelical service it is the praise of the congregation which particularly represents the element of subjective reality in revelation, i.e., man as he becomes the recipient of it in the Holy Spirit. In Eph. 5^{19} there is an early reference to ᾠδαῖς πνευματικαῖς[EN160]. But what is the meaning of πνευματικαῖς[EN161] in this context? What sort of possibility is it that man possesses here? If we are contemplating the Reformation period the answer is simple. At the end of 1523 Luther writes to Spalatin of his intention to publish a collection of psalms in German, and asks him for his co-operation in the task. The purpose of such *cantilenae spirituales*[EN162] is simply *quo verbum Dei vel cantu inter populos maneat*[EN163] (*W. A. Br.* 3, 220, 3). And more explicitly in 1524 in the preface to the so-called *Walther' schen Chorgesangbüchlein*: " ... in order that thereby God's Word and Christian doctrine may be applied and exercised in every sort of way. Accordingly I have also ... brought together some spiritual songs, to apply and make current the holy Gospel which hath now by God's grace once more arisen, so that we too may boast, as Moses doth in his song in Exo. 15, that Christ is our praise and song, and that we would know nothing else to sing or to say save Jesus Christ, as Paul saith in 1 Cor. 2" (*W.A.* 35, 474, 8). The intention of this programme is outwardly reflected in the fact that with four exceptions Luther himself did not compose freely, but imitated the Bible or the early and mediaeval Church. In Luther's case this was no makeshift: he was a poet of ability. It is simply that his concern was "not for his own interests, but for the Church and her faith" (L. Christ, *op. cit.* p. 367). This is decided by the actual content. Luther's hymns are completely lacking in all lyrical quality, i.e., in all emphasis upon the emotion of the subject. The one who speaks in them is neither giving to himself all kinds of accusatory, heartening, instructive and hortatory advice, nor is he constraining others with the challenge or invitation or demand to lay this or that upon their hearts. What these hymns contain is adoration and solid communication, confession of faith, confession of sins, proclamation. It would have to be a very strange reading that did not find in them the language of the Christian heart and its experience, or rather—no matter whether "I" or "we" is in the forefront as the subject of the hymn—of the community of God's children. It was in its name and on its behalf that Luther composed his hymns. But in these hymns we never find either God's child or God's Church preoccupied with themselves, but always turning to the recognition and praise of God and His acts, with the greatest concentration upon the second article as understood in all its biblical simplicity. It is in this way that there speaks the life, love, experience and actuality of subjective reality in revelation. And as regards purpose and basis the same is true of most of the hymn-writers of the 16th century, for instance, J. Decius, M. Weisse, J. Zwick, N. Hermann, Paul Speratus, J. Gramann, M. Schalling or N. Selnecker. The Reformed Church was marked by a strict adherence to the biblical psalms (in the renderings of Jorissen and Lobwasser). The result was that, although it had no very sure merit as poetry, in content its Church praise did maintain the same high

[253]

[EN159] to any and every delusion and deception
[EN160] spiritual songs
[EN161] spiritual
[EN162] spiritual songs
[EN163] so that the word of God might dwell among the peoples in song

level. It maintained it longer than the Lutheran, and in the stricter Reformed circles still does so to-day. But by the end of the 16th century, when academic orthodoxy had reached its peak, there had already been a remarkable change in the sphere of hymnology. It was not always equally radical, but its effects were felt at every point. In the first instance, of course, the object of faith is retained in spite of the change. But there is now a new preoccupation, and whole stanzas are devoted, not to this first theme, but to what is obviously a second centre of reflection, the heart, the soul, the I, the We, in all the problem of its relation to the former object. P. Nicolai, for example, is still deeply rooted in the 16th century in his "How sweetly shines the morning star." And the interesting feature of it is not that the bridal mysticism of the Song of Songs finds expression in the Evangelical Church. What really is interesting is that this is only a symptom of the formation of this new epicentre, which is almost palpable in this particular hymn. In the 17th century it made irresistible progress in men like J. Heermann, J. Rist, J. Franck, J. J. Schütz, Joachim Neander—and theologically there can be no doubt that Paul Gerhardt belongs to this series. Certainly the old Reformed note is not lacking in any of them. Paul Gerhardt is naturally the best from this standpoint. In fact, for broad stretches—in so far as they compose as orthodox theologians—it is impressively sounded. But the other note becomes clearer and clearer. On the one hand there is an intensifying of interest in the depths of the believing subject, his sin, his pardon, his sanctification, and in the perceptions, moods and feelings accompanying these processes. On the other hand, there is a widening of the element of religious meditation and reflection on the many aspects of the external existence of the subject in the various divisions of day and year, in calling, in good times and more particularly in bad, in life and especially in the expectation of death. In place of the drama of creation, reconciliation and redemption, which is

[254] the work of the triune God, another drama is staged. We hear a monologue of the soul, or a dualogue between the soul and God, or even at this early date of one soul with another. It is a serious and depressed and almost melancholy voice which we hear, and one which corresponds to the gloomy character of the history of the century. We must believe of these men that they struggled and strove and despaired and were comforted and established in faith. Sometimes they found unforgettable words to express it. But overlooking the change in the Reformation content of their hymns, it is in them and their self-confessions that we are forced to believe. And it is as self-confessions that their hymns harmonise remarkably well and not unnaturally with those of their contemporary, the convert and mystic J. Scheffler, *alias* Angelus Silesius. For good or evil, we must believe that he, too, was serious and ardent and profound in intention. But in what or in whom are we really believing? And in the glory of a newer, more gladsome and more self-conscious age this self-confession becomes richer, more luxuriant and more emotional as we pass into the 18th century. In the so-called rational theology, pietism triumphs theologically with its great slogan "not only doctrine but life too"; and at once the rivulets of poesy begin to gush in the direction of "not doctrine but life." It is a downright exuberant Christian feeling for life—quite in accordance with the general spirit of the age—which now meets us (even the tunes of the period begin to acquire a suspicious swing) in the songs of a Christian F. Richter, L. A. Gotter, B. Schmolck, J. J. Rambach, P. F. Hiller, Ernst Gottlieb Woltersdorf, and in his own particular way N. v. Zinzendorf. What first strikes one about them is the sometimes rather pompous but always very impressive way in which—the orthodox facade is still unbroken—they relate themselves to dogma and particularly to Christology. Nothing could be more moving, more triumphant or more solemn than, say, their language about Christ's active God-manhood in the three offices of prophet, priest and king. But the fanciful and fancy-breeding elaboration used shows at once the extent to which things have gone awry: confession and proclamation have now really given way to religious poetry. The objective element is now filled out and carried along by the ardour and the thankfulness and veneration and the laudatory rejoicing of the

subject. It is true that even this poetry is not devoid of confession and proclamation. The hymns do contain statements and verses which we are glad to read and sing, so gripped are we not merely by their emotional content but by their content of knowledge, biblical and reformed. But on the whole participation in the singing of these hymns implies a congregation which is highly self-impelled, highly self-activating and highly self-exalted, and no longer—we cannot fail to remark it—the congregation of Luther which is moved simply by hearing the Word in faith. It is a congregation which has grown far more godly, which makes far greater demands on itself. But above all it takes things much more seriously and importantly even in regard to its religious possessions. Children of God? Yes, but children of precocious wisdom and maturity, almost ready to leave school, already, it would seem, on a footing of comradeship with the Father. And then at the very peak of the century, there arise the two last great Evangelical hymn-writers, Gerhard Tersteegen and Christian Fürchtegott Gellert. The objective substance of the hymn has still not been abandoned: indeed it has hardly been touched. A fairly complete compendium of biblical and Church Christology could still be compiled from these hymns. But in both Tersteegen and Gellert is it not quite evident that that second epicentre has finally settled and hardened? The real substance of what they make the congregation sing definitely relates to this and not the former centre. The traditional Christology has turned unnoticed into an exoteric garment. In Tersteegen it is a garment for the exposition of a mystical experience of the Presence. In Gellert it is a garment for the exposition of a solid moral attitude. In both cases, however, it is a foreign body which adheres to the real substance not necessarily but a little accidentally. Listen to Tersteegen himself in the Foreword to his *Geistlichen Blumengärtlein inniger Seelen*, 1768: "Alas, that so [255] many hungry souls have so long allowed themselves to be supported and fed on dry, strengthless husk-and-shadow figures of truths, in which the spirit can find no solid or abiding satisfaction and peace, since in them the essential core-truths of the inward life of a Christian, still by God's grace to be experienced here in this pilgrim way, are, where not contemned, yet so little realised and known in their beauty and preciousness, that sympathy can never sufficiently lament it. Alas, men search far and wide and with many an effort for a treasure which they cannot properly find; yet they could have it so easily and so intimately, if only by God's help they would give themselves a chance of entering into the appropriate preparedness or disposition of the heart. Come, O souls called of God to His pure service of the spirit! Let us in the Lord's strength rid ourselves and let ourselves be rid of all visible things, of the senses, of reason, and of all idiosyncrasies, in order that, properly separated, simplified, pure creatures, we may enter into our spirit and soul-ground, and there find, behold and love God who is also a Spirit, and enjoy His peace which passeth all understanding." And listen to Gellert in the Preface to his *Geistlichen Oden und Liedern*, 1757: "Songs for the heart, for which music is particularly suited, must be so composed, that they let us feel everything that is lofty and touching in religion: the holiness of faith, the divineness of love, the heroism of self-denial, the greatness of humility, the loveliness of thankfulness, the nobility of obedience to God and our Redeemer, the good fortune of having an immortal soul created and redeemed for virtue and for eternal life; that they let us feel the shamefulness of vice, the bestiality of the desires and of sensuality, the vileness of greed, the pettiness of conceit, the frightfulness of lewdness, in a word, the attractions of virtue and the hatefulness of vice; of virtue as it is loved and commanded by God, and commanded for our good; of vice as it is rebellion before God, and for us shame, timeless misery, eternal pain." Compare with this what Luther wrote about the contents of a similar collection of hymns. It is hardly necessary to draw attention to the distorted products of pietism and rationalism which were so plentiful both then and later. It is not in the light of distortion but in the light of the pure form of the Neo-Protestant hymn as it reached maturity in Tersteegen and Gellert that we shall see what really happened. And it makes no essential difference whether we have a preference either for Tersteegen or for Gellert. Mysticism and morality are complementary opposites, which cannot seriously be played off one against the other except as a result of misunderstanding. If we really have to seek the subjective possibility of revelation, the Church, at the point where it has been unequivocally sought since the middle of the 18th century, it is better that this Church should sing both Tersteegen and Gellert, so as not to be guilty of partiality. What really happened at the peak of the development of the Evangelical hymn as it was reached in Tersteegen and Gellert was this. Not in a distorted form, but in its twofold classical form, the confession of Christ remains, but in the last resort, in relation to what those poets really intend and the congregation really sing and chant, it has become superfluous. Because it is no longer the one and all, because it has now become (unmistakably and irrevocably) a first side by side with a second, it is clear that it could be taken away altogether and nothing essential would be deducted from what was really intended to be sung and chanted. In the generation which followed Tersteegen and Gellert the Evangelical Church acquired a purely subjective hymnody. This was the age when 16th and 17th century hymns, including those of Luther and Paul Gerhardt, were allowed to disappear entirely or almost entirely from the hymn-books, or were subjected to such a lengthy transformation that they too came to say the only thing which people now wanted to say and to hear. Perhaps it would have been healthy and certainly instructive if this tendency had carried the day. It [256] would have brought it home clearly to the Church's consciousness that the Holy Spirit as men now thought they knew Him, being separated from Jesus Christ, was, in fact, a different spirit from the Spirit of Jesus Christ. He was the spirit of mysticism and morals but not the Spirit in whom the early Church and the Church of the Reformers had heard and believed the Word and nothing but the Word. But further development obscured rather than clarified the situation. When we turn to specifically modern hymnody, to men like Novalis, E. M. Arndt, A. Knapp, P. Spitta, we come across two facts. First, pietism and rationalism have now united in a single and all the mightier stream. But more than that, the radical tendency of the 18th century has obviously worked itself out and even been suppressed. The bias of tradition which clings to the life of public worship in a particular way, and the newly awakened sense of the value and dignity of history, have seen to it that the objective content of hymnody has apparently been restored. But, of course, there has not really been any change in content. The preponderance of the subjective element is still constantly increasing. In the 19th century the religious inwardness and moral seriousness of the Christian temper expressed in the hymn have really become its heartbeat and the measure by which it is measured. For obvious reasons, different from those in the 18th century, the congregation's confession has now really become its confession of itself. The further lesson has been learned, in a manner which was not even remotely possible in the 18th century, of poetically projecting the subjective, which is the real object of singing and speaking, upon the objective. The objective itself is thus transmuted into the subjective. Christ is glorified as the original type of all that is deepest and most powerful in the Christian heart and in the Christian congregation, as the aim, object and essence of all Christian convictions, wishes and longings. Here and there in this poetry one can still catch reminiscences of what the "spiritual song" of Luther and his contemporaries had still been in the century of the Thirty Years' War. And this awkward turning to the object involves automatically and involuntarily the possibility of the objective becoming articulate as such. But in principle we still have to say that the situation is now well-nigh hopelessly involved—doubly involved: for we are again in a position to compare the value of the old Protestant hymn with that of the modern. We again find it intelligible and usable. We can promote it to new honour. The idea arose out of the delightfully rich *Liederschatz der Evangelischen Kirche*, in which Luther and the Reformed Psalms, Paul Gerhardt and the poets of the late Baroque, Tersteegen and Gerhardt and the Romantics and Idealists, the poets of the Awakening and those of the mediating theology of the 19th century were all set peaceably side by side. Congregations were accustomed to the assumption, indeed, they were specifically educated in it, that the whole development had been normal and legitimate. In other words, even the very different first stage can confidently be regarded from the standpoint of the present. If Luther's "A safe stronghold our God is still" is sung with the same breath and intention as, say, E. M. Arndt's "I know whom I believe," then it just ceases to be Luther's hymn. Even Reformation praise of God disappears in the gurgling gullet of modern religious self-confession. All the same, the situation is not quite so involved that we cannot see the meaning of the way which the Evangelical Church has gone in this respect. Originally it did mean by a "spiritual song" a song in which, as in preaching and sacrament, but this time in the form of the congregation's answer, the Word of God is preached and heard. Then it found an interesting subsidiary theme in the experience which man produces by means of the Word. Then the sub-theme was allowed to become an independent theme. Then it was found to be obviously more interesting than the principal theme. Then it was raised to the status of principal theme. And finally, and most important of all, it was found that the most appropriate and effective way to treat this new principal theme was intensively to attract to it the old one, which in itself was now obsolete, but, regarded as an allegorical text, acquired a fresh although secondary glory. It is just this [257] last and conservative turn in the 19th century which should make clear to us the full extent of the reversal. In the 18th century it was thought for a time that the objective content of the hymn could simply be rejected. In the 19th century, however, it was found that it could be subjectively interpreted and utilised. And it is the latter fact which more clearly supports the view that so far as this way is to be considered the true way of its own inner development. Protestantism has followed the way of apostasy from the Reformation. The history of the hymn reveals to us the inner secularisation which has taken place. And it is the very sphere in which we find practically nothing in the way of its outward secularisation; in our modern hymn-books at least it is relatively seldom that we can fix an open heresy. It is far easier to find the hidden heresy involved in the whole development. This can be more or less clearly demonstrated in every section of our hymn-books. It is the heresy of the third article. The Holy Spirit has ceased to be the Spirit of Jesus Christ. To all appearances He is still a spirit of God, even a Christian spirit. In fact, however, He is the spirit of human inwardness and seriousness, the spirit of mysticism and morals. In that spirit we do not yet enjoy, or enjoy no longer, the communion with God which is realised in the revelation of God. On the contrary, for all our seriousness and with all our piety, we are simply alone with ourselves and by ourselves, ἐλπίδα μὴ ἔχοντες καὶ ἄθεοι ἐν τῷ κόσμῳ EN164 (Eph. 2¹²). Necessarily this hidden heresy had to manifest itself in other spheres. In the last resort the whole external secularisation of Protestantism in the specific form of modernistic Neo-Protestantism is only a symptom of the inner secularisation visible in the evolution of the hymn.

2. By the outpouring of the Holy Spirit it is possible in the freedom of man for God's revelation to meet him, because in it he is explicitly told by God's Word that he possesses one possibility of his own for such a meeting.

The Word of God which is revealed in revelation declares that man is not actually free for God. This is already expressed by the fact that it is actually the Word or the Son of God who is revealed. What happens is not just anything. It is the last and most peculiar thing which could happen from God's side. God comes forward Himself to be man's Saviour. This presupposes, and it is already proclaimed as a truth of divine judgment, that man cannot be helped in any

---

EN164 without hope and without God in the world

other way. It is not merely that man lacks something which he ought to be or to have or to be capable of in relation to God. He lacks everything. It is not merely that he is in a dangerous and damaged state, but in his being toward God he is completely finished and impotent. He is not only a sick man but a dead one. It was because the world was lost that Christ was born. Therefore from the very standpoint of Christ's birth we have to say, in the very strictest sense, that the world was lost. A statement like that is only possible from the standpoint of Christ's birth. But from that standpoint we have to make it. Man is free in many respects. He possesses many of the possibilities common to all creatures. And he possesses all the specifically human possibilities which do not appear to be realised except by him. But he does not possess the possibility of communion with God. He cannot be together with God in the way in which
[258] he can be together with his equals, and above all with himself, and in a wider sense of the term with all other creaturely realities. He does not possess a special possibility for this, nor do the rest of his possibilities give him any capacity for it. In this respect he is not free. We cannot say that to be a man means to be without God. But we can and must say, negatively, that to be a man does not mean to be with God. To be a man can certainly include to be with God, but only when it is overlapped by the definition: in Christ, that is, as a hearer and doer of the Word of God, in the Church. But this is the new thing added to our being as men by revelation. It is not included in our being as such. In fact, it is excluded. And as long as, and to the extent that, it is not added to that being as something new, the being is itself excluded from it. All this is as true as the Word of God itself. When the Word of God is acknowledged, it is also acknowledged that man is not free for God. But to acknowledge the Word of God means that he is actually free for God. Therefore it is part of the acknowledgment that his actual freedom to acknowledge is a miracle. It is not grounded upon any freedom or possibility for this acknowledgment which he possessed in his own right. It is grounded solely upon the freedom of the Word of God which has come to him. We cannot think away or ignore the negative content of this acknowledgment. On the basis of our own freedoms and possibilities we should never acknowledge the Word of God to all eternity. And an acknowledgment, grounded or even partly grounded in our own freedoms and possibilities, would *per se* not be recognition of the Word of God. The very intention of making our acknowledgment of the Word of God on the basis of our own freedoms and possibilities would make that acknowledgment quite impossible. And any subsequent attempt to explain that acknowledgment by our own freedoms and possibilities is to deny and therefore to destroy it. It is only as a miracle that it occurs at all. Similarly, it is only as a miracle that it is received and understood. Our own freedom and possibility to meet revelation must be completely talked out in order that the meeting may be possible. To become free for God we must be convinced that we are not already free. We must make room for the miracle of acknowledging the Word of God. The Word of God comprises in itself the necessary negation. If we do hear the Word of God, the

question whether we could hear it on the basis of some freedom of our own has already been discounted. If we do hear it, then *eo ipso* we know no other freedom but that of the Word of God itself. It is not a freedom which we have taken, but a freedom which God has given to us in His mercy, and in virtue of His omnipotence. And that is the very reason why it is in the act of hearing that we obviously know the force and validity of the negation. It has to be fulfilled in us, so that it is no longer expressed only in the Word as it is spoken by God, but in the Word of God as it is heard by us, and therefore in our own selves. It has to be made our own, so that we are quite unable to offer either the prac- [259] tical or theoretical resistance which denies and destroys the miracle of the acknowledgment, and therefore the acknowledgment itself.

But it is not our business either to talk out our freedom for God or to talk in the negation of that freedom. If we could, it would mean that we had in fact a freedom for God and His Word, and a very sovereign freedom at that. For before we heard the Word of God we should obviously know at least this much about its nature and essence: that what will meet us contrary to all our own capacity will be a miracle. But we should also know that our own abilities cannot attain to hearing this Word. And this twofold knowledge would enable us to teach ourselves about the negation, and therefore to dispose ourselves negatively, thus creating the condition by which we may be hearers of the Word of God. But the Word of God excludes every other freedom except its own. Therefore even the freedom to convince ourselves of our own unfreedom, to talk in the negation, is quite untenable. On the contrary, the fact that we are compelled to try to secure at least this freedom for God, the freedom to deny our freedom, is the proof that in practice we cannot attain that renunciation which the hearing of God's Word demands of us.

There is a way of asserting the *servum arbitrium*[EN165] and discoursing against the doctrines of the *liberum arbitrium*[EN166] ("God is everything, man is nothing and thou art a madman") which is too triumphant not to betray that the renunciation is still not made. It is the idea of a *liberum arbitrium*[EN167], of man's pride in his own decision, which triumphs in the very assertion of its opposite. That pride may only too well and gladly assume the form of a publican's Pharisaism. And even if we perceive this, our own last word will still be one form of that pride in decision.

What we concede to the Word of God will always be an attempt to make good a claim to our own freedom, to go on believing in our own possibilities. If we imagine that we can talk out this freedom ourselves, we have already talked it in again. Our talking out, however radical (and the more radical it is the more obviously this is true), is quite unable to talk out what really has to be talked out. It is better for us to recognise our total inability in this respect, to admit to ourselves that on the basis of our own possibilities we shall always be

---

EN165 will in bondage
EN166 free will
EN167 free will

men who require to believe in their own possibilities. The only power for this talking out is simply the power of the Word itself. In so far as we ourselves do the talking out, it is the power of the Holy Spirit. We must remember that what we have to do here is just to receive revelation as revelation. We have to see that this reception is the reception of revelation. We have to see that man is finally and actually confronted with God, with the Lord, as Creator, Reconciler and Redeemer. We have to realise that God's revealedness for us is God's own person and God's own work. All the comfort, all the power, all the truth of this

[260] revealedness depends upon the fact that it is with God that we are dealing. All our understanding of this revealedness depends upon the fact that we identify it with God Himself, ruling out all other possibilities but God's possibility. We have therefore to realise that as the recipient of revelation man is brought under God's judgment. It is only because of this that he is brought under God's promise. It is only because of this that God meets him as the One who intercedes for him, who undertakes and directs his cause, who does not therefore quench his own ability and will and accomplishment but subordinates it to His own, since man must always be subordinated to God, if God's glory is to triumph and man is to be helped. We are to understand, therefore, that for God to be revealed involves the dislodging of man from the estimation of his own freedom, and his enrichment with the freedom of the children of God. This negation, the negation of man through God's eternal grace and mercy, is only the obverse of his position as a child of God, as a member of the covenant between God and man. But this obviously means that the negation of man cannot be put into effect any more than his position as a child of God except through God's own action. Thus God's possibility triumphs over the very imprisonment in which we are involved, where we only fulfil our own possibilities and only believe in our own possibilities. The self-enclosed uniqueness of man, who only has and knows his own freedom, is overarched and enclosed and finally relativised through the uniqueness of God and His freedom, the freedom in which He is resolved to have fellowship with this man and once and for all to be his Lord. How could man ever foresee this triumph and the wonder of it? How could he ever anticipate this triumph or prepare himself for it? It is God's triumph. It is a state or position in which man may very well find himself, but only with amazement, only with gratitude, only in humble recognition of an accomplished fact, without any opportunity to think how it might come to pass, without possessing any need or capacity to derive it from his earlier state or to indicate the way which led from the one to the other. That earlier state was one of self-glorification and self-will. Apart from the triumph of God it would still be his state to-day. How else can he understand it, then, except as a state which is marked off as the old one, the state of his impossibility for God? He would again be forgetting or denying the triumph of God if in his new state or in the isolation, the relativising and the outdistancing of the old, he saw the activity of any other power than that which is the power of God

on and in us, and which with Holy Scripture we call the power of the Holy Spirit. That power and that power alone is his possibility. It is the possibility of that saving poverty, that saving humility, or that saving death, which carries with it existence in Christ, and the wealth and exaltation and life of that existence.

We read in Mt. 19²³ᶠ· that it is hard—it is easier for a camel to go through the eye of a needle—for a rich man to enter into the kingdom of heaven. The disciples are amazed at this saying (obviously and rightly they give it universal significance) and ask: "Who then can be saved?" But Jesus looked at them and said to them: "With man this is impossible, but with God all things are possible." It is from the same angle, of course, that the saying about the strait and narrow way (Mt. 7¹⁴ᶠ·) has to be understood. The "few" that find this way are not the clever or pious who might be supposed capable of finding it. They are those who are chosen by God (Mt. 22¹⁴) and who are therefore enabled to find what the many do not find. According to Mt. 7²⁴ᶠ· the proclaiming and hearing of the Word of Jesus means a judgment upon men, comparable with the storm and flooding which threaten a house. The encounter with Jesus will show whether the builder was a wise man, whether he has ears to hear (Mt. 11¹⁵); for if so, he will be not only a hearer but also a doer of His word: ὁ δυνάμενος χωρεῖν χωρείτω ᴱᴺ¹⁶⁸ (Mt. 19¹²). But who can "receive it"? He to whom the Son wills to reveal it (Mt. 11²⁷), those to whom it has been given to know the secrets of the kingdom of heaven (Mt. 13¹¹). Why is this the only possibility? Obviously because what has to take place is a "becoming like children" (Mt. 18³), a being "born again" (Jn. 3²); which clearly means to begin one's life all over again and quite differently. But that is just what no man "can" do—he has no possibility for it. "Repent and believe the gospel" (Mk. 1¹⁵). Yes, but what does μετανοεῖτε ᴱᴺ¹⁶⁹ mean? Do we, then, have the possibility or the ability to change our νοῦς ᴱᴺ¹⁷⁰, and, if so, where and how did we get it? No, it is with an unheard-of possibility that we have to do here. We hear of a lost son: "this thy brother was dead and is alive again" (Lk. 15³²). Who can that be? We hear also (Jn. 5²⁴; 1 Jn. 3¹⁴) that faith is a μετάβασις ᴱᴺ¹⁷¹ from death to life. Who has the freedom for such a μετάβασις ᴱᴺ¹⁷²? In Rom. 8¹⁰ we hear: "If Christ be in you the body is dead because of sin; but the Spirit is life because of righteousness." In Eph. 2⁵ we hear: "Even when we were dead in sins he hath quickened us together with Christ." How can this happen? In 2 Cor. 4¹⁶ we hear: "Though our outward man perish, yet the inward man is renewed day by day," and in 2 Tim. 2¹¹: "If we be dead with him, we shall also live with him." And in Col. 3⁹ᶠ· we hear a command: "Put off the old man σὺν ταῖς πράξεσιν αὐτοῦ ᴱᴺ¹⁷³ and put on the new man, which is renewed εἰς ἐπίγνωσιν κατ᾽ εἰκόνα τοῦ κτίσαντος αὐτόν ᴱᴺ¹⁷⁴." Who can be obedient to such a command? Let us be quite clear: the problem of this and of similar statements does not derive from their second part, as if it were dark and mysterious that we should come out of death into life, for then the first part, our being in death, is, as it were, a natural and self-evident starting-point. No, the starting-point, dying, destruction, putting off the old man, being dead, this too is obviously outside the range of our own possibilities, whether in the narrower sense of the terms, or in

---

ᴱᴺ¹⁶⁸ let the one who is able to receive it, receive it
ᴱᴺ¹⁶⁹ repent
ᴱᴺ¹⁷⁰ mind
ᴱᴺ¹⁷¹ crossing
ᴱᴺ¹⁷² crossing
ᴱᴺ¹⁷³ with its deeds
ᴱᴺ¹⁷⁴ for knowledge, according to the image of the one who created Him

the more comprehensive sense intended in these passages. Death is the boundary, the surrender and abandonment of our own possibilities. Dying is a sheer *contretemps*[EN175]. Therefore when Scripture speaks of this dying of the old life as the first step to the new, it never means a work which it is in our hands to fulfil. It most definitely does not mean what all the great mystics have described as the achievable process of self-surrender and ultimately of absorption. It means an event unachievable by man. It means a death which genuinely and properly confronts man. In Rom. 6[3f.] ("Are ye ignorant that all we who were baptised into Christ Jesus were baptised into his death? We were buried therefore with him through baptism into death; that like as Christ was raised from the dead through the glory of the Father, so we also might walk in newness of life"), and Phil. 3[10f.] ("that I may know him, and the power of his resurrection and the fellowship of his sufferings, becoming conformed unto his death; if by any means I may attain unto the resurrection from the dead"), this dying is brought into the closest connexion with Christ's death and with baptism which is given to us as the sign of it. "Because one died for all, therefore all died" (2 Cor. 5[14]). For "if any man be in Christ he is a new creature"; therefore it is true of him that "the old has passed away" (2 Cor. 5[17]). "In the Spirit" we have to break away from the ἐπιθυμία σαρκός[EN176] (Gal. 5[16]), indeed, we must mortify the πράξεις τοῦ σώματος[EN177] (Rom. 8[13]). It was the same in the Old Testament. It needed the presence of Jehovah to achieve the cry of "Woe is me! I am undone" (Is. 6[5]), without which the prophet could not be a prophet. "The breath of the Lord bloweth upon it," therefore "the grass withereth and the flower thereof fadeth" (Is. 40[7]). "Thine anger causeth us to pass away, and thy wrath that we must suddenly go hence" (Ps. 90[7]). "Thou hidest thy face, they are troubled; thou takest their breath, they die, and return to their dust" (Ps. 104[29]). Of itself the world cannot punish itself: but according to Jn. 16[8f.] it is the Comforter, the Holy Spirit, who shall punish them, who shall "judge them and kindle a fire" (Is. 4[4]). The judgment upon man is not his own but God's business. For that reason, in the Bible it is always associated with the righteousness of God. In the very act of judging God makes room for His own glory and co-opts man as His covenant partner (Is. 9[6], Ps. 33[5], Ps. 103[6]). The humiliation of man by God becomes something for which he is glad and thankful: "When thou humblest me, thou makest me great" (Ps. 18[35]). "I thank thee that thou humblest me and helpest me" (Ps. 118[21]). "It is good for me that I have been afflicted" (Ps. 119[71]). "I know, O Lord, that thy judgments are righteous and that in faithfulness thou hast afflicted me" (Ps. 119[75]). Genuine repentance will never speak in any other way. It will regard itself and therefore the subjective possibility of revelation even on its negative side as a divine and not as a human possibility.

[262]

In his 1516–17 lectures on the Romans, Luther does great honour to Christian repentance and humility in God's gracious judgment. But we should seriously misunderstand him if we missed the constant emphasis and reminder that it is the work of God and not of man if we are led to Christian repentance and humility. As Luther saw, the avowed purpose of the Epistle to the Romans was *destruere et evellere et disperdere omnem sapientiam et iustitiam carnis … et plantare et constituere et magnificare peccatum*[EN178] (on Rom. 1[1]; Fi. II, 1, 2). *Deus enim nos non per domesticam, sed per extraneam iustitiam et sapientiam vult salvare non quae veniat et nascatur ex nobis, sed quae aliunde veniat in nos, non quae in terra nostra oritur, sed quae de coelo venit*[EN179] (*ib.,*

[EN175] impossibility

[EN176] desire of the flesh

[EN177] deeds of the body

[EN178] to destroy and uproot and bring to nothing all wisdom and righteousness of the flesh … and to plant and establish and magnify sin

[EN179] For God wills to save us not through our own, but through an external righteousness and wisdom, which do not come, which are not born from ourselves, but which come to us from elsewhere; not which grows up from our land, but which comes from heaven

2, 7). But man can grasp and confess this only when he himself has become a real sinner. Has become—*est enim non naturalis*[EN180] (Rom. 3⁵, *ib.*, 71, 9). And: *rarum et arduum est peccatorem fieri*[EN181] (*ib.*, 71, 1). To become a sinner means to become a liar and fool, to be stripped of all our own righteousness, truth, wisdom and virtue, to be inwardly (in our own eyes), that which we are outwardly (before God) (*ib.*, 67, 10). But this is the very thing which of ourselves we cannot do: *nos non possumus introire ad nos et mendaces ac iniusti fieri*[EN182] (*ib.*, 67, 24). We have to believe that we are sinners: *sicut per fidem iustitia Dei vivit in nobis, ita per eandem et peccatum vivit in nobis*, i.e. *sola fide credendum est nos esse peccatores*[EN183] (*ib.*, 69, 10). But this means that we have to believe in God, and, of course, believe on His word, that *Deus per suum exire nos facit ad nos ipsos introire et per sui cognitionem infert nobis et nostri cognitionem. Quia nisi Deus ita prius exiret et verax fieri quaereret in nobis, nos non possemus introire ad nos et mendaces ac iniusti fieri*[EN184] (*ib.*, 66, 24; 67, 21). *Revelationi suae sive sermonibus suis debemus cedere ac sic iustificare et verificare eos ac per hoc nos ipsos (quod non cognoveramus) secundum eos peccatores confiteri*[EN185] (*ib.*, 67, 31). Therefore that *peccator fieri*[EN186] can be a reality only *spiritualiter*[EN187] (*ib.*, 71, 8); *humilitas*[EN188] can be real only as *spiritualitas*[EN189] (on Rom. 7²⁴, *ib.*, 175, 23). *Spiritualis et sapientis hominis est scire se esse carnalem et sibi displicere*[EN190]. (on Rom. 7¹⁴, *ib.*, 170, 5). Only the spiritual man can speak of himself as Paul does in Rom. 7¹⁴f. *Si non esset in luce spiritus, malum carnis sibi adiacere non videret nec gemeret*[EN191] (on Rom. 7²¹, *ib.*, 174, 32). *Qui odit peccatum, iam extra peccatum est et de electis*[EN192]. (on Rom. 8²⁸, *ib.*, 213, 6). *Verbum Dei facit opus suum*[EN193] i.e. *pavorem Dei in illis* (*ib.*, 214, 17). God's way (*natura*) is: *prius destruere et annihilare, quicquid in nobis est, antequam sua donet*[EN194] (on Rom. 8²⁶, *ib.*, 203, 4). In His *opus proprium*[EN195], as it stands before us in the humiliation and exaltation of Christ Himself, He is for us a hidden God, i.e., hidden behind the contradiction which it presents to our own thinking and being (*ib.*, 204, 11) .... *cum suam potentiam non nisi sub infirmitate, sapientiam sub stultitia, bonitatem sub austeritate, iustitiam sub peccatis, misericordiam sub ira absconderit*[EN196] (on Rom. 8²⁸, *ib.*, 208, 4). He attests His power (*virtus*) to the elect, by showing them their impotence, and hiding and destroying their own power, so that they cannot

[263]

[EN180] for he is not naturally so

[EN181] it is uncommon and difficult to become a sinner

[EN182] we cannot penetrate ourselves in order to become liars, and unrighteous

[EN183] Just as by faith the righteousness of God lives in us, so also by the same faith sin lives in us, that is, only by faith can it be believed that we are sinners

[EN184] God, through His own venturing out, causes us to enter into ourselves, and brings about in us both knowledge of Himself and knowledge of ourselves. For unless God had first ventured out and sought to become true in us, we could not have entered into ourselves and become liars, and unrighteous

[EN185] We ought to yield to His revelation and His words and so justify and vindicate them and thereby confess that we ourselves according to these (as we were previously unaware) are sinners

[EN186] becoming a sinner

[EN187] spiritually

[EN188] humility

[EN189] spirituality

[EN190] It is for the spiritual and wise man to know that he is carnal and displeases himself

[EN191] If he had not been in the light of the Spirit, he would neither have seen nor groaned that the evil of the flesh was fast by him

[EN192] Whoever hates sin is now set apart from sin and among the elect

[EN193] The Word of God does His work, that is, the fear of God in us

[EN194] first to destroy and annihilate whatever is in us, before He gives us what is His

[EN195] proper work

[EN196] since He has hidden His power only under weakness His wisdom under foolishness, His goodness under severity, His justice under sins, His mercy under wrath

boast of it any more (on Rom. 9^{17}; *ib.*, 229, 21). When this happens, it is evidence (*signum*) that we really have the Word of God and bear it within ourselves (on Rom. 10^{15}; *ib.*, 249, 12; cf. 214, 18; 227, 16).

Directly alongside this reminder of Luther's teaching we must set the well-known introductory chapter of Calvin's *Institutio* (I, 1). Calvin begins by insisting that the essence of all wisdom (*sapientia*) lies in the twofold *cognitio Dei et nostri*[EN197]—this raises the question which of the two precedes the other, which is the basis of the other. *Non facile est discernere!*[EN198] Calvin concedes at once that knowledge of God seems to be wholly based on self-knowledge, indeed on the knowledge of our *tenuitas*[EN199]. It is the *miserabilis ruina*[EN200], to which the fall has reduced us, which compels us to lift our eyes upwards. It is the sight of that whole world of wretchedness (*mundus omnium miseriarum*) which we now discover in man, the feeling of our own ignorance, fatuity, indigence, weakness, even perversity and corruption, which makes us realise that power, goodness, righteousness and truth have their *locus*[EN201] solely *in Domino*[EN202]. Before we begin to be dissatisfied with ourselves, we cannot long for Him. The self-satisfied man rests upon himself and has no need of God. Therefore it is *cognitio sui*[EN203] which impels us to seek God and sets us on the way to find Him. But how do we achieve a real self-knowledge? Only in the presence of God, condescending *ex illius intuitu ad se ipsum inspiciendum*[EN204]. Of ourselves we always regard ourselves as righteous and wise, unless we are convicted by unambiguous arguments to the contrary. But we can never be convicted by abstract self-examination. The eye is only able to grasp light in a very small measure, but we do not realise this as long as we direct it to the earth, only when we try to point it to the sun. Similarly, it is only when we think of God and His righteousness and wisdom and power that we see our own righteousness as *iniquitas*[EN205], our own wisdom as *stultitia*[EN206], our own power as *impotentia*[EN207], and we arrive at a real self-knowledge. That is why, according to Holy Scripture, man has no knowledge of his lowliness except when he stands terror-struck in presence of the revealed majesty of his God. Our knowledge of God may be limited by our corresponding knowledge of self, but in this conditioning relationship the first place decidedly belongs to the knowledge of God. That is why Calvin's exposition of the doctrine of man's unfreedom for God (*Instit.* II, 2, 1) begins with a reminder that sinful man has to renounce all wisdom and power of his own, because he must give God the glory. That is why repentance is derived strictly from faith, from *participatio*[EN208] in Christ (III, 7, 1). That is why *abnegatio nostri*[EN209], in which Calvin discerns the *summa vitat Christianae*[EN210], is derived from the statement: *Nostri non sumus, sed Domini*[EN211] (III, 7, 1). That is why it is clear that the *humilitas*[EN212] of faith in justification must not be confused with the virtue of modesty

---

[EN197] knowledge of God and of ourselves
[EN198] It is not easy to judge!
[EN199] weakness
[EN200] wretched ruin
[EN201] place
[EN202] in God
[EN203] knowledge of oneself
[EN204] from seeing Him to observing our own self
[EN205] wickedness
[EN206] foolishness
[EN207] impotence
[EN208] participation
[EN209] denial of ourselves
[EN210] height of the Christian life
[EN211] We do not belong to ourselves, but to the Lord
[EN212] humility

(*modestia*), but consists in the fact that when God is known in His Word nothing else remains except to hope in Him (III, 12, 6).

At this point we must mark off our teaching from a view which has recently been advanced in many quarters. This involves at least the possibility that we may have a bad conscience, that we may be disappointed in our arbitrary imaginings, even to the point of complete disillusionment. It involves the possibility of a collapse, and of our knowledge of the collapse, of all our ideologies and enterprises, the possibility of despair, the possibility that we may find in despair the controlling factor in our existence. In other words, it involves the possibility of a negative determination of our existence, a possibility which is integral to man, [264] an immanent anthropological point of contact with the revelation of God. Indeed, this possibility of a negative determination of our existence might objectively be identical with the wrath and judgment of God, and therefore subjectively, as our own experience, at least a necessary indication of it, and something which we should have to see and know as such. Therefore, to the extent that revelation is the manifestation of wrath and judgment (and yet indirectly, too, as the revelation of grace and salvation), it comes in answer to an existing possibility of our own, in answer to what man himself can already know about himself: it comes right into his own life. In that case what the Word of God talks us out of is only the positive possibility of receiving revelation. And at the same time we talk ourselves into the possession of a great negative possibility: in fact we must. In the very discontinuity which arises at this decisive point there is to be found a continuity between man and God, nature and grace, reason and revelation. In fact, we have here a neutral "feeler," the object of a natural theology under the third article. The truth behind this construction is, of course, self-evident. According to 1 Cor. 1²⁶ᶠ· God has chosen that which in the world's eyes is foolish and weak and ignoble and despised. According to Mt. 11²⁵ He has revealed the truth to babes. According to Lk. 1⁵² and James 1⁹ He exalts the meek. According to Lk. 6²⁰ and James 2⁵ the poor are blessed. According to Mk. 2¹⁷ the sick need the physician. According to 2 Cor. 12⁹ the power of God is mighty in the weak. In fact the connexion between God's revelation and the uncovering of the radical need for man's redemption is indissoluble. God's unveiling in revelation is invariably His veiling. Jesus Christ's resurrection and exaltation has for its presupposition His passion and His death, His profoundest humiliation. But not for one moment, even, can we abstract from this truth the fact that the connexion has its basis and meaning in Jesus Christ. Folly, humility, weakness, suffering and death—in short, the negative determination of man's existence as such does not in any way enjoy this connexion either generally or in itself. As an immanently anthropological possibility it has no merit or advantage compared with the various possibilities of a positive determination of our existence. According to 2 Cor. 7¹⁰ Paul knows of a "sorrow of the world" which "worketh death," just as sin does according to Rom. 7¹³. And in 1 Cor. 1²⁶ he says of those things which are foolish and weak and ignoble and despised, that God has chosen them—obviously from amongst similar things—and chosen them, "that no flesh should glory before God" (v. 29). If Luke, like James, emphasises particularly the connexion between Christ and the poor, the sick, the publicans, etc., on no less than three occasions (Lk. 7³⁶, 11³⁷, 14¹), the same Evangelist makes Him accept invitations actually to the table of a Pharisee—almost as if to warn them against the possible misunderstanding. A negative determination of existence is not as such identical with the saving exposure of our radical need of redemption. Moreover, the saving exposure of our radical need of redemption need not consist in a negative determination of our existence. On the contrary, if it is the exposure and therefore the foolishness and poverty and humility of which the New Testament speaks, it does not have its basis in a more or less negative determining, in an immanently anthropological limitation or even overthrow of our existence. To these latter, when we have exhausted every other aid, we can always react with irony, with scepticism, with apathy, with the greatest of all illusions, a so-called lack of illusion, and finally and in the last resort with suicide. It is not for the sake of these that we deserve to be blessed. Paul does not rejoice that the Corinthians were sad, but that they were sorry unto repentance, κατὰ θεόν[EN213] (2 Cor. 7⁹⁻¹¹). This λύπη κατὰ θεόν[EN214] is distinguished from "worldly sorrow" by the fact that we cannot react to it as we choose, that we can, therefore, very definitely be blessed for its sake. For that reason we must also say that it is not one of our own possibilities. It is not a determination of human exist-

[265] ence which can be fixed and understood according to an immanent anthropology. Luke's (6²⁰) "Blessed are the poor" is correctly interpreted by Matthew (Mt. 5²) in his "Blessed are the poor in spirit." This poverty, true and saving despair, is the gift of the Holy Spirit, the work of Jesus Christ. In this it resembles faith, of which it is a part. As the gift of the Holy Spirit and the work of Jesus Christ it is known decisively in the knowledge of our own sin and therefore and primarily in the knowledge of the divine compassion, forgiving us our sins. Before Damascus Paul first sees and hears his Lord, then he falls to the ground, a trembling comes over him, and he is blinded. As the gift of the Holy Spirit and the work of Jesus Christ, this poverty is a reality of faith. That is, it does not consist abstractly in our own experiences of poverty, no matter how powerful. It consists concretely in the poverty of Christ as it became an event upon Golgotha. This alone is the radical and the final exposure of our poverty and in that way the ground of our riches (2 Cor. 8⁹). As the gift of the Holy Spirit and the work of Jesus Christ, this poverty is a fundamental and comprehensive poverty. It is genuine despair, because it is saving despair. What is destroyed by it is not only our certainty, but also our uncertainty, and the disillusionments which lead up to it: not only our defiance but also our desperation, not only our illusions but also our complete absence of illusions, not only our good but also our bad conscience. It is despair about ourselves. Therefore it is despair even about the negative possibilities of the defining of human existence. Of course, it can and often enough—perhaps usually—does coincide with such negative possibilities. Concrete human folly, abjectness and weakness, which can be fixed and understood as such, are naturally intended in all those New Testament passages. And on the basis of divine election they may be sanctified as signs of that laudable poverty in spirit, of that divine sorrow unto repentance, of that true and saving despair. As such, they attest and declare it. To that extent they declare and attest God's revelation. But they are not necessarily correlated to it. We cannot maintain any general or necessary or logical connexion between them. If they are "feelers" on man's side, it is not in any neutrality as general human possibilities. It is only as signs sanctified by divine election. It is only on the basis of a revelation which has already been enacted and received. They do not belong, then, to anything that man can know about himself from his own standpoint. Consequently they are "points of contact" newly posited by God, not present already in the nature of man. Therefore they are not the object of a natural theology under the third article.

3. By the outpouring of the Holy Spirit it becomes possible for man in his freedom to be met by God's revelation, because in it the Word of God becomes unavoidably his master. From what has been said under 1 and 2, we are aware that we have to seek the subjective possibility of revelation, our freedom for the Word of God, only in the Word itself, in Jesus Christ. We have not to abstract from this objective factor and seek it in its effects on and in us. Therefore, in so far as it now becomes our freedom, we have to understand it as a miracle, and not in any sense as a natural freedom and capacity. But what is the significance

---

[EN213] toward God
[EN214] sorrow toward God

of this miracle of Jesus Christ actualised in us in the outpouring of the Holy Spirit; what is the import of this encounter, so that we can and must assert positively that it can confront us, that we do acquire a part in the divine possibility which is realised in it? That is the question which we now have to answer. In trying to answer it we need to keep before us what we established in 1 and 2. For the sake of saying something positive, we must not let ourselves be tempted [266] into speaking about a quality of grace poured into man, or a natural capacity and power for revelation. If we do, we turn our eyes away from Christ and towards man. And we do not say the positive thing that we really have to say. It is still the case that the subjective possibility of revelation is God's possibility, just as its objective and subjective reality is God's reality. But if that is so, what after all is the meaning of a man's participation in this possibility? One thing is certain. We can never make it comprehensible as our own participation, i.e., as our taking, conceiving, grasping and appropriating the share given us in this possibility. We can and should understand that it is to us that the possibility is given. Participation in it does not signify an abolition of our identity with ourselves. It is a frightful misunderstanding to try to interpret it along the lines of a possession or a trance. There are such states, but only when the consciousness of identity is removed. For that reason we must not interpret the miracle of the divine possibility along the lines of such unusual but not miraculous phenomena. In this miracle we are dealing with that miracle of God which is performed upon ourselves in our own identity with ourselves. Even if we did have to reckon with a removal of the consciousness of identity in the recipient of the revelation, if we were dealing with the miracle of this receiving, we should still have to say quite emphatically that it is performed upon a man who is really identical with himself. It does not take place in one who is outside himself—even the doctrine of the Holy Ghost must not lay itself open to a charge of Docetism. It takes place in the man who is himself and with himself. It is not to a transcendent *alter ego*EN215 (if there are such things) that the divine possibility in revelation is given to apprehend. It is given to me myself. I am the old and I am also the new man on the basis of this possibility. I in my apparently unrepeatable selfhood apprehend, or do not apprehend, am called or not called, am elected or rejected: I am judged, I am blessed. Therefore it is a question of our taking, receiving, laying hold of, appropriating the share in the divine possibility which is allotted to us. Moreover, we can and must realise that this participation is achieved in our own experience and activity, in that act of self-determination which we call our human existence. This participation has nothing whatever to do with a magical invasion of the inter-related totality of our physico-psychical human life by supernatural factors and forces. It does signify a limitation and interruption of our existence. Our existence is confronted by something outside and over against it, by which it is determined, and indeed totally determined. But it is determined as the act

---

EN215 second identity

67

of our self-determination in the totality of its possibilities. Yet not in such a way that we know in advance and can usually tell what form the fulfilment of this self-determination will take. Not as though we ourselves can decide upon a specific attitude to which the process of determination necessarily has to conform. Not as though, e.g., a passive, receptive attitude necessarily corresponds to the divine possibility: in certain circumstances an active, spontaneous attitude may correspond much better. Not as though the process of determination is necessarily fulfilled subjectively in the form of a state of uncertainty and despair. In certain circumstances it may be fulfilled subjectively in the form of an intensified or simply a healthy, normal sense of life. Antitheses of this kind are immanent antitheses. They belong together to the extent that they represent all the different possibilities within the act of our self-determination. But *per se*[EN216] they have nothing whatever to do with our being determined from without, with the divine possibility which is given to us in revelation. This is a relationship which they only acquire. It is important to make this point. We have to realise clearly that participation in the divine possibility does not mean that somewhere within our being, there is, so to speak, a vacuum for which we are not responsible and over which we have no control, but which we can abandon on the assumption that the divine possibility which is given to us will intervene. Where this happens the result is either enthusiastic magic or magical enthusiasm. This is related to the possibility given us by the outpouring of the Holy Spirit in the same way as idol worship is related to the worship of God. It approximates no less closely to the doctrine of an inpouring of grace than to that of the capacity of the natural man for revelation. But the possibility given us by the outpouring of the Holy Spirit is the possibility of a direct confrontation of the whole man by God. Man is confronted in the totality of his own possibilities, and therefore in all possible conditions and attitudes. In revelation, the whole man is addressed and challenged, judged and pardoned by God. In view of this totality of revelation to us we must not refer the revealedness in us to some obscure or even luminous place apart from our own experience and activity. We must not refer it to a place where we can exempt ourselves from all responsibility. We must not refer it to a place which enables us to count on the fact that God or "it" believes in us, from which we are therefore onlookers both of ourselves and God. In the presence of God there is no such back room. There is only the one well-known place for our physico-psychical existence, although it does include within it many alternative possibilities. It is in this totality that our existence participates in the divine possibility, or else we have no part in it. The point is that the whole area of our possibilities is again enclosed by the divine possibility. That is what we have to reckon with if we would understand our participation in this possibility. Therefore if we do not understand it, or if we can understand it only as a miracle, this does not mean that it is not we ourselves who are partici-

[267]

[EN216] in themselves

pators, we ourselves in our own experience and activity. What it does mean is that as participators in this possibility we are a riddle to ourselves. We know that we are set before God, but we do not know how it happened. We do not [268] know how we as such can stand and be before God. We do not know how we are worthy or capable of it. Again, we can and must know that all our experience and activity is involved in this standing before God. But we can never say how far this or that impression is our calling, this or that discovery our awakening, this or that decision our conversion, this or that conviction our faith, this or that emotion our love, this or that expectation our hope, and this or that attitude our responsibility and justification before God. For as participators in God's possibility, all that we see and find is simply ourselves, and all the very selfish, very human states and conditions and attitudes in which we actually find ourselves. We never can and never will comprehend how far the concretion of our situation and our attitude is the concretion of our participation in God's possibility. And this contradiction does not emanate from outside. It has nothing whatever to do with the philosophical difficulty of holding together our presence and God's presence, the visible and the invisible, reality and the idea. Philosophical hedges can be surmounted philosophically. And the necessary ways to do it have been discovered long ago, and are constantly rediscovered and applied according to the needs of the age. In an earlier context we have already said that the need for God, of which we are now speaking, is known only by the children of God. They alone really know the miracle of revelation. And in the light of this miracle they alone know the contradiction between the clear and certain fact and the not merely obscure and uncertain but utterly unknown means which alone corresponds to the fact. They know that they are accepted with God. But they know that they are great sinners. They know that they do stand before God. But they know that they cannot stand and live before Him. They know that the possibility of God which is given us is a content which the vessel of our activity and experience cannot contain. In face of the subjective possibility of revelation, as it is incontestably present in the reality of God's revealedness, they are bound to be a riddle. And they know that the riddle is insoluble. For it is not only that we cannot perceive the mystery of the Holy Spirit. We must not. That is the reason why we cannot. The one who crosses our way is God, and He is and will be the Lord. It is only in the most profound and wilful forgetfulness, or in the strict sense, only as we fall away from our status as the children of God—and because there can be no question of a child of God falling away, we have to say that we cannot possibly try to escape the contradiction between the clarity of the fact and the obscurity of the means. Yet this is our life in God's possibility, the receiving of God's grace in His judgment, clarity in obscurity, rest and peace and joy in those who, although they are awakened and called and converted and believing and loving and hoping, know themselves only too well before God, and are quite aware of the frailty of their impressions and discoveries and decisions and [269] emotions and expectations and attitudes. It is because the contradiction remains in force—not by them, nor by their insight and knowledge, but by God's gracious work and in God's knowledge—that their life in the divine possibility is grounded and maintained. God Himself maintains the contradiction in force. It is in Him that we do actually have Himself, the mystery of grace which we do not understand, or understand only as miracle. And what God does and knows in this context is the mystery of His Word as it has newly come to us. It is exactly the same if we say: the mystery of Jesus Christ. For the mystery of the Word of God coming to us and apprehended by us is this: that the mystery of Jesus Christ now stands in our life as a miracle, that as God there became man, for that reason we here have God. In Jesus Christ, the incarnate Son of God, the contradiction is maintained from above, from God: in all the almightiness of the merciful, condescending love of God. But in the same omnipotence the contradiction is also maintained downwards, towards man, when Jesus Christ comes to us as the Word of God. It is, therefore, maintained by the divine omnipotence. And the fact that it is maintained is manifested and manifest to us. For that reason, the contradiction is not one of those paradoxes which owe both their origin and their solution to our own acuity. It is not one of those contradictions which can be overcome if we have the sagacity and strength to bring them together in our own lives, to co-ordinate them in our thinking, to harmonise them in our feeling. The solution of the contradiction is not only in appearance. It is a genuine solution, proceeding from the reality of Christ's resurrection from the dead. Therefore life in this contradiction is not merely a life of acceptance, as we do actually accept some necessary and unnecessary contradictions, because we cannot remove them. On the contrary, life in this contradiction is already a life in reconciliation. Of course, there is still the contradiction and the conflict between the spirit and the flesh, between the new and the old man, between what we see and what God alone sees. But this very life in conflict is still a life in reconciliation. Our hearts and minds are preserved in the midst of conflict by the peace of God, which passes all understanding. They are preserved because and to the extent that Jesus Christ or the Word of God is unavoidably the Master of this life of ours.

We have now arrived at the two most relevant and helpful concepts in our attempt to describe positively the freedom of man for God's revelation. That freedom exists where the Word of God or Jesus Christ is to man the Master, and unavoidably the Master. Instead of master we might also say teacher, leader or lord. In this context the word "master" is particularly rich in content. Its counterpart may equally well be pupil, scholar, follower or adherent, or servant. And all this is involved in the freedom of man for the Word and by the [270] Word, of which we are speaking. But for the sake of clarity, we must at once add to the concept of "master" that of "unavoidable." *Analogia fidei*[EN217] it will be understood what is now meant by "master." There are indeed many masters and teachers, and leaders and lords. They are all of them distinguished from

---

[EN217] On the analogy of faith

this Master by the fact that they can be totally or partially avoided either altogether or from some particular point in time. To stand unavoidably under any other master is a sign of sickness. But to stand under this Master is not only the normal thing, it is the only possible thing. The outpouring of the Holy Spirit exalts the Word of God to be the master over men, puts man unavoidably under His mastery. The miracle of the divine revealedness, the power of Christ's resurrection in a man, consists in this event. In it the "God became man" is actualised in us as "man has God." It is a removal of the contradiction between a possibility which obviously is only God's possibility, and the human experience and activity, which only an unredeemed arrogance could claim as a fitting and worthy vessel for such a content. In this event man is a participator in this divine possibility. Through God he is free for God. We will now try to analyse the event.

(*a*) To have our master unavoidably in Jesus Christ means always to have found someone over against us, from whom we can no longer withdraw. We can withdraw from everything else that is over against us, whether it is the world or men. It is at once our misery and comfort, the source of our most serious aberrations and the help of which we simply must avail ourselves from time to time, that again and again we can withdraw to an inward solitude. The outpouring of the Holy Spirit makes this withdrawal impossible, at any rate in relation to the Word of God. We can say at once, of course, that it makes it impossible in principle. No matter who or where we are, whether we like it or not, whether we are worthy of it or not, parallel to our line of life, as a second constant, there runs the accompanying presence of the Word which is spoken to us, a presence which we can never frighten away. A man does not become a different person when he receives the Holy Spirit: why should he? But as the man he is, he cannot flee from this specific partner to any solitude. As the man he is, he stands in this specific relationship which he can no longer leave. In this specific relationship he must be secretly responsible. He must reckon with the fact that he is always engaged in a dialogue, whatever the content of that dialogue may be. Concretely, it may perhaps be with an element of biblical truth which has once illuminated him. It may be with a man in whom the Church once met him. It may quite simply be with the fact of his baptism. Generally speaking, it is with a *signum*[EN218] which was once factually a *signum*[EN219] of the Word of God as it confronted and met him. And the puzzling fact that he is bound in this way is the new life which he has as the child of God, a life which is independent of his own will and accomplishment but which carries with it the possibility of receiving the divine revelation.   [271]

We are not speaking of the omnipresence of God as philosophy understands it, but of the concrete theological omnipresence of which we read in Ps. 139[1-10]: "O Lord, thou hast searched me, and known me. Thou knowest my downsitting and mine uprising, thou

---

[EN218] sign
[EN219] sign

71

understandest my thought afar off. Thou searchest out my path and my lying down, and art acquainted with all my ways. For there is not a word in my tongue, but lo, O Lord, thou knowest it altogether. Thou hast beset me behind and before, and laid thine hand upon me. Such knowledge is too wonderful for me; it is high, I cannot attain unto it. Whither shall I go from thy spirit? or whither shall I flee from thy presence? If I ascend up into heaven, thou art there: if I make my bed in Sheol, behold thou art there. If I take the wings of the morning and dwell in the uttermost parts of the sea; Even there shall thy hand lead me, and thy right hand shall hold me." The man who can join in that prayer is through God free for God. What it involves is that "abiding" as the word is so pregnantly used, especially in the First Epistle of John; the abiding in us of Jesus Christ (3^{24}); of the Word ($2^{14.\ 24}$); of the love of God (3^{17}); of the anointing (2^{27}); of the divine seed (3^{9}); even of eternal life (3^{15}); even of God Himself ($4^{12.\ 15f.}$). It has, of course, its counterpart in our own "abiding" in the Word, in love, and in God.

(*b*) To have our master unavoidably in Jesus Christ means that we have discovered His supreme authority, to which in all our obedience or disobedience we are always responsible and subject. To other authorities we may make the most profound surrender. We may accept the strictest discipline in relation to them. But over against all of them we can still remain independent, at the deepest and truest level of reality. For every other authority is the kind which we still have to choose and recognise as such. Consequently our attitude to it stands or falls with our own choice and recognition of it. It has no power to dominate us unavoidably. Our thoughts at least—even if only our subconscious thoughts—are always free in relation to it. But the outpouring of the Holy Spirit means that man is placed under the Word, because it is God's Word. Obviously this does not involve any pronouncement upon the capacity or performance of man. Again, it is not a question of what he is in himself, but of the reality of the relationship in which he stands. Again, he has not become another person by receiving the Holy Spirit, and yet he is another person, so far as he stands in this relationship. The man who is really subject to the Word will not refuse to recognise that by the Word he is accused of disobedience at the very heart of his being. But this very impeachment of him confirms the reality of the relationship in which he is placed: supremacy on the one side, subordination on the other; claim on the one side, responsibility on the other; all the irreversible inequality of the relationship, in which he is now a partner. And this authority is not one which is freely chosen and later recognised: it is an original authority which has its basis in itself. In so far as man has to do with this authority, without any assistance or co-operation of his own, but concretely, in his own life, he is put in a position where freedom for God and the possibility of hearing His revelation is self-evident.

At this point we have to remember that in the Old Testament and New Testament the basic relationship between God and man is created by the establishment of an unequivocal superiority of God over man. Of Yahweh as of Jesus Christ the first thing which must be said concerning His action on man is that He rules over him. This is the case before anything else. Everything else is simply the working out of the reality that irresistibly and definitively man has acquired his King. The occurrence of revelation takes place within and on the basis of this basic relationship. It is not merely the background. It is the very atmosphere and setting in which reconciliation, grace, assistance, even judgment and punishment can arise on God's side—and faith and unbelief, obedience and disobedience on man's. The element which constantly surprises us, and the impression we receive from the whole Bible, is that in it not only the existence of God but His transcendence over man is proclaimed without any problems; it is the permanent presupposition of everything that we are told and taught. It all lives by this presupposition. It is true only because God's transcendence is already true. The Bible knows nothing of man in himself, man who can first hold himself aloof from God and then perhaps—or perhaps not—choose and recognise what is the will of God. In the Bible man appears at once as either the pious man or the sinner, either the servant of God or an arbitrary rebel against Him, either the believer or the unbeliever, either the one who gives thanks or the one who is in despair. He is never neutral. He never has the word or the breath for autonomous discussion. At the very points where he seems to speak most strongly, say in Job, or Ecclesiastes, or many Psalms, or, in the New Testament, in 2 Corinthians, where Paul seems to have such a surprising amount to say about himself, he is in fact most securely bound to that relationship, to that absolutely real relationship of super- and sub-ordination, which precedes all the expressions and experiences of his life with God, and which withdraws only in appearance, but is never completely obscured. It is in this relationship that the prophets and apostles see and hear the revealed God, and become His witnesses. The outpouring of the Holy Spirit which enables us to hear their witness, to apprehend revelation, obviously and necessarily consists in the fact that fundamentally we are placed in the same position, brought into the same relationship. It is here that the new life of the children of God begins. In this relationship we have ears to hear what is told us by God.

(*c*) To have our master unavoidably in Jesus Christ means that we are subject to a command, in face of which there can be neither subterfuge nor excuse. We can find excuses and subterfuges for the commands of all other masters, even when we obey them in whole or in part. We can have doubts about their meaning. We can insist that we did not hear or understand. We can reply that we have already fulfilled them; or, *vice versa*, that we cannot fulfil them, at any rate in the strict sense. But in face of this command those devices are impossible. The outpouring of the Holy Spirit means that men have received an order, by which they can now mark off their very existence. The outpouring of the Holy Spirit means that they themselves are utterly and absolutely commanded. No place is left to them at which they can devise subterfuges and excuses. The Word of God spoken to them strikes absolutely their very being. The content of the command is that their existence is an existence before and with Him, and in conformity with Him, that they must fear Him and love Him. [273] And as such it is always meaningful, perspicuous and clear. As such it is never fulfilled, but always unfulfilled. If we cannot actually fulfil it, that is the revelation of our guilt. It does not absolve us from the duty of obedience, from allegiance to Him. It simply lays that duty upon us. In this respect, too, it is not a matter of what man is in himself and becomes in himself. It is a matter of his real standing and walking in relation to the word spoken to him. This relationship consists in the fact that he is taken and bound and ruled. In this context what he is or becomes in himself, even his better efforts, is always shown to be disobedience. But it does not follow in the least that he has failed or that he ought to let himself fail; the result is that for the first time, however limited he can and must be in himself, he is really upheld from above. In his very disobedience he is called, challenged, claimed for obedience. He cannot take refuge either in activity or in passivity. It is not his activity or passivity, it is he himself in his activity or passivity who is the target. Therefore, as the target is aimed at and reached by this irresistible command, that which confronts us, that supreme power of which we were speaking, acquires actual concrete form. We cannot add anything to the fact that we are bound. We cannot alter it. Our human self-determination is still active, but it is imposed upon us. And in this fact we are free for God. We are capable of hearing His revelation.

At this point we may legitimately speak of the Pauline "bringing every thought into captivity to the obedience of Christ" (2 Cor. 10⁵). We may recall the $\dot{a}\nu\dot{a}\gamma\kappa\eta$[EN220], under pressure of which Paul exercises his apostolic office, for "woe is unto me, if I preach not the Gospel" (1 Cor. 9¹⁶). We may remember the $\kappa\alpha\tau\alpha\lambda\alpha\mu\beta\dot{a}\nu\epsilon\sigma\theta\alpha\iota$ $\dot{\upsilon}\pi\dot{o}$ $X\rho\iota\sigma\tau o\hat{\upsilon}$[EN221], which compels him to say: $o\dot{\upsilon}\chi$ $\ddot{o}\tau\iota$ $\ddot{\eta}\delta\eta$ $\ddot{\epsilon}\lambda\alpha\beta o\nu$[EN222] as well as $\delta\iota\dot{\omega}\kappa\omega$ $\delta\dot{\epsilon}$ $\epsilon\dot{\iota}$ $\kappa\alpha\dot{\iota}$ $\kappa\alpha\tau\alpha\lambda\dot{a}\beta\omega$[EN223] (Phil. 3¹²). We may recall the equivocal way in which he describes himself in Philem. 1, Eph. 3¹, 4¹, and 2 Tim. 1³ as the $\delta\dot{\epsilon}\sigma\mu\iota o\varsigma$ $\mathbf{I}\eta\sigma o\hat{\upsilon}$ $X\rho\iota\sigma\tau o\hat{\upsilon}$[EN224], or again, the subordination of his apostolic dignity to the prior $\delta o\hat{\upsilon}\lambda o\varsigma$ $\mathbf{I}\eta\sigma o\hat{\upsilon}$ $X\rho\iota\sigma\tau o\hat{\upsilon}$[EN225], Rom. 1¹, or again, the qualification of it by the added $\delta\iota\dot{a}$ $\theta\epsilon\lambda\dot{\eta}\mu\alpha\tau o\varsigma$ $\theta\epsilon o\hat{\upsilon}$[EN226] of 1 Cor. 1¹, etc., in accordance with which we then find the goal and content of his apostolate stated in the words: $\dot{a}\pi o\sigma\tau o\lambda\dot{\eta}$ $\epsilon\dot{\iota}\varsigma$ $\dot{\upsilon}\pi\alpha\kappa o\dot{\eta}\nu$ $\pi\dot{\iota}\sigma\tau\epsilon\omega\varsigma$ $\dot{\epsilon}\nu$ $\pi\hat{a}\sigma\iota\nu$ $\tau o\hat{\iota}\varsigma$ $\ddot{\epsilon}\theta\nu\epsilon\sigma\iota\nu$[EN227] (Rom. 1⁵). We recall further that the relationship of reconciled man to the righteousness of God and to God Himself is described in Rom 6¹⁸ ²² as a $\delta o\upsilon\lambda o\hat{\upsilon}\sigma\theta\alpha\iota$[EN228], and his relationship to the Holy Spirit in Rom. 8¹⁴ as an $\ddot{a}\gamma\epsilon\sigma\theta\alpha\iota$[EN229]. To look back from this point to the Gospels, it will surprise us how self-evidently the tone which Jesus adopts in His addresses is quite simply and directly the tone of command. It will surprise us how frequently the relationship of lord and servant or of king and subject seems to be the model for His relationship to His disciples. It will surprise us how frequently the Messianic challenge to faith is asserted as a challenge to obedience. In short, it will surprise us how clearly and powerfully the title *Kyrios* is applied to Jesus. A single example will illustrate the point: "But who is there of you having a slave plowing or keeping sheep, will say unto him, when he is come in from the field, Come straightway and sit down to meat; and will not rather say unto him, Make ready wherewith I may sup, and gird thyself, and serve me, till I have eaten and drunken; and afterward thou shalt eat and drink? Doth he thank the slave because he did the things that were commanded? Even so ye also, when ye shall have done all the things that are commanded you, say, We are unprofitable slaves; we have done that which it was our duty to do" (Lk. 17⁷⁻¹⁰). That is how the children of God hear the Word of God. Their hearing is really the hearing of an order and therefore obedience, a hearing which as such is necessarily a doing of the Word (Jas. 1²²: "Be ye doers of the word,

[274]

EN220 compulsion
EN221 being held by Christ
EN222 'not that I have already attained it'
EN223 I pursue so that I may also take hold
EN224 prisoner of Jesus Christ
EN225 slave of Jesus Christ
EN226 by the will of God
EN227 apostleship for the obedience of faith among all the nations
EN228 enslavement
EN229 being led

and not hearers only, deluding your own selves"). When we remember this we shall be on our guard against thinking that the commanding, ordering, or lawgiving of the Old Testament belongs specifically to the Old Testament, and confusing it with the *nomos*[EN230] of the Jews against which Paul contends in Romans and Galatians. In these Epistles Paul demonstrates the impotence of the Law for righteousness in God's sight. But the Law to which he refers is the commandment as it is heard unspiritually and without Christ. It is the commandment as it is heard without hearing the command within the commandment, without a fear and love for God the commander. It is the commandment which is not really a compulsory command. According to the *nomos*[EN231] of Israel the first of all the commandments is that we should fear and love God the commander: "I am the Lord thy God, which brought thee out of the land of Egypt, out of the house of bondage" (Ex. 20²). Paul himself stood under this Law, when he regarded and described himself as the servant and captive and bondman of Jesus Christ. He saw that believers, too, stand under the νόμος τοῦ πνεύματος τῆς ζωῆς[EN232] (Rom. 8²). In spite of the Reformers' dialectic of Law and Gospel, we can and must regard the whole possibility of our participation in God's revelation under the familiar concept of the divine Law. The Law speaks to us the command within the commandment. It demands that we should fear and love God. Therefore its purpose is not only to instruct and direct, to judge and to terrify. It is also to comfort, to give us hope and joy and help, to give us the very presence of God Himself in the act in which He Himself is ours, in which He binds Himself to us to save us. In the 119th Psalm we have an almost inexhaustible song of praise to the testimonies and commandments and statutes and laws and precepts and words and ways of God. But of the scriptural testimonies to revelation the 119th Psalm is one which we must not despise, but carefully consider. It is, as it were, a concretion of the saying about the omnipresence of God in Psalm 139: "Thy Word encompasseth me on every side."

(*d*) To have our master unavoidably in Jesus Christ is to exist in an ultimate and most profound irresponsibility. All other masters and teachers and leaders and lords load and burden us with responsibilities, i.e., with questions which we answer out of our own knowledge, with obligations which we satisfy by our own wish and action, with programmes which we have to fulfil and realise by our own achievements. For that very reason their power to command has exactly the same limitations. They give the orders, but then they leave us to execute those orders alone. They cannot command from us either fear or love. They cannot represent us. It is for that very reason that we can so easily make excuses and apologies in relation to their commands. But the Word of God has a limitless power of command. For it does not impose on us a new and final and frightful, because unending, responsibility. It claims our response. It claims our own will and action. It claims the achievement which is, of course, required of us. It claims all this, not as an autonomous work, the success of which we ourselves must guarantee, but as an act of service, in the fulfilment of which we are borne and covered by the work it does itself. From this aspect, [275] too, the outpouring of the Holy Spirit signifies the relativising of the question who and what we are in ourselves. By it we are put into this relation under the

---

[EN230] law
[EN231] law
[EN232] law of the Spirit of life

Word and under the command of the Word. And that means, of course, that as the people we are we have to participate in that work of the Word. Not as those who have to finish the work, to reach the goal, to bring in the results. In our very participation it is foreseen that we are men, and disobedient men, and therefore quite unsuitable for the work. Our participation does not depend upon our fitness for this work. It is a participation in spite of our unsuitability. It rests upon the forgiveness of sins. It is grace. It is a participation in fear and in love to the God who has mercy on us in that He calls us to it and permits it. That is just why it is not a participation which involves anxiety and worry whether we can really do what we are required to do. Of course we cannot do it. That is the presupposition of our participation. Only one thing is required of us. As those who cannot do it of ourselves, and never could, we have to participate when the Word does it. It is a matter of the receiving and adopting of man into participation in the Word of God. This participation corresponds to what took place in the incarnation of the eternal Son of God. It is the basis of the life of the children of God, that non-autonomous life which is a life only of grace and of faith. And when man is placed under the Word and under the command of the Word, he is really free. Free from worry about himself. But also free from worry about others. And free from worry about the whole development of human affairs in the Church and the world. In the ultimate and decisive question, the doing of the will of God in all these things, he has no worries at all, even when he ought to be weighed down in all the penultimate questions regarding himself and others and the Church and the world. That the will of God should be done in all things is what he can and should pray when the other burden seems likely to crush him, and then it will not crush him. But the very prayer, Thy will be done, is in fact an admission that I need not worry about it, because that is not my business. I am not responsible. This burden, the burden of my own and others' sins, does not lie upon me. It lies solely and entirely upon Jesus Christ, upon the Word of God. In the fact that I am bound to this Word of God consists the one and only thing which I can do for myself and others, for the Church and the world. What happens in this relationship will be good; what does not happen in this relationship will be bad. And when I am bound in this way I can never again take the burden on myself, I can never invest myself with the dignity of the Word, the dignity of Jesus Christ. Jesus Christ alone bears it and can bear it. Our relationship to Him must always consist in our knowing and saying and confirming and attesting and living out the truth: that He careth for you. And in this very freedom, [276] in this ultimate absence of responsibility, it is self-evident that we have to hear the freedom of God and the revelation of God.

The attitude of the men of the Bible and the recipients of revelation will again help us to see our way clearly at this point. It is marked by the fact that the strictness with which they are claimed for the things of God is directly paralleled by a particular attraction to the things of God. In the Old Testament prophets and especially in Paul in the New Testament, particularly in the latter case, we do not see anything of the rigidity or Zelotism or anxious zeal, in short, the spiritual cramp which always results when men think and act as if the *causa Dei*[EN233] were really their own anxiety and concern. They do not really aim to do what God does. They aim only to participate. They do not do the work: they assist. It is in this way that they are the recipients and witnesses of revelation. The commandments which they keep in love to God are God's commandments (ἐντολαὶ αὐτοῦ), and therefore not grievous (1 Jn. 5³). His yoke is easy and His burden is light (Mt. 11³⁰). They need not be ashamed of the Gospel, because it does not need their own dynamic. And it does not need it, because it is itself the δύναμις θεοῦ[EN234], and indeed εἰς σωτηρίαν[EN235] (Rom. 1¹⁶).

(*e*) To have our master unavoidably in Jesus Christ is to be subjected to a definite formation and direction. We can adapt ourselves to other masters. We can imitate them. We can model ourselves on them, or even on the caricature of them. No other master has the power to subordinate another man to his direction and leadership in such a way that the latter is completely himself and not a cast, and yet completely represents the form and the way of the master and not a caricature. The arbitrariness of all imitation is also its weakness. Just what imitation really intends, imitation cannot achieve. Therefore we can call it the tragedy of all other mastery, that at the very best it produces only imitation. The formation and direction of a man by the Word of God, which becomes a reality with the outpouring of the Holy Spirit, has nothing to do with imitation. We must again insist that under this formation and direction man remains the man he is. His own nature and thinking and willing and feeling, both in general and in detail, is not lost. But in the light of this his own being, he remains a sinner before God. Yet this very being of his as a sinner before God is subjected to the Word of God, and is therefore formed and directed by that Word. And because the subordination and therefore the formation and direction are perfect, there takes place at this point what imitation intends but can never achieve: the master acquires a pupil, a servant, a scholar, a follower, in whom he finds himself again and in whom accordingly he, the master, can also be found again by others. But the master is the eternal Word, which has assumed flesh. We are not the eternal Word, but flesh of that flesh, which in Him was made partaker of the divine nature. In that we are subjected to Him, the eternal Word, we are not only flesh, but in the flesh we are the children of God, the brethren of the First-born. That is the subjection of our being to the Word. Subjected to the Word, this being is no longer left to its own devices. It no longer grows wild. It still exists in the flesh. But in spite of and even because of this, its direction is from the Spirit, from the new birth, to the Word. It is the object of an attraction, a formation, a leading by the Word. From the standpoint of the being itself, this is, of course, inconceivable. It does not deserve it, nor can it contribute to it or co-operate in it. But that is just what makes it so necessary and irresistible. Only by a denial and rejection of Jesus Christ Himself, i.e., only in the absence of the Holy Spirit, can this attraction,

[277]

[EN233] cause of God
[EN234] power of God
[EN235] for salvation

formation and direction by Him be denied and rejected and rendered ineffective. Where and to the extent that He now acts in the Holy Spirit, He forms and directs the man who still exists in the flesh, who is still wandering as a sinner. Certainly this is a strictly hidden formation and direction, just as He Himself, the Master, is a hidden master. But His action upon us is just as real as He Himself is. And the aim of His action is that out of man's life there should come a repetition, an analogy, a parallel to His own being—that he should be conformable to Christ. Conformable to Christ does not mean that a man is a second Christ—which involves all the arbitrariness and weakness of a mere *imitatio*[EN236]. Conformable to Christ means that in all his humanity, for Christ's sake and in Christ, he is a child of God. It means, therefore, that he is directed away to the one for whose sake and in whom he is a child of God. This directing and integrating into Christ is the work of the Holy Spirit, and in it he can hear and receive the divine revelation. The possibility into which we have been inquiring is to be found in this actuality.

For a right understanding of this point, the decisive New Testament concept is one which is very important for the Synoptists, but also quite prominent in John. It is that of following Jesus. Ἀκολουθεῖν[EN237] points in quite a different direction from *imitatio*[EN238]. In the first place it is descriptive of someone who accompanies another, who takes the same road as he does. But more pregnantly, it indicates the follower who respectfully walks behind a master or prince, the scholar who strides along at a distance behind his teacher. And in cases like this imitation is not only unnecessary, but impossible. Further, we have to note that this following is distinguished from an arbitrary action, like imitation, by the fact that it is conditioned by the call of Jesus. It is therefore a Messianic gift. The individual who decides ("Lord, I would follow thee") to tread this way on his own initiative, at once proves that he is not suited for the kingdom of God (Lk. 9$^{61f.}$). Finally, the frequent inter-relating of the idea of following with that of self-denial ought also to prevent us from thinking that this is the kind of formation and direction which a man can undertake of himself. It is allowed and granted to him to participate in the existence of Jesus, in the salvation manifested in Him, and in His passion—that is what following is. In this following he becomes a μαθητής[EN239]. He can be taught by Jesus and can learn from Him. But he who does not follow Him is not worthy (ἄξιος[EN240]) Mt. 10^{38}, and cannot be His disciple (Lk. 14^{27}). In the same way we are told in 1 Pet. 2^{21} that in His passion Christ has left us a ὑπογραμμός[EN241], that we should follow in His steps, i.e., fashion our life according to the form of His passion. In the same connexion we must also think of Heb. 12^2, where Jesus is called the ἀρχηγός καὶ τελειωτής[EN242] of our faith, to whom we have to look if we are to run properly in the race which is set before us. But Paul also addresses the Galatians as children who seeing that Christ was still "openly set forth" before them in vain (Gal. 3^1) were not yet born again—in, as it were, the personal unity of the apostolic Word with the working of the Holy Spirit—but whom He had still to

[278]

[EN236] imitation
[EN237] Following
[EN238] imitation
[EN239] disciple
[EN240] example
[EN241] pattern
[EN242] author and perfector

labour to bring forth: μέχρις οὗ μορφωθῇ Χριστὸς ἐν ὑμῖν[EN243] (Gal. 4[19]). It is a matter of the μορφὴ δούλου[EN244] of Him who emptied Himself of His own God-form and humbled Himself to the death on the cross. It is of this that Christians must think if they are to revert from disunity to unity ἐν Χριστῷ Ἰησοῦ[EN245] (Phil. 2[1–11]). By the Spirit who is the Lord they are "changed into his (Christ's) likeness." The result is, therefore, that they become a mirror of the glory of the Lord. And in that very fact it is shown that, unlike the Jews whose hearts are covered when they read their Moses, they have freedom (ἐλευθερία) and therefore open eyes (ἀνακεκαλυμμένον πρόσωπον) for God's revelation (2 Cor. 3[12–18]). In that they become σύμφυτοι τῷ ὁμοιώματι τοῦ θανάτου αὐτοῦ[EN246], implanted into the Church, which by baptism we understand to be the image of His body given up to death for us, they will also participate in His resurrection (Rom. 6[5]). We have to put all these things in their general context if we are to gain even an inkling of what is meant by the very simple but pregnant Johannine τηρεῖν[EN247] of the Word and the sayings (Jn. 8[51], 14[23]) or commandments of Jesus (Jn. 14[15, 21], 15[10]; 1 Jn. 5[3]).

(*f*) To have our master unavoidably in Jesus Christ means finally and comprehensively that we have no concern of our own, but that His, Christ's concern, is our concern. No other master can master us so thoroughly, either for good or evil, that although we are in his service, or school, or following, we cannot still have our own concerns, and in the last resort have him as our master only for the sake of those interests of ours. But where the Word of God is master by the outpouring of the Holy Spirit, there enters in an interest or concern which does not allow any rivals, for the simple reason that in the Word of God it is always a matter of our own interest and concern. But it is our own interest and concern not as seen from our standpoint, but as seen from the opposite but beneficent standpoint of the wisdom of God, as judged by the righteousness of God, as adopted by the goodness of God. That is the Word of God: the work of God upon us: for us and therefore against us: the work of the kindness which we cannot grasp, which we have outraged, which does good to us, as to those who always do evil. Where it is heard as such, there is still an active will to assert and help ourselves, to maintain and justify and advertise ourselves, but it has been fundamentally broken and its vital power destroyed. At any rate it cannot exist in face of the Word of God—so that fundamentally it cannot exist at all. It can exist only as and to the extent that we exist under the Word. If that means humiliation, it also means comfort. If it means limitation, it also means liberation. If it means Law, it also means Gospel. It is a great affliction when our right to have our own desires and to pursue them is so radically questioned and finally taken away. But, of course, it is an even greater help, when the common necessity of worrying about our own situation is so radically relativised and in fact basically set aside. But however that may be, a central convulsion, indeed a revolution, has brought about the supplanting of

---

[EN243] until Christ is formed in us
[EN244] form of a servant
[EN245] in Jesus Christ
[EN246] conformed to the likeness of his death
[EN247] keeping

[279] our *causae*EN248 by the *causa Dei*EN249 (which does not demand our anxiety and activity but only our faith and obedience). In the light of this decrease on our side and increase on the other, we are again reminded of all that we have tried to say positively about the possibility of the revelation of God to man.

We will close with some words of John the Baptist in the Fourth Gospel, which again confront us with the riddle of the subjective possibility of revelation and the solution of this riddle: "A man can receive nothing, except it be given him from heaven. Ye yourselves bear me witness, that I said, I am not the Christ, but that I am sent before him. He that hath the bride is the bridegroom: but the friend of the bridegroom, which standeth and heareth him, rejoiceth greatly because of the bridegroom's voice: this my joy therefore is fulfilled .... He that hath received his testimony hath set to his seal that God is true .... The Father loveth the Son, and hath given all things into his hand. He that believeth on the Son hath eternal life" (Jn. 3²⁷⁻²⁹ ³³ ³⁵ᶠ·). Calvin (*Comm. on Jn.* 3³³, *C.R.* 47, 74) writes concerning the saying about confirmation of the veracity of God by our receiving of the witness of Christ: *Quantus est hic honos, quo miseros homunciones dignatur Deus, ut qui natura nihil sunt aliud quam mendacium et vanitas, idonei tamen censeantur, qui sacram Dei veritatem subscriptione sua comprobent*EN250. And concerning the saying about faith in the Son, into whose hand the Father's love hath given all things (*on Jn.* 3³⁵, *ib.*, 47, 75): *Facit enim hoc amor, quo Filium amplexus nos quoque in eo amplectitur, ut per illius manum nobis bona sua omnia communicet*EN251.

EN248 causes

EN249 cause of God

EN250 How great is this honour, which God bestows on wretched little men, such that they who are nothing by nature but falsehood and vanity, are nevertheless counted worthy to approve the sacred truth of God with their own signature

EN251 For He creates the love, by which he embraces the Son and also embraces us in Him, so that through His hand He may impart all his goodness to us

THE REVELATION OF GOD AS THE ABOLITION OF RELIGION

The revelation of God in the outpouring of the Holy Spirit is the judging but also reconciling presence of God in the world of human religion, that is, in the realm of man's attempts to justify and to sanctify himself before a capricious and arbitrary picture of God. The Church is the locus of true religion, so far as through grace it lives by grace.

1. THE PROBLEM OF RELIGION IN THEOLOGY

The event of God's revelation has to be understood and expounded as it is attested to the Church of Jesus Christ by Holy Scripture. It is within this concrete relationship that theology has to work. That is why when we asked how God does and can come to man in His revelation, we were compelled to give the clear answer that both the reality and the possibility of this event are the being and action only of God, and especially of God the Holy Spirit. Both the reality and the possibility! It was only for the sake of a better understanding that we could distinguish between the two. And what we had to understand was ultimately just this, that we must seek both of them in God, and only in God. Therefore we could not take the distinction seriously. We could not fix the reality of revelation in God, and yet find in man a possibility for it. We could not ascribe the event to God, and yet attribute to man the instrument and point of contact for it. We could not regard divine grace as the particular feature and man's suitability and capacity as the universal. We could not interpret God as the substance and man as the form. We could not, therefore, regard the event of revelation as an interplay between God and man, between grace and nature. On the contrary, as we tried to be faithful to Holy Scripture as the only valid testimony to revelation, we saw that we were committed to the statement that as an event which encounters man, this event represents a self-enclosed circle. Not only the objective but also the subjective element in revelation, not only its actuality but also its potentiality, is the being and action of the self-revealing God alone.

But this revelation is in fact an event which encounters man. It is an event which has at least the form of human competence, experience and activity. And it is at this point that we come up against the problem of man's religion.   [281]
The revelation of God by the Holy Spirit is real and possible as a determination of man's existence. If we deny this, how can we think of it as revelation? But if we do not deny it, we have to recognise that it has at least the aspect and

81

character of a human phenomenon. It is something which may be grasped historically and psychologically. We can inquire into its nature and structure and value as we can in the case of all others. We can compare it with other phenomena of a more or less similar type. We can understand it and judge it according to that comparison. But the sphere to which this problem introduces us is the sphere of religion. On their subjective side, too, we have tried as strictly and logically as possible to expound the reality and possibility of revelation as the divine reality and possibility. But how could we do that without having to speak no less definitely and concretely about an encounter and fellowship between God and man, about the Church and the sacrament, about a definite existence and attitude of man in the presence of God? And in speaking about these things we have spoken about things which are human. They are singular, perhaps, but not unique. They are astounding, but not inconceivable. And they are not unparalleled elsewhere. From this aspect what we call revelation seems necessarily to be only a particular instance of the universal which is called religion. "Christianity" or the "Christian religion" is one predicate for a subject which may have other predicates. It is a species within a genus in which there may be other species. Apart from and alongside Christianity there is Judaism, Islam, Buddhism, Shintoism and every kind of animistic, totemistic, ascetic, mystical and prophetic religion. And again, we would have to deny revelation as such if we tried to deny that it is also Christianity, that it has this human aspect, that from this standpoint it can be compared with other human things, that from this standpoint it is singular but certainly not unique. We have to recognise the fact calmly, and calmly think it through. If we are going to know and acknowledge the revelation of God as revelation, then there is this general human element which we cannot avoid or call by any other name. It is always there even apart from Christianity as one specific area of human competence, experience and activity, as one of the worlds within the world of men.

Cf. for what follows, Edvard Lehmann, "*Die Erscheinungs-und Ideenwelt der Religion*" (in Chantepie de la Saussaye, *Lehrbuch der Religionsgeschichte*, 1925, vol. 1, 23–130).

Always and even necessarily men seem to feel that they are confronted by definite forces which stand over their own life and that of the world and influence it. Even at the most primitive cultural levels they seem to be aware not only of nature but also of the spirit and of spirits and their operation. Human culture in general and human existence in detail seem always and everywhere [282] to be related by men to something ultimate and decisive, which is at least a powerful rival to their own will and power. Both culture and existence seem to have been determined or partly determined by a reverence for something ostensibly more than man, for some Other or wholly Other, for a supreme Relative or even the Absolute. There seems always and everywhere to be an awareness of the reality and possibility of a dedication, or even a sanctification of the life of man, on the basis of an individual or social striving, which is almost always and everywhere referred to an event which comes from beyond. As a result, the representation of the object and aim of the striving, or of the origin of the event, has always and everywhere been compressed into pictures of deities, with almost always and everywhere the picture of a supreme and only deity more or less clearly visible in the background. It is difficult to find any time or place when man was not aware of his duty to offer worship to God or gods in the form of concrete cults: by occupying himself with pictures and symbols of deity, by sacrifice, acts of atonement, and prayers, by customs, games and mysteries, by the formation of communions and churches. It is difficult to find any time or place when it was not thought that the voice of the deity had been heard and that it ought to be asserted and its meaning investigated. The Veda to the Indians, the Avesta to the Persians, the Tripitaka to the Buddhists, the Koran to its believers: are they not all "bibles" in exactly the same way as the Old and New Testaments? Are not at any rate the elements and problems in the basic outlook of all religions the same as those of Christian doctrine: the world's beginning and end, the origin and nature of man, moral and religious law, sin and redemption? And even in its supreme and finest forms, although it may be at the highest level, is not Christian "piety" on the same scale as all other forms of piety? And what are the criteria by which the highest place is necessarily accorded to it?

To allow that there is this whole world apart from and alongside "Christianity" is to recognise that in His revelation God has actually entered a sphere in which His own reality and possibility are encompassed by a sea of more or less adequate, but at any rate fundamentally unmistakable, parallels and analogies in human realities and possibilities. The revelation of God is actually the presence of God and therefore the hiddenness of God in the world of human religion. By God's revealing of Himself the divine particular is hidden in a human universal, the divine content in a human form, and therefore that which is divinely unique in something which is humanly only singular. Because and in so far as it is God's revelation to man, God Himself, and the outpouring of the Holy Spirit, and therefore the incarnation of the Word, can be seen from this side too, in the hiddenness which is obviously given to it along with its true humanity as a religious phenomenon, as a member of that series, as a particular concept within general observation and experience, as one content of a human form, which can have other contents and in which the divine [283] uniqueness of that content cannot be perceived directly.

We have to make the point even sharper by adding that the impression that we are dealing with human religion is no less strong and certain when the Church feels bound to speak about the divine revelation. Indeed, it is even stronger and more pronounced here than in other departments of religious history. It is no accident that expositions of the general phenomenology of religion usually take their most striking examples of the most various types of religious formation and action from the Bible (and the history of the Christian Church), as though we had here—in the phrase of A. v. Harnack—a "compendium of the history of religion." If it is true, as A. v. Harnack thinks, that the man who knows this religion knows all religion, then we certainly cannot isolate the "Christian religion" more easily from the general world of religion than we can all other religions. D. F. Strauss deserves a hearing at least when he makes the following criticism of those who defend the supernatural revealedness of Christianity: "Because the fruit is now before us, separated as ripe fruits usually are, from the twig and stalk which bore them, it is supposed not to have grown on a tree, but to have fallen direct from heaven. What a childish idea! And even when we can point out the very stalk by which it was attached to the maternal branch; even when in its growth we can see clearly its unmistakable relationship to other similar fruits; even when we can still find on its surface traces of the sun which has irradiated it and the hailstones which have bruised it, and the prick of evil insects which have attacked it: it is still argued that it cannot have sprung from any earthly stem or ripened in our atmosphere" (*Die chr. Glaubenslehre*, vol. 1, 1840, 352).

If we do not wish to deny God's revelation as revelation, we cannot avoid the fact that it can also be regarded from a standpoint from which it may in certain circumstances be denied as God's revelation. In fact, it can and must also be regarded as "Christianity," and therefore as religion, and therefore as man's reality and possibility. In this section we will have to show what exactly we mean by this "also." But first we have to see clearly the question which it poses, and the basic elements in the twofold possibility of answering it.

The question raised by the fact that God's revelation has also to be regarded as a religion among other religions is basically the plain question whether theology and the Church and faith are able and willing to take themselves, or their basis, seriously. For there is an extremely good chance that they will not take themselves and their basis seriously. The problem of religion is simply a pointed expression of the problem of man in his encounter and communion with God. It is, therefore, a chance to fall into temptation. Theology and the Church and faith are invited to abandon their theme and object and to become hollow and empty, mere shadows of themselves. On the other hand, they have the chance to keep to their proper task, to become really sure in their perception of it, and therefore to protect and strengthen themselves as what they profess to be. In this decision the point at issue cannot be whether God's revelation has also to be regarded as man's religion, and therefore as a religion among other religions. We saw that to deny this statement would be to deny the human aspect of revelation, and this would be to deny revelation as such. But the question arises how the statement has to be interpreted and applied. Does it mean that what we think we know of the nature and incidence of religion must serve as a norm and principle by which to explain the revelation of God; or, *vice versa*, does it mean that we have to interpret the Christian religion and all other religions by what we are told by God's revelation? There is an obvious difference between regarding religion as *the* problem of theology and regarding it as only one problem in theology. There is an obvious difference between regarding the Church as a religious brotherhood and regarding it as a state in which even religion is "sublimated" in the most comprehensive sense of the word. There is an obvious difference between regarding faith as a form of human piety and regarding it as a form of the judgment and grace of God, which is naturally and most concretely connected with man's piety in all its forms. That is the decision which has to be made.

[284]

We are touching upon one of the most difficult historical puzzles when we assert that in the manifestations of modern Protestantism in the 19th and 20th centuries, as it developed from its 16th and 17th century root, the great characteristic decisions have all gone on the side of the first alternatives. It was and is a characteristic of its theological thinking, so far as it here concerns us (in relation to its conception and formulating of the Church and its life), that in its great representatives and outstanding tendencies what it has discerned and declared is not the religion of revelation but the revelation of religion.

1. The Problem of Religion in Theology

As a text for what follows: "The word religion is introduced in the most decided opposition to the word faith so prevalent in the Lutheran, Reformed and Catholic Churches, and it presupposes the Deistic criticism of the universally Christian concept of revelation. Do we still want to assert that we are in the sphere of the Reformation?" (Paul de Lagarde, *Deutsche Schriften*, 4th impression, 46).

Thomas Aquinas (*S. Theol.* II 2, qu. 81 f.) spoke of the general (moral) virtue of *religio* and (*ib., qu.* 186 f.) of the specifically monkish *religio*[EN1]. Occasionally he described the object of theology as *christiana religio*[EN2] (e.g., in the Prologue to the *S. Theol.*) or as *religio fidei*[EN3]. But when he did this he had obviously no thought of a non-Christian "religion." What we call that seems then not to have been known by that name. And the concept of religion as a general concept, to which the Christian religion must be subordinated as one with others, was obviously quite foreign to him. In substance, the problem had been raised early in the Middle Ages by Claudius of Turin, John Scot Erigena and Abelard. But it did not and could not have any great importance until after the Renaissance.

After the humanistic fashion, Calvin spoke of the *religio Christiana*[EN4] even in the title of his *chef d'oeuvre*[EN5]. But when he did so he was not conscious of making *christiana*[EN6] the predicate of something human in a neutral and universal sense. What Calvin (*Instit.* I, 2, 2) describes as *pura germanaque religio: fides cum serio dei timore coniuncta, ut timor et voluntariam reverentiam in se contineat et secum trahat legitimum cultum qualis in lege praescribitur*[EN7]—is obviously a normative concept which he has derived from Holy Scripture, and in which the universal is sublimated in the particular, religion in revelation, and not *vice versa*. Certainly Calvin ascribes to fallen man an inalienable *semen*[EN8] of this religion (I, 3, 1 f.). But over against it he sets the knowledge that this *semen*[EN9] cannot ripen, let alone bear fruit in anyone (I, 4, 1; 12, 1). Therefore the concept of *religio*[EN10] as a general and neutral form has no fundamental significance in Calvin's conception and exposition of Christianity. For him *religio*[EN11] is an entity x, which receives content and form only as it is equated with Christianity, i.e., because as it is taken up into revelation and fashioned by it.

[285]

In general the older orthodox (J. Gerhard and L. Hutterus among the Lutherans, Bucan and H. Alting, Gomarus and Voetius, and even J. Cocceius among the Reformed) avoided any systematic treatment or discussion of the concept "religion." This was true even of some of the later ones, J. W. Baier on the one side, and F. Turrettini and P. v. Mastricht on the other. For Baier (*Comp. Theol. pos.*, 1686, Prol. I, 7 f.) religion is still only the essence of the possibilities of a *theologia naturalis*[EN12] which is inadequate for the knowledge of salvation. Neither materially nor formally is revelation related to religion. The two Basel men, Polanus and (his obvious disciple) Wolleb, are a striking exception even at the beginning of the 17th century. But even in these two the doctrine of religion is not placed at the head of the system under the theological principles of knowledge. Perhaps on the model of Thomas Aquinas, it is introduced under ethics, as an introduction to the exposition of the commandments of

---

EN 1 religion

EN 2 the Christian religion

EN 3 the religion of faith

EN 4 Christian religion

EN 5 masterwork

EN 6 'Christian'

EN 7 pure and genuine religion: faith joined to serious fear of God, such that fear also contains within itself free reverence and brings with it proper worship as prescribed in the Law

EN 8 seed

EN 9 seed

EN10 religion

EN11 religion

EN12 natural theology

the first table, and especially to commandments 2–4. And as in Calvin, it is filled out as the doctrine of the true, i.e., the one, necessary religion founded by God Himself, which is identical with the Christian religion, i.e., the Christian religion as inwardly apprehended by man (A. Polanus, *Synt. Theol.*, 1609, p. 3694 f.). Apart from Christianity there is only false and hypocritical religion and irreligiosity (p. 3718). For the natural man, who is a liar, is incapable of true religion, not only from the standpoint of the will but also from that of knowledge (p. 3710). *Vera religio sola proprie est, aliae non sunt, sed dicuntur esse*[EN13] (p. 3697). Therefore there can be no question of a freedom of choice between this and other religions (p. 3718). At the same time, we can find in J. Wolleb (*Christ. Theol. comp.*, 1626, II, 4, 1) the very thing which Polanus obviously tried to avoid. It is concealed and rendered innocuous by the context, but it is there all the same: a general and neutral definition of the concept "religion" (*Religio ... generali significatione omnem Dei cultum, specialiter cultum Dei immediatum, specialissime vero aut internum solum aut externum et internum simul denotat*[EN14]), to which the concept *vera religio*[EN15] (*ib.*, 4, 3) can be subordinated as a species. In a Dutch pupil of Polanus, Anton Walaeus (*Loci comm.*, 1640, 31 f.), and in the *Synopsis purioris Theol.*, Leiden, 1624, *Disp.* 2 17–20 (this disputation took place under the presidency of Walaeus himself), the concept "religion" occurs in a quite different and more captious context, namely in the proofs for establishing the authority and necessity of Holy Scripture. According to Walaeus this is supported by the fact that in Holy Scripture the *vera et salutaris religio*[EN16] is transmitted, i.e., the *christiana religio*[EN17], which has all the notes (*notae*) of the *vera et divina religio*[EN18]. The *notae*[EN19] are given as follows: (1) the *vera veri Dei notitia*[EN20], (2) the *vera ratio reconciliationis hominis cum Deo*[EN21], (3) the *verus Dei cultus*[EN22]. These *notae*[EN23] are found in the Christian religion taught in the Bible and not elsewhere. In them we recognise—and this is an unfortunate phrase—*conscientia hominum id ipsis dictante*[EN24] (*Syn.* 2, 18): *haec natura ipsa docet in religione vera requiri*[EN25] (Walaeus, 32)—the signs of true religion. And because of them we believe that the Bible is of divine origin and therefore necessary. This is an unambiguous hint at a general concept of religion which is known by virtue of the voice of conscience or of nature. It may be regarded as innocuous because it has importance "only" apologetically, in the content of arguments for the authenticity of Holy Scripture as against atheists on the one hand and the Papacy on the other. But once it is introduced, how long will it have "only" an apologetic importance ? Does it not actually have more weight with Walaeus than he himself concedes? We have to raise the question, for in him and in the Leiden Synopsis only a very incidental part is played by the reason for the recognition of the divine nature of Holy Scripture which was for Calvin (*Instit.* I, 6–8) the one and only reason beside which all other arguments (I, 8, 13) could be considered only as *secundaria nostrae*

[286]

[EN13] Properly speaking Christianity alone is the true religion, and others are not, but are only said to be
[EN14] 'Religion' means in general all worship of God, more particularly the unmediated worship of God, but most particularly worship that is either merely inward, or both inward and outward together.
[EN15] true religion
[EN16] true and saving religion
[EN17] Chrisian religion
[EN18] true knowledge of the true God
[EN19] Notes
[EN20] true knowledge of the true God
[EN21] true basis of the reconciliation of man to God
[EN22] true worship of God
[EN23] notes
[EN24] as the conscience dictates it to the very selves of men ...
[EN25] nature itself teaches that these things are required in true religion ...

1. The Problem of Religion in Theology

imbecillitatis adminicula[EN26] (with no mention at all of any argument *e vera religione*[EN27]). That reason is the *testimonium Spiritus sancti internum*[EN28]. But now does not the recognition rest upon these secondary arguments and therefore, as far as the *argumentum e vera religione*[EN29] is concerned, upon the general idea of religion which is supposedly known to us by conscience and nature? And what will that mean for the exposition and application of Holy Scripture? For Walaeus and the Leiden men it does not actually amount to much. But we can already foresee what it will amount to some day. A. Heidan (*Corp. Theol. ch~.*, 1676, L I, 7 f.) took up a highly individual position. Like many of his theological contemporaries, particularly in Holland, his obvious aim was to unite Calvin and Descartes. To the salvation of the Calvinist components, he equally obviously succeeded only in drawing some very remarkable parallelisms. No one can emphasise more strongly than he did the fact that faith and theology must be based on revelation. *Cum religio sit rectus Dei cultus, atque ille in vero de Deo sensu et recto erga eum affectu consistat, atque ille a nobis effingi non possit out debeat neque sit partus ingenii nostri, a Deo ipso cui cultus ille praestandus est, praescribi nobis debuit. Ille enim solus ideoneus est de se testis* (Calvin, *Instit.* I, 7, 4!) *qui quod sibi gratum est, docere nos possit et cui nihil gratum esse potest, nisi a se profectum et naturae suae conveniens. Quod quale sit nemo novit nisi ipse. At id quomodo innotescat, nisi nobis ab ipso patefiat et reveletur?*[EN30] (p. 12). It must seem that a general conception of religion was impossible on these premises. But then Heidan remembers the atheists of his time, and his Cartesian heart begins to flutter. There is a *naturalis Dei cognitio, quae singulis hominibus innata est*[EN31] (p. 8). If this were not the case, how could it become a reality in us by tradition and instruction? (p. 9). The existence of God can be proved *a priori*, by way of the ontological argument (p. 11). *Cum Deum cogito, concipio ens perfectissimum, numen potentissimum, sapientissimum*[EN32] ... (p. 12). And *ex hac notitia Dei ortum habet religio*[EN33] (p. 13). It seems that a general concept of religion has been reached. But Calvin stirs again and for his sake the deduction that *rectam rationem fuisse normam primaevae religionis*[EN34] is indignantly rejected: in fact, Adam had knowledge of God only by revelation (p. 13). *Deus non potest concipi sine verbo*[EN35]. Without revelation we can have no knowledge of God (p. 14). *Illa recta ratio est mera chimaera, cerebri humani commentum*[EN36] (p. 15). Obviously the introduction of the general concept is only an apologetic interlude. As soon as he forgets the atheists, Heidan again speaks only as a theologian of revelation. In his doctrine of Holy Scripture it is noticeable that he does not make any use of the *argumentum e vera religione*[EN37]. In his case,

---

[EN26] secondary supports from our weakness
[EN27] from true religion
[EN28] inward witness of the Holy Spirit
[EN29] argument from true religion
[EN30] Since religion is the right worship of God, and that consists in the true sense of God and the right attitude towards Him, and it cannot be created by us, nor should it be produced by our minds, that worship of Him must be made manifest by God Himself: it must be prescribed to us. For only that is a suitable witness to Him ... which can teach us what is pleasing to Him, and that nothing can be pleasing to Him unless it has proceeded from Himself, and conforms to His own nature. And what that is, no-one knows except Himself. But how could this become known unless he makes it plain and reveals it to us from Himself
[EN31] natural knowledge of God, which is innate in every single man
[EN32] When I think of God, I conceive of a most perfect being, and most powerful and most wise spirit
[EN33] from this knowledge of God, religion has its origin
[EN34] right reason was the norm of primeval religion
[EN35] God cannot be conceived of without the word
[EN36] That 'right reason' is a pure chimera, an invention of the human mind
[EN37] argument from true religion

too, the coming of a new outlook is only intimated. He obviously took it for granted that the contradictions amid which he moved would not be felt as contradictions by him personally. But it is evident that the problem could not be left at that stage. An important and serious step forward was made when M. F. Wendelin (*Chr. Theol. lib. duo*, 1634, I, 1) tried to make the *vera religio*[EN38] the *objectum theologiae*[EN39], distinguishing it from God as its *causa efficiens principalis*[EN40] and from Holy Scripture as its *causa efficiens instrumentalis*, and putting it at the head of his theological system as a form-concept. How does it come about that this subject, which was hardly referred to even incidentally by most of the older men, and was treated by Polan and Wolleb only in the context of ethics and by Walaeus as one "argument" with others in the doctrine of Holy Scripture, is now promoted to this high position? Now Wendelin is not guilty of filling out the concept *vera religio*[EN41] from *conscientia*[EN42] and *natura*[EN43], nor does he introduce it as an apologetic element into his doctrine of Scripture. On the contrary, the concept is filled out by him in a wholly objective and Christian way; *vera religio*[EN44] is the *ratio agnoscendi colendique Deum a Deo praescripta ad hominis salutem Deique gloriam*[EN45] or the *norma agnoscendi colendique Deum perfecta et mere divina in sacris literis consignata*[EN46]; to that extent it is *divinum quiddam et infallibile, a quo provocare nemini fas est*[EN47]. Wendelin obviously means that it is God's revelation in its subjective reality. But why is it emphasised in this way? we may ask—just as it is in the contemporary hymn. Yet it is still characterised and emphasised as God's revelation, and the secret catastrophe has not yet come to light. The same can still be said of F. Burmann. Of course, more striking accents are now noticeable: the compromises of Walaeus and Wendelin, an apologetic rationalising of the concept of religion on the one hand, and its systematic overemphasis on the other, are now seen in heightened form. As opposed to his teacher Cocceius, Burmann opens his *Synopsis Theologiae* (1678) with a big chapter, "*De religione et theologia*[EN48]," in which the main concept is that of the *creatura rationalis* striving after God, but attaining to God by God (I, 2, 1). Again we find the definition that *religio*[EN49] is the *ratio cognoscendi et colendi Deum*[EN50]. But now an ambiguous *recta*[EN51] replaces the addition which pointed expressly to revelation (2, 4): *a Deo praescripta*[EN52] or *in sacris literis consignata*[EN53]. And of this *religio*[EN54] as the *ratio recta cognoscendi et colendi Deum*[EN55] it can be said that *fluit ex ipsa Dei hominisque natura cum creaturam rationalem nihil aeque deceat, quam Dei ... excellentiam summasque virtutes venerare ac*

[287]

[EN38] true religion
[EN39] object of theology
[EN40] principal efficient cause
[EN41] true religion
[EN42] conscience
[EN43] nature
[EN44] true religion
[EN45] basis of knowing and worshipping God which is prescribed by God for the salvation of man and the glory of God
[EN46] rule for knowing and worshipping God, which is perfect and purely divine, as described in the sacred letters
[EN47] something divine and infallible, which no-one is allowed to gainsay
[EN48] 'On religion and theology'
[EN49] religion
[EN50] basis of knowing and worshipping God
[EN51] right
[EN52] prescribed by God
[EN53] described in the sacred letters
[EN54] religion
[EN55] right basis of knowing and worshipping God

1. The Problem of Religion in Theology

*colere. Inde religio necessaria et naturalis rationis sequela est; atque adeo datur religio naturalis*EN56 (2, 6–7). Yet the possible and apparently necessary deductions are not drawn by Burmann. As he sees it, the natural religion of the sinner does not attain its goal because he is a sinner (2, 11): *vera religio a solo Deo eiusque revelatione dependet*EN57, and the only *vera religio*EN58 is the *christiana religio*EN59 (2, 19). It is known to be *vera*EN60 by the fact that it has the characteristics of true religion; i.e., it gives us the *verum medium*EN61 and the *vera ratio*EN62 for communion with God (2, 18). We were told similar things in Walaeus. But as distinct from Walaeus, Burmann did not expressly point to conscience or to nature as the source of these *notae*EN63. And yet, like Wendelin, he did not expressly point to Holy Scripture. Perhaps in his case, too, we can accept the explanation: *huic ergo verae religioni unice adhaerescendum est*EN64 (2, 29); and the fact that from this point his Synopsis is a straightforward theology of revelation and Scripture. There were similar developments on the Lutheran side. This is true even of the representatives of Lutheran High Orthodoxy in the second half of the 17th century, e.g., in A. Calov, *Syst. loc. theol.* I, 1655, c. 2, in J. F. König, *Theologiae pos. accroam.* 1664, § 57 f., in A. Quenstedt, *Theol. did. pol.*, 1685, I, 2. In all of them (except Baier) we find that the chapter on Holy Scripture, the *principium Theol. cognoscendi*EN65, is preceded by one entitled "*De religione christiana*EN66," which is described as the *obiectum theologiae generale*EN67. But both theoretically and practically the *religio christiana*EN68 arises only in relation to the *religio paradisiaca*EN69 of Adam prior to the fall. It is expressly declared that the concept *religio*EN70 can be applied only *improprie, abusive, per nefas*EN71 to the worship of God by the heathen, Turks and Jews, or even Roman Catholics. And theoretically and practically the concept is filled out only from scriptural sources, or, to be more exact, only from what is regarded as Christian. *Religio vera*EN72 and *religio falsa*EN73, or, better, *religio*EN74 and *superstitio*EN75, are still opposed the one to the other like heaven and earth. In the entity described as *religio christiana*EN76 we can still recognise what we call the subjective reality of revelation. It is just that there is a change of emphasis. The question of the *religio christiana*EN77 has acquired an

---

EN56 it flows from the very nature of God and man, for nothing else is as proper for the rational creature as to venerate and worship the excellence and supreme virtues of God. Therefore, religion is a necessary and natural consequence of religion. It is for that reason that there is natural religion

EN57 true religion depends alone on God and His revelation

EN58 true religion

EN59 Christian religion

EN60 true

EN61 true means

EN62 true basis

EN63 marks

EN64 Therefore we must hold fast only to this true religion

EN65 beginning of the knowledge of theology

EN66 'On the Christian Religion'

EN67 general object of theology

EN68 Christian religion

EN69 pre-lapsarian religion

EN70 religion

EN71 improperly, incorrectly, wrongly

EN72 true religion

EN73 false religion

EN74 religion

EN75 superstition

EN76 Christian religion

EN77 Christian religion

autonomous interest. Even worse, as in Calov (*c.* 2, *sect.* 2, *qu.* 6), the discussion of the dangerous problem: *Utrum religio christiana vera sit?*[EN78] reveals a strange vacillation between spiritual and carnal argumentation. Yet even here no one can point to a single passage in which there is any notable deviation from the line adopted by Calvin. As a Lutheran parallel to Burmann we might mention D. Hollaz (*Ex. theol. acroam,* 1707). The corresponding chapter in his work is entitled "*De religione et articulis fidei*" (Prol. 2). The problem of a general concept of religion occupied him for the length of two questions. And he is distinguished

[288]

from Calov, König and Quenstedt, as Burmann is from Wendelin, by the fact that in the definition of *religio christiana*[EN79] as *ratio colendi Deum*[EN80] the addition of *A Deo praescripta*[EN81] is missing. Instead, the declaration of his predecessors, that this *ratio* definitely consists in faith in Christ, is in his case enriched by the addition *sincera in Deum proximumque caritas*[EN82]. Hollaz is one of the last and strictest representatives of the theory of verbal inspiration. Therefore theoretically he was a scriptural theologian. Yet the Bible was not so important to him that he had to mention it consistently at the point where mention of it has such a basic importance. Such was the power of that concern which was then about to make itself autonomous and all-powerful under the caption *religio*[EN83]. And yet later when he defines *vera religio*[EN84] (more clearly than in a Walaeus or a Burmann) he has at the very heart of it the qualification *quae verbo divino est conformis*[EN85]. And there can be no question that he finds the one true religion in that which is built upon the foundation of Jesus Christ (and which he identifies with the *religio evangelica, quae a ministerio Lutheri cognomen accepit*[EN86]).

In this as in other matters the catastrophe occurred, and Neo-Protestantism was truly and openly born, in the movement of so-called rational orthodoxy at the beginning of the 18th century. We can watch it happen in two theologians, on the Reformed side Salomon van Til (1643–1713, *Theologiae utriusque compendium cum naturalis tum revelatae* 1704), and on the Lutheran J. Franz Buddeus (1667–1729, *Institutiones Theologiae dogmaticae,* 1724). In form Buddeus was a disciple of Baier. But the difference in content is apparent at once, particularly in the present question. Dogmatics now begin quite openly and unilaterally—and in van Til it is the complete dogmatics of a *theologia naturalis*[EN87] constituting a first and autonomous section—with the presupposition of the concept and the description of a general and natural and neutral "religion," which as *religio in se spectata*[EN88] is the presupposition of all religions. *Ut enim a natura homo habet, quod ratione sit praeditus, ita, quod et Deum esse et eundem rite colendum agnoscit, mom minus naturae ipsi acceptum ferre debet*[EN89] (Buddeus I, 1, 3). As is the intellectual equipment, so is the knowledge of God? As a convinced Cartesian van Til appears ready to take even a further step when he declares: *Principium ex quo religio naturalis, quoad certam de Deo eiusque cultu demonstrationem hauriri debet est ipsum lumen rationis in mente hominis per notiones insitas et communes conspicuum, ita ut nemo attentior et praeiudiciis liberatus*

[EN78] Is the Christian religion true?
[EN79] the Christian religion
[EN80] the basis for the worship of God
[EN81] prescribed by God
[EN82] sincere love for God and neighbour
[EN83] religion
[EN84] true religion
[EN85] as it is in agreement with the divine word
[EN86] evangelical religion which received its name from the ministry of Luther
[EN87] natural theology
[EN88] religion examined on its own terms
[EN89] For just as man possesses from nature the gift of reason, so also it must be accepted that he has from the same nature the knowledge both that God exists and that He is rightly to be worshipped

illud ignorare possit^{EN90} (*Prael.* 4, 1). The definition of this *religio naturalis*^{EN91} is as follows: It is the *certum hominum studium, quo quisque pro sua sententia facultates suas in certi luminis contemplatione et observantia ita tenet occupatas, prout sibi existimat convenire, ut numen illud reddat sibi quocunque in casu propitium*^{EN92} (*Prael.* 2, 1). On the basis of this *religio naturalis*^{EN93} Buddeus (I, 1, 5–13) holds that there is knowledge of a supreme being (*ens perfectissimum, quod Deum vocamus*^{EN94}) who unites in Himself the perfection of knowledge, wisdom and freedom, who is eternal and almighty, and perfectly kind and upright, and true and holy, who is the final cause and ruling principle in all things, who is absolutely unique, to whom we owe obedience and responsibility, who opens up for us the prospect of an immortal life of the soul and an ultimate reward, without whose love we cannot be happy because He alone is the supreme good, who wills to be worshipped by us in word and work and thought, who imposes on us definite duties towards ourselves, our fellow-men and finally Himself. Van Til, in part I of his compendium, develops this natural theology in a broad doctrine of the nature and attributes of God, creation and providence, the moral law of nature, the immortality of the soul, and even sin. And all this can be known by man *facili negotio*^{EN95} (Buddeus I, 1, 5). *Cum ratio omnes homines luculenter edoceat eaque ita comparata sint, ut, siquis usu rationis polleat, sanaque mente sit praeditus, quam primum ista intelligit, statim praebere assensum teneatur*^{EN96} (I, 1, 14). Buddeus will not concede a substantial *verbum*^{EN97} or *lumen internum*^{EN98}, as taught by many mystics, i.e., he will not assert formally the existence of a second source of revelation (I, 1, 15). Nor will van Til allow anything of this kind; at all events in the *Dedicatio* of his work [289] he warns young theologians, *ne principium rationis eodem cum principio fidei habeant loco*^{EN99}, because the two are not equally evidenced. But what about that *prima scientia*^{EN100}, man's original knowledge of himself and God, which he then defines and describes as the presupposition of natural religion (*Prael.* 3)? Once we accept this knowledge, how far can we or ought we to say that after all it is not so well evidenced as that which comes from revelation? Be that as it may, at least Buddeus does not forget to make the immediate and well-known reservation of all exponents of natural theology: that the *religio naturalis*^{EN101} and its knowledge of God do not extend to eternal salvation, because with all these insights the means of fellowship with God, the supreme Good, and the right use of that means, have not yet been given to man. He therefore points us away to the indispensable supplementing of the *religio naturalis*^{EN102} by revelation (I, 1, 16–18). At a later stage, at the end of the first and the

---

EN 90 The principle from which natural religion, in as far as it is concerned with the certain proof of God's existence and how He is to be worshipped, is to be drawn is that light of reason in the human mind, evident from its natural and common thoughts, such that no-one who was attentive enough and free from prejudices could be ignorant of it

EN 91 natural religion

EN 92 that natural desire of men, in which each man by virtue of his reason so holds his faculties occupied by a contemplation and observation of certain light, that he intends to meet the fact that that spirit returns the favour to himself in whichever case

EN 93 natural religion

EN 94 the most perfect being, which we call God

EN 95 easily

EN 96 Since reason teaches all men excellently, and these matters are grasped such that, whoever is strong in the use of reason and has been endowed with a sound mind, as soon as he first grasps them, he is immediately constrained to offer assent

EN 97 inward word

EN 98 inward light

EN 99 that they should not consider the principle of reason as occupying the same place as the principle of faith

EN100 primal knowledge

EN101 natural religion

EN102 natural religion

beginning of the second part of his compendium, we finally come to the same reservation in van Til. And yet, according to Buddeus, we still have to say of this *religio naturalis*[EN103] that it contains the *notiones*[EN104] which are the *bases et fundamenta omnis religionis*[EN105]. It is by these *notiones*[EN106] that man has to be measured in respect of religion. It is on the ground of these *notiones*[EN107] that we can recognise as such the *religiones, quae revelatione nituntur*[EN108]. Whatever contradicts these *notiones*[EN109] of *religio naturalis*[EN110] is either not revelation at all or revelation misunderstood. According to Buddeus natural religion does us a twofold educational service. By its insufficiency it enables us to see the necessity for revelation. And by its directions it enables us to find true revelation. Buddeus thinks that he can guarantee that natural religion and revelation will never contradict each other, but always correspond (I, 1, 19–20). And in van Til natural theology culminates in a doctrine *De praeparatione evangelica*[EN111], in which: (1) from the presuppositions and data of natural religion there is logically postulated the necessity of a reconciliation between God and man; (2) again on the principles of natural religion the conditions of such a reconciliation are adduced; and (3) and lastly, the heathen, Jewish, Mohammedan and Christian religions are mutually compared, and the latter is shown to answer to the adduced conditions and is therefore recognisable as the revealed religion. *Theologia naturalis ... ad ista rationis dictamina religiones qualescunque explorat, ut inde elicias, religionem christianam (licet mysteria agnoscat naturalis scientiae limites excettentia) tamen plus quam reliquas cum lumine naturae consentire*[EN112] (*Praef. ad lectorem*). That is the programme which van Til and Buddeus set themselves and carried out to the best of their ability (the first time that such a programme was ever put forward in Protestantism without being condemned as unconfessional).

What they achieved, and all the leading theologians of the time co-operated, in the movement, can never be overestimated either in its basic significance or in the seriousness of its historical consequences. With these theologians there emerged clearly and logically what was perhaps the secret *telos*[EN113] and *pathos*[EN114] of the whole preceding development. Human religion, the relationship with God which we can and actually do have apart from revelation, is not an unknown but a very well-known quantity both in form and content, and as such it is something which has to be reckoned with, as having a central importance for all theological thinking. It constitutes, in fact, the presupposition, the criterion, the necessary framework for an understanding of revelation. It shows us the question which is answered by revealed religion as well as all other positive religions, and it is as the most satisfactory answer that the Christian religion has the advantage over others and is rightly described as revealed religion. The Christian element—and with this the theological reorientation which had threatened since the Renaissance is completed—has now actually become a predicate of the neutral and universal human element. Revelation has now become a historical confirmation

---

EN103 natural religion
EN104 notions
EN105 bases and foundations of all religion
EN106 notions
EN107 notions
EN108 the religions which depend upon revelation
EN109 notions
EN110 natural religion
EN111 On the preparation for the Gospel
EN112 Natural theology investigates various religions according to the dictates of reason rationes should read rationis] in order that you thereby may ascertain that the Christian religion (although it acknowledges the mysteries which surpass the limits of natural investigation) nevertheless agrees with the light of nature more than the others
EN113 goal
EN114 mood

of what man can know about himself and therefore about God even apart from revelation. [290]
"The light of nature goes even further. It shows me the true characteristics of this revelation.
No revelation is true, except it conform to the light of nature and increase it ... A true
revelation must prove itself such in my heart by a divine power and conviction which I clearly
feel ... which the light of nature teaches, which therefore leads me on and gives me a desire
to seek out and challenge such a revelation and in that way to demonstrate the true religion"
(C. M. Pfaff, *Einl. in d. Dogmat. Theol.*, 1747, 27 f., quoted from A. F. Stolzenburg, *Die Theol.
des Jo. Franc. Buddeus und des Chr. Matth. Pfaff*, 1926, 219 f.).

There is no need to tell in detail the sad story of more recent Protestant theology. Our two
examples, Buddeus and van Til, and the other theologians of that generation (C. M. Pfaff, S.
Werenfalls. J. A. Turrettini, J. F. Osterwald, J. L. von Mosheim) were all men of an admitted
seriousness and piety. And in points of detail they were outspokenly conservative. They knew
how to safeguard in their theology the full rights of revelation, at any rate in appearance.
Their aim was to find a more or less perfect agreement between the Bible and traditional
teaching on the one hand and on the other the postulates of *religio naturalis*[EN115] and the
claims to a genuine religion of revelation to which they give rise. Materially, therefore, they
did not make any very striking deviations from the line of 17th century orthodoxy. And they
were still a long way from the parlous stabilising of the relation between reason and revelation which was so soon to emerge in the philosophy of C. Wolff. The main point of this new
development was the fact that much the same evidence can be produced for both, and that
they should therefore give mutual guarantees of their right of ownership and also of peace-
able intercourse in a sphere common to both of them. This untenable compromise preceded the work of the so-called Neologians of the second half of the 18th century. The
Neologians could not convince themselves that all or even most of what had so far been
regarded as revelation could be substantiated before the critical authority of reason. They
thought it right, therefore, to submit Christian dogma, as well as the Bible, to a very severe
criticism on the basis of the *notiones*[EN116] of *religio naturalis*[EN117]. They were followed by Kantian rationalism which abolished the Neology, reducing *religio naturalis*[EN118] to an *ethica
naturalis*[EN119], and ultimately rejecting revelation, except as the actualising of the powers of
moral reason. Then Schleiermacher tried to find in religion as feeling the essence of theology, revelation being a definite impression which produces a definite feeling and then a
definite religion. Then, according to Hegel and D. F. Strauss both Christian and natural
religion are only a dispensable prototype of the absolute awareness of philosophy purified by
the idea. Then, according to L. Feuerbach in particular, there is room only for natural religion as the illusory expression of the natural longings and wishes of the human heart. Then
A. Ritschl taught that the Christian religion must be regarded as revealed and true, because
in it the supreme value of human life, i.e., (the opposite of Feuerbach) its liberation from
the world regarded as sensible nature, is most perfectly realised. Then E. Troeltsch taught us
that the main task of the theologian is to exercise himself in "entering hypothetically" into
the phenomena of general religious history, so that by a comparative assessment of the various worlds of religion he may then see that Christianity is relatively the best religion at any
rate for the time being and probably for all conceivable time (this side of the incursion of a
new ice age). And then at last and finally there came that tumultuous invasion of the Church
and theology by natural religion whose astonished witnesses we have been in our day. Of all

---

[EN115] natural religion
[EN116] notions
[EN117] natural religion
[EN118] natural religion
[EN119] natural ethic

this, of course, the doughty van Til and the equally doughty Buddeus never even dreamed. Yet they and their generation must still be regarded as the real fathers of Neo-Protestant theology, for which the way was not unprepared by the very different Reformation tradition. All these more or less radical and destructive movements in the history of theology in the last two centuries are simply variations on one simple theme, and that theme was clearly introduced by van Til and Buddeus: that religion has not to be understood in the light of revelation, but revelation in the light of religion. To this common denominator the aims and the programmes of all the more important tendencies of modern theology can be reduced. Neo-Protestantism means "religionism." Even the conservative theology of these centuries, the supra-naturalistic of the 18th and the confessional, biblicistic and "positive" of the 19th and 20th, has, on the whole, co-operated, making such concessions to the prevailing outlook that in spite of the immanent resistance which it has put up it cannot be regarded as a renewal of the Reformation tradition. C. E. Luthardt (*Kompend. d. Dogm.*, 1865, 2) quietly admitted the fact that since the 18th century theology has been "the science of religion"; "the science of Christianity only in the sense that the Church is the *locus* of Christianity"—no more. And at the end of the Foreword to vol. 1 of his dogmatics (1925) R. Seeberg calmly remarks that it might have been better to write a "philosophy of religion" instead of a dogmatics; but interested philosophers and historians would, of course, take it in that way without sharing his particular theological presuppositions. Weighing all the circumstances, we must regard an utterance of this kind as a more significant and serious symptom than the very worst pages in the books of a Strauss or a Feuerbach. It shows that at the end of the period which started with Buddeus theology had lost any serious intention of taking itself seriously as theology.

Why have we to judge this development negatively as a disruption of the life of the Church, and ultimately as a heresy which destroys it? Those who carried through the development, the great and with them the countless lesser theologians of Neo-Protestantism, have always felt that in opposition to mere tradition and its concerns they were the representatives of a free investigation of the truth even in relation to God and the things of God. They felt that they were this legitimately and by commission. And those who more or less resolutely opposed them demonstrated the purely immanent character of their opposition by the fact that on the whole they would not go so far in accepting the consequences of that reversal of revelation and religion. They made it clear that if not quite so logically they themselves stood right in the centre of that development. From the standpoint of a merely conservative outlook and attitude no serious objection or amendment could or can be alleged against the development. Against the basic proposition that truth must be freely investigated even in the field of theology, there is nothing to be said. As two hundred years of the history of theology have consistently shown, the man who rejects that proposition will inevitably and rightly cut a poor figure. Even if he does really represent the Church's interest as against that development, he is a poor and dangerous representative of that interest. And the question whether he really does intend the Church's interest, and is not at bottom howling with the wolves, can never be put to him too sharply as occasion offers. The motive for resisting that reversal ought not to be fear of its consequences.

It ought not to be fear of that reconstruction of dogma and biblical doctrine, as it was carried through in the 18th century by an application of the criterion of *religio naturalis*EN120. It ought not to be fear of Kantian moralism or Schleiermacher's theology of feeling, of Feuerbach's illusionism, of the Bible criticism of a D. F. Strauss or an F. C. Baur, a [292] Harnack or a Bousset, of the relativism of the history-of-religion school, etc. Of course, all these and much else are possible and actual consequences of that reversal, and they are still active to-day in spite of its relatively respectable antiquity. But we cannot be afraid of the consequences and repudiate them unless it is perfectly clear that we are not co-operating in that reversal of revelation and religion. To put it concretely, we are defenceless against the "German Christians" of our own time, unless we know how to guard against the development which took place in van Til and Buddeus, and even earlier: as early as König and Quenstedt, Wendelin and Burmann.

If we do not know this, if we argue against them in detail and not as a whole, and only from conservatism, i.e., fear, and not from knowledge, then we are lost, no matter how good may be our intentions or what victories we achieve in points of detail. What serves and helps the Church is not to soften or weaken the heresy which has infiltrated into it, but to know it, to fight it and to isolate it. If the dreaded results of the reversal of revelation and religion could really be claimed as the results of free, theological inquiry into the truth, then however novel or dangerous they might appear to be, the Church would have to recognise them as good and necessary, or at any rate as open to discussion and not disruptive of the fellowship of the Church. It is not because they are novel and dangerous, but because in fact they certainly are not the results of free, theological investigation of truth, that they can and should and must be opposed, radically and seriously opposed. The opposition must be directed— not contrary to the free investigation of truth but for the sake of it—against the point at which the results arise and emerge. But the point at which they arise and emerge is an uncertainty in the conception of revelation and the resultant relationship between God and man, which simply means an uncertainty, or decline of faith. If we are to try to explain that historical development, then—with all the caution and reserve which a judgment of this kind demands—we have to say that Protestant theology would never have conceived of reversing the relationship between revelation and religion if it had not shared with the whole Church of the time in a widespread vacillation concerning something which the Reformers had so clearly perceived and confessed. This was that the decision about man has been taken once and for all and in every respect in Jesus Christ. Jesus Christ is now his Lord, and man belongs to Him, and lives under Him in His kingdom, and serves Him, and therefore has all his consolation in life or death in the fact that he is not his own but is the property of Jesus Christ. Of course the Neo-Protestant theologians have said this. In fact they have usually left the confession of the Reformation "untouched." But the older Protestant theologians did not leave it untouched. They made use of it, i.e., when they pursued theology they thought or at any

---

EN120 natural religion

95

[293] rate tried to think in accordance with this confession. They reckoned inflexibly with the fact that things actually are as they said in the confession, and they did not reckon with the fact that in part they might be otherwise. That is why the theology of the Reformers, and at bottom of all the older Protestantism, was a free investigation of truth. For it meant that their theological thinking as such could always be free, free for its own inexhaustible object. It meant that having that object, it would remain true to itself. It did not need any other attractions or distractions or enslavements from alien points of view. Their theological thinking had the freedom of unconditioned relevance; the freedom of faith, we must say, because this unconditioned relevance was none other than that of faith. Of course, we cannot and must not reproach the later theology because the problem of human religion—we can put it more comprehensively and say the problem of man in general—both came to its notice and laid claim to its attention. The period of the 16th–18th centuries was in its own way a great period, when European man resumed the powerful offensive which had been made by Graeco-Roman antiquity, beginning to discover himself as a man, his nature, his possibilities and capacities, humanity. The discovery of "religion" belonged, of course, to the same movement. It was in the very nature of things that theology should have its part in that discovery.

To that extent we can only give partial approval to the belief of the older orthodoxy that the problem of religion ought not to be considered at all. It is a sign of the superiority of Calvin's theology that he was able quietly to incorporate this problem into his discussion and exposition. And if the development in the 17th and 18th centuries had been only a sign that Protestant theologians were openly participating in the spiritual movement of their day, we could hardly withhold our approval.

Ignorantly or stubbornly to ignore the anxieties and hopes of the immediate present is something which we do not expect or demand of theology for the sake of the Church. But it is quite a different thing openly to champion the predominant interest or even the demonism of an age, openly to identify oneself with that interest and to become the prisoner of that demonism. This is the very thing which theology must not do. Yet it is what it began to do in the 17th century, and was doing openly in the 18th. It fell prey to the absolutism with which the man of that period made himself the centre and measure and goal of all things. It was its duty to participate in this trend and lovingly to investigate it. But it was certainly not its duty to co-operate in it, which is what it did when in the time of Buddeus it openly turned "religionistic." But it was not what theology did that was really serious. It was what it did not do: its weakness and vacillation in the very substance of faith. In fact and in practice it ceased to regard the cardinal statements of the Lutheran and Heidelberg confessions as definite axioms. Originally and properly the sin was one of unbelief. It was that [294] belittling of Christ which begins the moment He is no longer accepted as our One and All and we are secretly dissatisfied with His lordship and consolation. Without denying the catechetical statements, this later theology thought that it should reckon seriously with man from another standpoint than that of the kingdom and ownership of Christ. It separated his own piety from the Word of God spoken to him, making of it a distinct and prior chapter. The danger was obvious that the chapter might become autonomous and, in fact, predominant, ultimately absorbing the chapter on the Word of God. And this was the inevitable result of that negation, that surrender in the very substance of faith. The real catastrophe of modern Protestant theology was not as it has often been represented. It was not that it retreated in face of the growing self-consciousness of modern education. It was not that it imperceptibly allowed itself to be told by philosophy and history and natural science what the "free investigation of the truth" really is. It was not that it unwittingly turned into a rather illogical practical wisdom. Of themselves, the modern view of things, the modern self-conception of man, etc., could not have done any harm. The real catastrophe was that theology lost its object, revelation in all its uniqueness. And losing that, it lost the seed of faith with which it could remove mountains, even the mountain of modern humanistic culture. That it really lost revelation is shown by the very fact that it could exchange it, and with it its own birthright, for the concept "religion."

It is always the sign of definite misunderstanding when an attempt is made systematically to co-ordinate revelation and religion, i.e., to treat them as comparable spheres, to mark them off from each other, to fix their mutual relationship. The intention and purpose may be to start at religion, and therefore man, and in that way to subordinate revelation to religion, ultimately perhaps even to let it merge into it. Again, the intention and purpose may be to maintain the autonomy and even the pre-eminence of the sphere of revelation by definite reservations and safeguards. But that is a purely secondary question. For all the many possible solutions, it is not decisive. The decisive thing is that we are in a position to put human religion on the same level and to treat it in the same way as divine revelation. We can regard it as in some sense an equal. We can assign it an autonomous being and status over against revelation. We can ask concerning the comparison and relationship of the two entities. And the fact that we can do this shows that our intention and purpose is to start with religion, that is, with man, and not with revelation. Anything that we say later, within this systematic framework, about the necessity and actuality of revelation, can never be more than the melancholy reminder of a war which was lost at the very outset. It can never be more than an actual veiling of the real message and content. In fact it would be better, because more instructive, if we accepted the logical consequences of our point of departure, and omitted our later efforts on behalf of revelation. For where we think that revelation [295] can be compared or equated with religion, we have not understood it as revelation. Within the problem which now engrosses us it can be understood only where *a priori*[EN121] and with no possible alternative we accept its superiority over human religion, a superiority which does not allow us even to consider

---

[EN121] at the outset

religion except in the light of revelation, far less to make pronouncement as to its nature and value and in that way to treat it as an independent problem. Revelation is understood only where we expect from it, and from it alone, the first and the last word about religion. The inquiry into the problem of religion in theology involves an either-or, in which the slightest deviation, the slightest concession to religionism, at once makes the right answer absolutely impossible.

We may well ask whether this is not much more clearly seen by the opposite side, by the strict exponents of a pure—a really pure—"science of religion," than it is by the theologian whose thinking and activity is informed by the "science of religion." A "pure" science of religion is one which does not make any claim to be theology. For such a science revelation is either (1) the phenomenon common to almost all religions, whereby their cultic, mythical and moral structure is traced back to the activity, imparting and ordering of the Deity, or (2) the strictly defined limiting concept of truth beyond and within the plenitude of religious realities, a concept which cannot as such be treated by the science of religion, let alone filled out in any concrete way. It would be too much to say that the concept of revelation is even respected by this procedure, for genuine respect would necessarily involve a quite different procedure. The purer the science of religion becomes, the more it drinks in that sea of religious realities (in which the phenomenon of revelations is only too plentiful), and the more it is reduced *ad absurdum*[EN122]. Yet from the standpoint of theology we must still describe its procedure as more sober and instructive and promising than the adulterated science of religion of theologians who, on the one hand, usually spoil the peaceful course of this investigation of religious realities by suddenly taking account of a religious truth of revelation, and, on the other, give evidence, by the philosophical standards of assessment and value which they apply, that they are dealing with something which they are in no position either to understand or to take seriously.

If we are theologically in earnest when we speak of revelation, we shall speak after the manner of those passages in the Catechism. It is a matter of Jesus Christ the Lord. It is a matter of man, therefore, only as he is reached by revelation in order that he may live under Him and serve Him, in order that he may belong not to himself but to Jesus Christ, in order that belonging to Him he may have comfort both in life and in death. But if we deviate only a nail's breadth from this confession, we are not theologically in earnest and we do not speak about revelation at all. Revelation is God's sovereign action upon man or it is not revelation. But the concept "sovereign"—and in the context of the doctrine of the Holy Spirit we can presuppose this as "self-evident" (although not at all self-evidently)—indicates that God is not at all alone, that

[296] therefore, if revelation is to be understood, man must not be overlooked or eliminated. And the same is true of religion, whether by that we mean the Christian religion in particular or human religion in general, to which the Christian religion belongs. But one thing we are forbidden. We must not try to know and define and assess man and his religion as it were in advance and independently. We must not ascribe to him any existence except as the posses-

---

[EN122] to absurdity

sion of Christ. We must not treat of him in any other sphere than that of His Kingdom, in any other relationship than that of "subordination to Him." We must not try to relate him to God's revelation only when we have first taken him seriously in this independent form. If we do, we say *a priori*[EN123] that—at least in the unconditional sense of those passages of the Catechism—Jesus Christ is not his Lord, and he is not the property of Jesus Christ. We have regarded both these truths as open to discussion. We have therefore denied revelation, for revelation is denied when it is regarded as open to discussion. In relating them in that way, we have not spoken about revelation, even though we may later have tried to do so in very earnest and clear and emphatic terms. We always have to speak about revelation from the very outset if we really want to speak about it later and not about something quite different. If we only speak about it later, then we are speaking, e.g., about a postulate or an idea. What we are really and properly speaking about is not revelation, but what precedes it, man and his religion, about which we think that we know so much already which we are not ready to give up. There lies our love, there our interest, there our zeal, there our confidence, there our consolation: and where we have our consolation, there we have our God. If we only come to revelation later there is nothing that can be altered. On the other hand, if revelation is not denied but believed, if man and his religion are regarded from the standpoint of those statements in the Catechism, then to take man and his religion seriously we cannot seek them in that form which has already been fixed in advance. There can, therefore, be no question of a systematic co-ordination of God and man, of revelation and religion. For neither in its existence, nor in its relation to the first, can the second be considered, let alone defined, except in the light of the first. The only thing we can do is to recount the history of the relationships between the two: and even that takes place in such a way that whatever we have to say about the existence and nature and value of the second can only and exclusively be made plain in the light of the first, i.e., in the course of God's sovereign action on man. It is man as he is revealed in the light of revelation, and only that man, who can be seriously treated theologically. Similarly, the problem of religion in theology is not the question how the reality, religion, which has already been defined (and usually untheologically), can now be brought into an orderly and plausible relationship with the theological concepts, revelation, faith, etc. On the contrary, the question is uninterruptedly theological: What is this thing which from the standpoint of revelation and faith is revealed in the actuality of human life as religion? [297]

If we are to maintain the *analogia fidei*[EN124] and not to fall into untheological thinking, we must be guided by the christological consideration of the incarnation of the Word as the *assumptio carnis*[EN125]. The unity of God and man in Jesus Christ is the unity of a completed

---

[EN123] at the outset
[EN124] analogy of faith
[EN125] assumption of the flesh

event. Similarly the unity of divine revelation and human religion is that of an event—although in this case it has still to be completed. As God is the subject of the one event, so, too, He is of the other. The man Jesus has no prior or abstract existence in the one event but exists only in the unity of that event, whose Subject is the Word of God and therefore God Himself: very God and very man. Similarly in the other, man and his religion is to be considered only as the one who follows God because God has preceded the man who hears Him, because he is addressed by God. Man enters, therefore, only as the counterpart of God. If we hesitate to trace back the different attitude of the older Protestant theology from that of more recent times to a deep-seated difference in faith, we can think of it simply and, as it were, technically in this way. It did not praise and magnify Christ in word only, as the newer theology definitely does in its own way. It could also praise and magnify Him in deed, i.e., by the practical ordering of its thinking about God. In other words, the discipline of the christological dogma of the early Church was still a self-evident presupposition with a real practical importance. On the other hand, it is obvious that the christological dogma was bound to become strange and incomprehensible to more modern theology, once it had ceased to be the practical presupposition of its actual thinking.

To sum up: we do not need to delete or retract anything from the admission that in His revelation God is present in the world of human religion. But what we have to discern is that this means that *God* is present. Our basic task is so to order the concepts revelation and religion that the connexion between the two can again be seen as identical with that event between God and man in which God is God, i.e., the Lord and Master of man, who Himself judges and alone justifies and sanctifies, and man is the man of God, i.e., man as he is adopted and received by God in His severity and goodness. It is because we remember and apply the christological doctrine of the *assumptio carnis*[EN126] that we speak of revelation as the abolition of religion.

2. RELIGION AS UNBELIEF

A theological evaluation of religion and religions must be characterised primarily by the great cautiousness and charity of its assessment and judgments. It will observe and understand and take man in all seriousness as the subject of religion. But it will not be man apart from God, in a human *per se*[EN127]. It will be man for whom (whether he knows it or not) Jesus Christ was born, died and rose again. It will be man who (whether he has already heard it or not) is intended in the Word of God. It will be man who (whether he is aware of it or not) has in Christ his Lord. It will always understand religion as a vital utterance and activity of this man. It will not ascribe to this life-utterance and activity of his a unique "nature," the so-called "nature of religion," which it can then use as a gauge to weigh and balance one human thing against another, distin-

[298]

[EN126] assumption of the flesh
[EN127] in itself

guishing the "higher" religion from the "lower," the "living" from the "decomposed," the "ponderable" from the "imponderable." It will not omit to do this from carelessness or indifference towards the manifoldness with which we have to do in this human sphere, nor because a prior definition of the "nature" of the phenomena in this sphere is either impossible or in itself irrelevant, but because what we have to know of the nature of religion from the standpoint of God's revelation does not allow us to make any but the most incidental use of an immanent definition of the nature of religion. It is not, then, that this "revealed" nature of religion is not fitted in either form or content to differentiate between the good and the bad, the true and the false in the religious world. Revelation singles out the Church as the *locus*[EN128] of true religion. But this does not mean that the Christian religion as such is the fulfilled nature of human religion. It does not mean that the Christian religion is the true religion, fundamentally superior to all other religions. We can never stress too much the connexion between the truth of the Christian religion and the grace of revelation. We have to give particular emphasis to the fact that through grace the Church lives by grace, and to that extent it is the *locus* of true religion. And if this is so, the Church will as little boast of its "nature," i.e., the perfection in which it fulfils the "nature" of religion, as it can attribute that nature to other religions. We cannot differentiate and separate the Church from other religions on the basis of a general concept of the nature of religion.

For a truly theological treatment of religion and religions the problem of *Nathan der Weise* is therefore pointless. Christian, Jew and Mussulman as such—and that is how Lessing sees them all, including the Christian—have no advantage over one another and have no real fault to find with one another. The way which Nathan/Lessing proposes as the solution to the conflict: "Let each be zealous for his uncorrupted, unprejudiced love ... " will only lead them deeper into the conflict from the theological standpoint, the standpoint of revelation. For religion and the conflict of religions arise from the very fact that each is striving after his love, which he will, of course, always regard as uncorrupted and unprejudiced. Where and when have religious men ever had anything but, at bottom and in general, good intentions? In the "eternal evangel" at the end of his *Education of the Human Race* Lessing was probably thinking only of the starting-point and goal of all religious history. Even theologically, he was justified to the extent that the mutual rivalry between religions is half-hearted and insincere. But Lessing did not see that after overcoming the false conflict between the various "religionisms," including the Christian, a genuine religious conflict might begin at a point which seems to lie quite outside the possibilities of his templars or his patriarchs. It might begin at the point where in opposition to all "religionisms" the proclamation of the grace of God is introduced as the truth of the Christian religion. Where Christianity does that—even as one religion with others—its self-consciousness is more than religious fanaticism, its mission is more than religious propaganda, and even in the form of one "religionism" with others it is more than a "religionism." But it will have to be radically different, or better: the grace of God will have to be very effective to be essential to Christians as grace, if we are to be able to say that about Christianity.

[299]

[EN128] place

101

§ 17. *The Revelation of God as the Abolition of Religion*

A truly theological treatment of religion and religions, as it is demanded and possible in the Church as the *locus* of the Christian religion, will need to be distinguished from all other forms of treatment by the exercise of a very marked tolerance towards its object. Now this tolerance must not be confused with the moderation of those who actually have their own religion or religiosity, and are secretly zealous for it, but who can exercise self-control, because they have told themselves or have been told that theirs is not the only faith, that fanaticism is a bad thing, that love must always have the first and the last word. It must not be confused with the clever aloofness of the rationalistic Know-All—the typical Hegelian belongs to the same category—who thinks that he can deal comfortably and in the end successfully with all religions in the light of a concept of a perfect religion which is gradually evolving in history. But it also must not be confused with the relativism and impartiality of a historical scepticism, which does not ask about truth and untruth in the field of religious phenomena, because it thinks that truth can be known only in the form of its own doubt about all truth. That the so-called "tolerance" of this kind is unattainable is revealed by the fact that the object, religion and religions, and therefore man, are not taken seriously, but are at bottom patronised. Tolerance in the sense of moderation, or superior knowledge, or scepticism is actually the worst form of intolerance. But the religion and religions must be treated with a tolerance which is informed by the forbearance of Christ, which derives therefore from the knowledge that by grace God has reconciled to Himself godless man and his religion. It will see man carried, like an obstinate child in the arms of its mother, by what God has determined and done for his salvation in spite of his own opposition. In detail, it will neither praise nor reproach him. It will understand his situation—understand it even in the dark and terrifying perplexity of it—not because it can see any meaning in the situation as such, but because it acquires a meaning from outside, from Jesus Christ. But confronted by this object it will not display the weak or superior or weary smile of a quite inappropriate indulgence. It will see that man is caught in a way of acting that cannot be recognised as right and holy, unless it is first and at the same time recognised as thoroughly wrong and unholy. Self-evidently, this kind of tolerance, and therefore a theological consideration of religion, is possible only for those who are ready to abase themselves and their religion together with man, with every individual man, knowing that they first, and their religion, have need of tolerance, a strong forbearing tolerance.

[300] We begin by stating that religion is unbelief. It is a concern, indeed, we must say that it is the one great concern, of godless man.

Outwardly crude things are only trifling compared with what is taught about growing pious with works, and setting up a worship of God according to our reason. For in this way the innocent blood is most highly dishonoured and blasphemed. The heathen have committed far greater sin by their worshipping sun and moon, which they regarded as the true worship of God, than they have with any other sins. Therefore the piety of man is vain blasphemy and the greatest of all the sins that he commits. Similarly the creature which regards it as an act of worship and piety to flee from the world is far worse in God's sight than any other sin, and this is the state of popes and monks, and of everything that seems good to the world, and yet is without faith. Therefore whoso will not obtain grace by the blood of God, for him it is better he should never come before God. For he but enrages the Majesty more and more thereby (Luther, *Pred. üb. 1 Pet.* 1[18f.], 1523, W.A. 12, 291, 33).

In the light of what we have already said, this proposition is not in any sense a negative value-judgment. It is not a judgment of religious science or philosophy based upon some prior negative judgment concerned with the nature of religion. It does not affect only other men with their religion. Above all it affects ourselves also as adherents of the Christian religion. It formulates the judgment of divine revelation upon all religion. It can be explained and expounded, but it cannot be derived from any higher principle than revelation, nor can it be proved by any phenomenology or history of religion. Since it aims only to repeat the judgment of God, it does not involve any human renunciation of human values, any contesting of the true and the good and the beautiful which a closer inspection will reveal in almost all religions, and which we naturally expect to find in abundant measure in our own religion, if we hold to it with any conviction. What happens is simply that man is taken by God and judged and condemned by God. That means, of course, that we are struck to the very roots, to the heart. Our whole existence is called in question. But where that is the case there can be no place for sad and pitiful laments at the non-recognition of relative human greatness.

That is why we must not omit to add by way of warning that we have not to become Philistines or Christian iconoclasts in face of human greatness as it meets us so strikingly in this very sphere of religion. Of course it is inevitable and not without meaning that in times of strong Christian feeling heathen temples should be levelled to the earth, idols and pictures of saints destroyed, stained glass smashed, organs removed: to the great distress of aesthetes everywhere. But irony usually had it that Christian churches were built on the very sites of these temples and with materials taken from their pillars and furnishings. And after a time the storm of iconoclasm was succeeded by a fresh form of artistic decoration. This goes to show that while the devaluation and negation of what is human may occasionally have a practical and symbolical significance in detail, it can never have any basic or general significance. And it must not, either. We cannot, as it were, translate the divine judgment that religion is unbelief into human terms, into the form of definite devaluations and negations. From time to time it has to be manifested in the form of definite devaluations and negations. [301] But we must still accept it as God's judgment upon all that is human. It can be heard and understood, strictly and exactly as intended, only by those who do not despair of the human element as such, who regard it as something worth while, who have some inkling of what it means really to abandon the world of Greek or Indian gods, China's world of wisdom or even the world of Roman Catholicism, or our own Protestant world of faith as such, in the thorough-going sense of that divine judgment. In this sense the divine judgment, which we have to hear and receive, can actually be described as a safeguard against all forms of ignorance and Philistinism. It does not challenge us to a venal and childish resignation in face of what is humanly great, but to an adult awareness of its real and ultimate limits, which do not have to be fixed by us but are already fixed. In the sphere of reverence before God, there must always be a place for reverence for human greatness. It does not lie under our judgment, but under the judgment of God.

To realise that religion is really unbelief, we have to consider it from the standpoint of the revelation attested in Holy Scripture. There are two elements in that revelation which make it unmistakably clear.

1. Revelation is God's self-offering and self-manifestation. Revelation encounters man on the presupposition and in confirmation of the fact that man's attempts to know God from his own standpoint are wholly and entirely futile; not because of any necessity in principle, but because of a practical necessity of fact. In revelation God tells man that He is God, and that as such He is his Lord. In telling him this, revelation tells him something utterly new, something which apart from revelation he does not know and cannot tell either himself or others. It is true that he could do this, for revelation simply states the truth. If it is true that God is God and that as such He is the Lord of man, then it is also true that man is so placed towards Him, that he could know Him. But this is the very truth which is not available to man, before it is told him in revelation. If he really can know God, this capacity rests upon the fact that he really does know Him, because God has offered and manifested Himself to him. The capacity, then, does not rest upon the fact, which is true enough, that man could know Him. Between "he could" and "he can" there lies the absolutely decisive "he cannot," which can be removed and turned into its opposite only by revelation. The truth that God is God and our Lord, and the further truth that we could know Him as God and Lord, can only come to us through the truth itself. This "coming to us" of the truth is revelation. It does not reach us in a neutral condition, but in an action which stands to it, as the coming of truth, in a very definite, indeed a determinate relationship. That is to say, it reaches us as religious men; i.e., it reaches us in the attempt to know God from our standpoint. It does not reach us, therefore, in the activity which corresponds to it. The activity which corresponds to revelation would have to be faith; the recognition of the self-offering and self-manifestation of God. We need to see that in view of God all our activity is in vain even in the

[302]   best life; i.e., that of ourselves we are not in a position to apprehend the truth, to let God be God and our Lord. We need to renounce all attempts even to try to apprehend this truth. We need to be ready and resolved simply to let the truth be told us and therefore to be apprehended by it. But that is the very thing for which we are not resolved and ready. The man to whom the truth has really come will concede that he was not at all ready and resolved to let it speak to him. The genuine believer will not say that he came to faith from faith, but—from unbelief, even though the attitude and activity with which he met revelation, and still meets it, is religion. For in faith, man's religion as such is shown by revelation to be resistance to it. From the standpoint of revelation religion is clearly seen to be a human attempt to anticipate what God in His revelation wills to do and does do. It is the attempted replacement of the div-

104

ine work by a human manufacture. The divine reality offered and manifested to us in revelation is replaced by a concept of God arbitrarily and wilfully evolved by man.

Hominis ingenium perpetuam, ut ita loquar, esse idolorum fabricam .... Homo qualem inlus concepit Deum, exprimere opere tentat. Mens igitur idolum gignit, manus parit[EN129] (Calvin, *Instit.* I, 11, 8).

"Arbitrarily and wilfully" means here by his own means, by his own human insight and constructiveness and energy. Many different images of God can be formed once we have engaged in this undertaking, but their significance is always the same.

Imagines Deus inter se non comparat, quasi alterum magis, alterum minus conveniat: sed absque exceptione repudiat simulachra omnia, picturas aliaque signa, quibus eum sibi propinquum fore putarunt superstitiosi[EN130] (Calvin, *Instit.* I, 11, 1). *In nihilum redigit quicquid divinitatis, propria opinione sibi fabricant homines*[EN131] (*ib.*). In the sense of this undertaking the final principles of the various philosophical systems are just as much idols as the idea of the uncanny in the outlook of the animistic religions; and the view of God expressed, say, in Islam, is no less defective than absence of any unitary idea or image of God in Buddhism or ancient and modern atheistic movements.

The image of God is always that reality of perception or thought in which man assumes and asserts something unique and ultimate and decisive either beyond or within his own existence, by which he believes himself to be posited or at least determined and conditioned. From the standpoint of revelation, man's religion is simply an assumption and assertion of this kind, and as such it is an activity which contradicts revelation—contradicts it, because it is only through truth that truth can come to man. If man tries to grasp at truth of himself, he tries to grasp at it *a priori*[EN132]. But in that case he does not do what he has to do when the truth comes to him. He does not believe. If he did, he would listen; but in religion he talks. If he did, he would accept a gift; but in religion he takes something for himself. If he did, he would let God Himself intercede for God: but in religion he ventures to grasp at God. Because it is a grasping, religion is the contradiction of revelation, the concentrated expres- [303] sion of human unbelief, i.e., an attitude and activity which is directly opposed to faith. It is a feeble but defiant, an arrogant but hopeless, attempt to create something which man could do, but now cannot do, or can do only because and if God Himself creates it for him: the knowledge of the truth, the knowledge of God. We cannot, therefore, interpret the attempt as a harmonious

---

[EN129] The mind of man is, so speak, a constant maker of idols ... Man imagines a certain god in his mind, and then goes to the work of making it. Therefore the mind conceives idols, and the hand gives birth to them

[EN130] God does not make comparisons among idols, as if he were favourable to one larger one, or another smaller one. Rather, without exception, He despises all images, pictures and other symbols, by which superstitious men have imagined that He would come closer to them

[EN131] It (i.e. Scripture) brings to nothing whatever divinity men make for themselves from their own imagination

[EN132] independently

co-operating of man with the revelation of God, as though religion were a kind of outstretched hand which is filled by God in His revelation. Again, we cannot say of the evident religious capacity of man that it is, so to speak, the general form of human knowledge, which acquires its true and proper content in the shape of revelation. On the contrary, we have here an exclusive contradiction. In religion man bolts and bars himself against revelation by providing a substitute, by taking away in advance the very thing which has to be given by God.

Non apprehendunt (Deum) qualem se offert, sed qualem pro temeritate fabricati sunt, imaginantur[EN133] (Calvin, *Instit.* I, 4, 1).

He has, of course, the power to do this. But what he achieves and acquires in virtue of this power is never the knowledge of God as Lord and God. It is never the truth. It is a complete fiction, which has not only little but no relation to God. It is an anti-God who has first to be known as such and discarded when the truth comes to him. But it can be known as such, as a fiction, only as the truth does come to him.

Notitia Dei, qualis nunc hominibus restat, nihil aliud est, quam horrenda idololatriae et superstitionum omnium scaturigo[EN134] (Calvin, *Comm. on Jn.* 3⁶, C.R. 47, 57).

Revelation does not link up with a human religion which is already present and practised. It contradicts it, just as religion previously contradicted revelation. It displaces it, just as religion previously displaced revelation; just as faith cannot link up with a mistaken faith, but must contradict and displace it as unbelief, as an act of contradiction.

In the Old Testament the rejection of heathen religion is directed with a surprising one-sidedness against its idolatry. Whatever god it may apply to, idolatry is to be rejected. As a reason for this judgment, it is consistently maintained, e.g., in Jer. 10¹⁻¹⁶ and Is. 44⁹⁻²⁰, that in all heathen religions man himself is originally the creator of his own god. I do not think it a likely explanation of these passages that the biblical authors did not know, or for the sake of vilification did not want to know, what the Catholic Church has always said in explanation and defence of its customary veneration of images, and what is to-day almost a commonplace of the science of religion, that the image of God is never originally and properly regarded as identical with the Deity represented, that the Deity is adored and worshipped in the image only as in its representative and substitute, and that to the image as such only a loosely intended δουλεία[EN135] is offered. I think it more likely that the reproach of "making idols" (Is. 44⁹, 45¹⁶) is made with a full knowledge of this fact, and that it is directed against [304] the spiritual idolatry which finds expression in the making of images. The people of Israel are forbidden to "cleave" or "fall away" to "other" or "strange gods," which is the one great sin. But these other gods are not called "other" just because they are the gods of other nations. And Yahweh is not zealous against them only for the sake of His own honour, because He is the one God of the people of Israel. On the contrary, they are "other" and

---

[EN133] They do not accept (God) as He offers Himself, but they imagine Him, rashly, to be as they have made Him

[EN134] The knowledge of God, as it is now among men, is nothing other than an abhorrent source of idolatry and all superstitions

[EN135] service

"strange" first of all to Himself. They are of a different nature and kind. And for this reason, that they can have such representatives and substitutes in the images which are made by human hands, whereas He, Yahweh, cannot be represented by any human work. For His name is holy. In His work, in His revelation, in His activity as the Lord of the covenant, in His commandments, in His Word enjoined upon the prophets, He wills to give exclusive testimony to Himself, to be His own Mediator. Behind the worship of other gods, as its idolatry reveals, there stands the caprice and arbitrariness of man. That is why Israel must not fall away to them. And this ban is emphatic; just as the ban on images is emphatic even though they may be meant to represent Yahweh. And they are emphatic because Yahweh is the God of the divine self-revelation, which contradicts the caprice and the arbitrariness of man. It is as such that He wills to be recognised and honoured. It is to be noted that what in the heathen seems primarily to be just folly, for Israel, and in the sphere of revelation and the covenant, is concretely revealed as the sin of unbelief. Because Israel has become participant in the divine self-revelation, it must neither participate in the idolatry of heathen religions nor make and venerate images of Yahweh. The latter no less than the former involves a radical repudiation of Yahweh.

The most remarkable New Testament development of this thought is to be found in the passages Rom. $1^{18f.}$ and Ac. $14^{15f.}$, $17^{22f.}$ (The passage Rom. $2^{11f.}$ does not come up for discussion here—for the general context of the chapter makes it clear that the heathen in whom the prophecy of Jer. 31^{33} has been fulfilled are Gentile-Christians.) The revelation of righteousness, i.e., of the will of God in Jesus Christ, graciously creating and bestowing righteousness on the earth—this fulfilment of all revelation has now made the distinction of the heathen from Israel a secondary one. The Messiah of Israel appeared and was rejected and crucified by Israel itself. In that way He has revealed Himself as the Lord of the whole world. This does not mean only that there is now a grace of God for all men of all nations. It also means that they are all drawn into the responsibility and accountability which formerly only Israel had experienced. It does not mean only that the covenant made between God and man has now to be proclaimed to all nations as good news which affects them too. It also means that the complaint of apostasy is now expressly and seriously levelled against them all. To use the words of Ac. 14^{16}: "The times have passed since God in the generations gone by suffered all the nations to walk in their own way." And with Ac. 17^{30}: "The times of ignorance therefore God overlooked; but now (in and with the Now inaugurated by Jesus Christ) he commands all men everywhere that they should repent." Where the forgiveness of sins is manifest, there sins are revealed and condemned and punished as such. The very revelation of the righteousness of God is also the revelation of the wrath of God against all ungodliness and unrighteousness ($\dot{\alpha}\sigma\acute{\epsilon}\beta\epsilon\iota\alpha$ $\kappa\alpha\grave{\iota}$ $\dot{\alpha}\delta\iota\kappa\acute{\iota}\alpha$) of men (Rom. 1^{18}). What is meant by that? According to Rom. 1 and Ac. 14 and 17 it does not mean what we usually understand by "ungodliness" and "unrighteousness." It does not mean a profane and secular attitude orientated away from the divine. It is rather the worship offered by man in a fine loyalty to what he regards as the divine. This loyalty and the truth of the divineness of this "divine" is roundly denied by God's revelation in Christ and man's confrontation by that revelation. It is this supposedly very best that men do, this worship of theirs, which is "ungodliness" and "unrighteousness." Their piety is "fear of demons" (superstition) Ac. 17^{22}. They worship the things which by nature are not gods at all (Gal. 4^8). So in and with their piety they are $\check{\alpha}\theta\epsilon o\iota$ [305] $\dot{\epsilon}\nu$ $\tau\hat{\omega}$ $\kappa\acute{o}\sigma\mu\omega$ EN136 (Eph. 2^{12}). And in the light of the revelation made and fulfilled in Christ we now have to say of all men what formerly, in the light of the revelation in Old Testament prophecy, we could only say of the renegade Israelites, that in the very best that they have done they are guilty of apostasy from God. It is in this way that they have "held the truth in

---

EN136 without God in the world

unrighteousness" (Rom. 1^{18}). But when Christ appeared and died and rose again, the grace of God became an event for all men, and all men are made liable for their being and activity, for their being and activity as it is revealed in the light of this event. For as the ultimate and profoundest human reality, this event is the self-revelation of the truth, and therefore of the truth about man. In the light of the self-revelation of the truth, our human being and activity is seen to be in its ultimate and profoundest reality a fight against the truth. It stands over against the truth self-revealed there at an angle of 180°. It is the assumption of Rom. 1 as well as of the speeches in Acts that in and with the proclamation of Christ the men to whom this proclamation is made and who in it learn about the relationship of God and man, i.e., about God's grace, have to admit that in this opposition they have a relationship to truth, which they deny and betray by this opposition. When the grace of God is proclaimed to them in Christ, they have to concede that "God has not left Himself without a witness" (Ac. 14^{17}). For in and with the proclamation of the grace of God in Christ there is disclosed to them the witness of God, from which they have fallen away and with which they have been brought into radical contradiction. As they come under the light of this proclamation, the witness awakens and arises and speaks and testifies against them, so that they stand before the God who meets them in this revelation unexcused and inexcusable (Rom. 1^{20}).

In the speeches of Acts the witness which is disclosed and awakens and accuses in this way, the witness which is promised to all men in and with the proclamation of Christ, is its knowledge of God as the Creator. "He did you good and gave you rain from heaven and fruitful seasons and filled your hearts with food and gladness" (Ac. 14^{17}). Yes, He! They come to know this afresh. And they come to know afresh that this was what they already knew. Is not this what they confirmed when "in ignorant worship" (ἀγνοοῦντες εὐσεβεῖτε, Ac. 17^{23}) they built an altar to the "unknown God"? In proclaiming to them God in Christ, Paul tells them: You knew about this, but this God has become an unknown instead of a known God, for now you worship Him ignorantly. Before this God, whom I now make known to you again, you stand therefore as men accused who cannot excuse themselves. I now tell you, from my own knowledge of Christ, I now guarantee to you as your own knowledge even in and in spite of your utter ignorance: that this God created the world and everything in it; that He is the Lord of heaven and earth; that He created man and directs the history of men. It is because this is the case, because men belong to this God, that they seek after God, if haply they might feel after Him and find Him, although—o folly of man!—He is not far from any one of us. For we actually live and move and have our being in Him. We do not need to seek after Him. The unknowing knowledge of one of your poets itself attests that "we are His offspring" and therefore that He is as near to us as a father is to his children. If that is true (and it is true), and if we know it (and we do), what is the meaning of this seeking and feeling after God, this trying to find God by which I see you gripped? It is only because God is the Creator and therefore the Lord—and in Christ this has been revealed for time and eternity—that we can commit the sin of idolatry. But why do we commit it? It is because we have to recognise that God is the Creator and therefore the Lord, as we are told—and in Christ we are told it as something well-known, something we have been told already—it is because of this that we have to recognise our idolatry as sin, as "ungodliness" and "unrighteousness"—why do we not do it? How can the Lord of heaven and earth, in whom we have our life and breath and [306] every thing, dwell in a temple made by hands and be served by human hands? How can we who are His offspring and children and who therefore already belong to Him, worship the Godhead in an image of our seeking and feeling and finding, an image made of gold, or silver or stone, graven by art and man's device, the image of our own attempts to draw near to Him? If God is the Creator, how can there be such a thing as a mediation which we ourselves establish? How impossible all these things are! And yet how real is the struggle against the grace of revelation in favour of a capricious and arbitrary attempt to storm heaven! In this struggle against grace the known God has become an unknown one. There is no future for opposition to the truth, now that it has as such been marked upon our body in God's revelation (Ac. 17^{24-29}). All that really remains for us—personally—to do is to "turn from these vanities unto the living God" (Ac. 14^{15}).

We meet with the same line of thought in Romans, but with a characteristically different emphasis. The witness which the apostle declares to the heathen in and with the preaching of Christ, which he therefore awakens in them and makes valid against them, is here emphasised to be their knowledge of God the Creator. The invisible and unapproachable being of God, His everlasting power and divinity, are apprehended and seen in His works from the creation of the world (Rom. 1^{20}). It is from a knowledge of God, a knowledge of Him on the basis of revelation, that men always start when revelation comes to them in Christ (Rom. 1^{19}). That is why they can be accused of a "holding of the truth," a *corruptio optimi*EN137 (Rom. 1^{18}). We must bear in mind that the very words which are so often regarded as an opening or a summons to every possible kind of natural theology are in reality a constituent part of the apostolic *kerygma*EN138, whatever contemporary philosophemes may be woven into them. To bring out the real meaning of the revelation of the righteousness of God in Christ (Rom. 1^{17}, 3^{21}), Paul reminds us in Rom. 1^{18}–3^{20} that the same revelation is a revelation of the wrath of God, i.e., that as we are told of the grace which has come to us, we have to perceive and believe our own abandonment to judgment. Grace and judgment are for both Gentile and Jew, both Jew and Gentile, Rom. 1^{16}, 2^9, and for both Jew and Gentile in the very best that they can do, their worship of God. It is a Christian statement presupposing revelation when in relation to the Jews Paul says that a knowledge of sin comes by the Law (Rom. 3^{20}). Similarly, it is presupposing the event which took place between God and man in Christ that he says that the knowledge which the Gentiles have of God from the works of creation is the instrument to make them inexcusable and therefore to bring them like the Jews under the judgment and therefore under the grace of God. Here, too, there is no difference. Because Christ was born and died and rose again, there is no such thing as an abstract, self-enclosed and static heathendom. And because Paul has to preach this Christ, he can claim the heathen on the ground that they, too, belong to God and know about God, that God is actually revealed to them, that He has made Himself known to them in the works of creation as God—His eternal power and divinity, which are none other than that of Jesus Christ. Therefore he can tell them that because of their knowledge they are inexcusable before God, if they have "imprisoned" the truth with their ungodliness and unrighteousness. We cannot isolate what Paul says about the heathen in Rom. 1^{19-20} from the context of the apostle's preaching, from the incarnation of the Word. We cannot understand it as an abstract statement about the heathen as such, or about a revelation which the heathen possess as such. Paul does not know either Jews or Gentiles in themselves and as such, but only as they are placed by the cross of Christ under the promise, but also under the commandment of God. The witness of the hope of Israel, the prophetic revelation, is fulfilled in Christ. By smiting its Messiah on the cross Israel founders on that revelation. It has now become a revelation to both Jews and Gentiles. It now concerns the Gentiles. Therefore the Gentiles have to bow [307] just as emphatically as the Jews to the claim and demand of revelation. Like the Jews, they are addressed on this basis: that from the creation of the world (ἀπὸ κτίσεως κόσμου, Rom. 1^{20}, i.e., in and with their own existence and that of the whole world)—not of themselves, but by virtue of the divine revelation—men know God, and therefore know that they are indebted to Him. The status of the Gentiles, like that of the Jews, is objectively quite different after the death and the resurrection of Christ. By Christ the Gentiles as well as the Jews are

---

EN137 corruption of the best
EN138 proclamation

placed under the heavens which declare the glory of God, and the firmament which telleth His handiwork (Ps. 19²). They are therefore to be claimed as γνόντες τὸν θεόν EN139 (Rom. 1²¹); but only to the extent that, like the Jews, they have not remained such (οὐκ ἐδοκίμασαν τὸν θεὸν ἔχειν ἐν ἐπιγνώσει EN140 Rom. 1²⁸). It is, therefore, not the case that Paul was in a position to appeal to the Gentiles, possession of a knowledge of the invisible nature of God as manifested from creation. He could not link up pedagogically with this knowledge. In his proclamation of Jesus Christ he could not let it appear even momentarily that he was speaking of things which were already familiar by virtue of that "primal revelation." At bottom the Gentiles did not achieve even in the slightest the knowledge of Ps. 19. That is, they did not give God praise and thanks as God (Rom. 1²¹). As the sequel shows, this does not mean only a quantitative falling away of their service towards Him nor an imperfection of their relationship to Him. It means rather that the δοξάζειν καὶ εὐχαριστεῖν EN141 which they owe God are not there at all. They have been ousted by another mind and thought and activity which at its root (in negation of the fact that God is revealed to man from the creation) does not have God as its object. "Their thoughts became vain and their foolish heart was darkened" (Rom. 1²¹). "They professed (themselves and others) to be wise, and in this they became fools" (Rom. 1²²). And the result was sheer catastrophe: "They changed the glory of the incorruptible God into the likeness of the image of corruptible man, yea of flying and four-footed beasts and creeping things" (Rom. 1²³). In this idolatry "they exchanged the truth of God for a lie, they worshipped and served the creature instead of the Creator, who is blessed to eternity. Amen" (Rom. 1²⁵). And in due course the exchange had terrible consequences in the indescribable moral confusion of the human race. Paul says nothing at all about the heathen maintaining a remnant of the "natural" knowledge of God in spite of this defection. On the contrary, he says unreservedly that the wrath of God has been revealed against this defection: "they which do such things are worthy of death" (Rom. 1³²). Just as revelation had always contradicted heathen religion in the sphere of Israel and on the soil of Palestine, so now, when Jesus Christ has died for all, it contradicts it "publicly," in its own heathen area, in an apostolic letter which remarkably enough is addressed to the Christians in Rome. There is no such thing now as an undisputed heathendom, a heathendom which is relatively possible, which can be excused. Now that revelation has come and its light has fallen on heathendom, heathen religion is shown to be the very opposite of revelation: a false religion of unbelief.

2. As the self-offering and self-manifestation of God, revelation is the act by which in grace He reconciles man to Himself by grace. As a radical teaching about God, it is also the radical assistance of God which comes to us as those who are unrighteous and unholy, and as such damned and lost. In this respect, too, the affirmation which revelation makes and presupposes of man is that he is unable to help himself either in whole or even in part. But again, he ought not to have been so helpless. It is not inherent in the nature and concept of man that he should be unrighteous and unholy and therefore damned and lost. He was created to be the image of God, i.e., to obedience towards God and not to sin, to salvation and not to destruction. But he is not summoned to this as to a state in which he might still somehow find himself, but as one in which he no longer finds himself, from which he has fallen by his own fault.

[308]

EN139 those who know God
EN140 they did not consider worthwhile holding on to the knowledge of God
EN141 glorifying and giving thanks

But this, too, is a truth which he cannot maintain: it is not present to him unless it comes to him in revelation, i.e., in Jesus Christ, to be declared to him in a new way—the oldest truth of all in a way which is quite new. He cannot in any sense declare to himself that he is righteous and holy, and therefore saved, for in his own mouth as his own judgment of himself it would be a lie. It is truth as the revealed knowledge of God. It is truth in Jesus Christ. Jesus Christ does not fill out and improve all the different attempts of man to think of God and to represent Him according to his own standard. But as the self-offering and self-manifestation of God He replaces and completely outbids those attempts, putting them in the shadows to which they belong. Similarly, in so far as God reconciles the world to Himself in Him, He replaces all the different attempts of man to reconcile God to the world, all our human efforts at justification and sanctification, at conversion and salvation. The revelation of God in Jesus Christ maintains that our justification and sanctification, our conversion and salvation, have been brought about and achieved once and for all in Jesus Christ. And our faith in Jesus Christ consists in our recognising and admitting and affirming and accepting the fact that everything has actually been done for us once and for all in Jesus Christ. He is the assistance that comes to us. He alone is the Word of God that is spoken to us. There is an exchange of status between Him and us: His righteousness and holiness are ours, our sin is His; He is lost for us, and we for His sake are saved. By this exchange (καταλλαγή, 2 Cor. 5^{19}) revelation stands or falls. It would not be the active, redemptive self-offering and self-manifestation of God, if it were not centrally and decisively the *satisfactio*^{EN142} and *intercessio Jesu Christi*^{EN143}.

And now we can see a second way in which revelation contradicts religion, and conversely religion necessarily opposes revelation. For what is the purpose of the universal attempt of religions to anticipate God, to foist a human product into the place of His Word, to make our own images of the One who is known only where He gives Himself to be known, images which are first spiritual, and then religious, and then actually visible? What does the religious man want when he thinks and believes and maintains that there is a unique and ultimate and decisive being, that there is a divine being (θεῖον), a godhead, that there are gods and a single supreme God, and when he thinks that he himself is posited, determined, conditioned and overruled by this being? Is the postulate of God or gods, and the need to objectify the Ultimate spiritually or physically, conditioned by man's experience of the actual superiority and lordship of certain natural and supernatural, historical and eternal necessities, potencies and ordinances? Is this experience (or the postulate and need which correspond to it) followed by the feeling of man's impotence and failure in face of this higher world, by the urge to put himself on peaceful and friendly terms with it, to interest it on his behalf, to assure himself of its support, or,

[309]

---

^{EN142} satisfaction
^{EN143} intercession

better still, to enable himself to exercise an influence on it, to participate in its power and dignity and to co-operate in its work? Does man's attempt to justify and sanctify himself follow the attempt to think of God and represent Him? Or is the relationship the direct opposite? Is the primary thing man's obscure urge to justify and sanctify himself, i.e., to confirm and strengthen himself in the awareness and exercise of his skill and strength to master life, to come to terms with the world, to make the world serviceable to him? Is religion with its dogmatics and worship and precepts the most primitive, or better perhaps, the most intimate and intensive part of the technique, by which we try to come to terms with life? Is it that the experience of that higher world, or the need to objectify it in the thought of God and the representation of God, must be regarded only as an exponent of this attempt, that is, as the ideal construction inevitable within the framework of this technique? Are the gods only reflected images and guarantees of the needs and capacities of man, who in reality is lonely and driven back upon himself and his own willing and ordering and creating? Are sacrifice and prayer and asceticism and morality more basic than God and the gods? Who is to say? In face of the two possibilities we are in a circle which we can consider from any point of view with exactly the same result. What is certain is that in respect of the practical content of religion it is still a matter of an attitude and activity which does not correspond to God's revelation, but contradicts it. At this point, too, weakness and defiance, help-lessness and arrogance, folly and imagination are so close to one another that we can scarcely distinguish the one from the other. Where we want what is wanted in religion, i.e., justification and sanctification as our own work, we do not find ourselves—and it does not matter whether the thought and represent-ation of God has a primary or only a secondary importance—on the direct way to God, who can then bring us to our goal at some higher stage on the way. On the contrary, we lock the door against God, we alienate ourselves from Him, we come into direct opposition to Him. God in His revelation will not allow man to try to come to terms with life, to justify and sanctify himself. God in His revelation, God in Jesus Christ, is the One who takes on Himself the sin of the world, who wills that all our care should be cast upon Him, because He careth for us.

... by this article our faith is sundered from all other faiths on earth. For the Jews have it not, neither the Turks and Saracens, nor any Papist or false Christian or any other unbeliever, but only proper Christians. So where thou come into Turkey, where thou canst have no preacher nor books, there say to thyself, be it in bed or at work, be it in words or thoughts. Our Father, the Creed and the Ten Commands; and when thou comest to this [310] article, press thy finger with the thumb or give thyself some sign with hand or foot, so that thou layest good hold of this article and makest note of it, And specially, where thou shalt see some Turkish stumbling-block or have temptation. And with thine Our Father, pray that God may keep thee from stumbling and hold thee pure and stedfast in this article, For in the article lieth thy life and blessedness. (Luther, *Heer-pred. wid. d. Türcken*, 1529, W.A. 30 II, 186, 15.)

2. Religion as Unbelief

It is the characteristically pious element in the pious effort to reconcile Him to us which must be an abomination to God, whether idolatry is regarded as its presupposition or its result, or perhaps as both. Not by any continuing along this way, but only by radically breaking away from it, can we come, not to our own goal but to God's goal, which is the direct opposite of our goal.

> Therefore I have often said that to speak and judge rightly in this matter we must carefully distinguish between a godly man (what philosophers call a *bonus vir*[EN144]) and a Christian. We too approve of being a godly man and there is nothing more praiseworthy on earth and it is God's gift, just as much as sun and moon, corn and wine and all things made. But that we may not mix and brew them indiscriminately, let a pious man have his praise from the world and say: A godly man is indeed a precious man on earth, yet he is not therefore a Christian. For he may be a Turk or a heathen (as in early times some have been highly praised). As indeed it cannot otherwise be, that among so many bad a good man must at times be found. But be he as pious as he will, he is and remains still for all such piety Adam's child, that is, an earthy man, under sin and death. But if thou ask about a Christian, you must go much higher. For this is a different man, who is not called Adam's child and hath no father and mother on earth. But he is God's child, an heir and nobleman in the kingdom of heaven. For he is called a Christian, because with all his heart he depends on the Saviour, who hath ascended to the Father, and believes that for His sake and by Him he hath God's grace and eternal redemption and life. That is neither mastered nor grasped, achieved nor taught by our own life and virtue and work by which we are called godly folk on earth, neither by righteousness according to the Law and ten commandments, which is yet necessary, as was said, and is found in every Christian. But this chief thing and righteousness is still far from achieved, of which Christ speaks and calls it righteousness. (Luther, *Pred. üb. Joh.* 16⁵⁻¹⁵, *Cruc. Somm. Post.*, 1545, W.A. 21, 365, 12).

A mistake which is not justified by its respectable antiquity, and which Luther himself had a share in confirming, is that of regarding the Old Testament as a document, and, where possible, as the classical document, of a religion of works, and therefore, because all religion as such is a religion of works, of religion in general. The Israel which understands the "Do this and thou shalt live" (Lk. 10²⁸) to mean that man has to justify and sanctify himself in his own works by fulfilling the Law, is not the true Israel. He wants to be under the Law, without wanting to listen to the Law (Gal. 4²¹). Sin has become "exceedingly sinful" καθ᾽ ὑπερβολὴν ἁμαρτωλός (Rom. 7¹³), making use of the Law (Rom. 7⁸·¹¹), committing the grossest act of treachery by means of the Law (Rom. 7¹¹). In face of the Law with its "Thou shalt not covet" it causes "desire" (ἐπιθυμία) to spring up in us (Rom. 7⁷). What is this desire and the sin that dwelleth in us (Rom. 7¹⁷)? According to the narrative of the fall of the first man (Gen. 3¹ᶠ·), it obviously did not consist primarily in the desire for fruit as such, but in the spiritual or pseudo-spiritual desire, by the enjoyment of this fruit to become as God, and to know good and evil. This is the "desire" which acquires a new and indeed its real power in Israel by the treacherous act which sin commits through the Law (Gal. 3¹⁹, Rom. 5²⁰, 1 Cor. 15⁵⁶). "They have a zeal for God, but not according to knowledge. For being ignorant of God's righteous- [311] ness and seeking to establish their own, they did not subject themselves to the righteousness of God"(Rom. 10²³). To the question of the scribe: "What must I do to inherit eternal life?", Jesus replies by simply directing to the Law. And how does the man take the direction? "But he wished to justify himself" (Lk. 10²⁵⁻²⁹; cf. 16¹⁵). That is the "desire" of a man betrayed by sin by means of the Law. It is not the true Israel which has succumbed to this desire, and it is not the intention of the Old Testament which is realised in this desire. This is the zeal of an

---

[EN144] 'good man'

113

Israel upon whose heart a veil has been put, even to this day when Moses is read (2 Cor. 3^{15}).
It is the zeal of an Israel which, in pursuit of a "law of righteousness," fails to attain the real
Law (Rom. 9^{31}). Israel is wrecked on the rock upon which it is built, because it will not
believe (Rom. 9$^{32-33}$). The Law given it by God is in truth a spiritual Law (Rom. 7^{14}). It is not
contrary to the promises (Gal. 3^{21}). Christ is the end of the Law: to justification for everyone
that believes (Rom. 10^4). By the Israel that crucifies his Messiah, the Law is not kept but
"weakened" (Rom. 8^3) and broken (Rom. 2$^{17f.}$). And that is why here as always the Law is
directed against Israel (Rom. 2^{12}, 3^{19}). The Law worketh wrath (Rom. 4^{15}). It killeth (2 Cor.
3^6; Rom. 7$^{5\ 13}$). The same curse which once came upon the fathers because of their disobedience to Moses, their persecution of the prophets, their whoredom with the Baalim—the
same curse now comes upon Pharisaic Israel, whose legalism is another form of its old lawlessness. "Thou gloriest in the law and dishonourest God by transgression of the law" (Rom.
2^{23}). "All the day long did I spread out my hands unto a disobedient and gainsaying people"
(Rom. 10^{21}). At root the new righteousness of works is simply the old idolatry. And at root
the old idolatry was simply a righteousness of works. To understand this equation we have to
read the speech of Stephen in Ac. 7$^{2-53}$, which closes with the annihilating verdict: "Ye
received the law by the ordinance of angels and kept it not" (Ac. 7^{53}). The way of the true
Israel, of the nation which the Lord by His Word has made to be the people of His covenant,
cannot have been the way from idolatry to the righteousness of works. The true Israel, i.e.,
the Isaianic remnant (Rom. 9^{29}), the seven thousand in Israel that did not bow the knee to
Baal (Rom. 11^4), was obedient to the Law of God in that it held all the other commandments
in and with the first one, which means that it received and accepted grace as grace, that it
lived by the Word of God, that it waited on God, that it looked to the hands of God, as the
eyes of a servant look to the hands of his master (Ps. 123^2). The true Israel could not depart
from the Law, but also it could not attempt to justify and sanctify itself by a misuse of the Law,
because the Law was put in its heart and written on its mind (Jer. 31^{33}; Rom. 2$^{28f.}$). as "the law
of the spirit of life" (Rom. 8^2): and in addition its transgression was forgiven and its iniquity
remembered no more (Jer. 31^{34}; Rom. 4^6). Given in this way, the Law was for it the direct
power of God, which necessarily preserved the justified and sanctified Israel from going
aside either to the left hand or to the right. The witness of this Israel, and therefore the
witness of the coming Jesus Christ, is the real meaning and purpose of the Old Testament. It
is not, therefore, the document of a religion of works. But with the New Testament it is the
document of the revelation which contradicts every religion of works and therefore all religion as such. Luther's attitude to this question is not reducible to a single denominator. As
an expositor of the Old and New Testaments, he often distinguished between Law and Gospel, commandment and promise, Old Testament and New, in a way which was utterly
abstract and schematic, with a Paulinism which was not that of St. Paul himself. But then (cf.
Theodosius Harnack, *Luthers Theologie*, 1862, new edn. 1927, vol. 1, 450 f.) he would again
perceive and understand the original and ultimate unity of the two with an astonishing clarity. We prefer this second Luther. At the end of his life, at the close of his Preface to the

[312] Romans (1546), he reduced the content of this apostolic writing to the following remarkable formula: So it seems as though St. Paul would in this epistle bring into small compass
the whole of Christian and Evangelical doctrine, and prepare an entrance into the whole of
the Old Testament. For undoubtedly he who has this epistle well at heart has the light and
power of the Old Testament beside him. Therefore let every Christian be constantly exercised in it. For which may God give His grace, Amen (*W.A. Bib.* 7, 27, 21). But if with Romans
we have the light and power of the Old Testament, then it is clear that even the Old Testament, and the light and power of its holy and righteous and most excellent Law, are necessarily grace, and the contradiction of grace against justification and sanctification by works
as the chief sin of man.

2. *Religion as Unbelief*

As regards the New Testament, do we not have to point out that, like the Old Testament, it is a Law, that is, an order and command and direction for the new life of the people and children of God? But it is not for that reason—not even partially—an authorisation and challenge to self-justification and self-sanctification. It is not a book of religion. From first to last it is the proclamation of the justifying and sanctifying grace of God. It is, therefore, a revelation of the unbelief which is in all religion. Again and again we have to point expressly to this fact. For the simple insight, that the New Testament is testimony to Jesus Christ and nothing else, can never be an insight which we have already won and can leave behind. It is one which we must win again and again as we wrestle with the errors of our ears and hearts. We constantly overlook the fact that the form of the New Testament witness, not only in the Sermon on the Mount, and the Epistle of James, and the paraenetic chapters of Paul, but everywhere, is the Law. We forget the clear and self-evident fact that the essence of the gracious work of Jesus Christ and the Gospel as it is experienced in the New Testament Church is His lordship over man. We forget that there can be no more direct or absolute an imperative than the simple claim made on man in the New Testament: that he should believe in this Jesus Christ. We forget that there can be no more stringent obedience than that which the New Testament describes as faith. None of the forcefulness with which the Old Testament claims man only and wholly for Yahweh has here been lost. We overlook this point. We break up the New Testament into evangelical and promissory and comforting sayings on the one hand, legal and ethical and imperative sayings on the other. We do not perceive its unity even as Law. We do not hear in the preaching of John the Baptist about the Lamb of God that taketh away the sin of the world the same preaching of repentance as is ascribed to him in the Synoptic Gospels. And then there easily creeps in a second error. It seems as though there is a kind of *nova lex*[EN145] in the New Testament side by side with the Gospel, i.e., side by side with the message of the reconciliation of the world with God achieved in Christ. It seems as though the Gospel only acquires a moral character because its appeal is not only to faith, but to something more and different, the free decision of the human will, because man is challenged to confirm the justification and sanctification achieved in Christ by specific attitudes and actions. It seems as though the word of reconciliation only becomes a serious matter in the light of this second word about the new life. The result is that when we listen to the New Testament message we constantly have to shift our gaze from one direction to another. At one time we have to think of Christ and His work, at another of the improvement of our own position. At one time we have to put everything into God's hands, at another to take everything into our own. At one time we have to believe, at another to love and to do all kinds of good works. Then the second error is almost inevitably followed by a third, the reversal of the relationship of the two constituent parts of the New Testament message as abstracted and characterised in this way. The second group of New Testament pronouncements, misunderstood as a *nova lex*[EN146], is undoubtedly much easier to understand and its meaning and bearing are more readily perceived than the first. From this we can tell that it speaks of supernatural grace, and Jesus Christ and His work, and the forgiveness of sin, and the gift of the Holy Ghost, only in an abstract way. Who is going to give time and attention to this obscure and lofty matter, which can so easily be misunderstood as intellectualistic? What we want to see is deeds. Life is urgent, with all its questions and tasks, and with all the possibilities which man always thinks that he has in relation to them. It is especially to these possibilities that the *nova lex*[EN147] seems to point as we think we see it in the New Testament. At bottom we are still alone when we weigh up the New Testament in

[313]

EN145 new law
EN146 new law
EN147 new law

115

this way. We are still in the sphere of our own ability and daring and enterprise and achievement. The whole mystery of the New Testament is our own mystery, with all the burdensome but beneficent responsibility which that involves. And why should we not weigh it up primarily in this way? Why should we not suppress the other side of it for special occasions, for the new efforts at ethical self-assertion which are necessary from time to time? Is it as indispensable as we affirm both before and after? Have we still any real place for it? Do we not find it a little disturbing that the New Testament seems consistently to have this other aspect? Be that as it may, the attentiveness and love and emphasis and zeal are no longer on this aspect, but on the much more practical matter of self-justification and self-sanctification, against the background of the assurance that either way the work of Christ and the gift of the Holy Spirit are, of course, the decisive starting-point. This threefold development is the process with which every reader of the New Testament is continually tempted to retranslate its message into a document of religion. It is, therefore, our task to make the process impossible at the very root: that is, at the point where the New Testament usually divides up into the two categories of (*a*) placatives and (*b*) motives. This division is quite unfounded. It would perhaps be better for us in the first instance to regard the New Testament as altogether Law than to think of it as divided into Law and Gospel. For, of course, it is true that faith in its message is both our justification and also our sanctification, both our new status in the sight of God and also our new life. And it is both, because it is simply faith in Jesus Christ. And we rightly understand it as such if in the first instance we understand it as outright obedience to the Lord Jesus Christ: which means that in the first instance the message of the New Testament is regarded as altogether Law. There is a good deal to be said for the view that sanctification, the fact that man is claimed by God, the fact that he belongs to God by grace (as Calvin develops the thought in Bk. III of the *Institutio*), is the main or at any rate the formally prior reality in faith. But whatever conceptual order we may adopt, in the New Testament faith is always faith in Jesus Christ. It may be taken more as trust or more as obedience. It may be taken first as trust and then as obedience, or *vice versa*. But one thing is always certain, that it can be understood only in the light of its object, Jesus Christ, i.e., in opposition to any claim which the believer might make for his own work. The believer in the New Testament sense is claimed by Jesus Christ with all his activity and work. He belongs to Jesus Christ. Therefore any claim on behalf of his own activity and work is decisively destroyed. He cannot expect to be able to help himself; he is not allowed even to wish to do so. Faith in the New Testament sense does not mean merely the superseding but the abolishing of man's self-determination. It means that man's self-determination is co-ordinated into the order of the divine predetermination. In faith, it loses its autonomy outside this predetermination, and therefore its significance over against God or in competition with God. It loses its significance as a sphere of ultimate and genuine decision, and therefore its character of ultimate and genuine seriousness. The only ultimate and really serious determination for the believer is that which proceeds from Jesus Christ. Ultimately and in the true sense he is no longer the subject. In and with his subjectivity he has become a predicate to the subject Jesus Christ, by whom he is both justified and sanctified, from whom he receives both comfort and direction. Proclaiming this faith, the New Testament has no room for a *nova lex*[EN148], which would have to be sought elsewhere than in the Gospel itself and as such. If John the Baptist preaches the Lamb of God, which takes away the sin of the world, it is in the same word, and not in a second which has to be heard along with the first, that he preaches repentance and amendment of life. An autonomous interest in the latter means the introduction of a foreign element into the New Testament message. For an autonomy of this kind can mean only that we have the "desire," first in secret, and then publicly, to resume that being as subject which

---

[EN148] new law

we lost in Jesus Christ, our self-determination outside the divine predetermination, and therefore to abandon our faith. All other desires are rooted in this desire, just as transgression of the first commandment inevitably involves that of all others. Sin is always unbelief. And unbelief is always man's faith in himself. And this faith invariably consists in the fact that man makes the mystery of his responsibility his own mystery, instead of accepting it as the mystery of God. It is this faith which is religion. It is contradicted by the revelation attested in the New Testament, which is identical with Jesus Christ as the one who acts for us and on us. This stamps religion as unbelief.

We cannot make this point without insisting expressly that it is only by the revelation of God in Jesus Christ that we can characterise religion as idolatry and self-righteousness, and in this way show it to be unbelief. Religion can, of course, be called in question from within, and we have to be aware of this and to distinguish it from the abolishing of religion by revelation. It is an observation which we can more or less clearly verify from the history and phenomenology of every religion that the religious man does not at all face up to his theoretico-practical aims, like a man who is sure of his business, straightforwardly. In his striving, then, he involves himself in a peculiar inward dialectic. He strangely contradicts himself. He scores through his thinking and willing, and uplifts and outbids it by a thinking and willing which he believes to be higher and better. In this way he necessarily calls himself in question, unsettling himself and plunging himself into uncertainty. But he also jeopardises more or less radically the whole of his religious activity—although without abandoning the religious attitude and appetite—but also without directing it to its real goal in this new and critical turn in the matter. The observation will not surprise us if we know the judgment which revelation has pronounced upon all religion. It is a confirmation of the fact that the verdict is true: Religion is always self-contradictory and impossible *per se*[EN149]. But we have to note that the critical turn at which the self-contradiction and impossibility are brought out is itself a moment in the life of religion. It has only an immanent significance. It does not give any ultimate or definitive answer to the question which it tries to answer. Therefore—and this is the point—it must not be confused with revelation. It does not show religion to be unbelief. For it falls under the same judgment. Even at the supposedly higher level where it tries to overcome idolatry and self-righteousness in its own strength and its own way, religion is still idolatry and self-righteousness. To be more specific, religion is called in question by a twofold movement which at root is only one: by mysticism on the one hand and atheism on the other. Our task is to show that even in these two supposedly higher and apparently inimical forms, whether in good or evil, in failure or success, religion is still thoroughly self-centred. [315]

The two primitive and as it were normal forms of religion are, as we have seen, the conception of the deity and the fulfilment of the law. It is always in

---

[EN149] in itself

these two forms that religious need first seeks its satisfaction. But it seeks satisfaction because it already has it—and that is why religious need differs from the need of man in faith in God's revelation. It is, of course, the need of man for a truth above and a certainty within, both of which he thinks he can know and even create for himself. Since the need is there, have not the starry heaven above and the moral law within long since brought this truth and certainty into the range and realm of his perception? He is not in any way lacking in advice or help. He knows that truth and certainty exist and are attainable, and he is confident of his own ability to achieve them. His need is not an absolute need, a strictly needy need, in face of which he does not know where to turn. His need is not in the least like the neediness of the believer, who with empty heart and hands finds himself thrown back entirely upon the revelation of God. To satisfy this need, he steps out in a bold bid for truth, creating the Deity according to his own image—and in a confident act of self-assurance, undertaking to justify and sanctify himself in conformity with what he holds to be the law. And in so doing he betrays the fact that even as he seeks satisfaction, potentially at least, in respect of his religious capacity he is already satisfied. He is like a rich man, who in the need to grow richer (which cannot, of course, be an absolute need) puts part of his fortune into an undertaking that promises a profit.

From this it follows that there is always an ultimate non-necessity about the origin and exercise of all religion. The life of religion, in which religious need seeks satisfaction and provisionally finds it, is fundamentally only an externalisation, an expression, a representation and therefore a repetition of something which previously existed without form or activity, but still quite powerfully, as the real essence of religion and to that extent as the peculiar religious possession of man.

Has the religious life as expressed and manifested any other necessity than the limited, loose, incidental and purely ornamental necessity of a children's game, or of serious or light-hearted art? If need be, could not religion's thoughts of God not be thought, its doctrines not be stated, its rites and prayers not be fulfilled, its ascetic and moral prescripts be freely disregarded? Does the religious outlook and desire really have to express itself in this way? Is it really bound to this expression once it has been made? Does it in any way cease to be what it is apart from it? The history and phenomenology of all religion show us that this is not actually the case: the outward and actual satisfaction of the religious need is a relative, but only a relative, necessity. If need be, the conception of Deity and justifying and sanctifying work of man are not indispensable.

[316]   And now we can add a second point. In all originated and applied religion, in all external satisfaction of the religious need, there is a very definite weakness deriving from the inward satisfaction which precedes it. At bottom, the external satisfaction will never be anything more or other than a reflection of what the man is and has who thinks he should proceed to this external satisfaction of his need. But what becomes of this reflection, if the original, religious

man, changes? Is it compatible with religion that it should change with him? Is it compatible with religion that it should not?

The religion of man is always conditioned absolutely by the way in which the starry heaven above and the moral law within have spoken to the individual. It is, therefore, conditioned by nature and climate, by blood and soil, by the economic, cultural, political, in short, the historical circumstances in which he lives. It will be an element in the habit or custom with which, quite apart from the question of truth and certainty, or rather at the very lowest and most rudimentary stages of his inquiry into it, he compounds with the terms of existence imposed upon him. But the terms of existence, and therefore custom, are variable. Nature and climate, or the understanding and technique with which he masters them, may change. Nations and individuals may move. Races may mix. Historical relationships as a whole are found to be in perhaps a slow or a swift but at any rate a continual state of flux. And that means that religions are continually faced with the choice: either to go with the times, to change as the times change, and in that way relentlessly to deny themselves any claim to truth and certainty; or else to be behind the times, to stick to their once-won forms of doctrine, rite and community and therefore relentlessly to grow old and obsolete and fossilised; or finally, to try to do both together, to be a little liberal and a little conservative, and therefore with the advantages of both options, to have to take over their twofold disadvantages as well. That is why religions are always fighting for their lives. That is why they are always acutely or chronically sick. There has probably never been a religion which in its fateful relation to the times, i.e., to change in man (or rather in its own liberalism or conservatism or in both at once) has not been secretly or openly sick. And it is a familiar fact that religions do actually die of this sickness, i.e., of an utter lack of fresh believers and adherents. They cease to exist except as historical quantities. The link between religion and religious man in his variableness is the weakness of all religions.

These two factors, the non-necessity and the weakness of all religions, constitute the presupposition for that critical turn which plays its specific part in the history and form of more or less every religion.

Usually the weakness of religion supplies the cause, its non-necessity the opportunity for this development. With the change of the times, that is, with his own alteration in time, man cannot be satisfied with the previous satisfaction of his religious need, i.e., as taught him by his fathers. The characteristics of the conception of God and the norms of the law of his religion are far too stiff or even far too fluid for him still to be able to feel at home in it. Its truth no longer speaks to him, its certainty is no longer valid. Doubt is aroused, and the desire for freedom—and, of course, because his religion has only that relative necessity both are possible—and they both seem to be trying to break out from the religion which has been passed down to him and taken over by him. It now seems—but only seems—that he is quite near to realising what revelation has to say of his religion, that he has been pursuing idolatry and self-righteousness. and that all his previous thinking and activity have been the activity and thinking of unbelief. Apart from revelation he will never reach this, the absolute crisis of his religion. He would have had to believe first to be able seriously to accuse himself of unbelief. And to believe, the revelation of God would have had to encounter him. Without this the outcome of the relative crisis in which he finds himself in relation to his religion will perhaps be this. A new religion with a new conception of God and a new law will quickly emerge and be established and proclaimed, being applauded and gaining historical breadth and form at the expense of the old. If this happens, then however great the historical catastrophe in which the change from religion to religion is consummated, the critical turn, at

[317]

119

which religion as such is called in question and the self-contradiction and the impossibility of religion as such are revealed, has not been reached. Where there is a more radical issue, as compared with the first possibility, it is a far more quiet and unassuming but also much more significant event. Of course, it is not as radical and significant as it pretends to be. But it is undoubtedly more radical and significant than the dying of an old religion and the emerging of a new.

Always presupposing the actual weakness and non-necessity of religion, it can happen not merely that the conception of God will be uncertain and the law oppressive, but that our own activity, the desire to form a conception of God, religious dogmatics, the fulfilling of the law, religious ethics and ascetics, will also be open to suspicion and doubt, and indeed impossible. It can happen that we become aware in principle of those presuppositions of the crisis of our religion, its weakness and non-necessity, as data which prevent us from escaping from our former religion to another or it may be to a new one, because we see only too clearly that the same problems will still meet us. But, of course, this is a proof that the need which has impelled our former religious life and activity was not in the strictest sense a needful need. It was the playful need to externalise a religious possession which exists prior to that externalisation and apart from it. In the crisis of our religion we are confronted by the real or supposed failure of that externalisation. In that externalisation as such we cannot accept even ourselves. We cannot participate in it any longer, at any rate inwardly and responsibly. Secretly or openly we abandon it. But we do not abandon our religious possession, which we have been trying to externalise. We do not abandon the formless conception of God, already present in the soul. We do not abandon the unrealised self-justification and self-sanctification, which we have already followed in the heart. We give up only in the sense that we consciously withdraw to the inner line from which we originally started. We do not lose anything by the withdrawal. We simply withdraw our capital from an undertaking which no longer appears to be profitable. The vitality and intensity which we applied to the conception of the divine image and the fulfilling of the law of our religion are now turned inwards and exploited in favour and in the direction of the formless and unrealised reality, unthought and unwilled, out of whose richness religion once sprang, only to
[318] be reabsorbed into it. The same acuteness of thought and the same power of will with which we once exerted ourselves positively and constructively, when we could still accept ourselves as religious believers, are now active negatively and destructively. The religious interest and desire which was once in play, expressing and manifesting itself, now prefers to live itself out without expression or manifestation. The same non-needy, religious need now seeks its satisfaction in a solemn non-satisfaction, in a pathetic renunciation of self-expression, in a pathetic silence, in a pathetic cessation of the soul, in the solemn emptiness which it thinks it would now prefer to its former equally solemn fulness. In our thinking and willing we have enough to do to define this vacuum in which there will be neither conception nor realisation, as in

fact there never has been. Our religious task is one of clearing out and tidying up in preparation for the expected fulness of the self-enclosed and self-sounding religious reality which will follow our emancipation from all representations. In view of this goal, there can be no thought of transition to another religion or the founding of a new one. That would only mean a loss of time and strength. Far better—and this is where our thinking acquires a new task—to convince ourselves that the previous attempt to externalise the conception of God was a misunderstanding which deceived us right at the outset when we were really wanting and seeking what is now known to be true: the religious reality of that formless and unrealised vacuum. Far better—and this is where our will is also claimed—that all the energy which we once directed to fulfil an outward law should now be concentrated on the task of inward loyalty, and therefore of loyalty to that nameless and impersonal and undirected will, which struggles within us for truth and certainty.

This is the new road on which religious man now moves towards the old theoretico-practical goal. He thinks the same thing, but he thinks it quite differently. At least he thinks that he thinks it quite differently. From a lofty watch-tower he looks down fiercely or sadly or indulgently on those who still think quite differently from what he does, but who possibly, probably, do not understand for a moment how very, very differently he now thinks. At any rate, in attitude, in seriousness, in the inwardness of faith, in the exaltation with which he gives himself to his task, the task of withdrawal, to his negations and destructions, to his work of liberation, probably even in what we might call his religious fanaticism, he still resembles his former self and all other religious men. Is it perhaps that he is mistaken in thinking that his road is so completely new? Still, even if it is in principle only a continuation of the old way, it cannot be denied that there has been at least a very sharp bend in the road.

So far we have described this relatively new road as a single one. But at a certain point in this road there is a fork, and it becomes the twofold way of mysticism and atheism. The difference derives from the relationship to the existing and hitherto accepted or predominant religion. Mysticism means that practically and basically we renounce that religion as regards its expression, externalisation and manifestation We do not think that we shall find truth in [319] its conception of God, or salvation and assurance in obedience to its law.

The word "mysticism" has, of course, two meanings: the one from μύειν, the other from μυεῖν. Μύειν means to close eyes and mouth; μυεῖν means to consecrate. Mysticism is the higher consecration of man, which he secures by exercising towards the external world, both passively and actively, the greatest possible reserve. Or it is the passive and active reserve towards the external world, which is at the same time dedicated to a higher consecration of man.

Mysticism means the basic liberation of man from that satisfaction of the religious need which hitherto he has sought "outside." Yet in its relationship to this "outside" it is the conservative form of that critical turn. For mysticism does not attack religion openly and directly. It does not negate it. It is not interested in iconoclasm or the refutation of dogmas or other open acts of liberation. It subjects itself to the prevailing doctrine and observance, and even respects it. It leaves religion in peace. Sometimes, indeed, it can apparently enrich religious dogmatics by certain particularly profound and serious epigrams, and contribute certain particularly meaningful forms (mysteries) to the cultus, and give new life to the universal fellowship by a particularly impressive expression of its principles and the assembling and exercising of the most faithful of its believers. Gladly and honestly it purports to be true "friendship with God." There is a radical withdrawal from the outwardly religious position. But in its mystical form it consists only in this: that the mystic insists upon interpreting everything that is taught and practised in any particular religion according to its inward and spiritual and vital meaning, i.e., in relation to the reality of that formless and unrealised vacuum, and not in any abstract externality. The mystic will give prominence to the fact, and emphasise it, that everything external is only a form and picture, that the transitory is only a parable, that its truth is only in its relation to the inexpressible, because undirected, essence from which it proceeded and to which it must also revert. The specifically mystical experience of renunciation, of silence, of the way of quietude, is that of understanding and indicating and interpreting an external form which has to be accepted and respected. The mystic will say the most dangerous things, e.g., about the secret identity of the within and the without, of the ego and God. But he will say them quite piously and always in connexion with a religious tradition which apparently asserts the opposite. He will, as it were, try to make the latter a witness against itself. He will claim freedom only for this interpretation of tradition, not freedom to supersede tradition. He may even go far beyond ordinary believers in outward conservatism. And all this not because of fear or dishonesty, the common complaints against the mystic, but because in his own way he has a sincere affection for the whole system of external religion. That is, he has an affection for it because he needs

[320] it. It is the text for his interpretations. It is the material for his spiritualising. It is the external of which he has to show the inward meaning. It is the point of departure for the great withdrawal, on which, as he thinks, a knowledge of the truth will be achieved. Where would mysticism be without its opposite numbers, religious dogmatics and ethics? If the latter perished, mysticism would "give up the ghost for want," just as it says that God would if man were to perish. It lives in fact by its opposite number, and for that reason it deals with it gently and even carefully.

There is therefore no contradiction, and it must not be taken as a mistake, when, e.g., Johann Scheffler, having caused the Ego and God to rise and set together, could then go on to sing:

"Claim thou never thy wisdom, however so clever thou art.
None there is wise in God, except in a Catholic part,"

and he could express himself similarly over a wide range of his poetical work. "This sensitive bard, who came from the very depths to dogmatics, who knocked at the door, who thought that he could remove stones with his seer's eyes, who tried to make dried rice green again by throwing himself into the thorns, by thrusting into the dead undergrowth with bared breast—he experienced something. A spider crept out of the thornbush, which sucked him dry of his heart's blood. And, suddenly, he hung in the thorns, himself like dry rice unsouled. The wind touched it, it still sang, in a last indestructible echo of its loving power. But intermingled with it there was the horrible sound of a crackling ghostlike twig. Scheffler became an orthodox fanatic ... " (Wilhelm Boelsche, in his edition of *Der Cherubinische Wandersmann*, 1905, LXIV f.; similarly Fritz Mauthner, *Der Atheismus u. seine Gesch. in Abendland*, Vol. 3, 1922, 190 f.). Even the champions of a radical mysticism could not show a greater lack of comprehension. As though mysticism did not claim to be the complement of existing and accepted religion! What is it to abandon, gouge out, reduce, or negate, if there is no such thing as religion? And how is it to exist as mysticism, if there is nothing left to negate? It is the genius and circumspection and economy of Angelus Silesius, in his investigation and presentation of this question of mysticism, that he recognised the fact that in this activity—together with friends in China and India and Arabia, who are much cleverer than their admirers in the modern West—he was always acting as an "orthodox fanatic."

From the same standpoint of its relationship to existing religion, atheism might be called an artless and childish form of that critical turn. Atheism means a blabbing out of the secret that so far as this turn involves anything at all it involves only a negation. Of course, even in its most radical forms, it is ultimately aiming at something positive. And in this respect its aim is the same as that of mysticism. Its positive goal is religious reality in that formless and unrealised vacuum, where knowledge and object are or again become one and the same thing—the Chinese *Tao*, the Indian *Tat tvam asi*, Hegel's in-and-for-itself of the absolute Spirit. For the sake of this positive goal, mysticism too must negate, and is prepared to do so. In the last resort it can only say No. Existing religion with its dogmatics and ethics is a structure which is taken over only to be broken up. But as far as possible, it will conceal this fact and say nothing about it. Atheism, however, shouts it out to the world. It hurls itself [321] against religion in open conflict. It loves iconoclasm, the refutation of dogmas, and, of course, moral emancipation. It denies the existence of God and the validity of a divine law. And its whole interest is in the denial as such. That is its artlessness. It fails to see what mysticism does not fail to see: that absolute denial can have no meaning except against the background of a relative affirmation. A herd cannot be periodically slaughtered, unless it is continually fed and tended, or at any rate kept in being. Atheism lives in and by its negation. It can only break down and take away, and therefore it is exposed to the constant danger of finishing at a dead end. But again, as compared with mysticism, atheism set out to be a purer and more logical denial of religion as such, of its God and its law. Much more clearly than in mysticism, the meaning of that common, critical turn is here seen to be a withdrawal from the dogma of religion and the way of certainty, which we once thought out and maintained, but now find incredible. Intensively atheism is more energetic than mysticism, but extensively it is more modest. It is satisfied to deny God and His law. It fails to see that, apart from religion, there are other dogmas of truth and ways of certainty, which may at any moment take on a religious character. In this respect, too, mysticism is the more astute and far-sighted. Sooner or later it extends to everything. It not only queries God; it carefully does the same of the cosmos and the individual as well. It proposes and practises a programme of comprehensive negation. But it keeps clear a way of retreat, or thinks it can. Atheism, on the other hand, does not deny the reality of nature, history and civilisation, of man's animal and rational existence, of this or that ethic or the lack of it. On the contrary, these are authorities and powers to which the atheist usually subscribes with the happiest and most naive credulity. Atheism nearly always means secularism. And more than that, atheism usually allies itself with these secular authorities and powers in the conflict with religion, with God and His law. It argues from their existence and validity. It accepts them as irrefutable data, from which it raises against religious authorities and powers the objection that they do not exist. But in so doing it exposes itself to the danger that all kinds of new and disguised, and sometimes not so disguised, religions may arise behind its back and wherever possible with its support.

It is because it is unguarded at these two points that atheism is the more primal, and unitary, and ultimately the stronger form of the critical turn that we are now considering. The meaning of this turn is here negation pure and simple. Specifically and concretely, it is the negation of the over-world of religion, the weakness and non-necessity of which are perceived, and which has become superfluous and irritating as a result of a change in the conditions of human existence. In essence, mysticism too is negation in ever new forms and [322]   degrees. Except in negations it cannot speak of the positive thing at which it ostensibly aims, the glory of the vacuum which takes into itself everything outward. And it is only to provide the necessary material that it deals gently and even carefully with religious positions. It goes to work more comprehensively, but in the last resort mysticism does specifically and concretely mean the negation of the over-world of religion. This world, not the cosmos or the ego, is the true and ultimate external which has to be made "inward," i.e., to be negated. Mysticism is esoteric atheism. But atheism still carries the banners and laurels of the work of liberation which is their common purpose. If the joint programme is practicable, it has the disadvantage of a lesser wisdom, but the advantage of a more direct and logical method—if only it did not betray right at the outset the fact that the common programme is not practicable. Its impracticability is shown by its inability to answer the following questions: (1) where does a denial of that over-world of religion finally lead?; and (2) how is the emergence of new and concealed "over-worlds" effectively to be prevented? Can the critical turn in religion—mysticism aiming at atheism, and atheism interpreting mysticism (that great artist in interpretation), lead anywhere, but nowhere: which in practice certainly means the stimulation of old religions and the formation of new?

When the atheist sees the danger of the sterile negation in which he finds himself, at the very last moment he usually borrows from his more cautious and far-seeing partner. That is why the great work which F. Mauthner wrote in praise of Western atheism concludes in the 4th vol. (1923), p. 372 f. with a section entitled "Der Friede in gottloser Mystik." In this section he again speaks of a "concept of God purified from the nonsense of theologians." He commends this to his readers, presupposing that they will regard it only as an "ordinary deception, a healthy lie, an unavoidable lifelong illusion," and that they will not accept it. Of course, the concept consists only in a "halting 'it'" (p. 446). Perhaps some may think that he does not let us go far enough. But others may be of the opinion that it is from this "halting 'it'" that all idolatry and self-righteousness derives. They may believe that at bottom and in spite of all reservations even this limited permission throws the door wide open again to every conceivable religious glorification. For if the atheist does not remain a pure atheist, if he tries to become a mystic again, let him see to it that, after the manner of Angelas Silesius, he does not finally and necessarily become a dogmatician and a moralist as well. And what if the atheist sees his other danger: that when his negation of the God of religion and of His law is complete, new religions may lift up their heads out of the nature and culture and history which are not negated, and out of man's own animal and national existence? Well, he may perhaps do as Otto Petras (*Post Christum*, 1936) did. He may address to himself and others (on the basis of some philosophy of history) a master-word to the following effect. To-day not only some but all ideologies and mythologies are dead, definitely dead, dead to all futurity. All that remains to modern man is a venture stripped of every dream of an over-world, the venture of a naked and dangerous existence, absolutely sterile and always con-fronted by death. This existence is typified already in certain soldiers in the world war, in the ocean flyer roaring forward in space between heaven and earth, or in this or that perverted modern industrialist: the man who. stripped of all illusions, hopes and fears, marches for the sake of marching, he knows not whence, he knows not whither. Very well! But then the [323] dilemma arises. Either this new form of existence is simply lived out and not preached by some who gladly surrender to this master-word. If that is the case, atheism is a private affair, and its critical function towards religion is at an end. Or this new form of existence is not only lived out but publicly proclaimed. But if that is the case it cannot dispense with some sort of basic, declarative ideology and mythology, i.e., some sort of over-world has to be dreamed into it too. And the result of this critical turning against religion is simply the founding of a new religion—and perhaps even the confirmation of an old.

To summarise: the critical turn against religion signifies in any case the dis-covery of its weakness and only relative necessity. But in its mystical form it cannot avoid combining its denial with a naturally not at all naive affirmation, but an affirmation all the same. And if it tries to escape this in its atheistic form, unwillingly but in fact it cannot avoid, if not preparing, at least opening up, a wide field for new religious constructs. But this means that even in these two extremely basic forms the critical turn against religion is not so radical and powerful that it knows how to make it clear, even in theory, how it really thinks to achieve the negation of religion, its God and its law. Of course, the will and purpose are clear enough: but the way is not clear. Historically we must say that those religions which have the innate capacity to be both conservative and liberal have so far given evidence of the longer wind and the more vital sub-stance in face of mysticism and atheism. If a religion died, it died because of the victory of another religion, not because of the more fundamental attack of mysticism or atheism. In fact, therefore, the weakness and the limited necessity of religion are not so fatal in their results as they might be. In its weakness and limited necessity religion is always there in different forms. And in the last resort mysticism and atheism can never prove that it might be otherwise, or how far it might be otherwise. For their own existence is far too closely bound up with the existence of religion. And if we tried finally to conceive the inconceivable and, according to all historical experience, the quite improbable; the historical existence of pure mysticism, which would necessarily be identical with that of pure atheism, its purity would obviously consist only in this: the negation which is ostensibly only a means to the end, a work of liberation, the dangerous negation—dangerous even to mysticism and atheism—which is so well adapted to bring in religion in one way or another, has now reached its goal. Man is finally and ultimately free of God and His law. He is free of all religious works and all religious working. He is free from all that striving for representation and expression. He is happy in that formless and unrealised vacuum, happy alone by himself, and therefore, alone, happy in the real world beyond the antithesis of the within and the without. But why should there not sometimes have been mystically or atheistically inclined individuals, able at any rate to imagine that they are happy in this way? If so, they will have tasted [324] and felt the great positive, which lies behind the critical turn against religion, and from which its negations alone derive their relative power, without mysticism and atheism always being exposed to betrayal to religion. But then, what about this positive? It is not so diametrically opposed to religion as its few fortunate and countless unfortunate devotees usually asseverate. It is really opposed to religion only as the spring is to the river, as the root to the tree, as the unborn child in the womb to the adult. It is the quiet religious possession. It is the contemplation of the universe and the creative power of the individual feeling which gropes after it in its nameless and formless and unrealised oneness. It is the power to be in the world and a man, which always precedes the "halting' it, '" but which will project out of itself that "halting 'it'" and later and quickly enough some sort of religion. The power to be in the world and a man, as man's own power, is identical with the power to devise and form gods and to justify and sanctify oneself. This power, and therefore the great positive beyond all negations, and therefore the happiness which the presence and the enjoyment of this positive can create, and therefore—if there ever has been or will be such a thing—pure mysticism or pure atheism can never be the real crisis of religion. This power belongs to the magic circle of religion: it is indeed its creative and formative centre and real point of departure.

If this statement is not accepted, its immortal proof is in Schleiermacher's *Talks on Religion* ("to the educated among its despisers"), 1799. Not only as an apologist, but as an expert expositor of religion, Schleiermacher was right not to accept at its face value the scorn of the all too uneducated, but to address them boldly in the name of the God "who will be in you."

A real crisis of religion is needed to affect this power, and this power first and decisively. It will not have to be content with easy successes against the theologies and ideologies and mythologies of external religion, extending only to temple buildings and ceremonies and observances. It will have to rush into that inner chamber shouting: Here is the *fabrica idolorum*[EN150] Here we lie and murder and steal and commit adultery! Here the cry must be: *Ecrasez l'infame!*[EN151] Here or nowhere: for if not here, religion and religions will grow from here like the heads of the Lernaean hydra, however zealously we may deny God outside and destroy His law. But a turning against the religions which can make this judgment on religion is manifestly impossible, whether in the form of mysticism or in that of atheism. For in making this judgment it will have to judge itself. We can be quite definite upon this point: it is as little likely to emerge in the future as in the past. The real crisis of religion can only break in from outside the magic circle of religion and its place of origin, i.e., from outside man. It is only in a quite different antithesis than that of religion and religious ability, only in the light of faith, that the judgment "unbelief, idolatry, self-righteousness" can be made on this sphere and therefore on man as a [325] whole, so that he can no longer flee from one refuge to another. This is what happens in the revelation of God. But to the extent that it does not happen in any other way, religion and religions are left at peace. There is development, but there is also a certain continuance, so that religion and religions are always there. Mystics and atheists cause a certain incidental and limited disquietude—when a greater or lesser historical transformation is due—but this belongs just as much to their innermost life as do the positive expressions and representations, the deities and laws, against which mystical and atheistical criticism is directed. The ebb as well as the flow belongs to the innermost life of the ocean. And it is in the purer forms—so far as they can be achieved—that the critical turn of religion is least hostile.

For to the extent that the purity of mysticism and atheism increases, and the work of liberation is achieved in specific individuals, and they attain either a real or an ostensible peace in that which is positively intended—to that extent the hostility to religion and religions will be definitely reduced. All the great "friends of God" and "deniers of God" have ultimately attained at any rate to a kind of toleration of religion; proving once again that the mother can never quite deny her child.

But the abrogation which is a genuine and dangerous attack on religion is to be found in another book, beside which the books of mysticism and atheism can only be described as completely harmless.

3. TRUE RELIGION

The preceding expositions have established the fact that we can speak of "true" religion only in the sense in which we speak of a "justified sinner."

EN150 idol-maker
EN151 Out with this infamy!

Religion is never true in itself and as such. The revelation of God denies that any religion is true, i.e., that it is in truth the knowledge and worship of God and the reconciliation of man with God. For as the self-offering and self-manifestation of God, as the work of peace which God Himself has concluded between Himself and man, revelation is the truth beside which there is no other truth, over against which there is only lying and wrong. If by the concept of a "true religion" we mean truth which belongs to religion in itself and as such, it is just as unattainable as a "good man," if by goodness we mean something which man can achieve on his own initiative. No religion is true. It can only become true, i.e., according to that which it purports to be and for which it is upheld. And it can become true only in the way in which man is justified, from without; i.e., not of its own nature and being, but only in virtue of a reckoning and adopting and separating which are foreign to its own nature [326] and being, which are quite inconceivable from its own standpoint, which come to it quite apart from any qualifications or merits. Like justified man, religion is a creature of grace. But grace is the revelation of God. No religion can stand before it as true religion. No man is righteous in its presence. It subjects us all to the judgment of death. But it can also call dead men to life and sinners to repentance. And similarly in the wider sphere where it shows all religion to be false it can also create true religion. The abolishing of religion by revelation need not mean only its negation: the judgment that religion is unbelief. Religion can just as well be exalted in revelation, even though the judgment still stands. It can be upheld by it and concealed in it. It can be justified by it, and— we must at once add—sanctified. Revelation can adopt religion and mark it off as true religion. And it not only can. How do we come to assert that it can, if it has not already done so? There is a true religion: just as there are justified sinners. If we abide strictly by that analogy—and we are dealing not merely with an analogy, but in a comprehensive sense with the thing itself—we need have no hesitation in saying that the Christian religion is the true religion.

In our discussion of "religion as unbelief" we did not consider the distinction between Christian and non-Christian religion. Our intention was that whatever we said about the other religions affected the Christian similarly. In the framework of that discussion we could not speak in any special way about Christianity. We could not give it any special or assured place in face of that judgment. Therefore the discussion cannot be understood as a preliminary polemic against the non-Christian religions, with a view to the ultimate assertion that the Christian religion is the true religion. If this were the case, our task now would be to prove that, as distinct from the non-Christian religions, the Christian is not guilty of idolatry and self-righteousness, that it is not therefore unbelief but faith, and therefore true religion; or, which comes to the same thing, that it is no religion at all, but as against all religions, including their mystical and atheistical self-criticism, it is in itself the true and holy and as such the unspotted and incontestable form of fellowship between God and man. To enter on this path would be to deny the very thing we have to affirm.

3. *True Religion*

If the statement is to have any content, we can dare to state that the Christian religion is the true one only as we listen to the divine revelation. But a statement which we dare to make as we listen to the divine revelation can only be a statement of faith. And a statement of faith is necessarily a statement which is thought and expressed in faith and from faith, i.e., in recognition and respect of what we are told by revelation. Its explicit and implicit content is unreservedly conditioned by what we are told. But that is certainly not the case if we try to reach the statement that the Christian religion is the true religion by a road which begins by leaving behind the judgment of revelation, that religion [327] is unbelief, as a matter which does not apply to us Christians, but only to others, the non-Christians, thus enabling us to separate and differentiate ourselves from them with the help of this judgment. On the contrary, it is our business as Christians to apply this judgment first and most acutely to ourselves: and to others, the non-Christians, only in so far as we recognise ourselves in them, i.e., only as we see in them the truth of this judgment of revelation which concerns us, in the solidarity, therefore, in which, anticipating them in both repentance and hope, we accept this judgment to participate in the promise of revelation. At the end of the road we have to tread there is, of course, the promise to those who accept God's judgment, who let themselves be led beyond their unbelief. There is faith in this promise, and, in this faith, the presence and reality of the grace of God, which, of course, differentiates our religion, the Christian, from all others as the true religion. This exalted goal cannot be reached except by this humble road. And it would not be a truly humble road if we tried to tread it except in the consciousness that any "attaining" here can consist only in the utterly humble and thankful adoption of something which we would not attain if it were not already attained in God's revelation before we set out on the road.

We must insist, therefore, that at the beginning of a knowledge of the truth of the Christian religion, there stands the recognition that this religion, too, stands under the judgment that religion is unbelief, and that it is not acquitted by any inward worthiness, but only by the grace of God, proclaimed and effectual in His revelation. But concretely, this judgment affects the whole practice of our faith: our Christian conceptions of God and the things of God, our Christian theology, our Christian worship, our forms of Christian fellowship and order, our Christian morals, poetry and art, our attempts to give individual and social form to the Christian life, our Christian strategy and tactics in the interest of our Christian cause, in short our Christianity, to the extent that it is *our* Christianity, the human work which we undertake and adjust to all kinds of near and remote aims and which as such is seen to be on the same level as the human work in other religions. This judgment means that all this Christianity of ours, and all the details of it, are not as such what they ought to be and pretend to be, a work of faith, and therefore of obedience to the divine revelation. What we have here is in its own way—a different way from that of other religions, but no less seriously—unbelief, i.e., opposition to the divine revelation, and therefore active idolatry and self-righteousness. It is the same helplessness and arbitrariness. It is the same self-exaltation of man, which means his most profound abasement. But this time it is in place of and in opposition to the self-manifestation and self-offering of God, the reconciliation which God Himself has accomplished, it is in disregard of the divine consolations and admonitions that great and small Babylonian towers are [328] erected, which cannot as such be pleasing to God, since they are definitely not set up to His glory.

To see how self-evident this standpoint is in Holy Scripture we have only to note the contexts in which from time to time the people Israel or the New Testament Church appears abstractly in its human existence—certainly as this nation or Church—but for a moment, as it were, behind the back of Yahweh or of Jesus Christ. We can think of Ex. 32: the scene which follows at the foot of Sinai immediately after the conclusion of the covenant and the giving of the Law: Israel, the congregation of Yahweh, the people of the revelation, under the leadership of Aaron, the head of his priestly class, in the full panoply of its religion. But Moses is temporarily missing, and with him obviously the concrete presence of the grace of Yahweh, which would make this religion true. The result: it is true, as we are expressly told in verse 5, that a feast of Yahweh is celebrated; but lo! it consists in adoration and sacrifice before the molten image of a calf. With a sacrificial zeal which cannot be denied they all gave of their best toward it. Aaron himself designed and made it. "And they cried: This is thy God, O Israel, which brought thee out of Egypt" (v. 4). "And the Lord said unto Moses, I have seen this people, and, behold it is a stiffnecked people" (v. 9). That is revealed religion as such. That is the actuality of revealed religion. That is revealed religion as seen for a moment in abstraction from the grace of revelation. And that was how above all the prophet Amos saw it. He described the sacrifices offered to Yahweh at Bethel and Gilgal by the bitter term "scandals" (transgressions R.V. 4^4), He warned them: "Seek not Bethel nor enter into Gilgal" (5^5). In the name of Yahweh he proclaimed: "I hate, I despise your feasts and will not smell your solemn assemblies. Yea though ye offer me your burnt offerings and meal offerings I will not accept them, neither will I regard the peace offerings of your fat beasts. Take thou away from me the noise of thy songs: for I will not heed the melody of thy viols" (5^{21-23}). In the most bitter earnest he flings the question: "Did ye bring unto me sacrifices and offerings in the wilderness forty years, O house of Israel?" (5^{25}). He also raises a question which relativises the whole of Israel's existence in a devastating way: "Are ye not as the children of the Ethiopians unto me, O children of Israel? saith the Lord. Have I not brought up Israel out of Egypt, and the Philistines from Caphtor, and the Syrians from Kir?" (9^7). In the light of all this we can quite understand why the priest Amaziah thought that he ought to denounce this man to the king as a "rebel," and to expel him from the royal temple of Bethel ($7^{10f.}$). It is equally significant that Amos expressly refuses to be a prophet or of the prophetic guild ($7^{14f.}$). With Amos there seems to open up an irreconcilable gulf between revelation and the religion of revelation. We have a similar uncovering of nakedness, of inward disobedience, and even of the religion of revelation in its actuality, its human exercise, in Is. $1^{11f.}$, Jer. $6^{20f.}$, Ps. $50^{7f.}$ It can (Jer. 7^{21}) be intensified to the cutting opposition: "Add your burnt-offerings unto your sacrifices, and eat ye flesh. For I spake not unto your fathers nor commanded them in the day that I brought them out of the land of Egypt concerning burnt-offerings or sacrifices: but this thing I commanded them, saying, Hearken unto my behests, and I will be your God, and walk ye in all the ways that I command you, that it may be well with you." And in Jer. $8^{8f.}$: "How do ye say, we are wise and we have disposal over the law of the Lord? How do ye say, We are wise and the law of the Lord is with us? But, behold, the false pen of the scribes hath wrought falsely. The wise men are ashamed, they are dismayed and taken: Lo, they have rejected the word of the Lord: and what manner of wisdom is in them?"

But, of course, we do not understand these pointed statements correctly, unless we understand them in the context of the general prophetic message of criticism, repentance and judgment. Of course, this, too, belongs to the life of Old Testament religion as such. It is directed from within against apostasy, against its falsification and degeneration, against cultic disloyalty and moral licence. But it has an unheard-of breadth of form. The radical nature of its criticisms and judgments and warnings beggars all comparisons. It cannot be explained until we see that we always have here something more than the opposition to the specific concrete aberrations and sins of Israel, which, of course, have to be taken seriously as such. What we have here is at every point the inevitable struggle of revelation against the religion of revelation, a struggle in which the prophets did not even spare prophecy itself. Is it not as if the whole religion of Israel is ground as between two millstones, between the Word of God, which so definitely institutes and orders and forms it, and the Word of God by which, one must almost say, every concrete obedience to this command is no less definitely unmasked as unbelief? May we not ask whether in this gruesome process an injustice is not done to this people, which is obviously so deeply and seriously religious, which in the end, in spite of all its mistakes and aberrations, tenaciously holds on to its religion through a thousand years of the most trying and difficult circumstances? We shall not ask this question, but we shall understand the process, if we realise that in it—and in this respect, too, the Old Testament has exemplary significance—the judgment of revelation upon religion as such does actually fall upon the religion of revelation. For that very reason the process can, and indeed must, close almost as a matter of course with the promise of salvation, which psychologically and historically is so difficult to explain. It has nothing whatever to do with a sentimental touch of sunset glow after the storm. It belongs so necessarily to the Word of judgment, because the Word of judgment is so comprehensive and profound. It points to the inconceivable divine acquittal. It shows us that the chastened are those whom God loves, that the killed are those who are to live. The Word always remains. The covenant of Yahweh remains, though broken and disgraced. Therefore Israel remains the people, and its religion the religion, of revelation: that is, up to Jesus Christ. With His rejection Israel did not as formerly commit one specific sin. With it, it did not merely break and disgrace the Word and covenant. It denied and abandoned it in substance. Again, and this time comprehensively, the fate of Israel is exemplary. The religion of revelation is indeed bound up with the revelation of God: but the revelation of God is not bound up with the religion of revelation. The prophetic criticism of religion is now seen to be prediction. The abstraction which for a thousand years was only a burning question threatening on the horizon is now achieved. What appeared only from time to time, invariably to be overcome by its opposite, is now revealed in all its nakedness, as human religion. Once it was the human answer to the divine revelation as demanded and ordered by God Himself. In its exercise it was accused and condemned of unbelief, but always readopted into grace. But now—the example had to be recorded—it is a rejected and an emptied religion. It is a religion deprived of its basis and object. It is the Jewish religion from which God has turned away His face. It is one amongst other religions and no more than they. Its only advantage is the terrible one that once it was more than they, but only once. It is so absolutely by the grace of God that the true religion is the true one, that it has to let itself be unmasked and condemned by grace as false religion. If it rejects grace, and therewith its unmerited acquittal, it can never be anything more than false religion, unbelief, idolatry and self-righteousness. If the Church knows what it is doing when it regards its religion, the Christian religion, as the true one, it must never close its eyes to this example or its ears to the warnings of Amos and Jeremiah.

[329]

[330]

It is just the same in the New Testament. When the disciples are seen as men, independently, as it were, of their commission, and of the directing and sustaining word of Jesus, when they stand for a moment on their own feet the far side of Easter and Pentecost, then in a transition no less sharp than that of Old Testament Israel, and obviously under the same order, they at once enter that peculiar shadow-world where their religion is seen to be a religion and therefore unbelief. The chief exemplary figure in this respect is the apostle Peter. The Roman Church would have been right to claim succession from this particular apostle if it had considered his part a little more closely. When Peter stands on his own feet, he is the man who does not mean the things of God but the things of men (Mt. 16²³). He is the doubter who ventures, and then immediately withdraws (Mt. 14²⁸ᶠ·). He can cut off the right ear of Malchus (Jn. 18¹⁰), but then deny Jesus thrice. He is the one to whom Jesus unequivocally says: When thou hast turned again, stablish thy brethren (Lk. 22³²). But what strange figures the rest of the disciples also cut. We remember the recurrent question: Who is the greatest in the kingdom of heaven? (Mt. 18¹). We remember the sons of Zebedee with their wish to sit the one on the right hand of Jesus and the other on the left (Mk. 10³⁵ᶠ·). We think of the despair of the disciples in the storm on the lake: "Why are ye so fearful?" "How is it that ye have no faith?" (Mk. 4³⁵ᶠ·). We recall their sleeping in the garden of Gethsemane (Mk. 14³⁷), and their rashness and helplessness in so many other cases. "Behold, Satan hath desired to have you, that he might sift you as wheat!" (Lk. 22³¹). There can be no doubt that what we are dealing with here is not just isolated or even frequent cases of omission and denial on the part of the disciples, but the extremely fundamental fact, that while Jesus has called them, and they are His followers, they belong to a γενεὰ ἄπιστος EN152 (Mk. 9¹⁹). They are wholly and utterly outside even while they are wholly and utterly inside. So far as they stand on their own feet, the four Gospels make it quite clear that they are wholly and utterly outside. It is clear that they have their religion, but it is equally clear that their religion is unbelief. If not, as in the confession of Peter (Mt. 16¹³ᶠ·) or the confession of Thomas (Jn. 20²⁴ᶠ·), then it is at once characterised as grace. Μὴ γίνου ἄπιστος, ἀλλὰ πιστός EN153, says the risen Christ to Thomas, when He lets him touch His wounds (Jn. 20²⁷). We have an explicit statement of the matter in Jn. 15¹ᶠ· The disciples are the branches in Jesus Christ the Vine. If a branch brings forth no fruit it is cut off. If it brings forth fruit, it is cleansed, that it may bear more fruit. "Ye are already clean for the word's sake, which I have spoken unto you. Abide in me as I in you. As the vine cannot bring forth fruit of itself, if it abide not in the vine, so neither do ye, except ye abide in me. I am the vine, ye are the branches. If a man abide in me, as I in him, he bringeth forth much fruit: without me ye can do nothing (χωρὶς ἐμοῦ δύνασθε ποιεῖν οὐδέν EN154). If a man abide not in me, he is cast out as a branch, which dries up and men gather them and cast them into the fire and burn them." The Acts, of course, shows us the acts of the same disciples, now as apostles, as fruitbearing branches "in the vine." But that "in the vine" must not be overlooked, the reminder "without me ye can do nothing" must not be suppressed, when in their person Christianity confronts the false religions of the Jews and the heathen as the religion which is unequivocally true. And it is not their person, but their office which is characterised in this way. It is the outpouring of the Holy Spirit which gives us the indispensable key to the story. That now as formerly the Christian religion can still be unbelief, when it is not by the grace of God faith, we see in the figures of Ananias and Sapphira (Ac. 5¹ᶠ·), or in the form of Simon Magus (Ac. 8¹³ᶠ·), or in a different way in the disciples of John at Ephesus (Ac. 19¹ᶠ·). In the apostolic letters the main passage which points in this direction is 1 Cor. 13 (which we shall best understand if for the

---

EN152 unbelieving generation
EN153 do not be unbelieving, but believe
EN154 without me you can do nothing

concept "love" we simply insert the name Jesus Christ). The chapter summarises the whole religious life of a Christian community at the time of Paul: speaking with tongues, prophecy, knowledge of mysteries, a faith that removes mountains, giving all one's goods to the poor, martyrdom in the flames to close—and of all this it is said that it helps the Christian not at all, absolutely not at all, if he has not love. For love alone never fails. Prophecy, speaking with tongues, knowledge, all these will be "done away." Their work is only partial. It is not the whole, and therefore it is nothing. It is childish thinking which must be left behind. It is the indirect reflection in a glass. At the very heart of the apostolic witness (which accepts the Christian as the true religion) Christianity could not be more comprehensively relativised in favour of revelation, which means a crisis even for the religion of revelation. [331]

Now it is not the case that this relativising of the Christian religion means that Christian faith is made weak or uncertain or hesitant, or that the decision for the truth of the Christian religion is robbed of its firmness and confidence. Christian faith does not live by the self-consciousness with which the Christian man can differentiate himself from the non-Christian. There is such a self-consciousness, and in its own place it, of course, is both right and necessary. But this self-consciousness has its natural limitations. It cannot possibly mean that the Christian would try to assert himself before God in a righteousness and holiness of his own. Unbroken in relation to man, it is broken in relation to God. It is because it is broken in the one case that it is unbroken in the other.

At this point we can adduce analogically what Paul says in 1 Cor. 4$^{2f.}$ about his attitude to criticism levelled against him in Corinth. He is not only not afraid to be judged by the Corinthians or by any other human court. He does not even think of judging himself; οὐδὲν γὰρ ἐμαυτῷ σύνοιδα [EN155]—an unbroken self-consciousness indeed! But—"I am not hereby justified: but he that judgeth me is the Lord ... He will reveal the hidden things of darkness, and make manifest the counsels of the hearts; and then shall every man have praise of God." The apostolic self-consciousness which is unbroken in relation to man is therefore breached in this way. Similarly in Rom. 4$^{1f.}$ Paul did not simply deny to Abraham as the father of Israel and all believers any "justification by works" or corresponding καύχημα [EN156]. He pointed to the fact that according to the word of Scripture there can never be any question of boasting before God. The justification of Abraham before God is the justification of a godless man. His faith is faith in that justification and not trust in his own works, in circumcision and the Law. In brief, it is not his religious self-consciousness.

It is with this delimiting of the religious self-consciousness that the knowledge of the relativising of even the Christian religion by divine revelation is concerned. We reach this delimiting in faith and by faith. How can it possibly signify a weakening of faith? On the contrary, faith will prove its power, and in the power of faith the Christian will live, in the very fact that faith continuously compels him to think beyond his religious self-consciousness, and therefore constantly to reckon with the relativising of his Christian religion by divine revelation. And, of course, in this light and only in this light the decision for the truth of the Christian religion can be taken with real power. Strong human

---

[EN155] for I do not judge myself
[EN156] boast

positions are only those which are fully abandoned to God: that is, positions which are seen to be quite untenable when measured by His will and judgment. Even from the standpoint of our own being and activity, we do not act prudently, but the very reverse, when we entrench ourselves against God in some tiny chink of our own being and activity, and try to secure ourselves. Not only our security before God, but the very security of our being and activity, and therefore our security in relation to men, rests absolutely upon our willingness in faith and by faith to renounce any such securities.

[332]

In this connexion we ought to consider the remarkable passage 2 Cor. 12$^{1f.}$. There can be no doubt that Paul is not here speaking of the religion of the Christian Church, as in 1 Cor. 13, but very personally of his own most intimate religious experience. There are great things of which he might glory in this sphere, of which, indeed, he could glory in truth, and without talking nonsense. He has been the recipient of ὀπτασίαι καὶ ἀποκαλύψεις EN157, and in particular, "fourteen years ago" he has known a rapture into the third heaven, into Paradise, associated with the hearing of "unspeakable words," which cannot be repeated. But who is it who can really glory in all these things? Three times (vv. 2, 3, 5) Paul speaks of him impersonally: "I know a man …." He calls him a "man in Christ." Undoubtedly he means himself. But—and this is the distinctive thing in the description of this ecstasy—he puts a space between himself and this man. And it is only at this remove that he will take part in the glory which this man—himself—has by virtue of these high things. "To the honour of this man I will boast; but to my own honour I will not boast, though it be because of weakness" (v. 5 acc. to Schlatter). He is restrained from being lifted up by these experiences (v. 7 f.), and is forced into this paradoxical glorying because of weakness. For, like a thorn in the flesh, an angel of Satan stands at his side to buffet him. Not even the most earnest prayer to Jesus Christ can frighten away this enemy. Indeed, Paul obviously does not now want to frighten him away. In his presence and activity he now sees the order in the power of which he is held outside the circle of these experiences: at the place where Christ dwells beside him, i.e., in his weakness. The Lord's answer to his prayer is this: ἀρκεῖ σοι ἡ χάρις μου · ἡ γὰρ δύναμις ἐν ἀσθενείᾳ τελεῖται EN158 (v. 9). He will therefore glory only in his weakness: "For when I am weak, then am I strong." But what is his weakness? Well, it is what is left of his Christian existence after deducting the religious experience of which he might reasonably and truly boast, i.e., humiliations, emergencies, persecutions, distresses for Christ's sake (v. 10). In these he sees the power of Christ dwelling in him. In these he knows that he is strong. In these he glories. And in Paul we can see how the real security of his being and activity, the power of his decision, the strength of even his outward position, the whole energy of his religious self-consciousness in relation to that of others, is rooted in the fact that he let everything, the Christian religion, and *in concreto* EN159 his own specific "revelations," be most definitely limited by revelation, by the Lord Jesus Christ: for "when I am weak, then am I strong."

We are here concerned with an order which can be forgotten or infringed only to the detriment of a real knowledge of the truth of the Christian religion. Again, to ascribe the demonstrative power for this truth to the religious self-consciousness as such is to the dishonouring of God and the eternal destruc-

---

EN157 visions and revelations
EN158 My grace is sufficient for thee, for my power is made perfect in weakness
EN159 concretely

tion of souls. Even outwardly, in its debate with non-Christian religions, the Church can never do more harm than when it thinks that it must abandon the apostolic injunction, that grace is sufficient for us. The place to which we prefer to look is only mist, and the reed upon which we have to lean will slip through our fingers. By trying to resist and conquer other religions, we put ourselves on the same level. They, too, appeal to this or that immanent truth in [333] them. They, too, can triumph in the power of the religious self-consciousness, and sometimes they have been astonishingly successful over wide areas. Christianity can take part in this fight. There is no doubt that it does not lack the necessary equipment, and can give a good account of itself alongside the other religions. But do not forget that if it does this it has renounced its birthright. It has renounced the unique power which it has as the religion of revelation. This power dwells only in weakness. And it does not really operate, nor does the power with which Christianity hopes to work, the power of religious self-consciousness which is the gift of grace in the midst of weakness, unless Christianity has first humbled instead of exalting itself.

By its neglect of this order Christianity has created great difficulties for itself in its debate with other religions. We can see these difficulties developing in three historical stages.

1. It was at the very least noticeable in the days of the early Church before Constantine. At that time Christianity had one great advantage. As a *religio illicita*EN160, an *ecclesia pressa*EN161, it was, as it were, automatically forced into something like the apostolic position, i.e., the apostolic weakness. The adherents of the Christian religion could not acquire any great credit by their cause, at any rate externally, in the field of politics, society or culture. They and their faith were alone against a hopeless, external super-power. They were fighting in a lost position. The angel seemed indeed to be buffeting them to prevent their reaching up to high revelations. They seemed to be automatically directed to boasting of nothing but this weakness of theirs, i.e., to resting in the sufficiency of grace. But the external super-power by which they were opposed, the later heathendom of antiquity, was a Colossus with feet of clay, as the apologists, the more primitive Church fathers and, of course, all the keener-sighted leaders of the contemporary Church were very well aware, in spite of all the pressure of persecution. Christian doctrine and practice possessed all the necessary qualities to commend itself against this heathendom, as the more profound and universal and serious religion. It was a real temptation, not merely to validate Jesus Christ against or for the sinful men of heathen religion, as the sacred books of the Church, the Old Testament and New Testament, demanded, but at the same time (and very quickly on a fairly broad front) to play off the Christian religion as better than the heathen, to contrast Christian possession—which can easily be demonstrated in many if not all

---

EN160 illegal religion
EN161 hard-pressed church

spheres of the spiritual life—with heathen poverty. When we read the apologetics of the second and third centuries, can we altogether avoid the painful impression that what we have here—as though the persecuted can only regard themselves as spiritually undeserving of the external pressure brought to bear on them—is, on the whole, a not very happy, a rather self-righteous, and at any rate a not very perspicacious boasting about all those advantages of Christianity over heathen religion which were in themselves incontestable but not ultimately decisive? In these early self-commendations of Christianity a remarkably small part is played by the fact that grace is the truth of Christianity, that the Christian is justified when he is without God, like Abraham, that he is like the publican in the temple, the prodigal son, wretched Lazarus, the guilty thief crucified with Jesus Christ. Instead, we have the—admittedly successful—rivalry of one way of salvation, one wisdom and morality with others, of a higher humanity consummated and transfigured by the cross of Christ with a decadent and defeated humanity which has rightly grown weary of its ancient ideals. How strangely did a man like Tertullian see the danger which [334] threatened at this point, and at the same time never really see it at all, but actually help to increase it. And to the extent that the fact that grace, that Jesus Christ, is the truth of Christianity was never completely concealed in the doctrine and proclamation of the Church, did not the fact that Christianity is the special religion of grace and redemption easily appear to be its final and supreme advantage, although it was robbed of its real meaning and power to convince by the fact that the Church was not content with grace? Both materially and formally that which is centrally and uniquely Christian was abandoned or replaced. To the extent that that took place, material and formal comparisons were everywhere made with the world, with the intention of prevailing over it at any rate spiritually. Against the power of syncretism, which was so integral to that passing spiritual world, only the might of spiritual poverty and the power of revelation within it could have emerged successfully. To the extent that this power constantly reappeared, the truth of Christianity spoke and shone forth. So far as the early Church was great, it was so by this power. If only the Early Church had not already trusted far too much to other powers, and thereby weakened itself, and paved the way for further weakenings.

2. At first the Church was exposed to external pressure. Because of this there was an external resemblance to the original apostolic situation. The Church was compelled constantly to reflect and to return to that which is ultimate and real. But all this came to an end with the developments which took place after Constantine and it quite disappeared in the whole period which was dominated by the idea of the *Corpus Christianum*[EN162]. Certainly this idea of the unity of Church and state has to be regarded as an extremely promising offer made to the Christianity of that period. But we must hasten to add that it then proved itself to be quite unprepared for the offer, not having out-

---

[EN162] Christendom

grown the temptations associated with it. As already the early Church had reflected more upon its intellectual than its spiritual superiority over against the heathen world around it, and had presumed more upon its monotheism, its ethics, its mystery, than upon its spirituality, upon the grace of Jesus Christ, so now as the acknowledged Imperial Church, in open alliance with the higher and lower political factors, it could find its greatness in the fact that it became increasingly a second world-power. It could make it its ambition—under the plea that it was, of course, a matter of the glory of God—to try to become the first and real world-power instead of the second. Where was the awareness of grace as the truth of Christianity in the days of the investiture-conflict and the crusades, or in the world of Gothic? To what extent was this a real concern in the great reform movement of Cluny and monasticism generally? To what extent could heathen and Jews find in the mediaeval Church a power which was genuinely different, a novel and unfamiliar power, not the power which men can always demonstrate, but the power of God which humbles and therefore blesses all men, the power of the Gospel? To what extent could the Church confront the Islam which oppressed it in South and East as something which was really original? To what extent could the Christian opponents of the Church, the imperial and national parties or the heretical sects, deduce from the action and attitude of the Church that there was any concern for the glory of God and not its own glory? Obviously much less as the spiritual alienation of the Church from its own centre and the inward secularisation that accompanied it, both of which had been prepared in the early period, now increased more and more. Christianity was moulded according to a definite universal, intellectual-moral-aesthetic form, which made possible, and inevitable, the complementary formation of all kinds of particular national Christianities, each with its own particular national-religious self-consciousness. To what extent was this form, either in itself or in its individual variations, an evidence of the truth of Christianity? Certainly it was evidence of a unique and rich religious self-consciousness, i.e., a testimony to the glory of Western man, educated and formed or stimulated and influenced by the Church as the (only too legitimate) heiress of ancient civilisation. But it could be an evidence of the [335] supreme, victorious truth of Christianity only in so far as in it it is secretly and ultimately a matter of the grace of Jesus Christ. And in spite of its zealous and absorbed activity in other respects, in this decisive respect the Church showed far too little vigilance and loyalty. The evidence of grace was not destroyed. It maintained its quiet force. Even in this world revelation shone out in the spiritual poverty of those who believed it as it is meant to be believed. But it did so in the Church only against the Church (i.e., against the tendency which dominated the Church, against the proud but treacherous idea of the *corpus christianum*[EN163]). On the very road on which it sought its strength, the Church of this time did the thing that was bound to weaken it at the critical point.

[EN163] Christendom

3. The way was prepared for the so-called "modern period" by the trends of the later Middle Ages, and the Renaissance. As concerns Christianity, it is characterised by a fresh collapse of the unity of the Church and state. Western humanity has come of age, or thinks it has. It can now dispense with its teacher—and as such official Christianity had in fact felt and behaved. Man finds himself as a "universum,"[EN164] and although he cannot at once throw off his respect for the teacher, he feels that he can at last go his way with head erect. Grateful for what they have received, but determined upon a secular factuality, politics, science, society and art all dare to stand on their own feet. The floods have receded, and behold, there is nothing much left after the thousand years of the apparent domination of Christianity except a little monotheism, morality and mysticism. As a whole, the humanity of the West does not seem to find in the Church or to ascribe to it anything more. Because of that, it does not feel compelled to remain tied to the Church. That is the joyous discovery which it now makes. Nor does the heathendom which surrounds the tiny peninsula of Europe and its transmarine colonies, or the fierce Judaism which continues to exist in the midst of Christianity, seem to have heard any more than this, or heard it with any emphasis from the mouth of the Church. In spite of the most favourable conditions of the Middle Ages, the Christian Church obviously could not impress world consciousness as anything more than a religious society. Under these favourable conditions it tried to bind and to dominate. But the increased secularisation of culture makes it plain that it has not been able to do this. So now again, as at the first, it is forced on to the defensive. At first, of course, there is no hint of outward repression or persecution. There is no reason for this. Certainly, it is opposed until well on in the 19th century, so far as it is a matter of liberation from mediaeval claims. But the moment it decides on a certain reserve and toleration, its freedom is conceded. There is no question of its being dangerous and of having to be radically persecuted, as had happened with full consciousness under the dying rule of antiquity. What is primarily in question in these centuries is the possibility that, assigned to its proper limits, the Church or Christianity may be an important and, under suitable oversight, a useful and usable force for education and order in the service of the new secular glory of Western man. And the non-Christian religions are on exactly the same level as inward Christian secularism, being content with a certain reserve and toleration on their own part and maintaining a mild indifference to the newer Christianity, so far as they come into contact with it. Of course, it might be dangerous for modern secularism and the non-Christian religions if the truth of Christianity, the grace of God in its radical and critical power, again found expression. It is significant that the only case in which there has been hostility to the Church in modern times, the persecution which early Protestantism had to suffer so long in many lands, was connected with the very fact that this

---

[EN164] universal

truth had again found utterance. But that is long ago. When the mediaeval dream was over, even Protestantism had, and knew how, to adapt itself to the existence of a religious society which modern man regards as ultimately unnecessary and innocuous. And as a whole the more, modern Christian Church never even gave a thought to retracing the false path prepared in early days or following what was openly neglected in the Middle Ages. In the recon- [336] sideration of itself and its possibilities imposed by the new situation, it did not attain again to the weakness in which alone it can always be strong. Instead, it inwardly affirmed the new situation, as it had previously affirmed the old. That is to say, it accepted modern man with his energetic attitude to himself, asking how best Christianity could be commended to that man. It took up the role allotted to it, and was at pains to make itself indispensable in it, i.e., by pointing out and demonstrating that if there is a truth in the Christian religion which can profitably be heard and believed, especially in the modern age, it consists in this, that properly understood, the doctrine of Jesus Christ, and the way of life which corresponds to it, has the secret power of giving to man the inward capacity to seek and attain the aims and purposes which he has independently chosen. In seeking after this new self-commendation, on the converging lines of Jesuistry, Pietism and the Enlightenment, it became secular anthropologic- ally, in the same way as in the Middle Ages it had been secular theologically. And it was in seeking after this new self-commendation that it arrived, among other things, at the discovery of the general concept of "religion," the theo- logical history of which we have briefly considered. Therefore it all amounted to this: that within the general anthropological concept, recognised by the non-Christian world as well, the particular "nature of Christianity" should be reliably disclosed and declared at the same human level, from the same view- points and on the plane of the same arguments used by those who thought that they could dispense with it, i.e., in the area of human and humanly per- ceived advantages and disadvantages, strong points and weak points, probabil- ities and improbabilities, hopes and fears. There was a certain resemblance to the situation under the Roman Empire—although without the corrective of outward persecution. But Christianity was now represented as a better founda- tion for philosophy and morality, as a better satisfaction of ultimate needs, as a better actualisation of the supreme ideals of modern man, than any of its vari- ous competitors. Just at this time and on these presuppositions, and supported by the Jesuits and the Protestant Pietists, there was a comprehensive readop- tion of the missionary task of the Christian Church. The result was a fresh confrontation of Christianity with the non-Christian religions. It was inevitable that both the mission and the confrontation should suffer most heavily from the fact that the sending Church was itself seeking its strength at a different point from where it could be found. And the debate whether the aim of the mission was the representing of an Americo-European or the founding of an autochthonous African and Asiatic Christianity, could not help towards a solu- tion of the hidden difficulty that either way the main concern was the "glory" of this or that Christianity in its relation to the needs and postulates of man. Now, in this third period, both in the Christian West and on the mission fields, it has always been the case that the truth of Christianity, the grace of Jesus Christ, has spoken, shone through and interpenetrated in the spiritual poverty of those who in this age believed in Him. But in this age, too, this was in contradiction to the tendencies and directions that dominated Church history. So far as these tendencies and directions dominated and determined the situation, it was inevitable that Christianity should surrender its truth to the continual fluctuations of modern man, that tossed about from one unclean hand to another its truth should seem to be the now absolutely authoritarian, now individually romantic, now liberal, now national or even racial truth of man, but not the truth of God which judges and blesses, and which it continually claimed to be according to the original and strangely enough unsilenced documents of Christianity. During this third period of its history Christianity and the Church have had experience of many victories—more than would have been dreamed at the peak of the period in the 18th century. But no one should be deceived about the fact that they were Pyrrhic victories. And the no less numerous [337] reverses, which it suffered on the same road, were more significant of the real state of things than the victories. And it may be that modern secularism for its part is still far from the end of its ways and possibilities. It may be that the powers of the heathen religions are far from being exhausted. If this is the case, it might become an ever more burning question, whether from the very standpoint of its existence as such, of its validity and task in the world, Christianity does not have cause to give a body blow to its own secularism and heathenism, which means—for everything else is secular and heathen—to set its hope wholly and utterly on grace.

We must not allow ourselves to be confused by the fact that a history of Christianity can be written only as a story of the distress which it makes for itself. It is a story which lies completely behind the story of that which took place between Yahweh and His people, between Jesus and His apostles. It is a story whose source and meaning and goal, the fact that the Christian is strong only in his weakness, that he is really satisfied by grace, can in the strict sense nowhere be perceived directly. Not even in the history of the Reformation! What can be perceived in history is the attempt which the Christian makes, in continually changing forms, to consider and vindicate his religion as a work which is in itself upright and holy. But he continually feels himself thwarted and hampered and restrained by Holy Scripture, which does not allow this, which even seems to want to criticise this Christian religion of his. He obviously cannot shut out the recollection that it is in respect of this very work of his religion that he cannot dispense with the grace of God and therefore stands under the judgment of God. At this point we are particularly reminded of the history of the Reformation. But in the very light of that history we see that the recollection has always been there, even in the pre- and post-Reformation periods. Yet the history of Christianity as a whole reveals a tendency which is quite contrary to this recollection. It would be arbitrary not to recognise this, and to claim that the history of Christianity, as distinct from that of other religions, is the story of that part of humanity, which, as distinct from others, has existed only as the part which of grace lives by grace. In the strict sense there is no evidence of this throughout the whole range of Christianity. What is evident is in the first instance a part of humanity which no less contradicts the grace and revelation of God because it claims them as its own peculiar and most sacred treasures, and its religion is to that extent a religion of revelation. Contradiction is contradiction. That it exists at this point, in respect of the religion of revelation, can be denied even less than at other points. Elsewhere we might claim in extenuation that it simply exists in fact, but not in direct contrast with revelation. But in the history of Christianity, just because it is the religion of revelation, the sin is, as it were, committed with a high hand. Yes, sin! For contradiction against grace is unbelief, and unbelief is sin, indeed it is *the* sin. It is, therefore, a fact that we can speak of the truth of the Christian religion only within the doctrine of the *iustificatio impii*[EN165]. The statement that even Christianity is unbelief gives rise to a whole mass of naive   [338] and rationalising contradiction. Church history itself is a history of this contradiction. But it is this very fact which best shows us how true and right the statement is. We can as little avoid the contradiction as jump over our own shadow.

We cannot expect that at a fourth or fifth or sixth stage, the history of Christianity will be anything but a history of the distress which Christianity creates for itself. May it not lack in future reformation, i.e., expressions of warning and promise deriving from Holy Scripture! But before the end of all things we cannot expect that the Christian will not always show himself an enemy of grace, in spite of all intervening restraints.

Notwithstanding the contradiction and therefore our own existence, we can and must perceive that for our part we and our contradiction against grace stand under the even more powerful contradiction of grace itself. We can and must—in faith. To believe means, in the knowledge of our own sin to rely upon the righteousness of God which makes an infinite satisfaction for our sin. Concretely, it means, in the knowledge of our own contradiction against grace to cleave to the grace of God which infinitely contradicts this contradiction. In this knowledge of grace, in the knowledge that it is the justification of the ungodly, that it is grace for the enemies of grace, the Christian faith attains to its knowledge of the truth of the Christian religion. There can be no more question of any immanent lightness or holiness of this particular religion as the ground and content of the truth of it, than there can be of any other religion claiming to be the true religion in virtue of its inherent advantages. The Christian cannot avoid abandoning any such claim. He cannot avoid confessing that he is a sinner even in his best actions as a Christian. And that is not, of course, the ground, but the symptom of the truth of the Christian religion.

EN165 justification of the ungodly

141

The abandoning and confessing means that the Christian Church is the place where, confronted with the revelation and grace of God, by grace men live by grace. If this were not so, how would they believe? And if they did not believe, how would they be capable of this abandoning and confessing?

> The passage in Gen. 32²²ᶠ·, on Jacob's wrestling at Jabbok, can throw light on this. It says of Jacob, who undoubtedly is already elected and called by God, that he wrestles with God until morning, and that God—obviously—does not overcome him. From the immanent stand-point he is and continues to be an enemy of grace. This is indicated by the new name Israel, which he acquires: "Thou hast striven with God and with men and hast prevailed"—a great distinction, but at bottom a shattering one, which reminds us of the religious history of the people whose ancestor Jacob was. The giving of this name to Jacob is a fulfilment of the judgment. But that is not the meaning and object of the history. After the conflict the sinew of Jacob's thigh is touched and dislocated by God. So, then, although he is not overcome by God, he is and continues to be a man weakened by God. Again, in his wrestling against God, Jacob will not let God go, because he desires to be blessed by Him. Again, God actually does bless this stedfast opponent of His. And finally, Jacob calls the place of this conflict with God "Peniel": "For I have seen God face to face and my life is preserved." The place where there is knowledge of the truth of the Christian religion will have to be such a Peniel, and it can be such a Peniel only where a man stands wholly and utterly against God, and in this resistance against God he is marked by God, and therefore cannot make any other request than: "I will not let thee go, except thou bless me," and in this very prayer of his he is heard and blessed, and in this very blessing he sees the face of God and in it he knows the truth.

[339]

We describe the victorious grace of God as the mystery of the truth of the Christian religion. But it must again be emphasised expressly that this means something more than that in its Reformation form at any rate Christianity claims particularly to be the religion of free grace, i.e., a religion whose doc-trine and life is now directly concentrated upon the reality described in the concept "grace." When we ground the truth of the Christian religion upon grace, it is not a question of the immanent truth of a religion of grace as such, but of the reality of the grace itself by which one religion is adopted and distin-guished as the true one before all others. It is not because it is a religion of grace that this happens, nor is it because it is so perhaps in a particularly insist-ent and logical way. But conversely, it is because this happens that it is a reli-gion of grace in an insistent and logical way. Of course, in its decisive features, the historical aspect of a religion of grace, even of a logical religion of grace, does not differ from that of other religions. In its immanent constitution it is involved absolutely in the contradiction against grace. Indeed, and at this point we cannot really try to save Protestantism—it may even assume the char-acter of a particularly emphatic revolt against grace. Even the religion of grace can be justified and constituted the true religion only by grace and not of itself. Of course, its election and truth are manifested in the fact that it is the religion of grace, and in consequence always understands and forms itself as such. The symptom of the surrender of every human claim, the confessing that we continually contradict God, will certainly not be wanting. It is inevit-able that in contradicting we know that we are thrown upon the One whom we contradict and who in a different way contradicts us, and we cannot fail to thank Him for the blessing of which we are so entirely unworthy. It is in this way, in the very encounter with God, the site of which we call Peniel or, it may be, Evangelical Reformed Christianity, that the face of God is seen, and therefore Peniel or Evangelical Reformed Christianity is the true religion. But we must not forget that it is not the symptoms, and therefore not the site we call by this name, which demonstrate the true religion, but that it is the truth itself which is the basis of the symptoms and distinguishes the site, so that we can call it this without being tied down to the site and symptoms. The truth itself is indispensable if in our consideration of the site and symptoms, however plain,   [340] we are not to be deceived concerning the truth of the Christian religion.

We can regard it as a wholly providential disposition that as far as I can see the most adequate and comprehensive and illuminating heathen parallel to Christianity, a religious development in the Far East, is parallel not to Roman or Greek Catholicism, but to Reformed Christianity, thus confronting Christianity with the question of its truth even as the logical religion of grace. We are referring to the two related Buddhist developments in 12th and 13th century Japan (i.e., during the life-times of Francis of Assisi, Thomas Aquinas and Dante): the Yodo-Shin ("Sect of the Pure Land," founded by Genku-Honen) and the Yodo-Shin-Shu ("True Sect of the Pure Land," founded by Genku's pupil Shinran). (Cf. for what follows: K. Florenz, "*Die Japaner*," in Chantepie de la Saussaye, *Lehrb. d. Rel. Gesch.²*, Vol. 1, 1925, 382 ff., and Tiele-Söderblom, *Komp. d. Rel. Gesch.⁶*, 197 ff.). The movements are a turning-point in the religious history of Japan. Their point of departure is the belief of Genku that the earlier forms of Japanese Buddhism, particularly that of the Zen-sects which flourished in the 12th century, were honourable and right, but that they were too severe for the mass of the people and therefore unattainable. What they had demanded had been that man should redeem himself by his own efforts, i.e., by his striving after a higher morality, mystical absorption, and contemplative knowledge as the "path of holiness." In its place Genku wished to see substituted a fundamentally much easier way of salvation. For this purpose he gave a central position to the god "Amida-Buddha." This god had been preached in China since the 7th century—there was a possible connexion with the Nestorian mission— and in Japan since the 8th. It was named "infinite light" or "infinite life," and in the popular mind at least was regarded as the supreme and personal God. This Amida, it was taught, is the Creator and Lord of Paradise, a "pure land (*yodo*) in the West." The life-problem of man is to be born again there after death, and from there to attain to Nirvana. "There in blessedness we shall sit cross-legged on lotus flowers, and in contemplation of Amida gradually develop to a full ripeness of knowledge, in order at last to enter Nirvana" (Florenz, 387). But how do we arrive at this new birth? Not by our own power, answers Genku, in sharp opposition to the other Buddhist sects. And he fastens decisively on a text which he took over from the Chinese tradition about Amida, heavily underlining it as the "primal promise." This text contained a vow of the God Amida himself, in virtue of which he himself, Amida, does not wish to accept complete enlightenment (Buddha-hood), unless all living creatures, who sincerely believe in him, and ten times desire of him regeneration into his country, participate in the fulfilment of this wish. So, taught Genku, we have to put all our trust not in our own strength, but in that of this other, Amida. We have to fulfil the one condition which he has attached to the attainment of salvation. We have to believe in Him, who has compassion on all, even sinners. We have to call on his name, and as we do so all his good works and meritorious acts stream into our mouths and become our own possession, so that our merit is Amida's merit, and there is no difference between him and us. We have to do this calling as often as possible. Particularly in the decisive hour of death we have to be sure when we call on this name that Amida will not reject even the greatest sinners, but will give them a corner in the paradise, which is the forecourt of Nirvana. Those who called on him, but with secret doubts, will be locked up for 500 years in the cup of a lotus flower in some corner of Paradise. And in a particularly significant way, those who did not succeed in relying wholly on faith and therefore on the efficacy of this calling, but who tried to secure themselves by the execution of so-called good works and religious practices, will find a preliminary lodging in the extreme West. The place provided is replete with heavenly delights, singing and dancing and playing. The obvious purpose of the purgatory is instruction, and from it they will depart to the fields of supreme blessedness. It was this doctrine of Genku and the Yodoshin which was systematically developed by Shinran, the founder of the Yodo-Shin-Shu. Both doctrinally and practically he made it basic. Everything rested on the primal promise of the compassionate redeemer Amida and on faith in him. But whereas Genku knew the worship of another Buddha as well as Amida, this was now strictly forbidden. In short, Buddha-Gautama took second place as a mere herald of the Amida doctrine. Genku had not contested the possibility of meritorious works. Shinran denied them absolutely. As he saw it, everything depends on the faith of the heart. We are too firmly embedded in fleshly lusts to be able to extricate ourselves from the vicious circle of life and death by any form of self-activation. All that we can do is simply to give thanks for the redemption assured by Amida without any activity at all on our part. In the Yodo-Shu doctrine the hour of death loses its emphatic and critical character, and calling on Amida loses the last remnant of the character of an achievement or a magical act. It becomes simply a sign of our thankfulness. Genku had said: "Even sinners will enter into life; how much more the righteous." But this was significantly reversed by Shinran: "If the righteous enter into life, how much more in the case of sinners." The redemptive significance of faith in Amida has nothing to do with feelings or joy of heart, or even the strength of the longing for salvation. There are, of course, ways of awakening and strengthening faith. For example, we ought to avail ourselves of the opportunity to be instructed in sacred doctrine. We ought to ponder its meaning. We ought habitually to hold discussions with religiously minded friends. We ought to recite the Amida-prayer in a gentle voice. In face of our utter sinfulness we ought to strengthen ourselves with the marvellous thought that because of the primal promise we are not rejected. But we must also know that even faith in this primal promise is ultimately a gift of God. Yet faith is for everyone, even for women—an unheard of innovation in the world of Buddhism. We shall not be surprised, then, to learn that Yodo-Shin-Shu knows nothing of bidding prayers, magic formulas and actions, amulets, pilgrimages, penances, fasts and other kinds of asceticism, monasticism. The cult-object in its rich temples is simply a picture or statue of Amida. Its priests have no mediatorial significance. Their function is to instruct believers and to carry out the practices of the church. They wear vestments only in the temple. They are subject neither to special laws of food nor to celibacy. Great emphasis is laid upon their activity in the way of instruction, preaching and edifying popular literature. The effect of faith in Amida, inculcated into the laity, is morality of life in the framework of family, state and calling. They are "to exercise self-discipline, to live in harmony with others, to keep order, to be obedient to the national laws, and as good citizens to care for the welfare of the state" (Florenz, 397). As distinct from the other Japanese sects Yodo-Shin-Shu has never let itself be supported legally or financially by the government. From the outset it has been completely free from the state, its main activity being in the large cities. We are not really surprised that St. Francis Xavier, who was the first Christian missionary to live in Japan (1549–1551), thought that he recognised in Yodo-Shin-Shu the "Lutheran heresy." But the question raised has an importance which is more than historical, for (according to Florenz,

[341]

398) half of the total population of Japan, at any rate a good third, still adhere to this church.

(In the same context we are also reminded of the Indian Bhakti religion. But even if we accept the parallel, it is not nearly so forceful as the Japanese one. Bhakti is an act of utter surrender and resignation. In it our own will is placed absolutely at the service of another's. It can easily be intensified into a personal act of inward inclination and love. The high or supreme God to whom Bhakti is offered can have any name or character. It is the emotion of love itself and as such which redeems man, which enables him to participate in the answering love of God, which even in earthly things allows him to be sympathetic and kindly, unselfish, patient and serene. There is mention of a certain neutralising of all other means of salvation. As a land of modest counterpart to the Protestant doctrine of justification, there is mention of a "cat rule," by which the soul of everything can be surrendered to God and does not need to make any effort, because God leads it to salvation in the same way as a cat carries its kitten. This is in contrast to a "monkey-rule," in which God's relation to the soul is characterised by the she monkey, to which the young must still cling even while they are carried. The most uncertain part played by the idea of God, the substitution of surrender and love for faith, and the utter and complete formlessness even of the concept of love, show that we are in a quite different world from that of the Japanese religion of grace, and an absolutely different world from that of Evangelical Christianity. It would be a very degenerate form of modern Evangelical Christianity which felt that the Bhakti religions could claim kinship with it.) [342]

It is only the "Japanese Protestantism" of Genku and Shinran which calls for serious consideration. When I said that its existence is a providential disposition, I meant that we ought not to be startled even momentarily by the striking parallelism of it to the truth of Christianity, but that we should be grateful for the lesson which it so abundantly and evidently teaches. And the lesson is this: that in its historical form, as a mode of doctrine, life and order, the Christian religion cannot be the one to which the truth belongs *per se*[EN166]—not even if that form be the Reformed. For obviously the form, even if Reformed, can never be proved to be incontestably original. Of course, no one in his senses would ever dream of speaking of an identity between Christian and Japanese "Protestantism." In practice no two natural or historical forms are ever the same. It is, therefore, well to note (1) that the starting-point of the Yodo-movement is obviously the popular demand for an easier and simpler road to salvation; but no one can say of either Luther or Calvin that they begin at that point. The consequence is (2) that among the Yodoistic ideas parallel to the Reformed, we miss any doctrine of the law and also of the holiness, or wrath of Amida. There is nothing to relieve the goodness and mercy of this God. There is nothing dramatic in his redemption of man. It does not have the character of a real solution. From this it seems (3) that in the Yodoistic antithesis to cultic-ethical righteousness by works there is lacking that accent of a struggle for the glory of God against the arbitrariness and boasting of man which is given its proper stress in Paul and later in the Reformers, especially Calvin. In this case it seems to be based entirely on a pastoral concern which, as such, is held to be obviously incontestable. (4) Yodoism and all Buddhism stand or fall with the inner power and validity of the stormy desire of man for redemption by dissolution; for entry into Nirvana, to which the "pure land" attainable by faith alone is merely the forecourt; for the Buddha-hood, whose perfection even the God Amida has not yet reached. In the Yodo religion it is not Amida or faith in him, but this human goal of desire which is the really controlling and determinative power. Amida, and faith in him, and the "pure land," to which faith is the entry, are related to this goal only as the means to the end. On a closer examination, therefore, there are not wanting

---

EN166 in and of itself

noteworthy immanent distinctions between the Japanese and Christian "Protestantism." An ever closer examination would show that they are even wider and deeper than stated. But to point out these distinctions is not to state the decisive factor. Yodoism can certainly be compared without violence to the simple Christian "Protestantism" which countless souls have thought of as the true Protestantism ever since the 16th century, which has found a definite self-conception and self-expression in Lutheranism especially, and which was to some extent that of Luther himself. Without being arbitrary, we can think of the magicians of Pharaoh, Ex. 7, who could at least do the same miracles as Aaron, even though he was the brother of Moses: the similarity was enough to make Pharaoh harden his heart. With so many similarities even the distinctions might give rise ultimately—perhaps as a result of contact with Christianity—to a further immanent development of Yodoism to an even purer form and in that way to an almost complete equality with Christian Protestantism. And this would mean that Yodoism would take its place with the purest form of Christianity as a religion of grace. But even if there were no question of this, we should still have good reason to see in the distinctions symptoms, but only symptoms, of the real difference between true and false religion. As symptoms they have no decisive or really determinative force. They are not as such the truth as against a lie. They are only the seal of a truth which we must first receive elsewhere. We have to reckon with them in theory. But in the last resort even if they were lacking we should still have no doubts concerning the difference between truth and error. In other words, the Christian-Protestant religion of grace is not the true religion because it is a religion of grace. If that were the case, then, whatever our view of the distinctions, we could quite reasonably say the same of Yodoism, and, with a rather more blunted sensibility, of the Bhakti religion. Indeed, why should we not say it of a whole range of other religions, for which grace in different names and contexts is not a wholly foreign entity? Only one thing is really decisive for the distinction of truth and error. And we call the existence of Yodoism a providential disposition because with what is relatively the greatest possible force it makes it so clear that only one thing is decisive. That one thing is the name of Jesus Christ. Methodologically, it is to be recommended that in face of Yodoism, and, at bottom, of all other religions, our first task is to concentrate wholly upon this distinction, provisionally setting aside whatever other deference we think we recognise. It is not merely a matter of prudentially weighing the various possibilities of heathen development, which might eventually catch up with the differences we teach, but of a clear insight that the truth of the Christian religion is in fact enclosed in the one name of Jesus Christ, and nothing else. It is actually enclosed in all the formal simplicity of this name as the very heart of the divine reality of revelation, which alone constitutes the truth of our religion. It is not enclosed, therefore, in its more or less explicit structure as the religion of grace, nor in the Reformation doctrines of original sin, representative satisfaction, justification by faith alone, the gift of the Holy Ghost and thankfulness. All this, as Figura shows, the heathen, too, can in their own way teach and even live and represent as a church. Yet that does not mean that they are any the less heathen, poor, and utterly lost. Our knowledge, and the life and churchmanship which correspond to it so badly, genuinely distinguish us from the heathen only to the extent they are at any rate symptoms of the grace and truth which is only Jesus Christ Himself and therefore the name of Jesus Christ for us—only to the extent that they are absolutely conditioned by this One and no other, and therefore tied to this name, their goal and content determined and fixed by it, strengthened and preserved by it. Christian Protestantism is the true religion to the extent that the Reformation was a reminder of the grace and truth determined in this name, and that this reminder is effective in it. The reminder was more a being reminded. And in the reminder it formed itself, or was formed (and with it in some measure the rest of Christendom) into what we now call accordingly an explicit religion of grace. Out of the reminder there sprang the doctrines of justification and predestination, the Evangelical doctrines of

146

the Church, the sacraments, and the Christian life and all the other distinctive features, which more or less clearly mark it off in this way. As symptoms, as predicates of the subject Jesus Christ—and we can take them seriously in retrospect—they have acquired, and had, and do have the force of truth: the force of the confession and attestation of the truth. How should it not be demanded and proper to proclaim the name of Jesus Christ, and in it the truth of the Christian religion? And now: in this symptomatic, confessional and attesting power, the not inconsiderable distinctions between the Christian and all non-Christian reli- [344] gions of grace become serious and important. We have good grounds for believing that even in respect of the twin-sided structure there is no real possibility of confusion. There can be no question, even in the future, of a real parallelism or coincidence between the doctrine and the life of the Christian and non-Christian religions of grace (however consistent). Instead, certain symptomatic distinctions will be visible here and there, in which the true and the essential distinction can always be perceived. But a conviction of this kind can be well-grounded only if it is based exclusively upon faith in the one and only Jesus Christ, for it is only from Him that the relative distinctions can have and constantly derive their relative light. Therefore the true and essential distinction of the Christian religion from the non-Christian, and with it its character as the religion of truth over against the religions of error, can be demonstrated only in the fact, or event, that taught by Holy Scripture the Church listens to Jesus Christ and no one else as grace and truth, not being slack but always cheerful to proclaim and believe Him, finding its pleasure in giving itself as promised to the service offered to Him, and therefore in being His own confessor and witness in the confession and witness of the Church. In fact, it all amounts to this: that the Church has to be weak in order to be strong.

That there is a true religion is an event in the act of the grace of God in Jesus Christ. To be more precise, it is an event in the outpouring of the Holy Spirit. To be even more precise, it is an event in the existence of the Church and the children of God. The existence of the Church of God and the children of God means that true religion exists even in the world of human religion. In other words, there is a knowledge and worship of God and a corresponding human activity. We can only say of them that they are corrupt. They are an attempt born of lying and wrong and committed to futile means. And yet we have also to say of them that (in their corruption) they do reach their goal. In spite of the lying and wrong committed, in spite of the futility of the means applied, God is really known and worshipped, there is a genuine activity of man as reconciled to God. The Church and the children of God and therefore the bearers of true religion live by the grace of God. Their knowledge and worship of God, their service of God in teaching, cultus and life, are determined by the realisation of the free kindness of God which anticipates all human thought and will and action and corrects all human corruption. For it does not leave anything for man to do except to believe and give thanks. And it teaches him to do this—not as his own work but as its own gift—which will never be denied to the man who believes and gives thanks. The Church and the children of God live under this ordinance. To that extent they live by the grace of God. But the fact that they do so is not the basis of their existence as the Church and the children of God. Nor is it the thing which makes their religion the true religion. From the standpoint of their own activity as such, they do not stand out decisively above the general level of religious history. They do not escape the divine accusation of idolatry and self-righteousness. For one thing, their life by grace hardly ever appears in history except as an occasional obstacle to the effective fulfilment even amongst them of the law of all religion. If the thought and will and action of Christians as those who live by grace were really the criterion of their existence as the Church and the children of God, with what confidence we could maintain their existence as such and the truth of their religion ! But we cannot maintain it on the ground of that criterion because it is not unknown for an apparent and sometimes a very convincing life of grace, and the phenomenon of the religion of grace, to appear in other fields of religious history. And yet by biblical standards we have no authority to speak of the Church and the divine sonship or of the existence of true religion in these other spheres. The decisive thing for the existence of the Church and the children of God and for the truth of their religion is something quite different. And therefore the decisive thing for their life by grace, in itself so equivocal, is also different. It is the fact that by the grace of God they live by His grace. That is what makes them what they are. That is what makes their religion true. That is what lifts it above the general level of religious history. But "by the grace of God" means by the reality of that by which they apparently but very equivocally live; by the reality of that by which men can apparently and equivocally live in other spheres of religious history. "By the reality" means by the fact that beyond all human appearance, beyond all that men can think and will and do in the sphere of their religion, even if it is a religion of grace, without any merits or deservings of their own, God acts towards them as the gracious God He is, anticipating their own thought and will and action by His own free kindness, arousing in them faith and thankfulness, and never refusing them. They are what they are, and their religion is the true religion, not because they recognise Him as such and act accordingly, not in virtue of their religion of grace, but in virtue of the fact that God has graciously intervened for them, in virtue of His mercy in spite of their apparent but equivocal religion of grace, in virtue of the good pleasure which He has in them, in virtue of His free election, of which this good pleasure is the only motive, in virtue of the Holy Spirit whom He willed to pour out upon them. It is of grace that the Church and the children of God live by His grace. It is of grace that they attain the status of the bearers of true religion. But we can see the concrete significance of this, we can see how different it is from any kind of higher principle of religion, which might be used in the assessment of all human religion, only when we are clear that "by the grace of God" means exactly the same as "through the name of Jesus Christ." He, Jesus Christ, is the eternal Son of God and as such the eternal Object of the divine good pleasure. As the eternal Son of God He became man. The result is that in Him man has also become the object of the divine good pleasure, not by his own merit or deserving, but by the grace which assumed man to itself in the Son of God. In this One, the revelation of God

[345]

among men and the reconciliation of man with God has been fulfilled once [346] and for all. And He gives the Holy Ghost. It is because of all these things and by means of them that there is in this One a Church of God and children of God. They are what they are, and they have the true religion, because He stands in their place, and therefore for His sake. They cannot for a single moment think of leaving Him with the intention and purpose of trying to be what they are in themselves, or to have the true religion in themselves. When they do in fact leave Him—as they are always doing—the result is that they become uncertain of their existence as the Church and the children of God, and therefore of the truth of their religion. But there can be no alteration in the objective content, that they are what they are, and therefore bearers of the true religion, only in Him, in the name of Jesus Christ, i.e., in the revelation and reconciliation achieved in Jesus Christ. Nowhere else, but genuinely so in Him. Therefore by the grace of God there are men who live by His grace. Or, to put it concretely, through the name of Jesus Christ there are men who believe in this name. To the extent that this is self-evident in the case of Christians and the Christian religion, we can and must say of it that it and it alone is the true religion. On this particular basis we must now expound and explain this statement under four specific aspects.

1. In the relationship between the name of Jesus Christ and the Christian religion we have to do first with an act of divine creation. That means that its existence in historical form and individual determinations is not an autonomous or self-grounded existence. The name of Jesus Christ alone has created the Christian religion. Without Him it would never have been. And we must understand this not only in the historical but in the actual and contemporary sense. The name of Jesus Christ creates the Christian religion. Apart from Him it would not be. For if we would speak of the Christian religion as a reality, we cannot be content merely to look back at its creation and historical existence. We have to think of it in the same way as we think of our own existence and that of the world, as a reality which is to be and is created by Jesus Christ yesterday and to-day and tomorrow. Apart from the act of its creation by the name of Jesus Christ, which like creation generally is a *creatio continua*[EN167], and therefore apart from the Creator, it has no reality. If we would speak of the Christian religion apart from the name Jesus Christ, only two possibilities remain. The first is the general religious possibility. Now, of course, this is open to the so-called Christian as well as to other men. But as such it can be realised in other non-Christian religions as well as in the Christian. In fact, as a possibility which is general by nature, it can be clearly realised only in a known or unknown non-Christian religion. In any case it is only an empty possibility, and therefore not a reality. The second possibility is the swiftly crumbling ruin of a construct very like religion which was once called and perhaps even was Chris- [347] tianity. But now that the root of life has been cut off from it, it no longer has

---

EN167 continuous creation

149

the capacity for life of a non-Christian religion. It can only decay, being replaced by another religion which has at least the power to be. That the Christian religion could never have entered history and therefore never existed without the creative power of the name of Jesus Christ in the strictest sense, is something which we hardly need to demonstrate. Without that name the men of the time could have existed as the bearers of a general religious possibility under the specific conditions under which it was the possibility of those men. There would then have existed a fairly quiet religious Hellenism of Jewish and Oriental and Occidental provenance and colouring. But Christianity as a missionary and cultic and theological and political and moral force has existed from the outset only in an indissoluble relationship with the name of Jesus Christ. And from the history of the Church during the last centuries we can learn that the existence of the Christian religion is actually bound up with this name and with the act of divine creation and preservation to which it points. Eliminate this name and the religion is blunted and weakened. As a "Christianity without Christ" it can only vegetate. It has lost its only *raison d'être*EN168. Like other religions, for other reasons, it can look only for a speedy dissolution. If we try to look away from the name of Jesus Christ even momentarily, the Christian Church loses the substance in virtue of which it can assert itself in and against the state and society as an entity of a special order. Christian piety (no matter whether it vaunts itself as a piety of head or heart or action) loses the substance in virtue of which it can be something distinctive alongside morals, art and science. Christian theology loses the substance in virtue of which it is not philosophy, or philology, or historical science, but sacred learning. Christian worship loses the sacrificial and sacramental substance in virtue of which it is more than a solemn, half insolent and half superfluous pastime—its substance, and therefore its right to live, and at the same time its capacity to live. The Christian religion is the predicate to the subject of the name of Jesus Christ. Without Him it is not merely something different. It is nothing at all, a fact which cannot be hidden for long. It was and is and shall be only in virtue of the act of creation indicated by this name. And it is because of this act of creation that along with its existence it also receives its truth. Because it was and is and shall be through the name of Jesus Christ, it was and is and shall be the true religion: the knowledge of God, and the worship of God, and the service of God, in which man is not alone in defiance of God, but walks before God in peace with God.

But note this. Because this name describes no less than the creation and the Creator of the Christian religion, we cannot act as though it were at our disposal, adding it to our supposedly Christian doctrines as an expository or confirmatory addendum, or even as a critical proviso, conjuring with it in relation to our supposedly Christian enterprises as with a magic force, interposing it as the pretext and purpose of our supposedly Christian institutions, like a stained-glass window in an otherwise completed Church. The name of Jesus Christ is cer-

[348]

EN168 reason for existence

tainly no mere *nomen*[EN169] in the sense of the famous mediaeval controversy. It is the very essence and source of all reality. It stands in free creative power at the beginning of the Christian religion and its vital utterances. If not, then what we bring in at the end or climax is not in any sense the name of Jesus Christ. It is simply a hollow sound which cannot transform our human nothingness into divine fulness. There is fulness instead of nothingness only where the name of Jesus Christ as the Creator of our doctrine and enterprises and institutions is really the beginning of all things. To understand the theory of this, it is best to look at it this way. The Christian religion is simply the earthly-historical life of the Church and the children of God. As such we must think of it as an annexe to the human nature of Jesus Christ. And we must remember what we are told concerning His human nature in Jn. 1¹⁴. There never was a man Jesus as such apart from the eternal reality of the Son of God. Certainly in the fulness of human possibilities, along the line from Abraham to the Virgin Mary, there was the possibility which found its realisation in the man Jesus. But it did not find this realisation independently, but in virtue of the creative act in which the eternal Son of God assumed the human possibility into His reality, giving to it in that reality the reality which previously and *per se*[EN170] it did not possess, and which, when it acquires it, it does not possess apart from His reality. The human nature of Jesus Christ has no hypostasis of its own, we are told. It has it only in the Logos. The same is true, therefore, of the earthly-historical life of the Church and the children of God, and therefore of the Christian religion. It is the life of the earthly body of Christ and His members, who are called out of the schematic, bare possibility into the reality by the fact that He, the Head, has taken and gathered them to Himself as the earthly form of His heavenly body. Loosed from Him they could only fall back into the schematic possibility, i.e., into the non-being from which they proceeded. They live in Him, or they do not live at all. By living in Him they have a part in the eternal truth of His own life. But they have the choice only of a part in His life or of no life at all. But a part in the life of the Son of God, as the heavenly Head of this earthly body, is simply the name of Jesus Christ.

2. In the relationship between the name of Jesus Christ and the Christian religion we have to do with an act of the divine election. The Christian religion did not possess any reality of its own. Considered in and for itself it never can. It is a mere possibility among a host of others. It did not and does not bring anything of its own to the name of Jesus Christ which makes it in any way worthy to be His creation and as such the true religion. If it is real, it is so on the basis of free election, grounded in the compassion and inconceivable good pleasure of God and nothing else. In a secondary sense we can, of course, explain the necessity of the rise of Christianity in the light of Judaistic development and the political, spiritual and moral circumstances of the Mediterranean world in the Imperial period. But in its reality we can never explain or deduce it from that source. Historically, we cannot seriously explain and deduce it except from the history of the covenant made with Israel. And we cannot do that with any strictness or discernment except when we explain and deduce it from the fulfilment of that covenant in the name of Jesus Christ, from the revelation as it is actually made and acknowledged and believed, and

---

[EN169] name
[EN170] in itself

[349]   therefore on the presupposition of that name. That it pleased God at that time
and place and in that way to reveal Himself in the name of Jesus Christ, is
something which had its necessity in itself, and not in circumstances and conditions prior to that name. From that day to this it is election by the free grace
and compassion of God if in virtue of the name of Jesus Christ the Christian
religion is a reality and not nothingness. As there is a *creatio continua*EN171 so
also there is an *electio continua*EN172, better described, of course, as God's faithfulness and patience. The name of Jesus Christ is not something mechanical. It
is not under any external constraint. It is not bound to what seems to have, and
claims reality as Christianity, as Christian doctrine and conduct and institutions, as pursued by ostensibly Christian men or the ostensibly Christian por-
tions of humanity. Where it is bound, it has bound itself. And the fact that it
has done so is always grace and not human or Christian merit. Grace, and to
that extent election, i.e., free grace, is simply the faithfulness and patience of
God. It is election if the Church is not only a favourite religious society, and
there are others, but the body of Christ, if it not only has aspirations but inspir-
ations, if its relation to state and society is a relation of genuine antithesis and
therefore of genuine fellowship. The fact that it controls the Word and sacraments, and has Holy Scripture and the Creeds, does not in any way alter the
fact that it is all election, unmerited grace. It is election if its worship is not only
a remarkably mixed development of Jewish Synagogue worship and the later
mystery cults, but worship in the Spirit and in truth. No tradition, however
faithful, and no consciousness of immediacy, however vital, can ever prevent it
from being only the former. If it is otherwise, if the alleged spiritual element is
genuinely of the Spirit, then it is only by the Holy Spirit who breathes as He
will, it is only because of a free and merciful turning on the part of God, it is
only by election, and not by any immanent aptitude for genuine spirituality. It
is election if theology is not a science without an object, if it does not hear and
expound the Word of God only in appearance, if it labours to serve the purity
of ecclesiastical doctrine. There is no method, or enlistment, or alignment
which compels us to say that theology is in any way different from rabbinic
scholarship or Greek speculation. If it is different, if it is the real learning of
the Church, it is so at every point on the basis of election, and not otherwise.
We could say the same of Christian piety, Christian custom, Christian philan-
thropy, Christian education and Christian politics. We have to remember that
the important adjective "Christian"—with which we expressly name the name
of Jesus Christ—can never be a grasping at some possession of our own. It can
only be a reaching out for the divine possession included in this name. It can
only be an inquiry about election. It can only be a prayer that God will not turn
away His face from us, that He will not weary of His unmerited faithfulness and

---

EN171 continuous creation
EN172 continuous election

patience. Where the adjective really means anything, election has already [350] taken place. And it is election, and only election, which makes the Christian religion the true religion. For there need be no fear that the thought of the decisive grace of God, which is not bound to any human or even Christian possession, will mean a weakening of the Christian certainty of truth. On the contrary, the thought may have a shattering effect upon all our self-confidence in regard to truth, and indeed it must. But it opens our eyes to the basis of real certainty. For the Christian religion is true, because it has pleased God, who alone can be the judge in this matter, to affirm it to be the true religion. What is truth, if it is not this divine affirmation? And what is the certainty of truth, if not the certainty which is based solely upon this judgment, a judgment which is free, but wise and righteous in its freedom, because it is the freedom of God?

From the standpoint of election, too, all the stress must be laid on the fact that the relation between the name of Jesus Christ and the Christian religion cannot be reversed. We remember Luther's translation of Ps. 100³: "Know that the Lord is God. He hath made us—and not we ourselves—to be his people and the sheep of his pasture." And Jn. 15¹⁶: "Ye did not choose me, but I chose you, and appointed you to go and bring fruit, and that your fruit should abide." Both these "sayings" are particularly directed to the religious community of the religion of revelation as such. For the Church and for the children of God there is a recurrent temptation to regard themselves as those who elect in this matter. It is their faith and their love, their confession, tradition and hope which is its proper substance. Its grounding in the name of Christ Jesus can then appear as a free concession. We may perhaps decide upon it very seriously, but by thinking that it is something which we ourselves can and should decide, we show that we no longer realise with what name we have to do. It is in this role of an elected and continually re-elected, but ultimately only an elected King, that the name of Jesus Christ occurs in almost all the theology and piety and Church life of the 18th to 20th centuries. In these centuries the Christian religion quite openly thought that it could live on its own substance, i.e., on Christian experience and morality and universal order as such. As a rule, this did not, of course, mean that the name of Jesus Christ was dispensed with, or that it was refused the necessary love and worship. The *beneficia Christi*ᴱᴺ¹⁷³ were thought to be seen in the substance of the Christian religion. Even within liberal, let alone conservative Protestantism, the individual radicals of the period, like Reimarus in the 18th, D. F. Strauss in the 19th and A. Drews in the 20th centuries, were like unwelcome brawlers in a passionately pious community. And it was as such that they were everywhere treated. But the mixture of pity and anger and obvious anxiety with which it was done was suspicious. So, too, was the pious and learned apologetic zeal, which all parties and not least the Liberals displayed, on one pretext or another to safeguard, or to restore and re-establish to the name of Jesus Christ, in opposition to the radicals, the traditional place of honour at the centre of everything. If it had actually enjoyed or regained that place, we might have been spared the trouble. Luther and Calvin did not need to aim at a "christocentric" theology, like Schleiermacher and later A. Ritschl and his pupils, because their theology was christocentric from the very outset, and without the singular attempt to make or call it so. It did not need to become christocentric. And how can theology or piety or Church life become christocentric, if it is not so at the very outset? The strainings and the unhealthy zeal and historical and systematic devices by which the moderns have tried to become christocentric bear clear and

---

ᴱᴺ¹⁷³ the benefits of Christ

[351]   eloquent testimony that they were not christocentric at the outset and therefore cannot be.
In a word, they bear testimony that, like the radicals, they believe that this is something
which we can choose for ourselves, though the actual choice is different. The belief that the
name Jesus Christ is something we can choose is the radically unauthentic element in the
Jesus-cult of Pietism and the revival movements of the period. It may well be said that the
positive concern of the period for the name of Jesus Christ is the clearest indication of the
basic rebellion of the Church of the time. For it was rebellion, if only pious rebellion, when it
was thought that we can affirm the name of Jesus Christ and therefore can and ought to
choose it from the secure haven of a religion which satisfies us in any case: when there was
the possibility of entering into a discussion of the matter. It was, of course, no accident when
in its concern with Jesus Christ—obviously for apologetic reasons—the theology of the
period made an abstract, human and historical life of Jesus Christ the particular object of its
endeavours. Here again that other aspect, which was so obvious to the Christology of the
early Church, was forgotten: that the human nature of Christ to which such an ingenuous
appeal was now made was not an independent reality, but even as a possibility, realised in the
eternal Son of God, it was the object of an externally unmerited and unpredictable election.
In a strange forgetfulness of what the New Testament itself clearly states, the piety or moralism or even demonism of Jesus of Nazareth was regarded as the element which can always be
acknowledged and presupposed, whereas His so-called "Messianic consciousness" gave rise
to a problem, and could be affirmed only after considerable thought, and with great reserve
and tentativeness. It escaped notice that in dealing with Christology in this way the theologians of the period merely revealed themselves in their own embarrassment: the great
certainty with which they claimed to be Christians, and in possession of Christian experiences and thoughts, and representatives of the Christian attitude, and the great uncertainty
with which they finally decided the question whether or not the name of Jesus Christ is
necessary. The very emphasis, the fact that no question is seen in relation to the one but a
real question in relation to the other, the naivete with which their own Christlikeness is
affirmed as compared with the hesitance of the final affirmation of Jesus Christ: all this
meant that directly as well as indirectly everything was lost and the confession of the name of
Jesus Christ was already abandoned. And it was tragic how the scientific seriousness, and
sincerity and profundity, and the deep and genuine piety, which were undoubtedly applied
to this hesitant affirmation, could only make the harm more apparent. Again, therefore, it is
not an accident if the psychology particularly of the theologians and churchmen of the
period (and especially about the turn of the 19th century) has for the most part been one of
a pronounced lack of humour, of weariness and depression, even of melancholia. Could it
be otherwise when for all the subjective solidity of the effort they were fighting for a kind of
lost cause? It might, of course, be objected: Is not the confession of the name of Jesus Christ
a free human decision and therefore a choice of this name? Of course it is: that is the
unequivocal teaching of Mt. 16[13f.], Jn. 6[67f.] We might also recall Josh. 24[15f.]: "And if it seem
evil unto you to serve the Lord, choose ye this day whom ye will serve; whether the gods
which your fathers served that were beyond the River, or the gods of the Amorites, in whose
land ye dwell: but as for me and my house, we will serve the Lord." But there is, of course, a
considerable difference between "choosing" amongst the Mesopotamian and Canaanite
gods, which is always possible for the people, and the being chosen by Yahweh, which Joshua
already has behind him. In fact there is no doubt that an election does take place: but it is an
election upon which, just because it is our own election, we can only look back as upon
something which has taken place already. In the act of electing we are not confronted by two
or three possibilities, between which we can choose. We choose the only possibility which is
[352]   given to us: "Lord, whither should we go?" Those who confess and therefore choose the
name of Jesus Christ choose the only possibility which is given to them, the possibility which

is given to them by Jesus Christ: "Thou hast the words of eternal life." They elect, but they elect their own election. There can be no question of a substance of the Christian religion which is their own, which antedates their electing and can play a part as a motive or criterion for electing the name of Jesus Christ. On the contrary, its decision has no independent validity. It is simply the recognition of a decision already made regarding them: and it is in the decision already made that they will alone find the substance of their more or less estimable religion. Their own decision, the decision of obedience to the decision made in the freedom of God, is what Scripture describes as the decision of faith and especially of faith in the name of Jesus Christ. The Reformers and the older Protestantism knew well enough what they were doing when with one breath they challenged man to this decision and to that extent undoubtedly appealed to his freedom, and then immediately (with greater or lesser emphasis) described predestination, i.e., the choice in the eternal decree of God, the election effected and perceived in Christ, as the proper object and content of the decision of faith. It is only in the decision of faith as ordered and understood in this way that we really have to do with the name of Jesus Christ. Ordered and understood in any other way, it may seem to be the name of Jesus Christ. It may be supposed to be that name. But in fact it is only a *nomen*[EN174], and as such it has no power and therefore it can never be affirmed with any power. The power of affirming the name of Jesus Christ is either its own power or it is impotence. And it is only in the decision of faith as ordered and understood in this way that the truth can emerge and become certainty. The truth illumines and convinces and asserts itself in the fulfilment of the choice whose freedom and power is only that of the name of Jesus Christ Himself. As such it becomes, it makes itself, the truth of the Christian religion, whereas in the alleged possession of an abstract Christianity we always look in vain for the truth of the name of Jesus Christ and therefore strive in vain for certainty of the truth of the Christian religion.

3. In the relationship between the name Jesus Christ and the Christian religion we have to do with an act of divine justification or forgiveness of sins. We already stated that the Christian religion as such has no worthiness of its own, to equip it specially to be the true religion. We must now aver even more clearly that in itself and as such it is absolutely unworthy to be the true religion. If it is so, it is so by election, we said. And now we must be more precise: it is so in virtue of the divine justification of sinners, of the divine forgiveness of sins. The structure of this religion (most acutely in its Protestant form) is certainly quite different from that of others. And this, too, we can understand and assess only as the work of the name of Jesus Christ. But it is not so decidedly different from others that in respect of it we can evade the judgment of the divine revelation that all religion is idolatry and self-righteousness. On the contrary, history in the Christian sense, whether the history of the Church as a whole or the life-story of the individual child of God in particular, stands always under this sign. The more closely we study it, or rather, the more clearly the light of revelation from Holy Scripture falls upon it, the more evident this is. Both as a whole and in particular it is a sinful story. It is not justified in itself. It is sinful both in form and also in its human origin. It is no less so than can be said of the story of Buddhism or of Islam. The hands into which God has delivered Himself in His revelation are thoroughly unclean. In fact, they are seriously [353]

[EN174] name

unclean. If our knowledge of the truth of the Christian religion were determined by the life of an immanent purity of the Church of God as its *locus*[EN175], or of the children of God as its vehicles, it would have been permanently concealed. Both are clean (even in their uncleanness) for the sake of the Word which is spoken to them. Otherwise it would be all up with our knowledge of the truth of the Christian religion. For we should be looking at the redeemedness of the redeemed. Or what is worse, we should be looking at our own redeemedness. We should not hear the Word by which the Church and the children of God are clean in their uncleanness and in all their unredeemedness redeemed. We should feel that the creation and election of this particular religion to be the true religion, even if it could be supported by many arguments, would ultimately be only a matter of arbitrary assertion, not borne out by the facts.

There is, of course, one fact which powerfully and decisively confirms the assertion, depriving it of its arbitrary character and giving to it a necessity which is absolute. But to discern this fact, our first task—and again and again we shall have to return to this "first"—must be to ignore the whole realm of "facts" which we and other human observers as such can discern and assess. For the fact about which we are speaking stands in the same relationship to this realm as does the sun to the earth. That the sun lights up this part of the earth and not that means for the earth no less than this, that day rules in the one part and night in the other. Yet the earth is the same in both places. In neither place is there anything in the earth itself to dispose it for the day. Apart from the sun it would everywhere be enwrapped in eternal night. The fact that it is partly in the day does not derive in any sense from the nature of the particular part as such. Now it is in exactly the same way that the light of the righteousness and judgment of God falls upon the world of man's religion, upon one part of that world, upon the Christian religion, so that that religion is not in the night but in the day, it is not perverted but straight, it is not false religion but true. Taken by itself, it is still human religion and therefore unbelief, like all other religions. Neither in the root nor in the crown of this particular tree, neither at the source nor at the outflow of this particular stream, neither on the surface nor in the depth of this particular part of humanity can we point to anything that makes it suitable for the day of divine righteousness and judgment. If the Christian religion is the right and true religion, the reason for it does not reside in facts which might point to itself or its own adherents, but in the fact which as the righteousness and the judgment of God confronts it as it does all other religions, characterising and differenti- [354] ating it and not one of the others as the right and true religion. We must observe that it is not a whim or caprice which is this confronting and decisive fact but the righteousness and the judgment of God. What takes place at this point is already perfectly in order, because however surprising it may be from

---

[EN175] place

our standpoint it is God's order which is manifested and operative. We are, of course, confronted by an acquittal which is utterly inconceivable from our standpoint. But the acquittal is a judgment. And although we have no insight into its motives, it is a righteous judgment. Therefore we cannot say that on the basis of that fact of God some other religion might have become the right and true religion. We perceive and acknowledge the judgment pronounced in this fact of God. And in doing so we have to accept it as it stands. We cannot juggle with the possibility that it might have been different. And we should again forfeit the absoluteness of the perception if we did not let it stand as wholly and utterly a perception of the divine judgment and therefore of the fact of God, if instead we tried to squint past the fact of God and to find certain conditioning factors of the judgment in the nature of the Christian religion as such. If we look at the Christian religion in itself and as such, we can only say that apart from the clear testimony of the fact of God some other religion might equally well be the right and true one. But once the fact of God is there and its judgment passed, we cannot look at the Christian religion in itself and as such. And it is only secondarily that we come to those thoughts of equality. They express the fact that in face of the righteous acquittal pronounced on the Christian religion in this judgment we have no merits or deservings of our own, to which we might point in confirmation. As we receive and accept it, we can cling only to the sentence itself, or the divine fact which proclaims it, and not to any glorious facts from the sphere of the Christian religion as such. The justification of the Christian religion is a righteous acquittal. It rests entirely on the righteousness of God. It is not in any way conditioned by the qualities of the Christian religion. It cannot, therefore, be understood in any way except as an act of forgiveness of sin. In that it is justified by that fact of God, its various qualities, far from being adduced as the basis of its justification, are not even considered or taken into account, but covered up. Of course they have to be covered up, and they cannot be considered or taken into account, if there is to be an acquittal. For the sum total of the qualities of even the Christian religion is simply this, that it is idolatry and self-righteousness, unbelief, and therefore sin. It must be forgiven if it is to be justified. And we can understand and receive its justification only if we understand and receive it as sheer forgiveness. If we understood or received it in any other way, we should again be by-passing the actual fact of God, by which the Christian religion is justified. We should again be missing the absoluteness of the knowledge of its truth. It is only as forgiveness that the truth adopts the Christian religion. It is only as [355] forgiveness that it can be known as a definition which in the last resort is inalienably peculiar to the Christian religion.

We ask: How is this justification in the form of forgiveness an act of the righteousness and judgment of God? On the basis of what right does God forgive, and forgive at this and not at some other point? And in answer to this question we have not only to point to the freedom and inscrutability of the divine judgment. We have also to bear in mind that this freedom and inscrutability is identical with the revealed fact of the name of Jesus Christ. It is quite in order to find forgiveness at this point and not at any other. It takes place according to the ordering of this act of God, that is, the name of Jesus Christ. It is this name which stands in relation to the world of religions, as does the sun to the earth. But it denotes a definite event, in which the world of religions acquires a definite part. For it denotes the unification of the eternal divine Word with the nature of man, and therefore with the rectification of that human nature, notwithstanding and in spite of its natural perversion, to humility and obedience to God. This rectification of human nature is the work of Jesus Christ from birth to death, and it is revealed to be such in His resurrection from the dead. But to the human nature readjusted in Jesus Christ there belongs the capacity from which, because of that nature, only religion as unbelief can and does proceed. In the human nature of Jesus Christ, instead of resisting God in idolatry and self-righteousness, man offers the obedience of faith. In that way he satisfies the righteousness and judgment of God. Therefore he really merits his acquittal, and therefore the acquittal, the justification of his religion. In the Christian religion it is a matter of the earthly life of the Church and the children of God. It is a matter of the life of the earthly body of which Jesus Christ is the Head; i.e., of the life of those whom He has brought into fellowship with His human nature and therefore to a participation in the acquittal which He has rightly and righteously merited. Christian religion is faith in the discipleship of the justifying faith of Jesus Christ which no man can imitate. If this is the case, then as a human faith it needs the divine forgiveness just as much as the faith of other religions. But it does actually receive and enjoy this forgiveness. And the forgiveness which it receives and enjoys is not a matter of whim or caprice. It is a strict and righteous award. In the first instance, of course, it is made only to Jesus Christ, the only man who has maintained and demonstrated the obedience of faith. But for the sake of Jesus Christ, i.e., for the sake of the fellowship and participation guaranteed to men by Jesus Christ, for the sake of the solidarity of our humanity with His bestowed by Him, for the sake of the faith in Him of discipleship, those whom He calls His brethren, and who in that faith in Him recognise and honour their first-born brother, are also (with their religion) the objects of that righteous award [356] of God. For them—as distinct from Him—this acquittal is a free and inconceivable forgiveness, a forgiveness which they did not merit, a forgiveness on the ground of His merit, yet a forgiveness with all the seriousness and emphasis of a valid award, a forgiveness which cannot be disputed or overturned. And in the same unconditional way it is a forgiveness even of their religion, of which, regarded in itself and as such, they would have to admit that it is unbelief, like the faith of other religions. The one decisive question which confronts the Christian religion, or its adherents and representatives, in respect of its truth, is this: who and what are they in their naked reality, as they stand before the all-piercing eye of God? Are they really His Church, His children, and therefore the adopted brethren of His eternal Son? If they are not, if their Christian religion is just a mask, then even if it is the most perfect and logical form of Christianity it is unbelief like all other heathen religions. It is falsehood and wrong and an abomination before God. But if they are, if they live by the grace of God, if they participate in the human nature of His eternal Son, if they are nourished by His body and His blood as earthly members of His earthly body in communion with Him as their heavenly Head: then for the sake of this fellowship their sins are forgiven, even the sin of their religion is rightly pardoned. Their Christian religion is the justified religion and therefore the right and true religion. Beyond all dialectic and to the exclusion of all discussion the divine fact of the name of Jesus Christ confirms what no other fact does or can confirm: the creation and election of this religion to be the one and only true religion. Of course, the one decisive question can never be spared the Christian religion and its adherents and representatives. It can never become irrelevant. It can never be regarded as settled. Whenever Christianity confronts other religions, or a Christian the adherent of another religion, this question stands over them like a sword. From that standpoint we can and must say that, in the world of religions, the Christian religion is in a position of greater danger and defencelessness and impotence than any other religion. It has its justification either in the name of Jesus Christ, or not at all. And this justification must be achieved in the actuality of life, of the Church and the children of God. But the achieving of this life is grace, the grace of the Word, which begets faith, and the Church and children of the Word, according to its free and inconceivable compassion. The possibility of a negative answer to that question is the abyss on the fringe of which the truth of the Christian religion is decided. A positive decision means a positive answer to the question. It means that the Christian religion is snatched from the world of religions and the judgment and sentence pronounced upon it, like a brand from the burning. It is not that some men are vindicated as opposed to others, or one part of humanity as opposed to other parts of the same humanity. It is that God Himself is vindicated as opposed to and on behalf of all men and all humanity. That [357] it can receive and accept this is the advantage and pre-eminence of Christianity, and the light and glory in which its religion stands. And as it does not have this light and glory of itself, no one can take it away from it. And it alone has the commission and the authority to be a missionary religion, i.e., to confront the world of religions as the one true religion, with absolute self-confidence to invite and challenge it to abandon its ways and to start on the Christian way.

The Christian religion will always be vital and healthy and strong as long as it has this self-confidence. But it will have this self-confidence only as its adherents and proclaimers can look away from themselves to the fact of God which alone can justify them. In so far as they still rely on other facts, this self-confidence will inevitably receive one inward blow after another and in the long run completely disappear. It makes no odds whether these other facts consist in ecclesiastical institutions, theological systems, inner experiences, the moral transformations of individual believers or the wider effects of Christianity upon the world at large. To glance aside at such facts will always and very quickly mean uncertainty regarding the truth of the Christian religion. For all these things may quite well be facts; but together and in detail they are facts which themselves need justification and therefore cannot be claimed as the basis of it. If the Christian or Christians who ask concerning the truth of their religion are wrapped up in themselves and their Christianity, forgetting that in this matter they have to do first with forgiven sin, then let them see to it how long they can protect themselves from the scepticism in this question which so irresistibly wells up in them. And if they can, if they are able to assign to these facts a credibility which in this field they cannot possibly have, that will be all the worse for them and the Christian religion than any open outbreak and admission of doubt. And again, those who believe in their Church and theology, or in changed men and improved circumstances, are on exactly the same road, the road to uncertainty. This is betrayed by the fact that all of them, incidentally but quite openly, and with the unteachable ferocity of a secret despair of faith, have to take refuge in reason or culture or humanity or race, in order to find some support or other for the Christian religion. But the Christian religion cannot be supported from without, if it can no longer stand alone. If it does stand alone it does not allow itself to be supported from without. Standing alone, it stands upon the fact of God which justifies it, and upon that alone. There is therefore no place for attempts to support it in any other way. Such attempts are a waste of time and energy. In fact, they are a renewal of the unbelief which is not unnoticed or unassessed by God, but covered up and forgiven. But such attempts are bound to be made if once we glance aside at other facts side by side with the one justifying divine fact. In that case unbelief has already returned. It already has the decisive word. And it will see in such attempts, not a waste of time and energy, but an urgent necessity. The secularisation of Christianity is then in full train, and no subjective piety will avail to halt it. And the result will be a loss of all outward health and strength and vitality.

4. In the relationship between the name of Jesus Christ and the Christian religion, we have to do with an act of divine sanctification. We said that to find the basis of the assertion of the truth of Christianity we must first look away from it to the fact of God which is its basis, and that we have constantly to return to this "first." When we ask concerning this truth, we can never look [358] even incidentally to anything but this fact of God. We cannot try to find the justification of the Christian religion apart from the name of Jesus Christ in other facts, not even in the inward or outward state of justification of the Christian religion. Yet this justification of the Christian religion only by the name of Jesus Christ obviously involves a certain positive relation between the two. Christianity is differentiated from other religions by that name. It is formed and shaped by it. It is claimed for His service. It becomes the historical manifestation and means of its revelation. We have compared the name of Jesus Christ with the sun in its relation to the earth. That must be an end of the matter. But the sun shines. And its light is not remote from the earth and alien to it. Without ceasing to be the light of the sun, it becomes the light of the earth, the light which illuminates the earth. In that light the earth which has no light of its own is bright. It is not, of course, a second sun. But it carries the reflection of the sun's light. It is, therefore, an illuminated earth. It is the same with the name of Jesus Christ in relation to the Christian religion. That name alone is its justification. But it cannot be transcendent without being imma-

nent in it. For it is only the Christian religion which is justified by it. And that means that it is differentiated and marked off and stamped and characterised by it in a way peculiar to itself. In the light of its justification and creation and election by the name of Jesus Christ, the fact that it is the Christian religion and not another cannot possibly be neutral or indifferent or without significance. On the contrary, even though Christianity is a religion like others, it is significant and eloquent, a sign, a proclamation. There is an event on God's side—which is the side of the incarnate Word of God—God adopting man and giving Himself to him. And corresponding to it there is a very definite event on man's side. This event is determined by the Word of God. It has its being and form in the world of human religion. But it is different from everything else in this sphere and having this form. The correspondence of the two events is the relationship between the name Jesus Christ and the Christian religion from the standpoint of its sanctification. It is not by the laws and forces of human religion and therefore of man, but in virtue of the divine foundation and institution, that this particular being and form are an event in the world of human religion. What becomes an event is unjustified in itself. It has no autonomous role or significance. It has simply to serve the name of Jesus Christ which alone justifies it. It can never—even incidentally—replace and suppress this name by its own substance. It can only attest it. It can only kindle and maintain the recollection and expectation of it. It can never claim to be itself the fact of God denoted by this name. It can only try to be its exhortatory and consoling sign. It can have a part in the truth only as it points to it and proclaims it. And in this pointing and proclaiming it can never have or claim any power or authority of its own. It will speak or be silent, work or rest, be known or not known, in virtue [359] of the power and authority of the name of Jesus, effectual in the outpouring of the Holy Spirit. That name alone is the power and mystery of the declaration which is the meaning of this particular being and form. That name alone expresses this being and form as the being and form of true religion. It is not justified because it is holy in itself—which it is not. It is made holy because it is justified. And it is not true because it is holy in itself—which it never was and never will be. But it is made holy in order to show that it is the true religion. At this point we link up with what we earlier described as the twofold subjective reality of revelation, which is the counterpart in our realm of the objective revelation in Jesus Christ. The Christian religion is the sacramental area created by the Holy Spirit, in which the God whose Word became flesh continues to speak through the sign of His revelation. And it is also the existence of men created by the same Holy Spirit, who hear this God continually speaking in His revelation. The Church and the children of God do actually exist. The actuality of their existence is quite unassuming, but it is always visible and in its visibility it is significant. It is an actuality which is called and dedicated to the declaration of the name of Jesus Christ. And that is the sanctification of the Christian religion.

§ 17. *The Revelation of God as the Abolition of Religion*

The covenant of God founded on grace and election acquired at once even with the people of Israel the evidence of a visible form, a seal which could be perceived by both the obedient and the disobedient, by both Israel itself and the heathen nations round about. It did so with the establishment of the Law. The whole aim and purpose of the Law was that it should be the sign of Yahweh's grace and election. But as the sign of Yahweh's grace and election, as the evidence of the covenant, the Law had to be observed and kept and sought out day and night. The founding of the covenant did not take place with the establishment of the Law, let alone with Israel's observing and keeping and searching of it. It took place prior to the Law with the reiterated calling of Abraham, Isaac and Jacob, and the sending of Moses, and the liberation of Israel out of Egypt. But because it took place as the basis of the covenant of God with this people, which had a human and historical existence like all other nations, it did not take place without the establishing of the Law. without claiming this people for obedience to the Law, without the promise of cursing and blessing attached to the observance or non-observance of it. The acceptance and observance of the Law was a recurrent guarantee that this people was the people of the covenant. The gift of the Law was the sanctification of this people, in answer to the grace of Yahweh, the necessary consequence of the revelation of grace, the inevitable historical form which could not be separated from it. And sanctification meant its separation and differentiation and characterisation as this people. How could it exist both as a human and historical nation and also as the people of Yahweh without undergoing a visible separation, differentiation and characterisation as this people? And how could it experience and adopt the grace which encounters it with its existence as this people, without being continually reminded of this visible separation, differentiation and characterisation, and constantly acknowledging it? Clearly the observance of the Law can only be a sign and testimony. It is only relative to the thankfulness for the promise, I am the Lord thy God, which can never be exhausted even by the strictest observance of any one of the commandments. But it is obviously a necessary sign and testimony. Its absence casts doubt both upon their thankfulness and even their existence as this people, automatically transforming the promise into a threat.

[360]

It is of a piece that in the New Testament we not only have the reconciliation of the world to God in Jesus Christ, but also, as a consequence and necessary adjunct, a "ministry of reconciliation," the establishing of a "word of reconciliation," a human request instituted in and with the reconciliation accomplished by God in Jesus Christ: "Be ye reconciled to God" (2 Cor. 5$^{18f.}$). It is a ministry "even as we have received mercy" (2 Cor. 4^{1}), a "ministration of the Spirit" (2 Cor. 3^{8}), a "ministration of righteousness" (2 Cor. 3^{9}). It consists in this, and only in this, that men may "reflect" the glory of the Lord "with unveiled faces" (2 Cor. 3^{18}; cf. 1 Cor. 13^{12}). Furthermore: "We preach not ourselves but Christ Jesus as the Lord" (2 Cor. 4^{5}). It is, therefore, a strictly subordinate and relative event, tied absolutely by the divine act of justification and the divine creation and election upon which it rests, absolutely dependent upon it. Where is the reflection which can last even for a moment without the object reflected? Where is the reflected light of the earth without the sun which illuminates it? Yet although tied and dependent in this way, the event which occurs in this "ministry of reconciliation" is a very real and necessary one. And the ministry must be executed without "fainting" (2 Cor. 4^{1}, 4^{16}) and in "joyfulness" (2 Cor. 3^{12}). Replacing the Old Testament Law, it is the sanctification of the congregation formed by the divine revelation and reconciliation. As the whole problem is presented to us in Paul's description of the sanctification of the apostolic office in the New Testament, it is the sanctification of the Christian religion which is accomplished once and for all in the name of Jesus Christ, but has to be continually reacknowledged and reaffirmed in obedience. It is because of this that we have to take seriously the fact that the Christian religion has a concrete historical nature and a concrete historical form: the distinction of that nature and form from those of other religions, the problems which arise concerning them, the possibility and danger of erring in respect of them and the need to make constant decision in relation to them. The name of Jesus Christ is not only the justification but also the sanctification of the Christian religion. But for that very reason these things have to be taken just as seriously as Israel had to take the Law, if it was to remain the people of the covenant. They have to be taken seriously in faith and obedience to the justifying name of Jesus Christ and therefore in the inescapable light of the question of truth which continually raises itself and demands an answer. The name of Jesus Christ justifies the Christian religion, without it being able to make even the slightest contribution to its justification as a human religion. This name is the authority and power which moves and transforms it in all its human sinfulness, continually erecting and maintaining a sign in this sphere, and seeing to it that it is observed. It is the authority and power which by this sign, by the sign of the Church and of the existence of the children of God assembled in the Church, continually exhorts and consoles this religion throughout its history, being revealed not only in the past, but by means of this sign in the present and future. It is perfectly true that Christians are sinners and that the Church is a Church of sinners. But if they are justified sinners—as Christians are—then in virtue of the same Word and Spirit which justifies them, they are also sanctified sinners. That is, they are placed under discipline. They are put under the order of revelation. They are no longer free in all their sinfulness. They remember the Lord who justifies them and they are bound to wait upon Him. To that extent, although they are still sinners, they are ready for Him and at His disposal. Both in general and in particular, Christianity as a historical form is readiness for the Lord, by whose name those who profess this religion, and with them the religion itself, are created and elected and justified. That is why the problems of the nature and form of this religion are serious problems: the question of canon and dogma, the question of creed, cultus and Church order, the question of correct theology and piety and ethics. They are not serious problems in the sense [361] that to win through to certain answers would enable Christianity to justify itself as the true religion. But they are serious problems in the sense that by the answers made to them it is decided whether Christianity is here and now ready for the Lord who justified it long ago, whether it really is justified and therefore the true religion, whether it does still participate in the promise which was made long ago and does not depend upon its merit or co-operation for validity. It is not a question of acquiring and maintaining an advantage when Christians and Christianity seek the truth concerning the visible nature and form of their religion, suffer and fight for the truth when it is known. The fact remains that the highest results of their seeking, suffering and fighting do not give them any advantage. It all amounts to this, that as they have to keep on breathing for animal life, so they have continually to struggle for their existence as Christians and Christianity, to be those who already have the advantage of knowing the name of Jesus Christ, and of being named after Him. It is a matter of the exercising and repeating of their existence as the Church and the children of God. They would not be what they are from eternity to eternity, if they were not so in time. They would not be what they are invisibly, if they were not so visibly and therefore, in this exercise and repetition. But the sanctification, to which they are subject in this exercise and repetition, is quite beyond their own striving and its successes and failures. No less than their justification, it is the work of Him for whose sake they are called Christians and Christianity.

§ 18

THE LIFE OF THE CHILDREN OF GOD

Where it is believed and acknowledged in the Holy Spirit, the revelation of God creates men who do not exist without seeking God in Jesus Christ, and who cannot cease to testify that He has found them.

1. MAN AS A DOER OF THE WORD

We have come a long way. We asked concerning the Word of God in its original form, and therefore concerning the revelation which is the object of the testimony of Holy Scripture, the source and norm of the proclamation of the Christian Church. Three answers were given, each of them complete in its own way. The first had special reference to the subject presupposed in the concept of revelation; the doctrine of God in His unity and trinity as Father, Son and Holy Spirit. The second had special reference to the event indicated in the concept; the doctrine of the incarnation of the Word of God in Jesus Christ. The third had special reference to the effect and goal of this event; the doctrine of the outpouring of the Holy Spirit. But there is still a gap in the last circle. We began both the christological and the pneumatological sections of our doctrine of revelation with a presentation first of the reality, then of the possibility of revelation, both on its objective side, as it derives from God, and also on its subjective side, as it comes to man. To put it in another way, we began with an exposition of faith, then of the related understanding, in regard to the freedom which God has for us and the freedom which we have for God, in regard to Jesus Christ and the Holy Spirit. There then followed an investigation of the concept of time in the christological section, and a corresponding investigation of the concept of religion in the pneumatological, which we have just concluded. But the christological section closed with a positive description of the real mystery of the person of Jesus Christ as the divine-human Reconciler, and of the miracle to which this mystery points. A corresponding discussion has still to be added to the pneumatological section. And since the section as a whole is concerned with revelation in its manward aspect, it is obvious that the object of this final discussion can only be man himself as the recipient of revelation, i.e., believing and perceiving man. In the true manhood of the Son of God, all those who believe in Him are taken up into unity with Him and into the unity of His body on earth. They become partakers by grace of the divine sonship which is proper to Him by nature. That is the full meaning and content of the revelation made in Jesus Christ as the Word of God by the Holy Spirit.

What has preceded will be a sharp warning that there is still no room for lyricism. We must not let ourselves be involved in a discussion of the Christian man abstracted from divine revelation instead of revelation itself, with a direct vision as the way and condition of knowledge instead of faith instructed by Holy Scripture. If we follow Scripture, there is no psychology of the Reconciler, but the strict doctrine of His true Godhead and humanity. Similarly there is no psychology of the reconciled. In both cases the only possible object of direct vision or psychology is the "flesh," of which we are told in Jn. 6^{63} that it profiteth nothing. Again, in Christology we had to hold to the Word that is made flesh. Similarly, if we are not to be betrayed into irrelevant prattling, we must now hold to the Spirit, who is involved in the redemptive conflict with our flesh. At this point we are specifically warned by the last section, in which it became evident that revelation is the removal of all religion, including the Christian. Christianity is the true religion only in virtue of the name of Jesus Christ, in the act and hiddenness of the divine grace, by dint of the divine creation, election, justification and sanctification. It is not the true religion in itself, or in such a way that the Christian is as such the master of truth. If we ignore this warning, if we insist upon the postulate of the Christian as such, apart from the Word and the Spirit and faith, we have to ask ourselves whether by allowing the Christian as such to assume such an unnecessary importance we are not risking something of vital importance: for the Christian abstractly considered is no longer a sinner, at any rate in any actual or serious sense. He is considered and explained only in his antithesis as a sanctified sinner. But the actual revelation which we receive in Jesus Christ by the Holy Spirit never ceases to tell us that we are sinners, in the strictest and most serious sense. It is only in and with this judgment upon us, not in ourselves but in Jesus Christ, that we are reconciled with God and therefore sanctified. Actual revelation does not know man in a partly achieved state of sanctification beyond the act of divine grace, but only as the object of this particular act, and therefore not in a peace or truce between the spirit and flesh, in which he can, as it were, be photographed psychologically, but only in the midst of the conflict which at no point reflects the predetermined issue to which it moves. If, then, we try to deal with the Christian *in abstracto*[EN1], or even think that we can, we must ask ourselves whether we have not lost sight completely of actual revelation, and whether in these circumstances we can catch any real glimpse of the Christian. For where else can he be seen except in the light of revelation?

But bearing in mind this limitation of our theme, which is the limitation of all theological discussion, we are forced to concede that man as he receives [364] and believes and confesses revelation does constitute a problem which has to

---

[EN1] in the abstract

be dealt with if our doctrine of the outpouring of the Holy Spirit, and therefore of revelation and the Word of God generally, is not to be incomplete at a critical point. According to Holy Scripture, revelation is the incarnation of the eternal Word and the outpouring of the Holy Spirit upon flesh. But if this is the case, then we must heavily underline the fact that it would not be revelation if man were to remain outside the closed circle of it, if the circle of his own existence were not intersected by this circle of revelation. The Christian *in abstracto*EN2 we must avoid—the Christian *in concreto*EN3 we cannot avoid. It is to him that the Word of God is directed and the gift of the Holy Spirit is made, and upon him that the light of revelation falls. We cannot see this light, which is, of course, always and exclusively the light of God, without seeing this man as well. But when we see man, we do not see any kind of being. Whatever it may or may not signify in detail or in a more general context, we see the being which is constantly realising its existence in acts of free determination and decision. And we the observers are ourselves the primary evidence.

To use the older terminology, we see a *creatura rationalis*EN4, a thinking, willing, feeling creature, a spiritual being which, with the angels, so far as we can gather, is unique of its land. The well-known passage in the Formula of Concord (*Sol. decl.* II, 19) does not say that man is a *lapis et truncus*EN5, but that Holy Scripture compares his heart with a *duro lapidi, qui ad tactum non cedat, sed resistat, item rudi trunco, interdum etiam ferae indomitae*EN6. The passage then continues: *non quod homo post lapsum non amplius sit rationalis creatura, aut absque auditu et meditatione verbi divini ad Deum convertatur; out quod in rebus externis et civilibus nihil boni aut mali intelligere possit, aut libere aliquod agere vel omittere queat*EN7. In every respect but one, man is "witty, intelligent and accomplished." But in *spiritualibus et divinis rebus*EN8 he is *similis* (!) *trunco et lapidi ac statuae vita carenti, quae neque oculorum oris aut ullorum sensuum cordisve usum habet*EN9. For he cannot see the wrath of God against his sin; he cannot see that he is threatened by death and hell; he will not receive either exhortation or instruction: *antequam per Spiritum sanctum illuminatur, convertitur et regeneratur*EN10 (20–21). As is said later, without the Holy Spirit he is actually worse than a stock, *quia voluntati divinae rebellis est et inimicus*EN11 (24). But: *Ad hanc Spiritus sancti renovationem nullus lapis, nullus truncus, sed solus homo creatus est*EN12 (22). As man and therefore as a *creatura rationales*EN13 man becomes the object of the divine action. But this means that *haec agitatio Spiritus sancti non est coactio, sed homo conversus*

EN2 in the abstract
EN3 concretely
EN4 rational creature
EN5 a stone, a dead weight
EN6 a hard stone that does not yield to the touch, a dead weight even though sometimes of a savage wild beast
EN7 not that man after the fall is no longer a rational creature, or can be converted to God apart from hearing and meditating on the divine word; or that in external and civil matters he can understand nothing of good or evil, or can do or neglect to do anything freely
EN8 spiritual and divine matters
EN9 like (!) a stone and a dead weight and a statue, lacking life, and having no use of eyes, mouth, or other senses of the heart
EN10 before he is illuminated, converted and regenerated by the Holy Spirit
EN11 since he is hostile and rebellious to the divine will
EN12 For this renewal by the Holy Spirit, no stone, no dead weight has been created: only man
EN13 rational creature

1. Man as a Doer of the Word

sponte bonum operatur^{EN14} (64). *Sic eum trahit, ut ex intellectu caecato illuminatus fiat intellictus, et ex rebelli voluntate fiat prompta et obœdiens voluntas*^{EN15} (60). If it does not belong to our freedom to put ourselves in this position, it is none the less our freedom which we exercise in this position. If there is no *cooperatio voluntatis nostrae in hominis conversions*^{EN16} (44), there can and must be once we assume the work of the Holy Spirit on man: *quantum et quamdiu a Deo per Spiritum sanctum ducitur, regitur et gubernatur*^{EN17}—if God were to withdraw His gracious hand from us, in that case *ne ad minimum momentum*^{EN18} (66).

We said earlier that in the very self-determination, without which he would not be a man, man becomes an object of the divine predetermination. It is in this way that the circle of his existence is intersected by the circle of revelation. [365] The grace of revelation is not conditioned by his humanity, but his humanity is conditioned by the grace of revelation. God's freedom does not compete with man's freedom. How could it be the freedom of the divine mercy bestowed on man, if it suppressed and dissolved human freedom? It is the grace of revelation that God exercises and maintains His freedom to free man.

It will be instructive to turn to the passage in Jas. 1^{21–25}, which is very important in this context. The emphasis is all upon man as the recipient of the Word of God. According to verse 21 this Word has "the power to save your souls." It is only of itself, only of the One who has spoken it, only "from above," that it has this power. James does not leave us in any doubt about that. But in this power this Word is "engrafted" in the man who believes and confesses it. It is something alien, the element of a new order. Yet it is as near to him as he is himself: "on thy lips and in thine heart" (Rom. 10⁸). But if it is really near to him, that means that it will be "received" by him. But this receiving means a very definite humbling of man. The self-righteousness which corresponds to his old and impure nature is reversed. He is reduced to that "meekness" which alone can do what is right in the presence of God. If the Word is really engrafted in us, this receiving and reversal are merely the self-evident and inevitable consummation of our existence as it is newly posited by God. We merely deceive ourselves if we try to be only hearers of this Word, and not doers because we are hearers (v. 22). As real hearers we are indeed taken prisoner by this Word. We surrender to it. Inevitably, therefore, the totality of our existence is evidence of what we have heard. According to Calvin's exposition of the passage (*C.R.* 55, 395), a doer of the Word is:. *qui sermonem Dei ex anima complectilur vitaque testatur, serio se credidisse, iuxta hanc Christi sententiam: Beati qui audiunt sermonem Dei et custodiunt cum*^{EN19} (Lk. 11²⁸). To want to be hearers only would mean to want to isolate the Word from our existence, to make ourselves onlookers at heart, and independent judges in our own consciences, to debate with the Word. In short, it would mean that we maintain our autonomy over against it as those who know the Word and are interested in it and reverence and adore it. But although we can do this with the word of man, we cannot do it with the Word of God. Because it is the Word of the Lord, to hear the Word of God is to

---

EN14 this action of the Holy Spirit is not coercion; rather the converted man does good of his own accord

EN15 Thus, He draws him, such that an enlightened understanding follows a blinded understanding, and a prompt and obedient will comes out of a rebellious will

EN16 co-operation of our will in the conversion of man

EN17 as much as, and as long as he is led, ruled, and governed by God through the Spirit

EN18 it would not be possible for the shortest moment

EN19 one who embraces the word of God with his soul, and bears witness in his life that he has earnestly believed as in this saying of Christ: 'Blessed are those who hear the word of God and keep it' (Luke 11.28)

obey the Word of God. Not to obey the Word of God is therefore to deceive oneself. The deception is twofold: first by dealing with the engrafted Word, as though it were not the Word of the Lord; and then by imagining that to ignore the engrafting is to rob it of its power, as though resisted grace does not become judgment by the very same power by which it may be blessing. As it says, vv. 23–24, we can see our natural face in a mirror, and then turn away and forget it again. But in the mirror of the Word of God we see ourselves as we are before God and therefore in truth. Once we have heard what this Word has to say to us, we can never forget it. We can only be what it says that we are. If we do not want to fall into the pit of iniquity, we must be doers of the Word. The man who, like Peter looking down into the empty grave of Jesus (Lk. 24^{12}, Jn. 20^5), stoops down and looks into the mirror of the Word of God, attains, as Calvin said, a *penetrabilis intuitus, qui nos ad Dei similitudinem transformat*[EN20]. This Word, this Law lays claim to us, and in doing so it lays claim to our freedom, i.e., our own free and spontaneous obedience. It does not claim individual works. It claims ourselves as the doers of the work which corresponds to its content. That is to say, it demands our confession, the confession of our existence. It demands our heart. It demands

[366]

that we leave the sanctuary of an abstract "inwardness," and give ourselves to the decision not merely of obeying, but of obedience, of accepting it as the truth without reserve, of submission to the truth. In this doing of the Word, which is true hearing, we are saved and blessed, the object of the divine good pleasure—not otherwise: *in ipsa actione sita est beatitudo*[EN21] (Calvin). A right understanding of this passage in James will show us at once why the concept "work," so long as it is not an evasion of Jesus Christ and of faith, has a very positive significance for Paul as well. For him, too, God will requite each "according to his works" (Rom. 2^6), and it is not the hearers but only the doers of the law who are justified (Rom. 2^{13}). Upon the one foundation, Jesus Christ, each individual builds his work, and it is this which will be made manifest one way or the other at the last judgment (1 Cor. 3^{13}). We all have to stand before the judgment seat of Christ and receive according to what we have done in this life (2 Cor. 5^{10}). In Gal. 6$^{3f.}$ it is deliberately emphasised that to avoid self-deception we must all look to our own work, by which we have both our own praise and our own burden. At times (Phil. 2$^{12f.}$) Paul can even regard the attainment of eternal redemption from the standpoint of κατεργάζεσθαι[EN22] (in the context the accent is not on this but on the ἐν φόβῳ καὶ τρόμῳ)[EN23], but, of course, he at once points to the obvious basis of it all: For it is God that worketh in you to will and to do of His good pleasure. Conversely, in Eph. 2$^{8f.}$, when he has just stated most strongly that we are saved by grace through faith, as a gift and not by virtue of our works, he can then continue: "We are His creatures, created in Christ Jesus to good works, for which God hath prepared us, that we should walk therein." From 1 Thess. 1^3 and 2 Thess. 1^1 we see that the concept ἔργον πίστεως[EN24] is a familiar one to Paul. And he can describe his own activity as an apostle as an ἐργάζεσθαι ἔργον κυρίου[EN25] (1 Cor. 16^{10}) and himself as the συνεργὸς[EN26] of God (1 Cor. 3^9). And we must add all those passages in which on very different grounds but always with the most unequivocal imperatives he summons Christians to good works. In none of these does he envisage any possible rivalry of the work of man with the work of Jesus Christ or the Holy Spirit. In Phil. 2$^{12f.}$ and Eph. 2$^{4f.}$ we can see clearly that although the presupposition of work or works cannot be thought away, it consists for Paul in an act whose Subject is God Himself and God

---

[EN20] a piercing insight, which transforms us into the likeness of God
[EN21] in that very action is located blessing.
[EN22] working
[EN23] fear and trembling
[EN24] the work of faith
[EN25] doing the work of God
[EN26] co-worker

alone, and whose power cannot be increased or diminished by the work or works, but only confirmed. In the Pauline doctrine of Christian works the question of anything more than this necessary confirmation does not arise. And after the uncompromising pronouncements of Romans and Galatians, there can be no question of any rivalry between human work and human faith. There can be no doubt that, according to Paul, it is in faith, and only in faith, that man is the object of that divine act, and therefore justified before God, because justified by God. And that is so because in faith he has Jesus Christ as his object, the One to whom he is drawn and committed and in whom he is established. In faith he confirms and acknowledges and affirms the divine act as something which has been done for him and to him. Because faith is faith in Jesus Christ, in faith it is true that he is a man reconciled to God. We can therefore describe faith as that work which confirms the divine action, upon which Paul lays such great stress. And in all the passages in which he describes that work as the criterion of our perseverance or non-perseverance before God, from his other statement it is obvious that he does not mean anything but the "work of faith," i.e., our life-work as ultimately and decisively defined as something which happens in faith. This work is our justification in the sight of God, not, of course, as a work of man, but for the sake of its object, because it is the work of faith in Jesus Christ. But this does not alter in the very least the fact that it is necesarily a human work, our life-work. It is man who believes. This does not justify him. What justifies him is the fact that he believes in Jesus Christ. But man believes. And when he believes, his faith is not an accidental or partial, but a necessary and total, determination of his existence. It may be a weak and tiny faith, but if it is not necessary and total even in its weakness and tininess, it is not faith, and Jesus Christ is not its object. It does not justify man because of its necessity and totality, but because of its object, for the sake of Jesus Christ. And yet it is not faith, it does not have Jesus Christ for its object, and therefore it does not justify, if it does not have this necessity and totality—or to put it more simply, if it is not man, man himself, the whole man, who believes. When we say man himself, the whole man, we come to what is in fact both in James and also in Paul, not the strict, mathematical centre (which can only be the name of Jesus Christ and faith in Him), but the central area which necessarily circumscribes and indicates that centre: the man who comes necessarily and totally under a new determination is the ἐν Χριστῷ EN27, the man who is the object of that divine act, the man who believes in Jesus Christ. His existence under this determination, his existence therefore under the determination of Jesus Christ and faith in Him, is what Paul so strikingly describes as his work or works. It is obvious that for Paul this work could as little be a rival of faith as it could of Jesus Christ and the Holy Spirit—or as little as in James the doing of the Word could be of the hearing. It is not additional to faith. It is the expression, the true and necessary expression of faith. In actual fact, faith is alone. But real faith—as opposed to what James calls a dead faith—is not an upward faith, as directed to Jesus Christ and therefore to justification. If it is to be faith at all, it is actually and necessarily a downward faith, as the faith of man, of man himself, of the whole man. We might also say that work is faith and faith is work, to the extent that it is the creation of the free God, and within those limits necessarily and totally the free decision and act of man.

[367]

If we are to speak fully and rightly of the grace of the Holy Spirit we cannot avoid the Christian *in concreto*EN28. And the Christian *in concreto*EN29 is the free man. whose freedom is safeguarded and maintained by God. If we remember that man's self-determination in Jesus Christ by the Holy Spirit stands under

---

EN27 in Christ
EN28 concretely
EN29 concretely

the sign and within the limits of the divine predetermination, we are faced with the problem which is usually described as the problem of theological ethics, or more practically as the Christian life. In this content we cannot do more than give a first and general outline. The fact of God's revelation as such raises the question what are we to do?—the question of the shaping of our life in conformity with this fact. Better, it commands our obedience. It is within these limits that we are forced to deal with the matter at this point. We will do so under the title "The life of the children of God."

I have to thank A. v. Harnack for this title. In 1925 I had a last direct conversation with him, upon the possibility and problem of an Evangelical dogmatics. He told me that if he had to write such a work himself, this would be his title. There is no doubt that if an Evangelical dogmatics did have to have a special title—and better not—this one could be used. Of course, even under this title its basic and decisive theme and centre would be the one Son of God and the Holy Spirit, its source would be Holy Scripture and its *locus* the Church. And obviously that is not what Harnack meant. His proposal was that dogmatics in the older sense ought now to be replaced by the personal confession of someone who has attained the maturity and serenity of final convictions and spiritual certainties, a confession determined at its very heart by the history of Christianity. For myself, I cannot see that this kind of confession is in any way a real substitute (or the function of dogmatics in theology and the Church. Harnack was obviously speaking for Neo-Protestantism, whose proper object of faith is not God in His revelation, but man himself believing in the divine. As it thinks and speaks under Holy Scripture and in the Church, theology cannot ascribe any such value or significance to man. But the impulse which led Neo-Protestantism on this particular track need not be repressed. It has a legitimate place within the doctrine of the Holy Spirit. I can perhaps do justice to it outwardly by adopting Harnack's proposal, even if not in his own sense. For the revelation of God does in fact create the life of the children of God. After what has been already said, I need hardly say that without any change in material significance we might just as well use the title "*The Life of the Church.*"

[368]

Human self-determination, and therefore the life of the children of God, is posited under the predominant determination of revelation. In a double sense our first definition of it is negative: God creates men who do not exist unless they seek Him, and who cannot cease to testify that He has found them. These negative formulations will later have to be replaced by positive ones. I use them first in order again to bring out the predominant determination, by which human self-determination is posited. The free decision of man, the act and work of man, the life of real men, is revealed in the fulfilment of revelation as the outpouring of the Holy Spirit. But it does not have its character as the life of the children of God from itself, but from the light in which it is placed. No positive—and we must add at once, no negative—description of what man does or does not do can clearly reproduce, in the strict sense, the "Christian" character of his life and activity and suffering. It acquires this character only "from outside," that is, from God. What is essentially "Christian" in this life and doing and not doing can only be the declaration: He and not I! He and not we! He, the Lord! He for us! He in our stead! The predominant determination of man by revelation, the basis of the life of the children of God, is the fact that this "He" avails for them, comforting, exhorting, ordering and limiting—and all with an unrivalled emphasis, because it is the reality of their own existence which is vindicated in it all, a reality which they can as little avoid as they can escape ourselves. But it is the hidden reality of their own existence. It is He, He who is the reality. He is not I. He is not we. Only indirectly is He identical with us and we with Him. For He is God and we are men. He is in heaven and we are on earth. He lives eternally and we live temporally. There is always this eschatological frontier between Him and us. But this means that it is only indirectly and not unequivocally that we can grasp that He and not I, that He and not we, as it is declared in the life and doing and not doing of man, and the effects of its comforting and exhorting and ordering and limiting in our human life. The reality of which we are trying to speak in respect of the life and doing and not doing of man is greater than, indeed utterly different from, anything that we can say about it, because He is this reality. It is clear that even with negative formulations like those mentioned we must not think that we can pass on to direct communication. In relation to Him they always say too little, in respect of human life and doing and not doing they say too much to be able to do [369] more than give a general indication or point in the right direction. But the pointing can be known as such and with its limitations by the fact that it takes place first in the negative formulation.

A first thing that we have to say is that if we think of the life of the children of God as a creation of the Holy Spirit we have to do with a determinateness of human life understood as *being* and *doing*. And with the necessary caution we can also say that we have to do with a determinateness of the inward and outward aspects of human life: its isolation and its fellowship.

These preliminary distinctions will all have to give way later to biblical concepts, and are only relative. In justification of them we can point at once to the biblical distinctions between regeneration and conversion, justification and sanctification, faith and obedience, the children of God and the servants of God. There can be no question of an antithesis between two quite different determinations of man; for He who determines, Jesus Christ and the Holy Spirit, is only One. We shall also find that the two lines which we are now separating constantly intersect. But it belongs to the indirectness of all our present consideration that we cannot possibly reduce what we have to perceive and state to a single denominator, or describe it in a single term. Apart from the loan-words "Christ" and "Christian," there is nothing in human life answering to that one name of Jesus Christ, in which, as we have seen, the two lines of our thinking converge in that quite different context.

In the revelation of God, man is claimed on the one hand as a specific subject and being. He is not merely newly qualified but really new, because newly made in the relationship created between himself and God. This is the Christian life regarded as being—and it is rightly and properly a benefit of revelation. But we have to remember that this being, as the being of a man, does not subsist of itself, but only in a specific doing on the part of the subject. The claim of revelation comes into force in this doing. In this doing, and to that extent in this being—because it is, of course, the doing of this subject and therefore of this being—we can, repeating the distinction, differentiate between the inward aspect, i.e., its meaning, intention and bearing, and the outward, i.e., the action and its effect, neither of which can exist without the other any more than being without doing, or doing without being. We again repeat the distinction when we say that, so long as we look at the being and inward aspect of man, as claimed in revelation, we see him in his isolation. For in his being as a new subject or in the intention of his activity he is isolated even in his social life, an individual even in the Church. He is confronted only by God, and no one can represent him in that confrontation. But if we look at the doing or outward aspect of this same man, we find that in spite of his isolation this same man is united in society as an individual with the whole Church, related, of course, to God, but in God to others. The impossibility of regarding him strictly from the one standpoint or the other means that we

[370]   cannot treat either of these insights as exclusive. The fact is that they belong together. It is only relatively that we can separate them.

Negatively defined, the first of the two, the being, the inward nature, the isolation of the Christian means that he cannot exist without seeking God in Jesus Christ. He is denied any other being than that which consists in the specific act of seeking. He is forced out of every other being and forced into that of being a seeker after God, and after God in Christ. Behind him there is only the impossible, the sin which he has committed and the abyss of death. It is true that that is always behind him and to that extent he is still a sinner, and under sentence of death. He is saved only in Christ. But it is behind him. He is saved in Christ. He is a sinner pardoned, a *peccator Justus*EN30. He lives in his activity as a seeker after God. That is his new creation by the Holy Ghost. In the Holy Ghost he actually hears and believes the Word of God, and the Word of God is the eternal Word, which assumed flesh and in that flesh raised up our flesh and the flesh of all those who hear and believe that Word to the glory of the Father. For that reason it is taken away from us, from the children of God. They can have it only as they have the Word, and therefore only as they seek the Word, only as they seek God in Christ, only as they "seek that which is above" (Col. 3¹ᶠ·). By the fact that, having heard and believed, they are forced into this search, they are new subjects, born again by the Holy Spirit. And this very search is the core of their life, the intention of their activity, the thing which in all their fellowship they can only be and do in isolation. And now we can name the biblical concept which speaks of this seeking after God by those whom He has found in His word. It is the love of God in the transitive sense, the love of man to God. That is the only being which remains when his other being is taken away from him, because he has risen with Christ.

Again, negatively defined, the second of the two, the doing, the outward

---

EN30 righteous sinner

172

aspect, the social nature of the Christian means that he cannot cease to testify that God in Christ has found him. Therefore his being makes necessary a very definite doing. He simply cannot suppress or conceal or keep to himself what he is. What is he? He is a man found by God. He did not seek, he was sought. He did not find, he was found. God in His eternal Word was free for him. And by the Holy Spirit he, man, was free for God. In the freedom of God he himself became free and the child of God. This is the irresistible summons to action. This is what he has to reveal and declare. This is what his whole existence has now to proclaim and attest and affirm. It is in this decision that he now lives. The freedom to decide otherwise is now behind him. It is true that it is always behind him. Again and from this angle, too, it is true that he is always a sinner, under sentence of death. For whatever is behind him is again the impossible, the sin which he has committed and the abyss of death. He is saved in Christ, [371] but only in Christ, and therefore in the decision to witness to Him. In face of the sin and death, from which he has come, as a real *Justus peccator*EN31, he can only live out and reveal and attest his salvation. The Spirit who has regenerated him compels him to do this work of revealing and attesting and confessing. And this inescapable confessing becomes the outward side of his life, his activity as a doing and working. And just at this point, for all the isolation of his inner path, he suddenly finds himself in the fellowship of the Church. And now again we can give the biblical concept which marks this fact. It is the attesting and confessing that we are found and saved: the praise of God. The praise of God is the action inescapably laid upon us when our freedom is transferred to another action under the sentence and judgment of God when we are dead with Christ.

All things considered, the Christian life, the life of the children of God, consists in these two concepts of love and praise. The children of God are those who seek after God and find their answer in God. It is in this apparently contradictory unity that they are what they are and do what they do. In fact, both sides are true: they ask because they already have the answer; they answer because they themselves are first asked. They are both true in Jesus Christ. And the two concepts together are the principle of what we call theological ethics: the love of God is our only remaining being and the praise of God is our necessary doing. Even in its consideration and doctrine of revelation dogmatics has already to ask what becomes of the man to whom the revelation of God comes? What have we to do who know that we have heard and believed the Word of God? And because it finds the problem of the Christian man in its basic considerations and treats it as its own problem, it takes ethics into itself, thus making a special theological ethics superfluous. For without ceasing to be dogmatics, reflection upon the Word of God, it is itself ethics.

EN31 righteous sinner

2. THE LOVE OF GOD

The Christian life begins with love. It also ends with love, so far as it has an end as human life in time. There is nothing that we can or must be or do as a Christian, or to become a Christian, prior to love. Even faith does not anticipate love. As we come to faith we begin to love. If we did not begin to love, we would not have come to faith. Faith is faith in Jesus Christ. If we believe, the fact that we do so means that every ground which is not that of our being in love to God in Christ is cut away from under us: we cannot exist without seeking God. If this were not the case, we should have failed to come to faith. And the fact that it is so is a confirmation that our faith is not an illusion, but that we ourselves as men do really believe.

[372] We remember what James says about doing and Paul about work. The faith of which Paul speaks is not an imaginary faith. According to Gal. 5⁶ it is a faith which is active in love, i.e., effectual, i.e., actual: ἐνεργουμένη EN32 He that loveth not knoweth not God, 1 Jn. 4⁸. If it is a matter of the way of faith, the way of the Christian, then love is the way, ἡ καθ᾽ ὑπερβολὴν ὁδός EN33 (1 Cor. 12³¹).

But there is also nothing beyond love. There is no higher or better being or doing in which we can leave it behind us. As Christians, we are continually asked about love, and in all that we can ever do or not do, it is the decisive question.

Paul expressly says of love in 1 Cor. 13⁸ that it οὐδέποτε πίπτει EN34. He means that it will still apply to the being and activity of the redeemed in the world to come. In eternity when we see God face to face, either we will be those who love, or we will not be.

Love is the essence of Christian living. It is also its *conditio sine qua non* EN35, in every conceivable connexion. Wherever the Christian life in commission or omission is good before God, the good thing about it is love.

According to Rom. 13¹⁰ love is the πλήρωμα νόμου EN36. According to 1 Tim. 1⁵ it is the τέλος τῆς παραγγελίας EN37. If ye keep my commandments, ye shall abide in my love (Jn. 15¹⁰). That is why in Mk. 12²⁹ᶠ· the Law and the prophets are summed up in the twofold commandment: Thou shalt love—God and thy neighbour. Love beareth all things, believeth all things, hopeth all things, endureth all things (1 Cor. 13⁷). In love the truth is honoured (2 Thess. 2¹⁰; 1 Cor. 13⁶; Eph. 4¹⁵). Love builds up the Church (1 Cor. 8¹; Eph. 4¹⁶). R. Rothe is right when he says "that every moral function (all the doing and non-doing) of the individual (apart from all else) is normal only in so far as, whatever else it may be, it is an act of love, and is done in love" (*Theol. Ethik²*, Vol. 1, 1867, p. 536).

But from this we may gather that as the living expression of the human

---

EN32 working
EN33 the most excellent way
EN34 never fails
EN35 necessary condition
EN36 fulfilment of the Law
EN37 the goal of the command

children of God, as the self-determination of human existence, neither in essence nor in actuality can love be understood in itself, but only in that sphere or light of the divine predestination, in which we stand when we hear and believe in the Word of God and are born again as the children of God. If love is the essence and totality of the good demanded of us, how can it be known that we love? Obviously it can be said that we do so only because something else can first be said of us, that we are loved, that we are men beloved. If there is nothing in the Christian life which can precede love, the love of God for man must first precede the Christian life as such, if it is to begin with love. It is not the case that we ourselves can put ourselves in the position in which all that we can do is to seek what is above. We do, of course, put ourselves in many awkward positions. We can even plunge ourselves into despair. But we cannot put ourselves in the position, that saving and blessed despair, in which we can only seek refuge in God. But God plunges us into this despair when He reveals Himself to us, when His Word is made flesh and the judgment of our flesh by the Holy Spirit, who opens our eyes and ears and therefore kindles our faith. When that occurs, the Christian life begins. We are born and live as the children of God. And then we are real men who really love. But only then. [373]

So it is a rare plant which groweth not in our garden, to love God with all our heart, etc. For "to love God" and to seek God's glory means to be hostile to ourselves and to the whole world. As Christ also says in Lk. 14: "If any man comes to me and hates not his father, mother, wife, child, brother, sister, even his own life, he cannot be my disciple." But we do not find that in us. Perhaps we love the letters GOD, but we do not love what the letters signify. We only curse and complain, especially when we are assailed and suffer (Luther, *Pred. üb. Lk.* 10$^{23-37}$, acc. to Rörer, *E.A.* 5, 70 f.). We have to think particularly of the passage in which we are told of Christian love that "the love of God is poured into our hearts by the Holy Spirit which is given unto us" (Rom. 5^5)—and for this reason, because in the death of Christ, God first showed His own love for us while we were yet sinners (Rom. 5$^{7f.}$). Herein is love, not that we loved God, but that He loved us (note the aorist ἠγάπησεν EN38), and sent His Son to be the propitiation for our sins (1 Jn. 4^{10}). "Abide in My love" says the commandment ; "for as the Father hath loved me, so have I loved you" (Jn. 15^9). "For the great love wherewith He loved us" God has given us this new status, quickened us together with Christ, saved us by grace and therefore set us on the way of good works (Eph. 2$^{4f.}$). Paul now lives his life in the flesh in the faith of the Son of God, "who loved me, and gave himself for me" (Gal. 2^{20}). The meaning of Deut. 30^6 is exactly the same (and we must note it if we are to understand Deut. 6^5) when Israel is told: "Yahweh thy God will circumcise thine heart, and the heart of thy seed, to love the Lord thy God with all thy heart, and with all thy soul, for thy life's sake." Of course love is our being and doing, if we love. But the fact that we love, and are those who love, which is the essence and totality of the life of the children of God, is no less a gift and work of God, a virgin-birth (in the extended sense of Jn. 1$^{12f.}$), than is the human existence of the eternal Son of God. It is for those who love God that there is prepared "what eye hath not seen, nor ear heard, neither have entered into the heart of man" (1 Cor. 2^9). Love is of God, and whoso loveth is born of God and knoweth God (1 Jn. 4^7). The fact that Christian love is grounded in the love of God for us was made a dogma at the *Conc. Araus.* II (529): *Prorsus donum Dei est diligere Deum. Ipse at diligeretur dedit qui non dilectus diligit. Displicentes*

EN38 'loved'

amati sumus, ut fieret in Moots, unde placer emus. Diffundit enim charitatem in cordibus nostris Spiritus Patris et Filli, quem cum Patre amamus et Filio[EN39] (*Can.* 25, *Denz.* No. 198). It is difficult to see what relationship there is between this and what Thomas Aquinas obviously thought that we should say, that *Deus potest a nobis amari naturaliter, etiam non praesupposita fide vel spe futurae beatitudinis*[EN40] (*S. Theol.* II 1, *qu.* 65, *art.* 5, 1). The biblical passages do not know anything of a natural love to God which is proper to us apart from divine revelation, or of a natural capacity for love which is prior to revelation. It is only the children of God by grace who love and can love God.

On the other hand, we must insist that the love of the children of God does become an event in an act or acts of human self-determination: it is a creaturely reality. A creaturely reality, let us say, which as such, as human self-determination, is re-created by God Himself in the sphere or light of the divine predetermination, thus being transformed, becoming love instead of non-love, but not ceasing on that account to be human self-determination and therefore a creaturely reality. We cannot therefore say that it is the product of a transformation of the creaturely into divine reality, nor can we say that in it the divine reality has taken the place of the creaturely. In strict analogy with the incarnation of the Word in Jesus Christ, what takes place in man by the revelation of God is this: his humanity is not impaired, but in the Word of God heard and believed by him he finds the Lord, indeed in the strict and proper sense he finds the subject of his humanity, for on his behalf Jesus Christ stands and rightly stands in His humanity at the right hand of the Father. For that very reason all that he can do is in his humanity to seek God in this Jesus Christ, and therefore to love Him. When the children of God love, they are the earthly members of His body, longing for their heavenly Head. The earthly members—that is why their loving, grounded as it is in the love of God, is not transmuted into a heavenly or divine loving.

[374]

As distinct from the sayings in Jn. 4[24]: πνεῦμα ὁ θεός [EN41], or 2 Cor. 3[17]: ὁ δὲ κύριος τὸ πνεῦμά ἐστιν[EN42] the saying in 1 Jn. 4[8 16]: ὁ θεὸς ἀγάπη ἐστίν[EN43] is an irreversible one. It does not say that even in any consummation God is what we know as love in ourselves. It does not know that what we know as love in ourselves is God. It does not teach the deity of love, but the love of the Deity. We have to take it quite strictly. The fact that God is love means not only that we ought to love but can and must love. According to 1 Jn. 4[9] the love of God is manifested in the fact that He sent His only-begotten Son, that we might live through Him. That is the incomparable and unattainable love of God. Only of that love can it be said that God is love. And as such, in essential contradistinction from all our loving, it is the basis of the loving of the children of God in all its creaturely reality.

[EN39] To love God is utterly the gift of God. He who loves although unloved, Himself grants that He be loved. We who displease Him have been loved so that there might be something in us whereby we might please Him. For the Spirit of the Father and of the Son whom we love with the Father, has poured out His love into our hearts

[EN40] God can naturally be loved by us, even without presupposing faith or hope in future blessedness

[EN41] God is spirit

[EN42] The Lord is Spirit

[EN43] God is love

2. The Love of God

It was Peter Lombard (*Sent.* 1, *dist.* 17) who maintained the doctrine that the love with which we love God and our neighbour is nothing but God. Indeed, as he saw it, it is the Holy Spirit Himself. For in the Trinity, according to Augustine, the Holy Spirit is the love of the Father for the Son and of the Son for the Father, and it is this Holy Spirit who is given to us. In the Christian life of man the Holy Spirit Himself replaces the human *motus animi*[EN44], although its effect is the same. Thomas Aquinas cautiously but very definitely rejected this view. Our love, he says, is only *quaedam participatio charitatis divinae*[EN45]. In itself, however, it is a human act of reason and will, with a human *principium. Oportet quod si voluntas moveatur a Spiritu sancto ad diligendum, etiam ipsa sit efficiens hunc actum*[EN46]. How else can our love be meritorious? (*S. Theol.* II 2 *qu.* 23, *art.* 2c). Apart from the last argument, we have to admit that Thomas is right. Furthermore, we must point out that at this point Lombard's conception of the operation of the Holy Spirit approximates closely to the magical and is in any case inadequate—as if the fact that the Spirit is given to man does not mean that man himself can hear and believe the Word of God; as if the miracle of the Holy Spirit does not therefore take place in the natural man as such, who is in himself free.

We must not do violence to the miracle of the Holy Spirit, the founding of the love of the children of God, even in its more precise form, by letting God be God and man man, but trying to explain the origin of love in man as a supernatural extension of natural human capacity. If we ask how it is possible for man to love, according to Holy Scripture, we have first to go back to faith, and then from faith to its object, Jesus Christ. It is in spite of and within the limitation of his natural capacities that man is met by Jesus Christ in faith in the promise. He is still a creature, afterwards as well as before. He is still a sinful creature. But he is met by Jesus Christ and sees and knows Him as very God and very Man, and therefore as the Reconciler. And that is the miracle of the Holy Spirit and therefore the founding of love in man.

[375]

It is at this point—as we saw a moment ago—that we part company with Thomas. In the passage cited he felt that he could make a concession to Lombard, and in line with his doctrine of grace generally he certainly could and indeed had to make it. It was this. He claimed that the *actus caritatis*[EN47] was possible only if there was added to the *potentia naturalis a forma habitualis superaddita, inclinans ipsam ad charitatis actum et faciens eam prompte et delectabiliter operari*[EN48]. What can we say about the introduction of this third principium which operates midway between the divine and the human? If we stress its divine character, we are involved in the same difficulties as those which Thomas himself raised against Lombard: where is the real man in this *forma habitualis*[EN49], who is, of course, supposed to be the subject of love? But if we stress its human character, where is the mystery of the origin of love, the miracle of the Holy Spirit? And with what right or consistency dare we introduce into the debate a third factor in the strict sense? No, if we want to find an answer to the question of the human possibility of love, i.e., a possibility which is in the sphere of man, we cannot take

---

[EN44] workings of the mind

[EN45] a certain participation in the divine love

[EN46] starting point. It is right that if the will be moved by the Holy Spirit to love, it (i.e. the will) is even so still the efficient cause of this act

[EN47] act of love

[EN48] natural potential, additional habitual form, inclining it (i.e. the natural potential) to the act of love and making it work promptly and with pleasure

[EN49] habitual form

refuge either in the "docetic" anthropology of a Lombard or the "Ebionitism" of a Thomas. We can only point to the fact that we live in the sphere of the Church, that we are therefore baptised and look to the fulfilment of the promise, that Jesus Christ died and rose again for us. This is the true *forma habitualis superaddita*[EN50], which does not ascribe to us either a miraculous extension of our own capacity, nor under the guise of this supernatural quality a liberty which abolishes grace *qua*[EN51] grace. If we do not entrust to the Church and baptism and the promise, the power of the Holy Spirit and therefore the power to found this love, what confidence can we have in this supernatural capacity? But if we do trust in the promise, how can we doubt that man as he is, real man without deduction or addition, can participate in the promise, and that the miracle of the outpouring of the Holy Spirit consists in the fact that this man with his natural capacity, which in itself is utter incapacity, does in faith participate in the promise and in faith begin to love? It was not the love of Lombard, which is identical with the Holy Spirit, or the love of Thomas which is thought of as a supernatural quality, but this love which in the human sphere is grounded only in the power of the promise and of faith, that Luther had in mind when in his exposition of 1 Jn. $4^{8\ 16}$ he dared to say of love: "He hath praised love, then, above everything else that can be named upon earth. For he maketh of it that which is called God; and he who hath it he honoureth not as a man or prince, a King or Emperor, but as a God, and setteth up that God not merely above lords and princes, nor yet in Paradise, but above all creatures, in God Himself; so that the two are one and the same. What then can we desire or think more precious or glorious than to be one with God and to abide where is High Majesty? What are all the Carthusians and monks compared with that man?" (*Pred. üb.* 1 *Jn.* $4^{16\text{ff.}}$, 1532, *W.A.* 36, 441, 30).

[376]   But it cannot be otherwise than that the love of God for us is the basis not only of the reality but also of the knowledge of Christian love. This means that we must not deduce the real meaning of love in this context from some arbitrarily if profoundly chosen master-concept of love in general, comprising the love of God for us on the one hand and our love for God on the other. Even in love there is only an indirect identification of the believer with God in Christ. How then can we ever set up or apply a master-concept of this kind? To know what love is, we have first to ask concerning the unique love of God for us. What our love is will necessarily appear when we ask about our response to this love of God for us and the confirmation and acknowledgment which we owe it. Only then, and by means of the standard which is given us in that way, can we assess the rightness or wrongness of a concept of love which is otherwise completely arbitrary.

To say the least, the definition of Christian love given by Thomas Aquinas (*S. Theol.* II 1, qu. 65, art. 5 c) is not very relevant. He speaks of *charitas*[EN52] as *amicitia quaedam ad Deum, quae quidem super amorem addit mutuam redamationem cum quadam communicatione*[EN53]. Is it not topsy-turvy to regard Christian love as merely a particular instance of the general possibility of "friendship"? As though in Christian love the *mutua redamatio*[EN54] had first to be reduced

---

[EN50] additional habitual form
[EN51] as
[EN52] love
[EN53] a certain friendship toward God, which indeed adds to love mutual love in return with a certain communication
[EN54] mutual love in return

to a presupposed *amor*[EN55], and the *communicatio*[EN56] between God and man to the *mutua redamatio*[EN57]. As though in Christian love the direct opposite was not the case: first and basically, a very one-sided *communicatio*[EN58] in God's revelation, which is as such the divine love; then and for that reason, although quite different from it (and not placed on the same level by the addition of the word *mutua*[EN59]) man's *redamatio;*[EN60] and only finally what we mean by the concept *amicitia*[EN61]. As a second example of what it is not, I will quote the description which Hegel (*Vorles. ub. d. Phil. d. Rel.* III 1, ed. Lasson, 75) gives of love: "Love is a differentiating of two, who are not at all divided for one another. The consciousness, the feeling of this identity, this being outside myself and in the other, is love: I have my self-consciousness, not in myself, but in the other. But this other in whom alone I am satisfied and am at peace with myself—and I only am as I am at peace with myself; without it, I am the contradiction which falls apart—this other, by being outside himself, has his self-consciousness only in me, and both are just the consciousness of apartness from self and identity, the perception and feeling, and awareness of unity. That is love, and all talk about love is empty talk if we do not see that it is the differentiating and the removal of the differentiation. God is love, i.e., the differentiating and the unreality of the differentiation is a game of differentiating, which cannot be taken seriously, the differentiation is posited as at once removed, i.e., the simple, eternal idea." The general possibility which Hegel equates with love is obviously that of an identity between identity and non-identity. But what resemblance is there between Christian love and this "game of differentiating which cannot be taken seriously"? God in His love for us acts in serious distinction from us, without either having his self-consciousness in us or losing it to us. "Not that we loved God, but that he loved us" (1 Jn. 4^{10})—that is how it is. And if we return God's love, that does not mean that we have our self-consciousness in God or lose it to God. Our differentiation before God is a serious thing, and it is only in this differentiation that we can and will love Him. The connexion between God's love for us and our love for God is not of such a kind that in the last resort it makes no difference whether it is God who speaks or man because the result is always the same, that both have their self-consciousness in one another; possessing and losing it, losing and possessing it in a movement which can cease and yet not cease only in the idea of this movement, which therefore deserves to be called God in a special sense. On the contrary, we have here an irreversible order of that which is above and that which is below, of predetermination and self-determination, of God and man. Finally, the relationship does not have the character of a continuous swinging or circular movement, or of the "simple, eternal idea" of it. It is essential to it that it should not be an idea but a drama or a history. On every side, therefore, the Hegelian presupposition proves unsuitable as an interpretation of the [377] concept of Christian love. And when we criticise current ideas of love, it would be as well not to forget the Hegelian, i.e., the Romantic, concept of the mutual losing of oneself in another. As a third example of what it is not, I take the definition of A. Ritschl (*Unterrichl i. d. chr. Rel.*, 1875, § 12, note d): "Love is the constant will which promotes another spiritual, i.e., like-minded, person to achieve his true and highest destiny, and indeed in such a way that the one who loves pursues his own final purpose (3rd edn.: individual purpose). This appropriating of the lifework of another does not mean a denial but a strengthening affirmation of ourselves." Here again—but this time in a more open anthropological, not to say *bourgeois*

[EN55] love
[EN56] communication
[EN57] mutual love in return
[EN58] communication
[EN59] mutual
[EN60] love in return
[EN61] friendship

form—love is equated with a general possibility, i.e., that of correspondence and equilibrium between the individual determination of the will and the social. That God in His loving pursues His own purpose is something which Ritschl would never have conceived or written if he had kept before him the revelation of the triune God, and particularly the person and work of Jesus Christ, instead of that master-concept. It is self-evident, of course, that in all that He does God does pursue His own individual purpose. But to insist upon this and to connect it with what He does to us in His love is to do such violence to the idea of divine love as almost to destroy it. On the other hand, Ritschl's definition does not fit our love to God, because in this case there can be no question of the one who loves (man) promoting "another spiritual and like-minded person (God), to achieve his true and highest destiny." On the same ground, we might even ask whether this can really be said of God in His love to us; and conversely whether the pursuit of our own individual purpose is a constitutive part of our love to God. In short, even in its Ritschlian form, the process by which we think we know what love is, and then apply this knowledge to divine and human love, does not hold out any invitation to follow it.

We will now try to give the briefest possible outline of what the love of God is which is the real basis of our love to God, determining its character. One thing is certain, that according to Holy Scripture it has nothing to do with mere sentiment, opinion or feeling. On the contrary, it consists in a definite being, relationship and action. God is love in Himself. Being loved by Him we can, as it were, look into His "heart." The fact that He loves us means that we can know Him as He is. This is all true. But if this picture-language of "the heart of God" is to have any validity, it can refer only to the being of God as Father, Son, and Holy Spirit. It reminds us that God's love for us is an overwhelming, overflowing, free love. It speaks to us of the miracle of this love. We cannot say anything higher or better of the "inwardness of God" than that God is Father, Son, and Holy Spirit, and therefore that He is love in Himself without and before loving us, and without being forced to love us. And we can say this only in the light of the "outwardness" of God to us, the occurrence of His revelation. It is from this that we have to learn what is the real nature of the love of God for us.

In this historical context we can point already to the sayings of Hosea and Jeremiah and Deuteronomy in the Old Testament: "When Israel was a child, then I loved him, and called him, my son, out of Egypt" (Hos. 11^1). "With cords as a man useth them, drew I them to me, with bands of love" (Hos. 11^4). "I have loved thee with an everlasting love, therefore with lovingkindness have I drawn thee to me, for me to have compassion on thee" (Jer. 31^3). "Because the Lord hath loved you and because he would keep the oath which he sware unto your fathers, hath the Lord brought you out with a mighty hand and with outstretched arm, and hath redeemed thee out of the house of bondage" (Deut. 7^8). "Behold the heaven and the heaven of heavens, and the earth and all that is upon it, unto the Lord thy God it belongeth. Only the Lord had a delight in your fathers to love them, and he chose their seed after them, even you, above all peoples, as at this day" (Deut. 10$^{14f.}$). Perhaps we might also add the distinctive abbreviations of the same message in passages like Pss. 11^7, 33^5, which say of Yahweh that He loves "righteousness" and the "law," at any rate to the extent that these concepts denote His redemptive action in Israel. We find the same teaching in the New Testament: "Behold, what manner of love the Father hath bestowed upon us, that we should be called the sons of God" (1 Jn. 3^1). "Greater love hath no man than this, that a man lay down his life for his friends. Ye are my friends ... " (Jn. 15$^{13f.}$). "Walk in love, as Christ also

[378]

180

hath loved us, and hath given himself for us" (Eph. 5²). "In all these things we are more than conquerors through him that loved us" (Rom. 8³⁷).

In Holy Scripture the love of God to us speaks the language of this fact—the fact of His election, guidance, help and salvation—and it is in this language that it has to be heard and understood. But all the expressions of this factual language meet in the name of Jesus Christ. In this name the approach of God to man consists in one fact alone. This is, of course, the event of revelation and reconciliation in the one Word, which is the Son of God. It is the fact that God intercedes for man, that He takes upon Himself the sin and guilt and death of man, that laden with it all He stands surety for him.

At this point, above all other texts, and remembering the many others which say the same thing, we recall the central saying of Jn. 3¹⁶: "God so loved the world, that he gave his only begotten Son, that whosoever believeth on him should not perish, but have everlasting life." In the light of this we understand Luther's anger against Erasmus: *Christi ne uno quidem iota merttionem facis, ac si sentias, christianam pietatem sine Christo esse posse, tantum si Deus natura clementissimus Mis viribus colatur. Quid Hie dicam Erasme?*[EN62] (*De servo arb.*, 1525, W.A. 18, 609, 18).

This self-sacrifice of God in His Son is in fact the love of God to us. "He gave Him," which means that He gave Him into our existence. Having been given into our existence He is present with us. Present with us, He falls heir to the shame and the curse which lie upon us. As the bearer of our shame and curse, He bears them away from us. Taking them away, He presents us as pure and spotless children in the presence of His Father. That is how God reconciles the world to Himself (2 Cor. 5¹⁹). We can, indeed, speak of the love of God to us only by pointing to this fact. It is the work and gift of the Holy Spirit that the fact itself speaks to us, that in the language of this fact God says: "I have loved thee ... fear not, then; for I am with thee" (Is. 43⁴ᶠ·). No other saying is needed, for this one says all there is to say.

"If God be for us, who can be against us? He that spared not his own Son, but delivered him up for us all, how shall he not with him also freely give us all things? ... Christ Jesus that died, yea rather, that is risen again, is even at the right hand of God, who also maketh intercession for us" (Rom. 8³¹ᶠ·).

In this passage it is as well to note that the love of God for us—how else could it be?—is the [379] love of our Creator. When in that fact He says, "I love thee," He speaks as to One to whom we owe our existence, without whom we did not exist and without whom nothing existed, the One who has made heaven and earth. If we hear this fact we hear that the Creator of all things loves us: in other words, in face and in the midst of His creation, and our existence as such in the content of the natural and historical cosmos which is "our world", we can no longer feel that we are unloved or only partially loved. The act of creation was and is itself an act of the love of God to us. Jesus Christ is the "first-born of all creation"—"by him were all things created, that are in heaven, and that are in earth, visible and invisible" (Col. 1¹⁵ᶠ·). But if this is the case, then how can we who are beloved of God in Jesus Christ be unloved or only

---

[EN62] You make not even one tiny mention of Christ, as if you think that there can be Christian piety without Christ, as if God who is most merciful by nature is worshipped only with full strength. What should I say to this, Erasmus

partly loved within this creation, in the sphere of nature and history? Nay, "I am persuaded, that neither death, nor life, nor angels, nor principalities, nor things present, nor things to come, nor powers, nor height, nor depth, nor any other creature, shall be able to separate us from the love of God, which is in Christ Jesus our Lord" (Rom. 8$^{38f.}$). There is, of course, no question of any actual or known basis of the love of God apart from Christ. We are the beloved in nature and history, not through any powers of reconciliation and revelation proper to nature and history, but because nature and history are in the hand of their Lord, who causes everything to work for good to them that He loveth (Rom. 8^{28}). "It was the good pleasure of the fulness (of God) to dwell in him (Jesus Christ) and by him (in the life of his ἐκκλησία EN63 to reconcile all things to himself, making peace by him through the blood of his cross: by him, whether things in earth or things in heaven" (Col. 1$^{19f.}$). By Him and therefore not by any powers and orders of the created world in itself and as such. He is the Son of God who according to Heb. 1^3 upholds all things τῷ ῥήματι τῆς δυνάμεως αὐτοῦ EN64, i.e., in His revelation—and as the Reconciler καθαρισμὸν τῶν ἁμαρτιῶν ποιησάμενος EN65 the One who sat down on the right hand of the Majesty on high, and is greater than all the angels (Heb. 1^4). We cannot speak of a love of God the Creator *in abstracto*, supposedly active and manifest in nature and history as such. The *Heidelberg Catechism* was right when in its exposition of the first article of faith (*Q.* 26) it laid down as its main assertion, that "the eternal Father of our Lord Jesus Christ ... for the sake of His Son Christ is my God and my Father," adding all its other statements about the operation of God as Creator and the benefit which we owe to God as Creator merely as the predicates of this subject.

Therefore when we try to describe to ourselves the love of God, we can only express and proclaim the name of Jesus Christ. That is what it means to speak concretely of the love of God, i.e., in face of the complementary question: What then shall we do? In this connexion it is perhaps as well to remember only one thing. We have touched upon it already: that God has no need to love us, and we have no claim upon His love. God is love, before He loves us and apart from it. Like everything else that He is, He is love as the triune God in Himself. Even without us and without the world and without the reconciliation of the world, He would not experience any lack of love in Himself. How then can we for our part declare it to be necessary that we should be loved by Him? It is, in fact, the free mercy and kindness of God which meets us in His love.

[380]

This is a thought which is emphasised by Augustine: *Ibi enim gratia amor est, ubi non aestuat indigentiae siccitate sed ubertate beneficentiae profluit* EN66. That is why the love of God necessarily kindles our answering love: it comes to those who could not be prepared for any such thing to come to them. It is the love of *Deus iudicans* EN67 for *homo peccans* EN68 (*De cat. rud.* 4, 7). And in another passage it is asked whether the love of God means that He needs us (*frui* EN69) or that He uses us (*uti* EN70). There is as little question of His needing us as there is

---

EN63 church
EN64 by the power of His Word
EN65 as made purification for sins
EN66 For grace is love where it does not trickle, dry and sparing, but flows forth in abundant goodness
EN67 God the judge
EN68 man the sinner
EN69 needs
EN70 uses

of the light needing the radiance which it spreads itself: the good which we have is either God Himself or that which comes from God—how then can He need us? But if that is the case there can be no question of God using us as though this were necessary to meet a divine need. If God uses man, it is only in the service of His kindness to man: *Ille igitur usus, qui dicitur Dei, quo nobis utitur, non ad eius, sed ad nostram utilitatem refertus, ad eius autem tantum bonitatem*EN71 (*De doctr. chr.* I, 31–32). "That there should be a God and that He should love the world and grudge it no good thing, passeth all our reason, mind, comprehension and skill. If I were God, who knoweth the world inside out, of what sort it is, I should have wished it hell fire, and done it. That is what I should have done. But what doth God? Instead of His wrath which the world hath well deserved, He hath loved the world, and in such surpassing and incomprehensible wise, that He giveth His only Son to the world. His bitterest enemies. I have no rhetoric or eloquence to encompass this *Artificium*EN72, or adequately to draw out these *magnificas figuras*EN73. Were it not more than enough That God had bidden the world good morrow? But He goeth further and loveth the world, the shameful fruit. For it is *omnium odibillissimum et maxime inamabile objectum*EN74, the image of all that is most hostile and unholy. That is what the world is in very truth. A stall full of wicked and shameless people, who misuse most shamefully all the creatures of God, blaspheming God and ascribing all their ills to Him. And it is these shameful folk that God loveth. That is a love transcending all love. Verily He must be a good God, and His love must be a great, inconceivable fire, much greater than the fire which Moses saw in the bush, yea much greater than the fire of hell. Who would despair, for that God is thus minded towards the world? It is too high and above my skill, I cannot amplify nor adequately represent it, as it is in fact and in verity" (Luther, *Pred. üb. Jn.* 3^{16–21}, 1532, E.A. 4, 124 f.).

We now turn to the second question, that of our loving, which we can understand as an answer to the love of God for us. This must be the standard for all that we have to say. It must be set over against our presentation of the fact. It must be a description of the human self-determination which occurs in the sphere and light of the divine predestination. It must correspond on man's side to that which is said by God on His Side. We cannot deny or hide the fact that in one way or another we all think we know already about human loving, and we continue to do so even when confronted by the fact of the love of God to us. If, then, we are asking about Christian love, let us say what we know. But only in the limits and under the discipline of this canon. If we forget it or pass it by in favour of some preconceived idea of love in general, to that extent we will derive our definition of Christian love from a false source. At this as at other points, there is no absolute guarantee against such a possibility. But at this point, too, we can find a relative guarantee. In other words, we can use the concrete method of exegesis, as we did in § 15, 2, when we took Jn. 1^{14} as the *locus classicus* on the incarnation. The biblical witness of revelation and therefore of the love of God to us does not leave us in the lurch even in respect of a [381] proper human love to God, because the outpouring of the Holy Spirit is an

---

EN71 Therefore that use, which is attributed to God, whereby He uses us, is directed not to His, but to our utility, and according to his great goodness.

EN72 artistry

EN73 magnificent sayings

EN74 the most detestable of things, an utterly unlovable object

element in this revelation. Without arbitrary selection, we can take as our *locus classicus*[EN75] the words of the synoptic Jesus in Mt. 22[37f.], Mk. 12[29f.] and Lk. 10[27f.] In these passages He is asked which is the "first" or "great" commandment, or (acc. to Luke): "What must I do to inherit eternal life?" And He replies with a conflation of the Old Testament sayings in Dt. 6[5] and Lev. 19[18].

In Mt. and Mk. these two sayings are divided into a "first" or "great" commandment and a "second" (which according to Matthew is "like" unto the first). But in Luke, who does not even repeat the verb ἀγαπήσεις[EN76], they can obviously only be understood as a single command. In point of fact, of course, the unity as well as the distinctness is brought out in all the versions.

We must now examine point by point its most explicit form as we find it in Mk. 12[29-31]: The first (commandment) is this: Hear, O Israel; the Lord our God is one Lord: and thou shalt love the Lord thy God with all thy heart, and with all thy soul, and with all thy mind, and with all thy strength. And the second is this: Thou shalt love thy neighbour as thyself.

1. Only Mark records the address and presupposition of the commandment in Dt. 6[4]: Hear, O Israel, the Lord our God is one Lord. But this is most helpful in placing us in the right context. First of all, the address: Hear, O Israel. The commandment to love is not directed to humanity, or to men in general in their natural or historical groupings. Humanity or men in general are not even considered as the recipients of this commandment and as those who will fulfil it. The commandment is given to Israel. Indeed, it is given to Israel only in the sense of the synoptic Jesus. It is given to the community declared in the twelve apostles as representing the new twelve tribes. It is given to the community of believers in the Messiah, both Jews and Gentiles. It is given to the true Israel, the Church of Jesus Christ. The decision which it demands is, of course, possible for everyone. But it is not possible for everyone to hear the commandment which claims this decision. Even at its roots, in the invitation and summons to love as a Christian, Christian love is something actual. Not every man is in fact what it is decisive to be: Israel elect and loved of God, an earthly member of the earthly body, whose heavenly Head is Jesus Christ. Israel, the people of believers, is indissolubly bound to the redemptive Word of God, to the only-begotten Son of God who was sacrificed for us. But who is Israel, who is it that belongs to this people, to this community? The "Hear, O Israel" shows that this is something which is constantly being decided afresh. According to the witness of the Old Testament, Israel in the national sense, Israel "according to the flesh" has as such no claim to be this Israel. Even if it be hearing Israel, which observes the commandment to love, it has to remain Israel by ever hearing anew. If no one can hear without being a child of God, no one can be a child of God without ever hearing anew. Let us imagine for a moment that both conditions are fulfilled: men who hear because they are children of

[382]

[EN75] proof-text
[EN76] you shall love

2. *The Love of God*

God, children of God who as such hear—human self-determination in the sphere and light of the real, divine predestination, yet in that sphere and light a corresponding self-determination which is no less real. The result is a very definite understanding of the commandment itself. Then: Thou shalt love, as the text itself suggests, also and basically means: Thou wilt love. Loving becomes a self-evident and necessary act on the part of the beloved, hearing Israel. To hear this command means to hasten to fulfil it. But the power and seriousness and value of the fulfilling do not lie in what the beloved, the men of hearing Israel, can do in themselves, but wholly and utterly in what the beloved have heard as the men of hearing Israel, in the promise under which their being stands, that God is for them. Because it is true that they are therefore the beloved of God, it is also true that their activity will be love. When they hear the commandment and in that way maintain themselves as Israel, the beloved of God, they lay hold of their own future as men who love, but in such a way that their love consists only in the fact that they are loved and therefore has its power and seriousness and value only in the One who loves them, in Jesus Christ. In Jesus Christ God is for them. Therefore in Him, when they hear the commandment, they lay hold of their own future as lovers, their fulfilment of the Law.

2. This is even more plain when we consider the presupposition of the commandment, that the Lord our God is one Lord. Even in the Old Testament passage it is remarkable enough that the emphasis on the commandment to love is linked up with a reference to the uniqueness of Yahweh. The Lord is referred to by Moses as "our God," i.e., the God who has entered into covenant with us from the days of the Fathers. And according to the saying of the synoptic Jesus, the same Lord is "one Lord" for those who believe in Him, i.e., as their Master He does not belong to a *genus*[EN77], in which there are others who can also rule over them. Apart from His, there may be all sorts of other so-called, supposed and apparent spheres and therefore all sorts of other so-called, supposed and apparent lords. But no one else rules and is the Lord as He is, i.e., in deed and in truth. That is, He is the only one who does what He does. He acts towards them in a matter in which none but He can act: in the matter of their deliverance from the shame and curse of their human existence, from sin and death. And in this matter He again does what He alone can do: He intercedes for them; He gives Himself to be the bearer of their shame and curse; He suffers in their place, that they may be acquitted and free. For that very reason His control is a unique control. It is a control which at first sight is quite definitely not what we mean by ruling and commanding. It is not a matter of demands and claims and orders. On the contrary, it is all gift and offer and promise. But just because it is this promise made to man, it is an [383] unparalleled rule with its demands and claims and orders. In virtue of His promise, God takes the place of man. He takes the matter which is for man a

---

[EN77] category

185

matter of life and death right out of his hands and makes it His own business. Therefore man belongs to this Lord. What other lords can be compared with Him? They are only so-called, supposed and apparent lords. Therefore "the Lord our God is one Lord." But when we say this, the content of the commandment is in fact decided: what it is that God who is the one Lord will order and demand of man. Certainly He does not require that man should again take into his own hands this matter which is a matter of life or death, either wholly or in part. Certainly He does not require that he should try to purify himself from the shame and curse, to free himself from sin and death, to make himself out to be holy and righteous and living. Certainly He does not require that he should try to do something to repay God for what He is and does for him: "All this I did for thee: what wilt thou do for Me?" If he were to do things of this kind man would be disobedient to the one Lord. He would in fact insult and deny God as the one Lord. For he would deny the necessity and sufficiency of His unique work. And in so doing he would deny the uniqueness of His lordship and therefore of His being as God. Ceasing to acknowledge the uniqueness of his Lord, and therefore His being as God, he would open up the way for the thought that there may perhaps be other real lords side by side with this Lord. And then it is not long before the hour comes when he calls upon other gods and worships them side by side with the real God.

What was the recurrent sin of Israel against its God? Obviously it was the constant tendency to forget that God and God alone had delivered it out of the house of bondage, Egypt. It was the constant arrogance of wanting to dispose of its own weal and woe, of triumphing or murmuring as though it were not the people of God's own possession, by virtue of the deliverance which God accomplished for it. There was an incipient idolatry in this emancipation from God as sole helper, even before the emergence of actual idolatry. And what was and is apostasy in the Church of Jesus Christ? Is it not again and again the refusal to let Jesus Christ be Jesus Christ? Is it not the attempt to set up alongside Him a specifically Christian righteousness, holiness and vitality? And for all its appearance of obedience, this attempt is in fact profoundly disobedient. It always involves secularisation: an inevitable surrender of faith and love and hope, the betrayal of the Church and its message and order to the powers and values and principles of the world.

The commandment of God as the one Lord is obviously heard and respected only where it is interpreted as a commandment to love Him. Love and love alone can correspond to the uniqueness in which He is the Lord. And whatever love may consist in, by virtue of the uniqueness of God, it will always be the one *diligere*[EN78], the one choice, in which man chooses God as his Lord in the sense in which God has already chosen Himself and decided on His own lordship—that is, as the One who interceded for us and represents us, as the One who already loved man before man could and would love Him, as the One who has done literally everything for man, so that there is nothing left for man himself to do. To choose this Lord, to let Him be the Lord, means to love Him,

[384]

[EN78] love

186

and that is what man is enjoined to do by this Lord. Again, when we say "the Lord our God is one Lord," the fulfilment of the commandment to love God is also decided. For although it is enjoined upon man and man himself has to achieve it, neither inwardly nor outwardly nor in any other way will the fulfilment be in something which man can accomplish of himself. The uniqueness of the lordship of God is again denied and trampled underfoot if man presents Him with a love which is his own. Love to God consists decisively in recognising that we have nothing of our own to offer Him. We cannot offer a love which is the work of our own hands or heart. We have to recognise that He intercedes for us and represents us, that what is our own, even our own love for Him, can never be anything but our shame and our curse. The love with which we reply to the love of God for us can begin and grow only when we go beyond what we can claim as our own love, when we recognise that we the unloving are beloved by Him. In other words, it can begin and grow only in the recognition of Jesus Christ and therefore in Jesus Christ Himself. That is how—in all the seriousness of our reality before God and in God as the one Lord—it really becomes our own love to God.

3. The commandment tells us "Thou shalt." As we have already seen, within the "Thou shalt" there is a "Thou wilt" which is indeed the presupposition of the "Thou shalt." But this does not indicate any weakening of the "Thou shalt." On the contrary, how can the commandment as such have real and ultimate seriousness and emphasis if it does not demand the fulfilment of man's nature, if it comes to him, as it were, as an alien body, which he can deal with as he himself decides, which he can assimilate or not as he pleases, the choice being left entirely to himself? The law which does not have its basis and meaning in the Gospel, in the declaration of a revelation, benefit and election which are made already, of the grace of God as it is already operative in Jesus Christ—that law is no real Law. For an abstract law like that, however fiercely it may be represented and asserted as the Law of God, can never really claim man, and therefore judge him and therefore force him to obey. From the "Thou shalt" which is not rooted in the "Thou wilt" of the Gospel we can always withdraw in a light-minded despair or a despairing light-mindedness. And if it is the commandment of God which is compressed into "Thou shalt love," how can it be a commandment if as such it stands, as it were, in the air, if it comes to man from without, if it does not demand the fulfilment of his inmost being?

It is singular to read in G. Kittel's *Wörterbuch zum Neuen Testament*, concerning the concept of love in the Old Testament (vol. 1, 25 f.), that clothed in the garments of law the commandment to love reduces the Law *ad absurdum*[EN79], since it is the border at which all human *and* divine lawgiving ceases, and it demands an ethical way of life that transcends the Law. What the commandment to love reduces *ad absurdum*[EN80] is not the Law, but the idea of a law which confronts man from outside, instead of being posited with his being in covenant with God and therefore claiming him from within. What the commandment to love reduces

[385]

[EN79] to absurdity
[EN80] to absurdity

ad absurdum[EN81] is the kind of formulation which we find in the same passage (p. 29): "Thou shalt exercise the totality of the power which indwells thee, so as by the affect (!) of love to give rise to a disposition which will determine life's conduct (!); thou shalt give thy whole personality to the development of thy relationship with Yahweh." How we can ever come to be challenged by so fantastic a demand is quite inconceivable.

Love to God can be demanded and is demanded from those who already belong to God—to the God who is Lord in this unique sense. From them, as we have seen, *love* is indeed demanded. And it is *demanded*. God intercedes for them. God takes their affairs, their life's concern in the strictest sense of the concept, out of their hand. Therefore with all their existence they are cast back upon God and directed to Him. Their choice, *diligere*, has already been fixed. Love to God is the only possibility which is open to them. The "Thou shalt love" summons them to this sole remaining activity, which they themselves now find to be necessary, self-evident and indispensable. For them it is a real "Thou shalt," like an imperious physical demand. It is a genuine "Thou shalt," beside whose obedient fulfilment disobedience is a manifest impossibility, an absurdity.

At first sight, it might appear that there is a contradiction in the fact that love to God is demanded from the children of God and is therefore an act of obedience. But this is not the case. On the contrary, only love can make a real demand, i.e., the demand which really comes from God and really comes to man. And it is only in love that there can be real obedience. And conversely real love, which is the love of God, can only be the fulfilment of a command and therefore obedience. It would not be the commandment of God if, whatever else its content, it did not demand from us the most voluntary thing of all, love. And it would not be the love of God if it were not a voluntary decision for Him, if it had any taint of an act of human caprice.

Is vere demum se Deo in obsequium addicet, qui cum amabit …. Deus coacta hominum obsequia repudiat, vultque sponte et liberaliter coli: discamus interea, sub Dei amore reverentiam, quae illi debetur, notari[EN82] (Calvin, *Comm. on Mt.* 22[37], *C.R.* 45, 611). It was therefore significant that when Polanus (*Synt. Theol. chr.*, 1609, p. 3856 f.) gave eight reasons which ought to move us to love God, numbers 2–8 were as follows: because God is our supreme good, because He overwhelms us with His benefits, because love to Him is the necessary proof of the knowledge of God, because it is the sign of our fellowship with Him, because it is the sign of the love of God for us, because it conforms to the example of Christ, the angels and the saints, because God Himself is its reward—but the first and obviously decisive reason is: *Quia ipse nobis hoc mandat*[EN83], in proof of which he adduces this text and also Deut. 11[1], 30[16]; Josh. 22[5], etc. S. Kierkegaard (*Leben und Walten der Liebe*, 1847, ed. Schrempf, 29 f.) has rightly taken the phrase "Thou shalt love … " to mean that what is Christian "does not have its origin in the heart of man," from which he deduces that "only the obligation to love forever

---

[EN81] to absurdity

[EN82] He truly offers himself in obedience to God, who loves Him … God rejects the forced obedience of men, and wants to be worshipped spontaneously and freely: here we should also learn that by 'love for God' is meant the reverence that is due to Him

[EN83] Since he commands it of us

protects love against all change, making it eternally free in its blessed independence, and safeguarding its happiness eternally against all despair." But in order that it may become for us this happy obligation, in the words of H. F. Kohlbrügge (*Pred. üb. Luke* 10$^{25f.}$, 1854, *Schriftausl. Heft* 15, 2, 507). "we must completely renounce the love of God as a commandment." "Having come to Christ, having come under the lordship of free grace, we continue as we are under this grace, clinging to Christ—and as we continue clinging to Him, our experience is that His yoke, i.e., the obedience of faith, is easy and His burden, that is, the keeping of His commandments, abiding in His word, is light." Obviously a hard yoke, or a heavy burden, in the sense of the words of Mt. 11$^{29f.}$, upon which Kohlbrügge plays, would not be the happy obligation intended by Kierkegaard, and for this reason, that it would not be the obligation imposed upon us. If it is to be imposed upon us we have to "cling to Christ," i.e., to be in faith the beloved of God in Him. But as His yoke and His burden, it is "easy" and "light," because although it does not have its origin in our hearts, it is not an alien demand which comes to us from without, but it is the demand to be what we are. It is only in this way that it is the commandment of God, not one which proceeds from our own heart, but one which is inserted into our heart by Him, which is appropriated by our heart and which in its divinity is a means of blessing to us in the sense of Kierkegaard. Neither the obligation nor its fulfilment is "hard" and "heavy." What is "hard" and "heavy," impossible and absurd, for those who "cling to Christ," is its non-fulfilment, the disobedience, which would be a denial of their very being. It is by an abstract "law," i.e., by an abstract consciousness of duty, that we become "weary and heavy-laden." But when we respond to the "Come unto me" of Jesus Christ, we are neither burdened by the fact that love is now demanded of us, nor are we absolved from obedience to the commandment by this demand to love, nor pointed to some "ethical way of life" which transcends the Law. But by responding in faith to the Saviour's call and coming to Christ, we become what we are, i.e., we love in all our actions. What is inserted into us and appropriated by our hearts as we "cling to Christ" is Christ Himself, the One who loved us and took our place as Saviour. Being loved by Him, and having Him as our Lord, we have no future apart from Him, and therefore no future without love. For us "Thou shalt love" can only mean: Thou shalt not try to evade or escape thy future as opposed to thy present. Thou shalt go further. Thou shalt live. Is there any other categorical imperative apart from this? It is categorical, even though and indeed because it is an easy yoke and a light burden.

4. "Thou shalt love the Lord thy God." As the children of God are what they are and in that way fulfil the law, their love has its counterpart or object in God. That is so even though, and indeed because, He gives Himself to be theirs in faith. How else could He be objective for them, if He did not become theirs in faith? But how could He become theirs in faith, if He were not objective for them, if He did not confront them as another? God alone—because He is God and man's Creator—can confront man as another. But His confrontation means that He gives Himself to be man's own. And therefore in this confrontation, which is not the removing but the form of His presence in the heart, He can and will be loved by man. The decisive element which is revealed in this fact is that love is love for another. Of course, this element is real only in love to God, and in the love to the neighbour which it includes and posits. All other [387] loving is compromised as such by the uncertainty of the objectivity or otherness of the one who is loved, by the possibility that the one who supposedly

loves is perhaps really alone. Where there is no otherness of the one who is loved, where the one who loves is alone, he does not really love.

It is at this point that we must guard against an idea which played a singular part in the theological concept-world of the early Church and has continued to do so right up to the present time. That is the idea of a "self-love" which is not merely justified but commanded. The main biblical support for the idea is to be found, of course, in the "Thou shalt love thy neighbour as thyself." But appeal can also be made to Mt. 7^{12}: "All things whatsoever ye would that men should do unto you, even so do ye unto them"; Phil. 2^{12}: "Work out your own salvation ... "; and 1 Tim. 4^{16}: "In doing this thou shalt save both thyself and them that hear thee;" and with a touch of humour (Polanus, *op. cit.*, p. 4183) Prov. 12^{10}: "A righteous man regardeth the life of his beast." Concerning the "as thyself" we shall have to speak later. But in any case the "as thyself" does not stand side by side with God and our neighbour in such a way that we can agree with Augustine, who was guilty of reading into the passage when he commented: *in quibus tria invenit homo, quae diligat: Deum, se ipsum et proximum*[EN84] (*De Civ. Dei* XIX, 14). Similarly, the presupposition that according to Mt. 7^{12} we will all manner of things that people should do unto us cannot be equated with a commandment. And if Phil. 2^{12} does not teach self-redemption, neither does it teach self-love: even faith, in which we affirm and grasp our redemption by Christ, ought to be very different from an act of self-love. Now Augustine (and before him Tertullian and Chrysostom) was of a different opinion. *Nihil est tibi te ipso propinquius. Quid id longe*[EN85]? *Te habes ante te*[EN86], he could declare (*Sermo* 387, 2), concluding with the exhortation, to love ourselves first, then our neighbour, although both, of course, in God and in the corresponding limits (*De Doctr. chr.* I, 22 f.). Thomas Aquinas gave to this view its speculative basis, that love is a *virtus unitiva. Uni cuique autem ad se ipsum est unitas, quae est potior unione ad alium. Unde sicut unitas est principium unionis. ita amor quo quis diligit seipsum, est forma et radix amicitiae*[EN87] (*S. Theol.* II 2, qu. 25, art. 4, c). Even Polanus (*op. cit.*, p. 4182 f.) has a chapter entitled "*De caritate hominis erga seipsum,*"[EN88] beginning with the luminous statement: *Unusquisque sibi ipsi primum proximus est, deinde aliis*[EN88]. And the 18th century Church used to sing—

> That I should love myself, O God, it is Thy will,
> And as Thou hast prescribed, let me this task fulfil,
> Hold back in holy bounds the urge in me,
> Which Thou implantedst, happy and blessed to be.

(*Lieder für den öff. Gottesdienst*, edited by J. J. Spalding, 1780, 213.)

Even Kierkegaard (*op. cit.*, 24 f.) still thought that the commandment to love our neighbour states, in the right sense, the reverse as well: Thou shalt love thyself in the right way. But there were two who did not agree, Luther and Calvin. *Igitur credo, quod isto precepto "sicut te ipsum" non precipiatur homo diligere se, sed ostendatur vitiosus amor, quo diligit se de facto, q.d. curvus es totus in te et versus in tut amorem, a quo non rectificaberis, nisi penitus cesses te diligere et oblitus tui solum proximum diligas .... Sicut et Adam est forma futuri i.e. Christi, alterius Adam. Sicut in Adam*

[EN84] Here man finds three things to love: God, himself, and his neighbour

[EN85] There is nothing more neighbouring to you than yourself. What are you looking for in the distance

[EN86] You have yourself before you

[EN87] unifying power, Each person has a unity to himself which is stronger than the union with another. Therefore, just as this unity is the principle of union, so also the love by which one loves himself is the form and root of friendship

[EN88] On the love of man for himself.

[EN88] Each one is closest first to his own self, then to others

*mali sumus, utique sic in Christo boni esse debemus; comparatio hic, non autem imitatio exprimitur*EN89 (Luther, *Röm. Brief,* 1515–16 on Rom. 15², *Fi.* II, 337, 8). And irrespective of the authority of Augustine, Calvin inveighed against the representatives of this view: *Evertunt non interpretantur verba Domini, qui inde colligunt (ut faciunt omnes Sorbonici) amorem nostri semper ordine priorem esse: quia regulatum inferius sit sua regula. Inprobitas, inscitia*EN90 and [388] *fatuitas*EN91 were revealed in this exposition. *Asini sunt, qui He micam quidem habent caritatis*EN92. Our self-love can never be anything right or holy and acceptable to God. It is an affection which is the very opposite of love. God will never think of blowing on this fire, which is bright enough already. His demand is that the impulse should be "reversed," *evertatur in caritatem*EN93 (*Comm. on Gal.* 5¹⁴, *C.R.* 50, 251 f.; cf. *Comm. on Deut.* 6⁵, *C.R.* 24, 724; *Comm. on Mt.* 22³⁹, *C.R.* 45, 612). We have to admit that the Reformers were right. Of course, there is the man who loves himself: this is assumed in our text and in Mt. 7¹². But there is no commandment to do this. Self-love is not on the same level as the commanded love to God and our neighbour. Where the latter begins, the former ceases, and *vice versa*. Loving himself, man does not love or no longer loves in the sense of the children of God: and to the extent that this love is the only true love, we must add that loving himself he does not love or no longer loves at all. Loving himself, he is alone. That is the predicament of most of what passes for "love." Man is supposed to love, but the truth is that man is concerned only with himself and therefore does not love at all. Love must always have an opposite, an object. It is only an illusion that we can be an object of love to ourselves. But it might be objected at this point that there is a self-knowledge. But in the only real self-knowledge (which is radically different from the "know thyself" of antiquity), the self-knowledge of repentance, we are not in any sense objective to ourselves. It is by the mirror of the Word of God, by Jesus Christ, that we learn the truth about ourselves. What we love—if we love at all—is always something else or someone else. Of much apparent loving of another we have to ask whether the other really is another, whether it has in fact a basic object, and therefore whether it is real love at all. And in spite of Augustine the invention of a commandment to love oneself was a cardinal error. As the wrath of Calvin rightly felt, it meant the elevation of something negative in itself into a principle. It was obviously the dictum of a "natural" theology and anthropology, that there is in man—manifestly unaffected by the fall—the life principle of an original *unitas ad se ipsum*EN94 of all life, on the basis of which self-love is something good and possible, taking precedence over love of one's neighbour. If that was the real view, it ought to have been subjected to a critical examination in the light of our text and Holy Scripture generally, which would no doubt have led to its dissolution. But it was preferred uncritically to take the "natural" view as a standard for the exposition of our text. The right thing is to avoid this result from the outset.

EN89 Therefore I believe that in this statement 'as yourself', a man is not commanded to love himself; rather a wicked love is indicated, by which he in practice does love himself. It is saying that you are wholly turned in on yourself and directed to loving yourself, by whom you will not be justified unless you repent, stop loving yourself, forget yourself and love your neighbour … Just as Adam is a type of the one to come, that is, Christ the second Adam; just as in Adam we are wicked, so thus in Christ we must be good. So here also the comparison is not identical

EN90 They overturn the words of the Lord, rather than interpret them, when they conclude from this (as do all those in the Sorbonne) that love for ourselves is always first in rank, since the norm itself is inferior to what it governs., Wickedness, ignorance

EN91 stupidity

EN92 They are asses, who have not even a grain of love

EN93 should be turned into love

EN94 unity to oneself

In love to God man is not alone. On the contrary, in love to God he has to do with a genuine partner—with the One who loving him first has given Himself to be his own, and therefore made Himself a genuine partner. Only of love to God can it be said that it has a genuine partner, for it is only in love to God that there is love to one's neighbour. For that reason only the love of God can be called real love. And it is the Lord who wills to be loved as the other. We again think what that means. The one Lord, the Lord of all lords, the Lord who is not only called Lord but actually is the Lord by coming to man as the Revealer of Himself and by taking his place as the Reconciler, that One is Lord in such a way that His lordship is known by man in every circumstance: if not in goodness, in severity, if not as assistance, as opposition, if not in the presence of His revealedness, in the times of His forbearance which can also be times of warning: times to remember and await His revealedness. In all these things He never ceases to be the Lord, and in that eminent sense in which it can be said only of the Son or Word of God who became flesh for us. It is a matter of the love of this Lord, and of this Lord as "thy God." Being this Lord, i.e., acting upon me as this Lord, He is in fact my God. All that I know of God and can know and should know and indeed ought to know, I know by an exercise of lordship, of which I am the object. It is not possible for me even to think of a God who is not this Lord. And how can He be the Lord He is, if He is not God? His lordship is the action of deity. This Lord is identical with God Himself. And the uniqueness of the Lord in whose hands I am means the uniqueness of God. The knowledge of the uniqueness of God is not the result of a philosophical consideration of the nature of God. It is the answer to His revelation as the Lord. The philosophical consideration of the nature of God can never lead us beyond the dialectic of the concepts of monotheism and polytheism, pantheism and atheism. It is only in the revelation of God as the Lord that the decision is made: I am the Lord thy God—I: not the idea of the unity of God, not the beings which want to be gods, not anything or everything which can be divine, not thou thyself in thine own divinity, but I—thou shalt have none other gods but me.

In this text the New Testament κύριος [EN95] is an exact equivalent for the Old Testament name for God, Yahweh. The meaning of the Old Testament formula, "Yahweh thy God" or "Yahweh our God," does not differ in the slightest from the developed form. When Yahweh reveals His name to Moses, He makes (or re-makes) the covenant between Himself and Israel. The decisive factor in this covenant is that the Yahweh revealed to Israel should act towards Israel in the way peculiar to Himself, to salvation, and that in this action He should be acknowledged by Israel as God, and in view of the uniqueness of His action as the only possible Lord of Israel, to be respected and worshipped as the only God. It is customary to distinguish the so-called "henotheism" of certain strata of Old Testament tradition as an earlier, and from the standpoint of the history of religion a lower, stage as compared with the later and supposedly higher "monotheism" of the prophets. But as such, even where it is not explicit on the point, even where, like St. Paul (1 Cor. 8⁵), it actually recognises the existence

---

[EN95] Lord

of other gods, faith in Yahweh has as its main point a recognition of the uniqueness of the deity of Yahweh. And the strength of the later "monotheism" of the prophets—that which distinguished it more sharply from heathen monotheism than from the so-called earlier henotheistic stage in its own area—was the simple power of faith in Yahweh, the power of the knowledge of the unique history, in which Israel was confronted by its Lord.

5. But what does it mean to love?—to love this other, the Lord thy God? As we have considered the text we have already formed certain preliminary definitions. To love means to become what we already are, those who are loved by Him. To love means to choose God as the Lord, the One who is our Lord because He is our Advocate and Representative. To love means to be obedient to the commandment of this God. In every case, therefore, love is an accepting, confirming and grasping of our future. In it this future is identical with [390] the reality of God, who in the most pregnant sense of the word is "for us." It is therefore an accepting, confirming and grasping of the God who is our future. And as such it takes place in an order and connexion which proceed from God, and is therefore an act of obedience. But from what we have just said we learn the following further lessons. If love, as distinct from the illusion of self-love, is love for another, and if this other is God the Lord, then our loving must be defined as the nature and attitude of man, conscious that he is of a different kind from that object. Love to God takes place in the self-knowledge of repentance in which we learn about ourselves by the mirror of the Word of God which acquits and blesses us, which is itself the love of God to us. The man who loves God will let himself be told and will himself confess that he is not in any sense righteous as one who loves and in his loving before and over against God. On the contrary, he is a sinner who even in his love has nothing to bring and offer to God. The love of God for him is that God intercedes for him and represents him even though he is so unworthy, even though he can never be anything but unworthy and therefore undeserving of love. He is accepted and confirmed and grasped by this love of God to him. In it is both his own future and the commandment of God: how can that have any other meaning than that he is driven to repentance and held there? He can and will love only as even in respect of his loving he allows and willingly allows this to happen.

At this point I should again like to quote H. F. Kohlbrügge: "The feeling of sin and misery begins and remains in us, the more we are irradiated by the sun of righteousness. Whoso is born of God has his supreme good in God alone; nothing else can satisfy him. Idols must all give place one after the other. But the more the love of God increases in the heart, the more knowledge there is of inability, and, even with the best of wills, unwillingness, to love God the Lord, and to love Him with all the heart and soul and mind and strength. The spirit will not come from the flesh. The love of God and neighbour cannot be found in man, in the flesh, but only hatred of God and neighbour. The love of God is poured into our hearts by the Holy Spirit given to us. That is the knowledge and experience of all the saints. In themselves, that is, in their flesh, they find no good thing and therefore no love to God .... Only by the fact that they are perfect in Christ Jesus do they have the assurance that they are perfect in love. But the more Christ has become their peace, the more they humble themselves in the dust before God, and are rejected utterly because of their lovelessness, and find the basis of their hope only in the love with which God has first loved us, and in the grace of Jesus Christ, in which He is so rich towards us in all patience and mercy." According to Kohlbrügge there are definite marks of a sorrowful kind by which the children of God can know that the love of God is in them. These are weeping, groaning, crying, sorrow and concern because in their hearts they find only perversity and hostility, only the love of sin and the world and the things which are seen, because they have no desire at all for God and His love, but a cold, sluggish, hard and stony heart, filled with all kinds of evil considerations and other sinful thoughts. Therefore the children of God must at all points humble themselves before the holiness of God. They must bow beneath His holy law. They must be crushed and broken in respect of [391]   the love of God and neighbour. They must be humbled to the very core. They must apply to themselves what the apostle Paul says in the seventh chapter of Romans, especially of the sin which the regenerate find in themselves in the light of God's law. For the fact that they are overwhelmed in this way proves that the love of God is in them (*ibid.*, pp. 502–504).

The very necessity of this knowledge of the otherness of the one who loves as compared with the one who is loved will perhaps make it clear that to love God is to seek God. Those who are found by God in His great love for us are the very ones who must and will seek Him. In seeking Him they assure and affirm and apprehend their own future and therefore Himself. They are obedient to His commandment. In seeking Him, therefore, they love Him. We cannot be satisfied with repentance as such (especially if it is sincere). We cannot be satisfied with self-knowledge (especially if it does not mean assurance but a burning need). Beyond our own quite conscious lovelessness, and therefore without even dreaming that with our love we can offer anything to God, we begin genuinely, and in need, and with a consuming desire to know, to ask about the One who has first loved us. As those who are in need but also have a consuming desire to know, we know God as the one God, the one God because He is the one Lord, one in His revelation, one in His activity on our behalf, the One who is Himself alone our hope. As those who are in need but also have a consuming desire to know, we know that this one God is our only refuge and salvation—indeed He is the only possibility of our existing at all. In all the otherness in which He confronts us, we actually belong to Him—in all our otherness over against Him. If we are quite clear about His lordship and therefore His love on the one hand, and our own lovelessness and unworthiness of love on the other, it will strike us quite clearly that the autonomy of our existence has been taken from us. He has taken it to Himself; He has not taken away our existence from us. We have not ceased to be ourselves. We are still free. But in that existence He has left us without root or soil or country, "having transferred us to the Kingdom of the Son of his love" (Col. 1^{13}), having Himself become our root and soil and country. From the standpoint of His incarnation and exaltation, the fact that we are "translated into the kingdom of the Son of God" means that as the Second Adam He has assumed human nature, that He has united it to His divine person, so that our humanity, our existence in this nature, no longer has any particularity of its own, but belongs only to Him. And from the standpoint of the reconciliation and justification effected in Him, it means that, bearing our punishment, achieving the obedience we did not achieve and keeping the faith we did not keep. He acted once and for all in our place. We cannot, therefore, seek our own being and activity, so far as they still remain to us, in ourselves but only in Him. Strictly speaking, our being and activity as such can only be this seeking. We misunderstand this seeking if we think of it as a special art or striving on the part of those who have [392] already proposed and undertaken the task, or as a wonderful flower of piety which has grown in the garden of those who are already particularly situated and gifted for it. Even the works and wonders of mystical love to God are still part of our own being and activity, which has as such to be abandoned in its entirety in the sight of God, as something which is loveless and unworthy of love. Our own being and activity stands wholly and utterly under this judgment (including, therefore, all the works and wonders which are possible within it, but also in its dark lethargy and wildness). Yet this being and activity acquires a direction at the point where everything is done for us, the direction Godward in Jesus Christ. And this is no special work. It is far more. It is the work of all works. It is no special miracle. It is far more. It is the miracle of all miracles. And as such it is the simplest necessity of nature: even more necessary than breath to our body. But it takes place quite irrespective of any works or wonders of which we may be capable, or of the lethargy and wildness which is inherent in all our being and activity, including our highest efforts as well as worst periods of unconcern. What matters is emphatically not the fact that we are seeking. What matters is that if we accept and adopt this direction, we are always seekers. Of course, that means that we are seeking. But in all that seeking we are again in the sphere of our lovelessness and unworthiness of being loved. In spite of our seeking, we can still be rejecting. Our seeking may be upright, inward and profound, but as such it will stand in constant need of the forgiveness of sins. What justifies the seeking is only the fact that we seek as real seekers. And that means that it is only He whom we seek and who has again and again made us seekers, who in our existence has thrown us back utterly upon the forgiveness of sins through Him. That we should be those who always seek Him is what the commandment to love enjoins. It is the love which is the fulfilling of the law.

And now there is really only one other thing to add. If we are seekers of God, and to that extent lovers of God, this can be definitely and unequivocally proved and maintained of the children of God only by the one thing: that in all circumstances and in every connexion they rejoice if their seeking is not in vain, if therefore the One whom they seek allows Himself to be found by them, if in that way He confirms the fact that He has sought and found them, before they ever sought Him. How can they not rejoice when God really confronts them, when the One whom they loved loves them again and anew, as He had already loved them before, when He is therefore present to them in His Word, in Jesus Christ, when He speaks with them, and acts on them? Is He not a faithful God, because He does so? And how can they not rejoice that He is so faithful? But we have every reason to think that it is not self-evident that we

[393]

should rejoice. We seek many things in which we do not rejoice when we find them—which shows, of course, that even our seeking is impotence and error. Supposing that this is the case here, with the children of God in their seeking after God?

> Often enough we can see in others, and especially in ourselves, that it is possible to be a regular and genuine and serious seeker after God, out of a passionately sincere heart, or a real sense and experience of the many compulsions of life and conscience—only to give it all up when our apparent seriousness is suddenly taken seriously, in a situation in which our seeking could really be a finding, because a being found; and simply because the God we find, who has let Himself be found, is not the One of whom we can joyfully confess that it is Him we have sought. We love Him or think that we love Him at a distance, but we do not love Him near at hand. We prefer to withdraw to that pretended love at a distance. But is not that love unmasked and adjudged as non-love?

Let us be more precise. This is something which can never happen with the children of God. They will prove and maintain that they are what they are, those who really love, not merely subjectively honest, but quite genuine seekers after God, by the fact that they do not withdraw but stand fast, and joyfully, with a Yes which comes from all their heart and soul and mind and strength, even when they find God. When they do find God, when the love of God reaches its goal, this means that they hear and feel and taste afresh that they have an incomparable Lord and that they can be free only in obedience to Him. When they do find God, they are met by grace, which means that they accept, that they receive the gifts proffered, that they approve what is done for them, that it may be done to them. But grace shows that in themselves they are poor and impotent and empty: indeed, that they are adversaries and rebels. Grace points them away from self, frightens them out of themselves, deprives them of any root or soil or country in themselves, summons them to hold to the promise, to trust in Him, to boast in Him, to take guidance and counsel of Him and Him alone. Grace is the discipline which does not permit them any idolatry or self-righteousness, but bids them say, even when they have done all that it is their duty to do, that they are unprofitable servants. Grace does not allow of any arrogance, even at a later stage. Grace keeps down. Grace reveals the lethargy and wildness which lie like a heavy load upon even their best thoughts and undertakings. Grace demands of them that they trust only in grace, and live only by grace—and by grace really live. If that be God, the Son of God and the Word of God, who can rejoice at it? Who in seeking after God ever sought after that? We can only reply that the children of God rejoice in it. This and this alone is what the children of God have sought. Therefore the children of God are not disillusioned or embittered. They do not turn away, they do not return to that pretended love at a distance, when the Beloved One is seen to be like this, and meets them in this way. For the children of God there is nothing bitter about the severity of the Law from which there is no escape, the mercy which reveals our misery, the freedom and glory of God, which take from us all claim, the order which obtains here and which right to the very core of our being is always and unreservedly an order of humiliation, the light which falls right into our darkness. There is nothing shameful about it. They do not need to flee from it. It is all sweet. It is the greatest possible honour. They seek after it with the greatest possible diligence. They do not ask anything more, or different, or higher, or more dignified. They love it just as it is. They can never let it be repeated too often, or hear it or see it too often, or allow it to sink into their feelings and conscience and will too often. It is in this way that they desire to be treated and ruled. They love the One who deals with them in this way. And that proves that they have really sought after God and loved God. It is proved by the fact that they continue to love God, that they love the One whom they sought all the more now that they have found Him, now that He has found them afresh. God sees and knows that they do. He knows His own. At heart, man is a hypocrite. In respect of love he can easily make out to himself and others that he is something which he is not. We have to answer to God, if we think we should confess that we love Him, not only in the way in which we seek Him, but in the way in which He gives Himself to be found, because that is what He is. God sees and knows whether we love Him in this way. But if it is true before Him, that we love Him in this way, if we can say before God that it is true—as the children of God can—then we are not only permitted to be sure about our loving and therefore our fulfilment of the Law, but we are forbidden to doubt. If we rejoice to hear the actual Word of God to man, we love God. The very fact that we rejoice to hear the Word of God means that the assurance which we are not only permitted but commanded has nothing to do with the forbidden arrogance of the *homo religiosus*[EN96].

6. It might be asked whether the addition, that thou shalt love God, "with all thy heart, with all thy soul, with all thy mind and with all thy strength," really adds anything new and specific to what we have already said. I think that this is actually the case. For obviously these concepts, which we must not isolate, of course, but take as a whole and in their total effect, are an emphatic reminder that man himself, the whole man, is challenged by the commandment to love, not only that he love, but that he should be one who loves, and therefore (in the twofold sense of the word) one who is condemned, and therefore a seeker after God, as we have seen already. It is to be noted that the words "all" and "thine" are repeated four times. And the four main words, heart, soul, mind and strength, which obviously describe the sphere of human capacity as such, at once indicate that when the commandment claims this being for love, it is concretely the actual and whole being of man which is claimed. We ourselves, with all that we have and are as men (and have not and are not), are either those who love or those who do not. There can be no division between the man I am visibly in myself and the man I am invisibly in Jesus Christ, and then on the basis of this division a dismissal of the former because of the duty to

[394]

[395]

[EN96] religious man

love. It is as the man I am visibly in myself that I am invisibly in Jesus Christ. And it is the fact that I am invisible in Jesus Christ that imposes upon me as the man I am visibly in myself the duty to love. Rightly, then, there can be no question of any division of my visible being, or of any restricting of the duty of love, to particular aspects and capacities of this being, whether to my so-called inward parts or to my so-called deeds. Of course the commandment to love claims my inward parts. But in doing so, it claims that I should not only think and feel but, as I do so, live and act out of the love for which it claims me. It claims my life and activity, but in doing so it claims that they should be love from the inmost parts. Again, there is no question of a division between the different times and situations and tasks of human love; as though love were commanded at one time and not commanded at another, as though it were left to our judgment to love, or not to love or to love less. The addition is a guarantee, therefore, against every division, and therefore against every reservation or exception in love. Or positively, it means that Christian love is characterised as a total constitution and attitude of man. It is one man who is pardoned by Jesus Christ, one man who is the sinful creature which he is in himself: one in his existence within and without; one at every stage and in all the circumstances and encounters of his way. As this one man he is either a man who loves or a man who does not. Clearly, the addition reaches back to the presupposition, that "the Lord our God is one Lord." It is, as it were, a proof that the One who is loved in Christian love is really God. God is the one Lord. That He is the One who is loved is shown in the fact that He is loved without division, reservation and exception; either in that way or not at all: there is no question of any other alternative. It will be rewarding to take a backward look from this standpoint.

In its relationship to that presupposition, the addition shows us that there is a similarity between the love with which God loves us and the love for Him which He has enjoined upon us. For all the majestic superordination of the one over the other, we can still describe them both by the same concept. To the exclusiveness with which God and God alone is our Lord, there corresponds the exclusiveness with which our being and activity must be a seeking after God and that alone. From a new angle this similarity may draw our attention to the grace in the law of love imposed upon us. It is grace that God wills not only to love us but to be loved by us in return. Just as He does not need to love us, in the same way and even less He does not need to be loved by us. But that is what He wills. And as He is our exclusive Lord, He wills our exclusive love: all thy heart, all thy mind, all thy might for this one thing, to love Him. He therefore [396] wills—and by His Word and His Holy Spirit He creates—that similarity between Him and us. What He is for us in His sphere as God, Creator and Reconciler, we can be for Him in our sphere as sinful creatures. We can therefore love. And in loving we can participate in His perfection.

"Ye shall be perfect, even as your Father in heaven is perfect" (Mt. 5⁴⁸). This is not a law

198

which crushes and kills. It would be so only if we were to hear it, not from the mouth of Jesus Christ, from which it comes to us as a law fulfilled by Him, but as a human regulation, which we would have to fulfil. Heard from Him it is indeed the Law, but the Law as the promise and form of the Gospel, the Gospel in the Law. Is there any news more glad and comforting than that God wills this similarity between Him and us and has already created it in Jesus Christ?

In the second place, the addition again and especially lights up the voluntariness of the obedience given in Christian love. We shall seek after God undividedly and unreservedly, as the commandment demands, only when the commandment to do it has reached and touched not only our heart, our soul, our reason, but all these as our own capacity and all of them completely; so that all of them, in their good points and bad points, in the strength and splendour which may be proper to them as such, and in the perversity and shame which are quite certainly proper to them before God, become our own total act of love. Love as the totality of our being and activity excludes the slavery of law, which obeys only out of fear or has an eye for the gifts of God instead of Himself. Love as a totality excludes an obedience which is melancholy and burdensome because it is secretly resisted. Love as a totality cannot leave in us any fear of God because of sin unforgiven. Where forgiveness reigns, there is, of course, an inevitable fear of God, but it is only a form of love, the seeking of that without which we can do nothing. Again, as a totality love cannot play with God, as though He were a means to achieve all kinds of good ends. Of course, we do have all kinds of good and not so good ends. And a kind of heathen automatism often lets us ascribe to God the role of Fulfiller of the wishes corresponding to them. But in love to God do not our wishes necessarily become of themselves the desire that His will should be done? Again, love as a totality cannot co-exist with a fear of the world or of ourselves: as though there were still powers and forces, which made us obey only sluggishly and under duress. Such powers and forces do, of course, exist. But what is the concern which they cause us compared with the one concern, to love God aright? Love is the freedom into which the love of God has transferred us. Does it not absorb and suck up all the reservation which we can and do make against it. Does it not transform them into reasons for and not against a willing and joyful obedience?

Calvin was a preacher especially of the majesty of God and the Law and obedience, but it was the voluntariness of love which he particularly emphasised in his comments on this passage in both its Old and its New Testament contexts: *Deum non oblectant extorta et coacta obstquia .... Nihil Deo placet quod affertur ex tristitia vel necessitate, quia hilarem datorem quaerit ... Deus se nobis amabilem reddit, ut libenter et qua decet alacritate amplectamur quicquid iubet*[EN97] (*Comm. on Deut.* 10[12], *C.R.* 24, 723), ... *vultque sponte et liberaliter colt*[EN98] (*Comm. on Mt.* 22[37], *C.R.* 45. 611). From these words of Calvin we turn to the texts in Rom. 8[15] and 2 Tim. 1[7]. [397]

[EN97] Obedience extracted and coerced does not please God ... Nothing which is brought forth out of sadness or necessity pleases God, since He seeks a cheerful giver ... God makes Himself attractive to us, so that we might freely and with appropriate speed accept whatever He commands

[EN98] He desires to be worshipped spontaneously and freely

which speak of the "spirit of adoption" or the "spirit of power and of love and of a sound mind" which we have received, and of the "spirit of bondage to a new fear," and "the spirit of despondency" which we have not received—and above all to 1 Jn. $3^{19f.}$, $4^{17f.}$, which speak of our heart condemning us and not condemning us, that if we are of the truth we can assure our heart, that God is greater than our heart and knoweth all things, while we, on the other hand, can be confident that whatsoever we ask we receive of Him, as those who keep His commandments and do those things that are pleasing in His sight. They also speak of the judgment of God in which we stand, that in it love may reach its end with us, giving us the same confidence: φόβος οὐκ ἔστιν ἐν τῇ ἀγάπῃ ἀλλ' ἡ τελεία ἀγάπη ἔξω βάλλει τὸν φόβον[EN99]. Fear can only be the punishment of those who are not perfect in love. We are perfect in love and therefore without fear; for we love, because God has first loved us.

Third, we learn from the addition that love cannot be lost. The expressions "all thy heart," "all thy soul" undoubtedly point not only to a cross-section of man's existence but to a long section. From this standpoint, in respect of the individual acts of human life in their temporal succession, they say of that existence: The commandment to love claims you totally and therefore undividedly and without reserve. There can be no question of any limitation of that love. The addition underlines the fact that, because the divine "thou shalt," is a true and proper one, as distinct from all law which is not real or which we do not count as real law, it affects the body, and in such a way that we cannot distinguish our own existence from it. "Thou wilt love," it says with an emphasis from which there can be no escape, because it does not point us to any acts which we can do or not do, but to our future life. If we accept this, we cannot think of love as a possibility beside which our future might hold other possibilities. We can think of ourselves only as its captives, and as its captives for our whole future. The same is true when we remember that in love there is actualised a similarity between God and His children, the similarity between the exclusiveness with which He is the Lord, and the exclusiveness with which we must therefore seek after Him. Once this circle is closed, once the similarity is actualised, how can there be any going back, or giving up, or limitation? The same is true again when we remember the voluntariness of love. Obviously we can think of love ceasing only if in or with it there is a place for those elements of fear whose presence would mean that it is not voluntary and therefore not love. If love does not have these elements of fear and is therefore real love, how can it possibly cease? The addition "all thy heart, all thy soul" (and this must be decisive for our whole consideration of the matter) reflects the once and for [398] all revelation and reconciliation which has come to us as the Word of God, for which the Holy Spirit has opened us, which is the basis of the love to God in us, which has irresistibly challenged us to love, which has made it possible for us to love even in our total incapacity for love. Are we to think the absurd thought that God, the triune God, can cease to be God, and that that kingdom of His into which we have been placed by faith can actually have an end? The operation of human-creaturely impressions and experiences can certainly cease.

[EN99] there is no fear in love; perfect love casts out fear

2. *The Love of God*

Human purposes and enterprises can cease. What we have called the works and wonders of love, what takes place in the sphere of the human being and activity even of the children of God, and therefore stands under the judgment of God, and therefore has its visible limits: all that can cease. But how can love itself cease, that direction of man's being and activity which involves a judgment upon even the greatest works and wonders possible in this sphere, but in which above all the forgiveness of sins and the covering of shame is already achieved and thankfully accepted? How can it ever be really possible for man to lose this direction again? Whatever can be lost has never been love.

Against the fact that love cannot be lost, the text in Mt. 24¹² has been alleged, in which we are told that in times of persecution the increase of ἀνομία EN100 will mean that the love of many will grow cold (ψυγήσεται). But does this really refer to those who are genuinely obedient to Jesus' commandment to love? There are, of course, all kinds of other love: the love of relatives and friends, which, according to the sayings of Jesus, can in time of temptation turn not only into indifference but even into hate. It is impossible that Jesus should have meant and said the same thing about the love to God and neighbour of the commandment. The verse in Rev. 2⁴ has also been recalled: "I have this against thee, that thou didst leave thy first love." But does not this epistle speak of the constancy (ὑπομονή) of the then Church? Can ἡ ἀγάπη σου ἡ πρώτη EN101—whatever it may be—signify Christian love as such? As we see from what follows, does it not refer to specific works in which it no longer reveals itself and ought to do so? Against these two texts we can set 1 Cor. 13⁸: ἡ ἀγάπη οὐδέποτε πίπτει EN102. And Rom. 11²⁹: ἀμεταμέλητα γὰρ χαρίσματα καὶ ἡ κλῆσις τοῦ θεοῦ EN103. And Rom. 6¹⁴: "Sin shall not have dominion over you: for ye are no longer under the law, but under grace." Also the passages from 1 Jn.: "Whosoever abideth in him sinneth not: whosoever sinneth hath not seen him, neither known him" (3⁶). "Whosoever is born of God doth not commit sin, for his seed remaineth in him; and he cannot sin, because he is born of God" (3⁹). And (of particular significance as the basis) 5¹⁸: "We know that whosoever is born of God sinneth not; but He that is born of God (Christ) keepeth him, and that wicked one toucheth him not." This is in the same letter, in the opening of which it is so strongly declared, that "if we say that we have no sin, we deceive ourselves, and the truth is not in us. If we confess our sins, he is faithful and just to forgive us our sins, and to cleanse us from all unrighteousness. If we say that we have not sinned, we make him a liar, and his word is not in us" (1⁸ᶠ·). There cannot, therefore, be any reference to or recommendation of a perfectionist self-righteousness, complacency or assurance in these passages. Obviously, we have to speak of sin as a reality when it is a question of knowing ourselves on the basis of truth and the Word of God with reference to what we have been right up to the present moment. But we cannot speak of sin as a possibility when it is a question of knowing ourselves on the basis of the same truth and Word of God, in relation to what we will be in the knowledge of the commandment and its promise given to us. It is only as the impossible, the excluded and the [399] absurd, only on the supposition that we are not we, and that Jesus Christ is not Jesus Christ, that sin can be thought of as our future. The same consideration has to be taken into account in the difficult chapter Heb. 6. To understand it, we have to start at the end of the chapter (vv. 13–20). We are told that God had given to the heirs of the promise a "strong

---

EN100 lawlessness
EN101 your first love
EN102 love never fails
EN103 for the gifts and calling of God are irrevocable

encouragement" by "two immutable things" (διὰ δύο πραγμάτων ἀμεταθέτων, v. 18), first by the promise itself and as such, and then by the oath which (acc. to Gen. 22$^{16f.}$) He swore by Himself, seeing there was none greater than Himself (v. 13). "The oath serves for confirmation to the ending of all strife" (v. 16). On the basis of this twofold certainty—that we have the Word of God and have it as God's Word—we can and should "flee to lay hold of the hope set before us. We have it as an anchor of the soul which is sure and stedfast, and enters into that which is within the veil, whither as a forerunner Jesus entered for us, that he might be the high priest for ever according to the order of Melchisedek" (6$^{18-20}$). On the basis of this very presupposition we cannot think of resting on what the beginning of the chapter (vv. 1–8) calls the λόγος Χριστοῦ τῆς ἀρχῆς,^{EN104} i.e., we cannot be content with a promise which is still empty and unfulfilled, as though it were not fulfilled in advance in view of the oath which God sware by Himself, and the divinity of the One who has made it. We cannot stop at a foundation upon which there is to be no further building. But on the basis of this presupposition we can and should "go on to perfection" (ἐπὶ τὴν τελειότητα φερώμεθα). "And this will we do if God permit" (vv. 1–3). But this perfection is a future from which there is no return. Those who hear and receive the Word of God are like the earth watered by the rain, which, thus blessed by God, brings forth fruits meet for use (v. 7). Could it not bring forth thorns and thistles as well? Of course, but it is then accursed, and its fruits are to be burned (v. 8). As the blessing of God the Word would not then be heard or received. There would be no returning from the future posited by the Word, only a proof that for us that future had not been posited at all. The Son of God would then be crucified and put to shame by us. We would participate afresh in the transgression with which Israel confirmed its rejection (v. 6.). Now, of course, this transgression is the past which we have to confess openly. And again and again we shall have to realise and confess that we are guilty in respect of our past as this transgression. But it cannot at the same time be our future. "For it is impossible for those who were once enlightened, and have tasted of the heavenly gift, and were made partakers of the Holy Ghost, and have tasted the good word of God, and the powers of the age to come"—the text continues: "if they shall fall away, to renew them again unto repentance" (vv. 4–6). Therefore in the context of the letter, we have here an obvious warning against the idea that the future quietly includes both the possibility of sin and also the possibility of a fresh renunciation of sin. This idea of a divided future alternating between sin and repentance is the very thing which is excluded by the presupposition—or as we might say in our own context—by the totality of the commandment to love based on the presupposition. Those who have heard the good Word of God and tasted the powers of the world to come cannot reckon with this bilinear but only with the unilinear future: that they will love as they are loved. How can they have that sure and certain anchor of their hope "within the veil," how can they see Jesus, who stands as High Priest at the right hand of the Father, how can they be His contemporaries, if at the same time they can and want to compromise the turning-point of all ages, and therefore of their own age, which is His age, by the idea of a twofold future of sin and repentance? As such, they neither know a present repentance, nor will they owe that future repentance which is always commanded of those that love God, when they look back to the sin which they have done and do and time and again will do, as those that belong to the past. The possibility of future repentance presupposes that we love God with all our heart and soul, and therefore affirm and accept Him, and in Him our only future. There is a saying which in the Middle Ages and even later was ascribed to Augustine, and in content it is quite right: *Charitas, quae deseri potest, nunquam fuit vera*^{EN105} (*De salutaribus documentis* 7). By comparison, the biblical testimony was weakened when Thomas

[400]

---

^{EN104} the elementary teaching about Christ
^{EN105} The love which can be abandoned was never true

2. The Love of God

Aquinas conceded the impossibility of losing love *ex virtute Spiritus sancti*[EN106], the impossibility of sin in the act of love itself, and the impossibility of losing *charitas patriae*[EN107], i.e., the love with which we shall meet God face to face, but then continued: *charitas autem viae ... non semper actu fertur in Deum, unde quando actu in Deum non fertur, potest aliquid occurrere per quod charitas amittatur*[EN108] (*S. theol.* II 2, qu. 24, art. 11c). It was, of course, a mistake to set against this the doctrine of love as a *habitus a Spiritu sancto infusus*[EN109], as occasionally propounded by the later Calvinists (e.g., by Polanus, *Synt. Theol. chr.*, 1609, p. 3867), for the concept *habitus*[EN110] approximated too closely to the quite unbiblical idea of a supernatural qualifying of the believer and therefore a jeopardising of the knowledge of the freeness of grace in respect of the believer. In and with the love of God, our loving of God, too, is a promise addressed to us, and grasped as such in faith. It is not, therefore, a supernatural quality, a "*habitus*[EN111]." Yet the meaning behind this equivocal expression is a right one: that we cannot perceive and understand love in those "acts" in which it is offered or not offered to God, but only in the being of man as determined in faith by the Word and the Holy Spirit. And it would involve a negation of this, and indirectly of the Spirit of God, to carry through the thought that it can be removed and lost by the vacillations which we can definitely anticipate in relation to the "acts" of love (by the judgment under which these acts as such invariably stand and will stand). Christian love does not find comfort in itself and its acts, but only in its foundation and object. Its cessation, therefore, does not belong to any possible future, but only to the impossible.

The fourth thing we learn from the addition "with all thy heart ... " is that Christian love cannot be understood except as the thankfulness which the believer owes to God in His revealing and reconciling work. The totality in which God wills to be loved by us according to His commandment excludes all self-glorying, all claims which he who loves might make to the loved One on account of his love. If he does make such claims, to that extent he ceases to love. His heart, or reason, or some part of his nature or capacity, moves to dispense him from loving, at any rate in part, allowing him both to search and to have edifying but vain thoughts about the beauty and value of the search. Where this happens, his gaze is not exclusively upon God in Jesus Christ. His heart is divided, and his attention vacillates between God and himself. The similarity between his loving and God's loving tends in the same direction, because he obviously does not let God be the one Lord. Nor can there be any further question of a genuine voluntariness in his love. And what is to prevent it degenerating into a love which can be lost, if it is not only confidence in God, but also to some extent confidence in self, in the power and beauty of the being and activity of the children of God, or even in the works and wonders corresponding to this being. No, it can only be understood as thankfulness. Negatively that means that love is grace, but not *gratia gratum faciens*[EN112]. Its

---

[EN106] because of the power of the Holy Spirit

[EN107] the love of heaven

[EN108] but love in the meantime, in this age ... is not always directed to God, and when it is not directed towards God, something through which love might be lost can obstruct it

[EN109] disposition infused by the Holy Spirit

[EN110] disposition

[EN111] disposition

[EN112] grace making grace

[401] relationship to the love with which God loves us is irreversible. The love of God is its basis, and it rests upon it. It cannot therefore justify itself. How indeed could it, if it is the seeking of that Other who justifies us, and therefore the recognition that we cannot justify ourselves by our own being and activity, even by our being and activity as the children of God? And the positive meaning of it is that love is nothing more and does not wish to be anything more than the obedient erecting of the sign of divine grace. Indeed, what God in His love wills from us to His glory is that our existence in the determination which we ourselves give to it should be a sign of the fact that we stand under His predetermination. The fulness of His love is not only that He rescues us from the sin and death to which we would fall victim if left in the determination which we would have given ourselves, but that He claims us for the proclamation of His glory. That is what takes place in the fact that we may love Him. Therefore the love of God—and it is at this point that it merges into the praise of God—means that in our own existence we become a sign of what God as the one Lord has done and is for us. How can love to God be inactive? It is all activity, but only as man's answer to what God has said to him. As this answer it is a work, and it produces works. But it is a work, and produces works, in the fact that it is the witness of God's work, and therefore a renunciation of all self-glorying and all claims.

3. THE PRAISE OF GOD

Rather strangely, the emphasis in Mk. 12 falls on the last part, the "second commandment," "Thou shalt love thy neighbour as thyself." From what we said at the outset, and fundamentally, about the relationship between the love and the praise of God, and from what we have just said in our exposition of the commandment to love, this really comes under our new heading. As anticipated, the whole meaning and content of the commandment to love our neighbour is that as God's children, and therefore as those who love Him with all our heart, soul, mind and strength, we are summoned and claimed for the praise of God as the activity and work of thankfulness which, by reason of our being as those who love, we cannot avoid. The "second" commandment has no other meaning and content apart from and in addition to: "Bless the Lord, O my soul, and all that is within me bless his Holy name." And *vice versa*, it is by the "second" commandment that we experience point by point and exhaustively what is the praise of God, what is the meaning and content of the revealing, manifesting, attesting, confessing, living out and showing forth of the lordship and redemption which has come to the children of God. Therefore we have to say just as strictly that no praise of God is serious, or can be taken seriously, if it is apart from or in addition to the commandment: "Thou shalt love thy neighbour as thyself." Whatever else we may understand by the praise [402] of God, we shall always have to understand it as obedience to this commandment.

Cf. for what follows, R. Bultmann, *Jesus*, 1926, 102 f.; E. Fuchs, *Was heisst: 'Du sollst deinen Nächsten lieben wie dich selbst? Theol. Bl.*, 1932, 417–48

First, we will simply continue the exposition which we have begun and ask what we are to think of the remarkable duplication or repetition of the commandment to love as such? In what sense is there obviously a second loving of the children of God alongside the first? In what sense does the "neighbour" obviously stand alongside God as the object of this loving of theirs? We cannot be too cautious in our reply—at any rate in relation to all preconceived and imported concepts of God and man and love.

In the sense of the text as we have so far expounded it, as a commandment to love God, the commandment to love is one of unequivocal absoluteness and exclusiveness according to all our present findings. To think back for a moment over what we have said, it is obviously *the* commandment, the one commandment, the commandment of all commandments, and the commandment in all commandments. Therefore, if the commandment to love our neighbour is placed alongside it and expressly described as a separate "second commandment," there seem to be only three possible explanations. Either we have another absolute demand in the strict and proper sense. If that is the case, we will have to repeat all that has been said about love to God and apply it to love to our neighbour. Or there are not really two demands at all, but one absolute demand. Love to God and love to the neighbour are identical; the one has to be understood as the other. If that is the case, we will have to show that God is to be loved in the neighbour and the neighbour in God, and in what way. Or there is only the one absolute demand of love to God, and the demand of love to the neighbour approximates to it as the first and most important of the particular, relative and subordinate commands, within which, as in Luther's catechism, the commandment to love God forms the real nerve and content, the commandment in the commandments and the commandment of all commandments.

First, we must abandon at once as quite impossible the idea that there are two absolute commandments side by side. Exegetically, it is not legitimate to compare the brief saying on love to the neighbour with that about love to God simply by transferring all the definitions of the one to the other. On this explanation, it is impossible to see any way of avoiding the conclusion that the text speaks of the love of two Gods. But God is the one Lord and God. We are enjoined to love Him, and to love Him with that totality and exclusiveness. The same love cannot, therefore, be demanded as love to the neighbour.

The second solution, to regard the two loves as identical, is in itself a useful [403] and illuminating solution. But it does not stand up to closer investigation. It is only by the severest pressure that it can be introduced into the text: it does not say, as on this presupposition it would have to say, that we must love our neighbour with all our heart, with all our soul ... and the Lord God as ourselves. Certainly, the two commandments belong together. That is clear. But it is just as clear that the commandment to love our neighbour is a "second" commandment. The final and almost unavoidable logic of this solution would be the damnable confusion and blasphemy: that God is the neighbour, the neighbour is God. But we need not press it as far as that. If we try to interpret love to God as love to the neighbour and love to the neighbour as love to God, we have to make certain anthropologico-theological presuppositions which are quite illegitimate because they cannot be based on the biblical witness to revelation, and are in fact contrary to it.

In other words, as the basis of this identification we have to ascribe an inherent value (1) to the neighbour as representing the human race, and (2) to our relationship to him as the fulfilment of individual humanity, to the human thou, and therefore to the human ego in its relationship to the thou. And this value is not derived but autonomous, and therefore has to be brought into a more or less direct connexion with God or with something divine. It is because of this twofold value, because of the self-based sanctity and dignity and glory both of man in himself and also of the fellowship between man and man as such, that according to this conception religion is also humanity and love to God is love to the neighbour (meaning love to man). Of course, it is usually more or less strongly emphasised that humanity must also be religion and love to man must also be love to God. But it is inevitable that the distinctive features of a love to God which cannot be seen should be known and therefore necessarily determined by a love to man which is very much seen and supposedly well known. Love to God is, then, the quintessence and hypostasised expression of what we know in a concretely perceptible and practical form as love to man. Love to God is the idea, the supreme norm of this known love to man. But it is clear that in these circumstances love to God cannot be what it is in Holy Scripture, the response of man to the being and activity of One who has first loved us. The converse, that true love to man must also be love to God, comes too late to be a real converse. The statement has no importance, if the real cardinal and interpretative principle of love is in the preceding statement, that true love to God will have to be love to man. It is too late for love to God to be decisive and meaningful in the biblical sense. There is no praise of the God who has first loved us, breaking forth in love to the neighbour. Instead, there is praise of the sanctity and dignity and glory of man, with a somewhat equivocal love for the God created according to the likeness of this man. The meaning and place given by Holy Scripture to love to God are quite different. Holy Scripture speaks of man always and exclusively from the standpoint of his sin and reconciliation. It addresses man only in the name of Jesus Christ. It does not, therefore, participate in this praise of man. As Scripture sees it, man as such has no dignity of his own, nor has the fellowship of man with man. What

[404]

he is as an individual and in fellowship, he is under judgment and as a new creation of the love of God. The only humanity there is is this lost humanity, founded anew by the Word and Spirit of God, revealed in Jesus Christ and to be grasped in faith in Him. There is no humanity based on itself. If such a humanity has to be presupposed in order to identify love to God and love to the neighbour, then the identification cannot be made. Love to God in the sense of Holy Scripture, and this love to the neighbour, are opposites which mutually exclude each other.

Of course, we might find some other basis for the identification. We do not need to base the commandment to love the neighbour in the idea of humanity, and therefore in a doctrine of the inherent dignity of man and of the fellowship of man with man, and certainly not in a general doctrine of man existing either as an individual or in society, as it were, in a vacuum. There are other ways of showing the identity of this commandment with the commandment to love God. Inveighing roughly against all forms of idealism, we can replace the idea of humanity by an appeal to history, that is, to all those real and historically visible orders, marriage, the family, calling, nationality, the state, in which we all undoubtedly exist and in which we no less definitely have to recognise and respect the ordinances of creation and therefore the ordinances of God. The reason why I live as a human I in relation to the human thou is because in virtue of my creation it is arranged that I should stand in these orders and therefore be a father, son, brother, husband, compatriot, citizen, etc., and as such that I should definitely confront and be confronted by the thou, that I should be directed and pledged and indebted to it, in short, that I should be wholly and utterly bound up with it. The thou appointed for me by the ordinances of creation, is my neighbour. It is not that he has a value in himself or for me. It is rather that he is ineluctably posited for me in the framework of these ordinances. That is the basis of the commandment to love one's neighbour. Love to God is, therefore, necessarily love to the neighbour, because obviously I can only honour God by submitting to what He as Creator disposes regarding me and therefore by accepting my responsibility to the thou in the framework of His ordinances. But is this historical basis of the identity of love to God and love to man really so very different from the first humanitarian basis as it pretends to be? Is the idea of order which lies at the root of it so very opposed to the earlier decisive idea of humanity, because when the Bible speaks of God it will not at any price speak of man, but speaks all the more confidently and definitely of these ordinances? Have not the idea [405] of humanity and that of order this in common, that they both rest upon an inherent value which is presupposed without question—although there is perhaps the distinction that in the one case the emphasis is upon the presupposedness, in the other upon the value? Can we not interpret humanity as an order of creation and all the orders of creation as orders of humanity? Do we speak any the less about man when for a change we prefer to speak more about the supra-personal bonds in which he stands than about the inner freedom of his humanity? Here, too, under another aspect, are we not really speaking about love to man rather than love to the neighbour? It may be objected that the idea of order is obviously superior to that of humanity because it derives from the divine creation. But in the last resort cannot the champions of humanity claim that in dealing with it as a pure presupposition they, too, are thinking of the divine creation? We have to put the same question to both the humanitarian and the historical schools: whether the so-called humanity or the so-called ordinances are given and known by us in the sphere of the created world in such a way that in them we can recognise the divine creation? whether in this sphere of sin and reconciliation there can be any direct knowledge of God and His commandments, i.e., a knowledge which is based directly upon creation apart from revelation? Only if this is the case dare we openly equate what humanity or the ordinances seem to command with the biblical commandment to love the neighbour, and therefore this commandment with the commandment to love God. If it is not the case, then the idealism of the humanitarians and the realism of the historicists both lead us to the same empty cistern: to the knowledge of a God who is made in our own image, the content and idea of our own freedom and our own relationships. The freedom of the children of God begins only where the freedom, which we think we experience in our humanity, ends. Their real relationship begins only where the relationship with what they think they experience and know as ordinances in history ends. If we compare the connexion with our fellow-man, which seems to be laid upon us in virtue of the freedom and relationship supposedly learned from creation, with the biblical commandment to love our neighbour, and if we again compare the latter with the commandment to love God—how far we have gone from the commandment to love God as it was laid down by Jesus and fulfilled in Him! Instead—and either way—how near we have come to the blasphemous inference (which was not, of course, intended either way), that God is the neighbour, i.e., man, and that man is God!

But it might still be argued that we do not need to define and fill out the concept neighbour according to the teaching of philosophical idealism or realism. Can we not define and fill it out quite legitimately, i.e., from the standpoint of the biblical testimony to revelation, and still identify the commandment to love God and the commandment to love the neighbour? Now we must certainly affirm that what the neighbour is can and ought to be determined, not by the idea of humanity or order, but by Holy Scripture. And we can already anticipate and say that in the light of Holy Scripture the neighbour certainly cannot be identified with God, but must always be thought of as a man and therefore as a creature. But that means that love to him cannot be equated with love to God, but must be distinguished from it, and that only in that distinction can it be brought into a most definite connexion with it. If we have a legitimate concept of neighbour the chances of establishing an identity of the two commandments are at their very slenderest.

[406]

3. The Praise of God

The collapse of the second possibility regarding the relationship of love to God and love to the neighbour seems logically to leave only the third alternative: to separate the commandment to love the neighbour from the absolute commandment to love God, and to regard it as one of the relative, derived and subordinate commandments, although perhaps the first and most important; to regard it perhaps as a summary of the commandments of the second table, and yet as such only a repetition and commentary on the first commandment, the commandment to love God. This solution, too, is in its way simple and illuminating. It means that, ultimately and in fact, the life of the children of God can still be described in a single phrase. Fundamentally only the one thing has to be said of them, that they live in love to God and therefore in rendering obedience to the absolute commandment of the Father. Beside the fulness of this life, their life in love to the neighbour can have only the significance of a free sign. Now there can be no doubt that in view of all that we have said about love to God this third solution brings us nearer to the underlying truth than either of the other two. Yet it cannot be worked out in this form. For at the very outset we meet the difficulty that Holy Scripture does not treat the commandment to love the neighbour in such a way that when it is a question of the neighbour we are, as it were, at a lower stage of the divine commanding, on a field of secondary decisions, which merely follow or accompany love to God. It is the praise of God which breaks out in love to the neighbour. And in Holy Scripture the commandment to praise God rings out on at any rate the same note of central and absolutely decisive urgency as that of love to God. If we look at the texts with this in mind, we might even ask whether the first solution with its two absolute commandments is not preferable to this third with its contrasted absolute and relative commandments; or whether after all we will not have to come back to the doctrine of the identity of the two commandments.

In the text in Mark the two commandments are referred to as πρώτη EN113 and δευτέρα EN114. But there is no indication that this enumeration is meant to express a subordination of the second to the first. Indeed, we can only understand the statement in Mk. 12³¹: μείζων τούτων ἄλλη ἐντολὴ οὐκ ἔστιν EN115, if in it their parity over against all other [407] commandments is presupposed. And in Mt. 22³⁸f. we are told expressly that αὕτη ἐστὶν ἡ μεγάλη καὶ πρώτη ἐντολή. δευτέρα ὁμοία αὐτῇ ἀγαπήσεις τὸν πλησίον σου ὡς σεαυτόν EN116. And it then adds that "on these two commandments hang all the law and the prophets." Note further that "Love thy neighbour as thyself" appears in Mt. 19¹⁹ as Jesus' answer to the question: What must I do to inherit eternal life? this time as the conclusion and summary of a recapitulation of the commandments of the second table (and quite apart from the commandment to love God). In Jas. 2⁸ again "Love thy neighbour as thyself" is called "the royal law" quite apart from the commandment to love God, and in what follows it

---

EN113 first
EN114 second
EN115 there is no other commandment greater than these
EN116 This is the first great commandment. The second is like it: you shall love your neighbour as yourself

is equated with the "law of freedom" which in James undoubtedly embraces the totality of the divine Law. And we find the same in Paul: in 1 Thess. 4⁹ he calls Christians θεοδίδακτοι εἰς τὸ ἀγαπαν ἀλλήλους EN117. "The whole law is fulfilled in one word, even in this; Thou shalt love thy neighbour as thyself" (Gal. 5¹⁴), and in the same epistle: "Bear ye one another's burdens, and so fulfil the law of Christ" (Gal. 6²). And unequivocally in Rom. 13⁸ᶠ: "He that loveth another hath fulfilled the law." All the commandments of the second table are "summed up" (ἀνακεφαλαιοῦνται) in the saying: "Love worketh no ill to his neighbour. Therefore love is the fulfilling of the law," or according to Col. 3¹⁴ the σύνδεσμος τῆς τελειότητος EN118. We are also definitely told in Jn. 13³⁴ (cf. 15¹² ¹⁷): "A new commandment give I unto you, that ye also love one another." In addition and finally, there is a whole series of extremely emphatic pronouncements in 1 Jn. According to 1 Jn. 2⁸ᶠ, to live in light or in darkness is the same as to hate or to love one's brother. It is a lie for a man to think that he can love God and hate his brother, for a failure to love the brother that he has seen, proves that he cannot love the God whom he has not seen (4²⁰). In 3¹¹ "the message that ye have heard from the beginning is that we love one another." It is because we love the brethren, that we know that we have passed from death to life (3¹⁴). If we recognise love in the fact that He laid down His life for us, then "we ought to lay down our lives for the brethren" (3¹⁶, cf. 4¹¹). The commandment which God has given us is that we should believe in the name of His Son Jesus Christ and that we should love one another (3²³, cf. 4²¹). We may well ask whether the effect of all these passages as regards the life of the children of God is not to put love to God to some extent on the periphery as no more than a presupposition, making love to the neighbour the true and essential act of Christian decision? If the life of the children of God had been described in a phrase, would it not be love to the neighbour rather than love to God? Well, such a conclusion would be foolish. And it would be no less foolish to allow these considerations to force us back to the assumption of two absolute commandments or to the awkward doctrine of the identity of the two commandments. Yet on these grounds it is obviously impossible to assign to the commandment of love to one's neighbour a position which is in any way subordinate. If there can be no question of restricting the first commandment, obviously we have always to reckon with the fact that in its own way the second comes no less seriously or urgently or incisively than the first.

We must also ask the radical question whether it is even possible to conceive of a commandment of God which is subordinate, derived and relative? Is not the commandment of God always and whatever it says an absolute commandment? If we postulate two commandments of God, a primary one which demands love to Him, and a secondary which, comprising all sorts of individual injunctions, demands "only" love to the neighbour, does not this inevitably give rise to the idea that in the latter we do not have to do with the commandment and judgment and grace of God in the same sense, that we are [408] not bound to obey with all our heart, and all our soul ... that we have entered the sphere of free human interpretation and explanation of the Law, that basically it is not a matter of obedience, but of our own selection of what is most fitting according to the dictates of conscience and our view of the existing situation? Such an idea cannot be held in relation to any of the individual commandments of the so-called second table, or in fact to any commandment

---

EN117 taught by God to love one another
EN118 common bond of perfection

of God, which might be its occasion and actual content; how much less, therefore, to the summary of all individual commandments (as opposed to the
"great one" of love to God), as we have it before us in Holy Scripture in the
commandment to love one's neighbour! If Jesus calls this a "second" commandment. He is obviously pointing us to a way which is different from the
first and cannot be substituted for or confused with it; to a distinctive sphere or
meaning of the love which is commanded. But in the one case as in the other,
it is obviously a question of the love which is commanded, not in a weaker
sense, but in the emphatic sense of the first commandment. There is certainly
no question of conduct in which we can even partially excuse ourselves from
obedience and go our own way. According to Holy Scripture there is no freedom except as we are bound to the commandment of God. Obedience itself is
what Holy Scripture means by freedom. If, therefore, it speaks so clearly of a
"second" commandment, we must ask carefully how far we are commanded to
love in a second and different way, in a second sense or sphere. And we shall
have to insert quite definitely that without any reservation, distinction or diminution we are still dealing with the question of the commandment and of
obedience to it.

The connexion and the difference between the two commandments are
plain when we remember that the children of God, the Church, now live, as it
were, in the space between the resurrection and ascension of Jesus, and in the
time of the forbearance of God and their own watching and waiting. In effect
they live in two times and worlds. And in both of these their one undivided
existence is claimed absolutely by God, subjected to His command and
engaged to obedience. There can be no question of any other Lord but God
claiming our love, or of any other object but God wanting to be loved. But the
love of the children of God corresponds to their twofold existence in two times
and worlds. The resurrection and ascension of Jesus Christ have taken place.
On this basis they are already members and participants of the new world created by Him, by faith in the manifestation of the Son of God in and with the
human nature which He has adopted, in and with the flesh which He has
united to His deity and glorified by His power. Represented by Him, *peccatores
iusti*[EN119], in His person they are already assembled before the throne of God,
citizens of His everlasting kingdom, participators in eternal life. They are in
Christ; and it is in the totality of this their hidden being, which is none other
than their actual human and creaturely existence here and now, that in the
way described they are put under the commandment to love God, to seek after [409]
the One who has first sought and found them. But by virtue of the coming but
not yet visible lordship of Jesus Christ, in faith in His coming, comforting
themselves with the promise of the forgiveness of sins, given in the Word made
flesh for all flesh, they always stand in need of the comfort and warning of this
promise, because although the former time and world are past they still lie,

[EN119] righteous sinners

211

indeed are, behind them. They have to wait and watch for their Lord as *iusti peccatores*[EN120]. They have to serve Him in the relationships, connexions and orderings of a reality which has, of course, been overthrown and superseded by His resurrection, but not yet visibly abolished and replaced by His second coming, in the space between the times, where it doth not yet appear what they shall be. They "walk" in the light in face of darkness, and in this visible pilgrimage in all its hope and peril, which is simply the totality of their actual human and creaturely activity here and now, God has placed them under the commandment to love their neighbour. With this in mind we can try to bring out the elements of truth in the three rejected answers to the question of the relationship between the two commandments.

1. We are in fact (and this is the basic truth in the first solution) dealing with two different demands, both of which have to be regarded as in the same sense the commandments of God. They are both commandments of the one God. They are both concretely directed to His children living between and in the two times and worlds. They both claim them absolutely, and absolutely for God. And yet because of the twofoldness in which they exist before God and for God, they are not one but two commandments. The first one, the commandment to love God, is intended for the child of God in his completed existence in Jesus Christ as the heavenly Head of His earthly members. The second commandment, to love the neighbour, is intended for the child of God in his not yet completed walk and activity as an earthly member of this heavenly Head. It is the same God speaking to the same man. He speaks to him in two ways, because he exists in two ways. But because it is the same God who speaks and the same man who listens, in both cases an absolute obedience is demanded. Two absolute commandments? No, but two commandments of the one absolute Lord, so that they both have absolute significance for the same man as God has determined and without competing the one with the other.

2. In both commandments (and this is the basic truth in the second solution) we have to do with the one claim of the one God on the whole man. In both cases we are concerned with His revelation in Jesus Christ by the Holy Spirit, with the order of grace, in which His Church, His children, are placed. It is His revelation which underlies the twofold reality and aspect of human existence. It is by means of this revelation and in the light of it that there is the transition, the movement of the one time and world to the other, and therefore the twofoldness of the demand made upon man. In the revelation of God it is indeed a unique and absolute demand, just as the God who gives it and the man who receives it are one. But again, by positing and illuminating the twofoldness of our existence, the divine revelation underlies the fact that the demand is also a twofold demand, the unity of which can be believed but not perceived. To dissolve love to God into love to the neighbour, or love to the

[410]

[EN120] righteous sinners

neighbour into love to God, would be to deviate from the divine revelation, and to lose again the unity in which love to God and love to the neighbour are commanded. If we try to love God as the neighbour, it will not be the God whom we are commanded to love. And if we try to love the neighbour as God, it will not be the neighbour whom we are commanded to love. If we are not to deviate from the divine revelation, if we really want to obey the one commandment of God, we can only love God and our neighbour. The desire to experience the unity of these commandments, and corresponding speculation about that unity, must be suppressed for the sake of the true unity of the commandment and of obedience to it. The Word and the Spirit of God are the true unity which we seek. But to find this true unity we have to listen to the Word and the Spirit and therefore to listen to the twofold commandment of love in the divine revelation.

3. To the extent (and this is the basic truth in the third solution) that the commandment to love God refers us to our existence in the time and world which comes and remains, the commandment to love the neighbour in the time and world which now is and passes, we are in fact dealing with a first and a second commandment, a primary and a secondary, a superior and a subordinate, an eternal and a temporary. The two times and worlds are not symmetrical. They do not balance each other. The one prevails over the other. That which comes and remains has the priority and superiority over that which now is and passes. This is something which belongs to the nature and essence of both of them as they are posited and illuminated by the divine revelation. It is therefore quite right that in the text of Matthew the commandment to love God should be described not only as the first, but also as the "great" commandment. It is in fact the basic and comprehensive commandment, the greater circle which includes in itself the lesser commandment of love to the neighbour. Because of the time and world which comes and remains, by virtue of the shadow which it has thrown, by virtue of the light of divine forbearance which it has cast, our present time and world is that which, now is and passes. And therefore love to the neighbour is undoubtedly commanded for the sake of love to God and in and with the commandment to love God. Love to God is the real cause and expository principle of love to the neighbour. Love to the neighbour is in fact the token of love to God. To that extent, as something commanded in respect of our existence which now is and passes, by its very nature it can be the erecting of a sign, and not of a completed and eternal work. But we must be careful not to treat it arbitrarily. It is also right that the [411] second commandment should be put alongside the "first" and "great" with the express declaration that it is "like" it. If we do not want to deviate from revelation, we can never think of achieving the unity of the two commandments by identifying love to God and love to the neighbour. But on the same presupposition, we cannot express the priority and superiority of the first commandment, as though they were of our disposing, by ascribing to the second a lesser degree of divine seriousness and emphasis, by regarding and treating the

sphere designated by the second commandment as a sphere of free human reflection and decision side by side with the sphere of the divine predestination. No: the commandment of love to the neighbour is enclosed by that of love to God. It is contained in it. To that extent it is inferior to it. But for that very reason it shares its absoluteness. In and with it, it has all the seriousness and emphasis of the commandment of God, in face of which there is no room for arbitrariness, but only for unceasing responsibility. The sign of love to the neighbour is a sign which is demanded from us. It is not one which is left to our own arbitrary choice. For the time and world, as members of which this second demand addresses us, is the time of the judgment and patience of God. It is, therefore, no less the time of God than the time and world which comes and remains, as members of which we are summoned to love to God.

Now that we have purified the presuppositions in respect of the relationship between love to God and love to the neighbour, we can turn to the specific question: What is love to the neighbour? What does it mean when it says: "Thou shalt love thy neighbour as thyself?"

1. Here again our best plan is to go forward step by step. We will begin by considering what can be the force of the "thou shalt." According to the findings we have just made, there can be no doubt that in the full range of the concept it has the significance of the commandment and the claim of God regarding His children. In this case it applies to His children, so far as they are still members of the world which now is and passes, when it doth not yet appear what they shall be; but even so it is still the commandment and claim of God. It does not cease to be true that they should love Him with all their heart and all their soul ... that in their totality they are challenged by Him and for Him. But now the totality and absoluteness of the commandment acquires the concrete shape which corresponds to the world which now is and passes.

That is why Polan (*Synt. Theol. chr.*, 1609, p. 4187) gives as the main reason why we should love our neighbour *sedulo el libenter: quia a Deo nobis mandata est*[EN121].

[412] It is actually the case that in the midst of the world which now is and passes, they cannot cease to attest that God has found them. For they cannot exist without seeking Him as members of the eternal time and world, for which He has made them. The twofold determination of their existence, that they are members of both the coming and the passing world, cannot involve any limitation of the commandment and of obedience to it. On the contrary, it is because they are found, and therefore members of the coming world, that they are also members of the passing world. The second commandment, that they should love their neighbour, reminds them of the unity and therefore of the totality of their existence as the children of God. But if we think of love to the neighbour as in this sense based on love to God and therefore enclosed by it, here, too, we cannot understand the "thou shalt" apart from the promise:

[EN121] seriously and willingly: because it has been commanded us by God

"thou wilt." When it is a matter of the neighbour, it is a question of our walk and activity as those who love God, of the inevitable outward side of that which inwardly is love to God. If love to God is its content, the "thou shalt" simply shows to the children of God the future which is definitely before them: thou wilt be what thou must be as one who is loved by God; thou wilt seek the One who hath found thee. But this being the case, obviously the second commandment, if love to the neighbour is its content, can only show them the future which is before the one who hears the first command and is therefore to be addressed as one who loves God. The one who loves God, the second commandment tells us, will love his neighbour as himself. This is no less the Gospel than the first commandment. If not, if it does not presuppose the renewal of our being in Jesus Christ, if it does not come to us as those to whom it can come, how can it really be to us a law, how can it really claim us? Neither from the content nor the form of this commandment can we abstract Jesus Christ as the One who utters it any more than we can in the case of the first commandment. If those to whom the commandment comes only love God because they are first loved by Him, it is only on this presupposition that they will actually love their neighbour as themselves, and that the fact that they do so can be stated and understood.

Il est certain, que jamais nous n'aimerons nos prochains, sinon que nous ayons aimés Dieu auparavant: car la vraye charité procède de ceste source là[EN122] (Calvin, *Serm. on 1 Cor.* 10[15f.], *C.R.* 49, 668).

But on this presupposition it is a real fact, and it can be stated and understood, that the children of God will love their neighbour as themselves. We will take this first in its general significance: in their existence as members of the world which now is and passes, they cannot lose or surrender or suppress the characteristic that they are citizens of the world which comes and remains. It is provided that this citizenship should continue to be hidden so long as this world lasts, so long as they live this side the second coming and the bodily resurrection of the dead. For they are not Jesus Christ Himself, but the earthly [413] members of the earthly body of this their heavenly Head and Lord. The praise which Jesus Christ has offered to God in His resurrection and ascension, the Gospel of the forty days, is something which they His Church will not repeat. But they could not be what they are if their life did not stand under the constraint to declare and attest that unique and irrepeatable praise of God; under the presuppositions and conditions of this present passing world, and in the flesh which still clings to them. They are still in this world. They are still in the flesh. But in that they believe in the risen and exalted Jesus Christ, they are held and moved here in a very definite way by the commandment of God. The commandment constrains and compels them even in this world, but as citizens

---

[EN122] It is certain that we would never love our neighbours, unless we have loved God first: for true charity proceeds from that source

of the world which comes, to live by their faith and therefore to seek God in Jesus Christ. And the same commandment obviously constrains and compels them, as citizens of the world which comes, but in this present world, to live by their faith. From this standpoint it is simply the commandment to love their neighbour. It is not now a question of seeking the One without whom they cannot live. In that sense it is only the One in whom they believe who can be the object of their love. We cannot believe in our neighbour, nor are we required to do so in this second commandment. To confuse or confound the two demands, to be related to our fellow-man in such a way that we believe in him, that we give to him what we owe to God, is to make us incapable of fulfilling what we do owe to him. Yet we cannot seek the One in whom we believe and without whom we cannot live, we cannot love God, without this loving, as it were, manifesting itself, not as a second, repeated light of revelation, but as the light of our human and earthly witness to revelation, in the praise of God commensurate with us in our humanity within this world and time. This love is our answer to His loving. It is a loving with all our heart, all our soul .... It therefore puts us in a position of sheer thankfulness. And being put in that position in the totality of our existence, we cannot allow ourselves to understand and treat it, and with it our relation to God, as an affair of the heart, as the matter of a self-sealed inwardness. Nor as men living in the limitations of their humanity and under the presuppositions and conditions of this world, can we take refuge in the excuse that we are not Jesus Christ, and that we cannot praise God in some miraculous intervention like His resurrection and ascension. By the very fact that Jesus Christ is risen and ascended, we are compelled and constrained in our simple sphere, which has not to be confused with His, which is the very sphere in which we can and must be the children of God, to let our walk and activity be the walk and activity of those who are thankful. Not to do this, not to desire it, to hold back, is to deny the position in which we are put, to deny our love to God and therefore the fact that we are loved by Him, to deny in fact our very status as children. If we cannot do this, we cannot help but testify. By what we might again call a necessity of nature, in our very existence we become a sign and testimony.

[414]

It is obviously in this sense that in the Sermon on the Mount Jesus says to His disciples: "Ye are the light of the world," explaining that a city which is set on a hill cannot be hidden, and that there is no sense in a man trying to put a light under a bushel instead of on a lampstand (Mt. $5^{14f.}$).

Yet although this is something which we become ourselves, we have no arbitrary choice in the matter. It is God in His revelation who defines and ordains the testimony, when it is really the testimony of His own children, born again by the Word and Spirit. How can the praise which freely breaks forth from heart and soul and mind and strength be the praise which is well pleasing and acceptable to God, unless it takes place in strict obedience to His commandment? If we were left to ourselves in this matter, the most marvellous constraint and unconditional enthusiasm and ecstasy by which we might feel impelled could, of course, lead to unusual and even sensational eruptions and explosions, to all kinds of remarkable movements and evanescent developments—but with all our enterprises and achievements we would still be exposed to the corruption and transitoriness of this world and of our own old nature as determined by this world. There would certainly not be any real testimony to the resurrection and ascension of Jesus Christ, any serious and as such effective manifestation of our love to God. We must be quite clear that every expression of our love to God, however well intended, is inexorably exposed to the law of the corruption and transitoriness of this world and of our old nature, to the extent that it is only an expression of our own arbitrariness or is accompanied or followed by it. What comes from our own experiences and discoveries is most certainly not the praise which is well pleasing and acceptable to God. For it to be such, the order of divine revelation and the commandment of God must be established and revered. And this commandment is the commandment to love one's neighbour. It is this commandment with its "thou shalt" which once again, in this second dimension, shows us the future which is before us. This time it is our future in this world, our future in the time still left to us under the judgment and forbearance of God. But for us even this future is an assured one. More than that, it orders us and it is therefore ordered. That is the first general lesson of the second commandment side by side with the first.

2. But who and what is the "neighbour" of whom this commandment tells us that we should love him as ourselves? How does he come to be, as it were, the material of this sign and testimony of our thankfulness? The explanation that he has this role and significance because of some inherent value in himself as such, or in the relation to him as such, is one which we have already rejected. We have also rejected the cognate explanation that we are directed to our fellow-men because of the existence of certain original orders of human life in society. If we are to regard the commandment as a genuine commandment, [415] our best plan at first is not to give place to any explanation. To obey a command does not mean to be convinced by its import that it is good, and then to applaud it and, of course, actively to endorse it. If we first tried to reason out why we should love our neighbour, we would never love him at all. Do we even know why we should love God? All that we can say on this point is merely a later explanation of the fact that we should do so. To continue asking what is the import of the first commandment is necessarily to continue breaking it. In respect of the second commandment we shall have to try later to explain what it is all about that we are commanded specifically to love our neighbour. But the fact that it is commanded is a fact of revelation which is quite independent of this explanation and which claims primarily to be understood and evaluated as such. The true content of the two explanations remains, of course, and we can assume it at once: that in the neighbour set before us by the commandment we have to do (in a sense which has still to be defined more accurately)

with our fellow-man, whom we did not choose as such ourselves, but who is posited as such.

That is the meaning of the biblical terms πλησίον, ἕτερος, ἀδελφός [EN123], and the reciprocal genitive ἀλλήλων [EN124], all of which obviously try to describe both the proximity and the distinctiveness, and also the givenness, of the entity referred to, and invariably mean our fellow-man. But in quite a number of important passages express use is made of the vocable ἄνθρωπος [EN125]: Mt. 6^{14}, 7^{12}, 10$^{32f.}$; Lk. 5^{10}; Rom. 12$^{17f.}$; 2 Cor. 3^2; Col. 1^{28}, etc. There can, therefore, be no objection when Calvin on one occasion sums up the content of the commandment in this way: *Ubi ergo cognoscitur Deus, etiam colitur humanitas* [EN126] (*Comm. on Jer.* 22^{16}, *C.R.* 38, 388).

The fellow-man posited as such constitutes, as it were, the material, the opportunity for the necessary maintaining of our faith in the sphere of this world. It is in relation to him that our love to God is manifested.

In this connexion Calvin was quite ready to speak of a *probatio* [EN127] or *examen* [EN128] or *experimentum* [EN129] of our faith (e.g., *Comm. on Ps.* 15^2, *C.R.* 31, 144; *Sermon on Gal.* 5$^{4f.}$, *C.R.* 50, 680; *Comm. on Gal.* 5^{14}, *C.R.* 50, 251).

As those who love God we have to accept the fact that this is the only way in which we can maintain our faith. Therefore we do not need to try to find other and supposedly better and more impressive ways. To do so is only to deviate from the revelation and commandment of God. No matter who or what he is, the neighbour is our future, and indicates the order in which God wills to be praised by us. It will always be to Him and before Him and in relation and responsibility to Him that this praise of God can take place, if it is to be a praise which is well pleasing and acceptable to God. The same God who willed to love us, and wills to be loved by us, also wills that we should love this neighbour. He wills both in the same unsearchable compassion. To try to withdraw from His [416] compassionate will in relation to our neighbour is necessarily to renounce His mercy for ourselves. In this respect, too, He is unsearchable. But not more so than in respect of love to Himself. If it is a real miracle that we can love God, it is necessarily a real miracle that we can love our neighbour.

When we try to come to closer grips with the question, who or what is this neighbour, we must not be confused by the fact that loving our neighbour is described in Holy Scripture as serving, helping, doing good, sacrificing ourselves, in short as a payment of something which we owe, so that with corresponding frequency reference is made to his poverty and want and need of assistance and the like. It is not the fact that he is in need, and there is some-

---

[EN123] neighbour, other, brother
[EN124] one another
[EN125] man
[EN126] Therefore where God is known, there also humanity is nurtured
[EN127] proof
[EN128] test
[EN129] experiment

thing we can give him, which makes him the neighbour whom we should love.

In this respect we shall have to treat with some reserve the advice frequently given by Luther, that we must seek our neighbour within the orders of life and society in which we actually find ourselves: the husband in his wife, the children in their parents and brothers and sisters, the master in the servant, the inferior in the superior and *vice versa*, the national in the fellow-national and so on. This advice might easily lead to the idea that the neighbour is one to whom we have a definite duty, who has a claim upon us. Of course, he has: but we cannot possibly think of our neighbour as Holy Scripture does if we think of him from that standpoint as an embodiment of the Law, or rather of a Law separated and emptied of the Gospel. It is right that when the Old Testament speaks of the neighbour who is to be loved, the primary reference is to fellow-Israelites. But note that in the Old Testament the "people" is not primarily a national community of blood. The "neighbour" also includes the frequently mentioned and by no means unimportant "stranger that is within thy gates." And the nation itself and as such is primarily the people of God, the people of the covenant and the *cultus*[EN130]. Even in the Old Testament it is only secondarily that it is this within the framework of a closed, but never absolutely closed, national community of blood. The neighbour in the Old Testament sense is primarily the member of the covenant of Yahweh. In the light of the New Testament the secondary definition of neighbour cannot become primary (not even by extending it to all sorts of other orders of life and society). The neighbour cannot, therefore, be thought of as a kind of content of the mandate, claimed by human society in all its various forms. The mandate does, of course, exist, but it owes its dignity and validity to a form of the neighbour in which he does not face us as the representative of the mandate, or as an authority to which we owe obedience and service.

The primary and true form of the neighbour is that he faces us as the bearer and representative of the divine compassion. Where he is only Law, where he means confusion, accusation, the discovery of our wickedness and helplessness, wrath and judgment, we see him in a veiled form. And even if we cannot have him or see him in any other way, he could not meet us even in this veiled form, he could not seriously claim and judge us unless he were primarily and properly set before us in quite a different, as the instrument of that order which is so necessary and indispensable for us in this time and world, in which God wills to be praised by us for His goodness. That there is this instrument of the order is itself divine goodness which we ought to recognise and praise as [417] such before we ever ask about the claim to which it gives rise.

It is the context of the Lucan version of our text, the pericope of the Good Samaritan (Lk. 10[25–27]), which is calculated to help us most in this respect. What first strikes us in this account is that the twofold commandment of love is not introduced as a saying of Jesus, but as a saying of the lawyer (νομικός), who is trying to "tempt" Jesus. To his question: What shall I do to inherit eternal life? Jesus answered with a counter-question: "What is written in the law? How readest thou?" (v. 26). And it is by way of answer to this counter-question that the lawyer recites the twofold commandment (v. 27). Purposely in his mouth, the unit, of the two commandments seems to be more strongly emphasised, by omitting the distinction into a first and second, than is the case in Matthew and Mark, where the twofold commandment

---

EN130 cult

is introduced as a formulation of Jesus Himself. There is, therefore, in the third Evangelist an awareness of the fact that a twofold love is demanded of the one man who as the rest of the account makes clear is neither ready for nor capable of it. Of course, it is not by nature or of himself that the lawyer knows what he recites. He is in fact a doctor of the Law in Israel. Therefore outwardly and in appearance, by his very calling, he belongs to the community of Yahweh. In an important function he lives in the sphere and by the tradition of this community, claiming to be a member and in fact a prominent member of it, with a special claim to participate in the associated promises. The word of faith is nigh him, as it says in Rom. 10^8, in his mouth and in his heart. It is false exegesis to assume that he is necessarily guilty of subjective insincerity. But whatever his subjective sincerity, he betrays the fact that he does not really know the near word, the two commandments, which he can recite so faithfully. Jesus praised him for his good knowledge and faithful recitation: ὀρθῶς ἀπεκρίθης EN131. But he then challenges him to do the very thing which he knows and can express so well, and in that way (for this was his original question) to inherit eternal life. Why does he not go and do it? Why does he ask what he should do when he obviously knows so well? Indeed, why? The reason is evident, for he goes on to ask: "And who is my neighbour?" (v. 29). He had answered rightly, very rightly, in respect of love to God. But he does not ask: And who is God? That is something which he seems to know and thinks he knows. He asks only in regard to the unperspicuous latter part of the doctrine which he has so weightily advanced. He asks only in regard to a single concept in the second of the commandments advanced by him, the concept neighbour. It is only this concept which he wants clarified. But from the very fact that he can ask this question the physician Luke regards him as mortally ill. He thinks that the question reveals that this doctor of the Law does not actually know the second commandment at all, and therefore not the first. Luke does not, of course, express it in this way. He goes further back. He finds the real reason for the question in the fact that the man "wished to justify himself" (v. 29). The lawyer does not know that only by mercy can he live and inherit eternal life. He does not want to live by mercy. He does not even know what it is. He actually lives by something quite different from mercy, by his own intention and ability to present himself as a righteous man before God. Or he thinks that he can live in that way. He wished to justify himself. That this is the case is revealed by the question: And who is my neighbour? If a man does not know who his neighbour is, if he does not or will not know what mercy is, if he does not live by mercy, then obviously his intention and effort is to justify himself. But how can he understand the second commandment if this is his relation with his neighbour? And how can he understand the first apart from the second? Why does he not go on to ask: Who is God? what is loving? above all—the most obvious question in the light of what Jesus had just said: what is the "doing" which these commandments require? But, of course, if he had asked all the things which have to be asked he would have known the two commandments and stopped asking. But by asking "only" about his neighbour, he shows that he does not really know either of them, even though he can recite them: and that is why he wants to justify himself. The converse must also be stated: that because he wishes to justify himself, he does not really know the two commandments at all, although he can recite them. If he had no wish to justify himself, he would know the commandments in that case, and he would then know who is his neighbour, and everything else that has to be known at this point. Again, if he had known who is his neighbour, he would know the commandments, and would not wish to justify himself. Which is the first and basic element in his perversion? His self-righteousness, or his lack of knowledge of revelation? Who is to decide? The one certain thing is that in this man the two go hand in hand and confirm each other. So then, to the question: And who is my neighbour? and the background that "he wished to justify

[418]

EN131 You have answered correctly

himself," Jesus answers in the Lucan version (vv. 30–35) with the story or parable of the good Samaritan: the man who fell among thieves, who lay wounded and half-dead by the roadside, whom the priest and Levite saw and passed by on the other side, until at last the Samaritan appeared, who took charge of him without hesitation and with unsparing energy. What is the meaning of this story as an answer to the question? We might expect—and current exegesis of the text is in accordance with this obvious expectation—that Jesus would have said to the teacher of the Law: This Samaritan did not ask questions like you. He found his neighbour in the man that had fallen among thieves. He treated him accordingly. Go and do thou likewise. But the assumption on which (v. 37b) this final challenge is reached, according to the statements of the text, which in themselves are quite clear, although obstinately surrounded by traditional exposition, is really quite a different one. The question with which Jesus concludes the story is which then of the three (i.e., priest, Levite and Samaritan) proved to be a neighbour to the man who fell among thieves? And the teacher of the Law himself had to reply: "he that showed mercy on him," i.e., the Samaritan. This man as such, as the one who showed mercy, is the neighbour about whom the lawyer was asking. And that is the only point of the story, unequivocally stated by the text. For the lawyer, who wants to justify himself and therefore does not know who is his neighbour, is confronted not by the poor wounded man with his claim for help, but by the anything but poor Samaritan who makes no claim at all but is simply helpful. It is the Samaritan who embodies what he wanted to know. This is the neighbour he did not know. All very unexpected: for the lawyer had first to see that he himself is the man fallen among thieves and lying helpless by the wayside; then he has to note that the others who pass by, the priest and the Levite, the familiar representatives of the dealings of Israel with God, all one after the other do according to the saying of the text: "He saw him and passed by on the other side;" and third, and above all, he has to see that he must be found and treated with compassion by the Samaritan, the foreigner, whom he believes he should hate, as one who hates and is hated by God. He will then know who is his neighbour, and will not ask concerning him as though it were only a matter of the casual clarification of a concept. He will then know the second commandment, and consequently the first as well. He will then not wish to justify himself, but will simply love the neighbour, who shows him mercy. He will then love God, and loving God will inherit eternal life. But now the text takes a last surprising turn. In fact, the lawyer does not see his own helplessness. He does not see that the priest and the Levite bring him no help and the Samaritan does. He does not really know his neighbour. Therefore he does not know either the second commandment or the first, although he can recite them so well. Therefore he does not love, he does not do what he must do to inherit eternal life. What advice or help can be given to him? The section closes with the again quite unexpected challenge flung out at him by Jesus, v. [419] 37b: "Go and do thou likewise" (ὁμοίως). From what precedes, we might have thought that He would summon him to that threefold knowledge. But that is not the case. He is merely summoned to do what the Samaritan did. He is summoned to be the neighbour who must bring comfort, help, the Gospel to someone else. Once he is, he will no longer want or need to ask: And who is my neighbour? He who is merciful—at this point we can and should remember Mt. 5[7]—will receive mercy. We see and have a neighbour when we show mercy on him and he therefore owes us love. We see and have a neighbour when we are wholly the givers and he can only receive. We see and have him when he cannot repay us and especially when he is an enemy, someone who hates us and injures us and persecutes us (Mt. 5[43f.]). The Samaritan also receives: he receives from the man who fell among thieves, by giving to him. The fact that he becomes a good neighbour to him is merely a witness that he himself has found a compassionate neighbour in the man who is half-dead. And those who do likewise, as neighbours who exercise mercy—and who therefore themselves see and have a neighbour—really know both the second and the first commandments. They know them because they keep them. Their intention and attempt to try to justify themselves is smashed. They can only respond to the mercy which has met them. They can only love. They praise God. And in so doing they know what they must do to inherit eternal life. At this point we might ask whether and how it was possible to summon the lawyer—who obviously does not see or have a compassionate neighbour, who lacks all the necessary presuppositions—to go and do likewise and in that way to praise God. Well, it is Jesus Christ who gives the summons, and we cannot abstract Jesus Himself from the summons which He gives. On His lips the "Go and do thou likewise" is only Law because it is first Gospel. The good Samaritan, the neighbour who is a helper and will make him a helper, is not far from the lawyer. The primitive exegesis of the text was fundamentally right. He stands before him incarnate, although hidden under the form of one whom the lawyer believed he should hate, as the Jews hated the Samaritans. Jesus does not accuse the man, although judgment obviously hangs over him. Judgment is preceded by grace. Before this neighbour makes His claim He makes His offer. Go and do likewise means: Follow thou Me. There the story ends. We do not hear what becomes of the lawyer, whether he finally learns to know the Law in doing it or whether he only continues to recite it. But his question: Who is the neighbour, his neighbour? has been unmistakably answered.

In the biblical sense of the concept my neighbour is not each of my fellow-men as such. It is not, therefore, a matter of telling myself and realising that humanity as such consists of mere individuals, who are all my neighbours.

This is a point at which Calvin's exegesis is obviously wide of the mark. He thought that instead of telling him the parable, Jesus might just as well have said to the lawyer: *proximi nomen ad quemvis hominem promiscue extendi, quia totum humanum genus sancto quodam societatis vinculo coniunctum sit*[EN132]. As he sees it, "Love thy neighbour as thyself" can be *clarius*[EN133] (!) put in this way: *Dilige unumquemque hominem sicut te ipsum*[EN134]. For: *ut quis nobis sit propinquus, sufficit esse hominem, quia nostrum non est communem naturam delere*[EN135]. The contrasting of the priest and the Levite with the Samaritan signifies a *propinquitatem, quae nos ad mutua officia obligat, non restringi ad amicos vel consanguineos, sed patere ad totum humanum genus*[EN136]. And the attitude of the Samaritan *demonstrat natura duce et magistra, hominem hominis causa esse creatum: unde colligitur mutua inter omnes obligatio*[EN137] (*Comm. on Lk.* 10^{30}, *C.R.* 45, 613 f.). This is more a Stoic than a New Testament doctrine. It is not supported either by the text or by any other part of Holy Scripture. To prove it, Calvin had to do what so many other expositors have done and studiously overlook the fact that according to vv. 36–37a of this chapter it was not the three, let alone the whole *genus humanum*[EN138], but only the Samaritan who was neighbour to him that fell among thieves.

[420]

In the biblical sense of the concept my neighbour is not this or that man as such. Nor is he the member of this or that larger or smaller group, or of the

---

[EN132] the word 'neighbour' is to be extended indiscriminately to every person, since the whole human race is joined by a certain common bond of partnership

[EN133] more clearly

[EN134] Love each person as yourself

[EN135] It is enough, for someone to be a neighbour to us, that he be a man, since we must not eradicate our common nature

[EN136] close association, which obliges us to serve one another, not to be restricted to friends or kin, but to be open to the whole human race

[EN137] shows by the guidance and teaching of nature, that man has been created for the sake of man. From this the mutual obligation among all men is derived

[EN138] human race

group which comprises the whole of humanity. It is not therefore the case that the question: Who is my neighbour? really means: Is this or that individual one of my neighbours? On the contrary, my neighbour is an event which takes place in the existence of a definite man definitely marked off from all other men. My neighbour is my fellow-man acting towards me as a benefactor. Every fellow-man can act towards me in this way, not, of course, in virtue of the fact that he is a man or that he is this particular man, but in virtue of the fact that he can have the commission and authority to do so. But not every fellow-man does in fact act towards me in this way. Therefore not every man is my neighbour. My neighbour is the man who emerges from amongst all my fellow-men as this one thing in particular, my benefactor. I myself, of course, must be summoned by Jesus Christ, and I must be ready to obey the summons to go and do likewise, that is, to be myself a benefactor, if I am to experience as such the emergence of a fellow-man as my benefactor, and therefore to see and have him as my neighbour. Therefore I myself have a decisive part in the event by which a fellow-man is my neighbour. But when we say this, do we not simply say that the whole matter is that of an event?

What is the meaning and content of this event, and therefore of the benefit which comes to me through my neighbour? To begin with, we can only reply that it consists in this: that through my neighbour I am referred to the order in which I can and should offer to God, whom I love because He first loved me, the absolutely necessary praise which is meet and acceptable to Him. It is not at all self-evident that in the midst of the world which now is and passes the children of God are referred to this order and borne along by and concealed within it. It cannot be taken for granted that they really can here and now really praise God. In this present transitory world they might have had to manage without any such reference. Here and now they might have been left to themselves. And in that case, what they offered as praise of God would, as we have seen, be subject to all the corruption and transitoriness of this world and of their own former nature. And in that case and in those circumstances what would become of their faith, of their love to God, of their citizenship in heaven? Being lost here, would they not also be lost there? Could they and would they still believe and love and hope in this world and therefore belong to that world? No: they would "fall among thieves" and be left half-dead and helpless by the roadside. And in that need there would be no man to help [421] them; not even the representative of the Church, to the extent that he is only a man, as the parable so drastically shows with its assessment of the priest and the Levite. They would simply die. They would simply cease to be what they are. They can only be what they are as the children of God if in respect of their twofold existence they are surrounded and borne along by the mercy of God. In their existence in the world which comes and remains they are surrounded and borne along by virtue of the high priestly advocacy and intercession of Jesus Christ. But this advocacy and intercession of Jesus Christ has its counterpart in the world which now is and passes. There is a painstaking mercy of God which follows them even here, seeking for them the very best, even in respect of the praise of God which is so necessary to them and so inseparable from their love of God and their existence as the children of God. The bearer and representative of this temporal as well as eternal mercy of God is simply my neighbour, i.e., the fellow-man who emerges from amongst all others as my benefactor. To what extent my benefactor? To the extent that, in virtue of a special commission and authority here and now, he proclaims and shows forth Jesus Christ within this world, thus giving to my praise of God direction and character: the character and direction in virtue of which it is meet and acceptable to God, not arbitrary and subject to the corruption of everything which takes place in this world, but confirming and maintaining my love to God, enabling me even as I offer it really to live in this world really by faith. That is the Samaritan aid which my neighbour gives to me. That is the meaning and content of the event in which he is to me a neighbour and not merely a fellow-man. Of course, I have my own part. I have to go and do likewise. I myself have to be a neighbour and therefore a bearer and representative of that divine mercy in the world. I have to be a child of God. It is only then that this will come to me through the neighbour. But again that does not alter the fact that this thing has to come to me through my neighbour, In respect of the necessary offering of my praise of God, I am referred to the fact that I am not alone. It is in virtue of the presence of my neighbour that I stand under and in the order in which God receives the praise which is proper and acceptable to Him.

We ask further: To what extent has a fellow-man commission and authority to emerge in this way, and therefore to be in a position to act towards me as the bearer and representative of the mercy of God? Our first general and decisive answer is: To the extent that there is within the world a Church, created by the Word and Spirit of God to be the earthly body of the heavenly Head, Jesus Christ, the great sign of revelation in the time between the ascension and the second coming of Jesus. It is the Church which introduces the Good Samaritan. To understand this, we must first remember that the Church as such and [422] in itself is simply the work of the service which men render one another by mutually proclaiming and showing forth Jesus Christ. For the proper praise of God within this world the Church and this ministry are necessary. In the Church it is true that the Lord does not leave His own as orphans in this world, in this sphere of the judgment and the patience of God (Jn. 14[18]). In the Church He is with us alway even to the end of the world (Mt. 28[20]). He is this by means of the service which is offered in the Church. Who and what a neighbour is, we can best realise from those who founded the Church, the biblical prophets and apostles. What they do is the purest form of that work of divine mercy which is assumed by the children of God. They bear witness to Jesus Christ. In that way they order the praise of the children of God; they make it possible as a real praise of the real God. But the same thing happens wherever the Church is the Church. Where it has the form of the priest and Levite, that is, where this service is not offered, it is not the Church. In the Church we cannot wish to justify ourselves, we cannot try to live by self-will, but only by mercy. In the Church we flee to Jesus Christ proclaimed, that is, to our neighbour, who offers us the service of proclaiming Jesus Christ.

But although this general reply is decisive, it is not of itself enough. It is not enough for this reason. As the Bible sees it, service of the compassionate neighbour is certainly not restricted to the life of the Church in itself and as such. It is not restricted to those members of the Church who are already called and recognisable as such. It is not restricted to their specific action in this capacity. Humanity as a whole can take part in this service. The Samaritan in the parable shows us incontestably that even those who do not know that they are doing so, or what they are doing, can assume and exercise the function of a compassionate neighbour. The Church in fact does not exist only for itself, inwards. It does not exist only for those who are already consciously and visibly its adherents and members. The fact that there is a Church has also a significance outwards. Within world-history, humanity, it points to the fact of a calling, a limitation and determination, which applies both to the whole and to each individual within the whole. By virtue of the reconciliation effected in Jesus Christ the existence of the Church in the world has a representative significance. Even though the humanity around it does not belong to the Church we can no longer think of it as untouched by or not participating in the mission which in the Church man acquired and accepted for his fellow. The existence of the Church means that a summons is given to the humanity which is around it but does not belong to it. It means that a *character indelibilis*[EN139] is imparted to man as such. In this, although he may not be aware of the Church, although he may be indifferent or hostile to it, yet even as one who is outside and over against it, he still has a part in its existence in his own way. Not as though every man as such is my neighbour. Even within the Church it is only a promise that he is this, and that this service is done to man. The actuality of it is always an event. But because there is a Church every man does actually stand under the promise of this event. It is impossible to be absolutely outside the Church, to have absolutely no part in it. We will see why in a moment. Whatever a man makes or does not make of it, whether it means for him grace or judgment, whether he himself will sooner or later belong to the Church or not, every man is actually related to the Church by the fact that he exists with it in the space between the ascension and the parousia of Jesus Christ. To that extent he is actually involved in the calling to that service which is offered in its true and explicit form in the Church: the service of proclaiming Jesus Christ. It is in the light of this summons, of the fact that simply as he is, as a man, he can be a neighbour to me here and now at any moment, as the Samaritan was to the man half-dead by the roadside, it is in this light, and not in the light of the fact that he is an outsider, that I must regard him from within the Church. I

[423]

EN139 ineradicable distinguishing mark

could not believe in the Church if in it and by it I did not find hope even for man as such.

We could call this awareness of the destiny of man the Christian conception of humanity. It is distinguished from the Stoic in three ways. First, it is not based on the perception and assessment of a so-called "nature" of man. Second, in ascribing to man as such a *character indelibilis*[EN140] it does not mean statically a quality of his own. Third, it does not ascribe to him only—which is not enough—a so-called disposition or capacity which may perhaps be developed by instruction and education. It means actually and concretely his destiny, a historical differentiation of man and humanity, which consists in a mission and authorisation, and is fulfilled in an actual confrontation with the Church of Jesus Christ. It was in the light of this historical differentiation that in a particularly impressive way Paul (and, of course, all the mission of the primitive Church) considered the Gentiles, and the possibilities of order and culture amongst them, and the fact that in more than one connexion it can be claimed expressly that they render considerable services to the Church for which all thanks are due: not in the light of a significant and promising nature of man, not in the light of an education which is always due for future completion, but in the light of the actual and therefore significant and promising encounter of the Gentiles with the Church of Jesus Christ. The Church would not take itself seriously if confronting the world it did not regard it as a world already changed by this fact, if it did not find hope for man, not as such and before it has claimed him, but simply because it exists and will claim him. How can it ever cease to see him in advance in the light of "thou wilt," by which it lives itself? How can it rest towards him in a barren "thou shalt" and therefore "thou art not"? The Christian conception of humanity is, therefore, a very different one from the Stoic. But it is to be distinguished from it not by a lesser, but by a disproportionately much greater intensity and definition. What kind of power can and will that conception have which deals only with the "nature" of man and the still to be realised possibilities of education which must be weighed against it? Again and again it will be corroded by a very justifiable scepticism, not only in respect of human nature, but also in respect of all human education. It is only in the Church or from the Church that there has ever been a free, strong, truly open and confident expectation in regard to the natural man, a quiet and joyful hope that he will be my neighbour, a conception of humanity which is based on ultimate certainty.

[424]   How do we ever come to the point, either within or of necessity also without the Church, where we can count at all on the possibility of this fellow-man emerging to help, and therefore on the event of the neighbour, as described in the parable of the Samaritan? How can we ever trust that a man will be my neighbour like that? What is the real mission and authorisation in which he can? In answering this question we must keep strictly to what the biblical testimony to revelation has to say concerning it. Our fellow-man becomes to us the compassionate neighbour because he is seen in the reflection of the sign which gives to the great sign of the Church, in all its meaning for humanity generally, its origin, basis and stability, in the reflection of the human nature of Jesus Christ. In the resurrection and ascension of Jesus Christ there took place a glorification of suffering, crucified, dead and buried man in his unity with the person of the Son of God. And it was in that glorification, in the Gospel of the forty days, that the praise which is meet and acceptable to God became

---

[EN140] ineradicable distinguishing mark

event in its original and most proper form. Proclaiming Himself, Jesus Christ has rendered us the benefit of setting up the order of praise without which we would be lost in this world. It is really an order which is set up at this point, a destiny which is fulfilled. Because in this One human existence became once for all and uniquely a testimony to the fact that God has assumed it, there can and must be a praise of God by other men, even by those who are not Jesus Christ, even by those who, like all of us, have to move within the limitations of this present, passing world and their own former nature. This original order, this new destiny of man is operative in the existence of the prophets and apostles, by whom Jesus Christ is proclaimed, and of the Church, in which this proclamation is perpetuated. In this proclaiming we again have an event, in a secondary form: a glorification of man the sinner abandoned to death. Man himself now becomes a sign. He can and must show mercy. He can and must summon to a genuine praise of God, and in that way render to the children of God that necessary service. He can and must be my compassionate neighbour. He can and must and will, not by his own capacity and will, but because the Son of God has made Himself my neighbour in His incarnation and revealed Himself my neighbour in His resurrection. The service of the Church—where the Church really is the Church—rests on the fact that Jesus Christ won human brethren of this kind, that He has become a neighbour to individual men who can as such be good neighbours to us, because in them Jesus Christ is present to us, and in hearing them, we hear Him (Lk. 10^{16}). The Church means the service of testimony. But the Church and all that takes place in it exists only representatively for the world, just as it has its own life only representatively in its heavenly Head. It is not the churchman in particular, but man generally, every man, who in the Church comes into the light of the promise: "Ye shall be my witnesses" (Ac. 1^8). For that reason we must expect to find the witness of [425] Jesus Christ, and therefore our neighbour, not only in the Church, but, because in the Church, in every man. Not simply to find: if we are to find him, the event of divine beneficence has to be real. But to expect to find: for if in the prophets and apostles we see men to whom Jesus Christ has become a neighbour, and they themselves have become helpful and compassionate neighbours by bearing witness to Him, if it has become a general possibility in the Church that men can have this function, then we must obviously be prepared and ready for the fact that man, our fellow-man generally, can become our neighbour, even where we do not think we see anything of the Church, i.e., in his humanity he can remind us of the humanity of the Son of God and show mercy upon us by summoning us in that way to the praise of God.

We can expect this hidden neighbour, who stands outside the visible Church, just because there is a visible Church. We are obviously referred to him by at least some of the statements made in Scripture about the Gentiles. The Gentiles, with their worship of false gods, are the dark background before which the redemptive dealings of God with His people and Church take place. They are also the object of the Church's mission and proclamation. As those who are one day to be assembled on Mount Zion, they are the content of one of the prophecies of the last days. But in individual figures whom we must not overlook, they also have a present place in the redemptive history attested by the Bible. They are strangers, and yet as such adherents; strangers who as such have some very important and incisive things to say to the children of the household; strangers who from the most unexpected distances come right into the apparently closed circle of the divine election and calling and carry out a kind of commission, fulfil an office for which there is no name, but the content of which is quite obviously a service which they have to render. We can think of the Balaam, Num. 22–24, who is to curse Israel, but instead he must irresistibly bless. We can think of the harlot Rahab who, according to Josh. 2¹², "had mercy" on the Israelite spies, and who was therefore justified by her works according to Jas. 2²⁵, and saved by her faith according to Heb. 11³¹. We can think of the Moabitess Ruth and her loyalty to the humiliated Israelitess Naomi, a loyalty which has no less reward than that she is made the ancestress of David and given prominence as such in Mt. 1⁵. We can think of the co-operation of Hiram, King of Tyre, in the building of Solomon's temple (1 K. 5¹⁵ᶠ·). We can think of the sayings and gifts of the Queen of Sheba (1 K. 10¹ᶠ·). We can think of the Syrian captain Naaman (2 K. 5¹ᶠ·). We can think of the wonderful role which is ascribed to the Persian king Cyrus, not only in Deutero-Isaiah but also in the book of Ezra. And in the New Testament we can think of the wise men who come with their offering from the East (Mt. 2¹ᶠ·); of the centurion of Capernaum, who, according to Mt. 8¹⁰ᶠ, had such a faith as Jesus had not found in Israel, and led Him to speak of the many who shall come from the East, from the West and shall sit down with Abraham and Isaac and Jacob; of the Syro-Phoenician woman (Mk. 7²⁴ᶠ·); of the centurion at the cross with his messianic confession (Mk. 15³⁹); of the centurion Cornelius at Caesarea, in whose house Peter learns that "in every nation he that feareth him and worketh righteousness, is acceptable to him" (Ac. 10³⁵). That these biblical figures must be regarded as in any way the representatives of a general revelation is excluded by the context of all these passages. The most remarkable of them all is the Melchisedek, King of Salem, and a "priest of the most high God," who brings bread and wine to Abraham, and blesses him and receives from him a tithe (Gen. 14¹⁸ᶠ·). He

[426]   reappears in the royal Ps. 110⁴, again mysteriously as the representative of an otherwise unmentioned priestly order, by which even the Elect of Yahweh seems to be measured. According to Heb. 5⁶ᶠ, 6²⁰, 7¹ᶠ·, he is the type of Jesus Christ Himself and of His supreme and definitive high priesthood. It is therefore not merely legitimate but obligatory to regard the figure of Melchisedek as the hermeneutic key to this whole succession. It is not on the basis of a natural knowledge of God and a relationship with God that all these strangers play their striking role. What happens is rather that in them Jesus Christ proclaims Himself to be the great Samaritan: as it were, in a second and outer circle of His revelation, which by its very nature can only be hinted at. It must be noted that no independent significance can be ascribed to any of the revelations as we can call them in a wider sense. There is no Melchisedek apart from Abraham, just as there is no Abraham apart from Jesus Christ. They have no Word of God to preach. They are not witnesses of the resurrection. They have no full power to summon to the love of God. In this they differ permanently and fundamentally from the prophets and apostles, as does their function from that of the Church. Their witness is a confirmatory and not a basic witness. But granted that there are prophets and apostles, granted there is a people of God and a Church, granted that God is already loved, they have the authority and the power to summon those who love God to the praise of God which is meet and acceptable to Him. If we know the incarnation of the eternal Word and the glorification of humanity in Him, we cannot pass by any man, without being asked whether in his humanity he does not have this mission to us, he does not become to us this compassionate neighbour.

By virtue of this characterisation our fellow-man becomes to the children of

God a confirmatory witness to Jesus Christ. In Holy Scripture the characterisation is brought out by the use of the strong term brother. In the Old Testament it is used with neighbour to describe a member of the nation or covenant. In the New Testament, with one or two exceptions, it completely replaces the term neighbour. What the Church expresses and affirms when it makes this term the term for our fellow-man is the nearness of our neighbour, his indispensability, the, as it were, natural impossibility of leaving him, of trying to be the children of God alone and without him. But as the term which institutes the neighbour, in its biblical sense it can only be understood christologically, i.e., from the standpoint of the incarnation, the resurrection and ascension of Jesus Christ. The fatherhood of God and the sonship of man is originally and properly true in Jesus Christ. It is only true for us by transference, through Him. Similarly, brotherhood and brotherliness amongst men are not a requisite of their humanity, but a new creation of the revelation and reconciliation of God. Brotherhood arose amongst men because Jesus created it between Himself and individual men, by calling them into relationship with Himself, that nearness of brothers which cannot be destroyed or doubted but is absolutely necessary and indisputable; by allowing their humanity to enter into blood relationship with His; by giving them His Father to be their Father. It is that way, in Himself and not otherwise, that He made them brethren one to another. Any confirmation of their brotherliness one to another can consist only in the fact that each recognises in the other the original and proper brother Jesus Christ and is therefore summoned to the praise of God by him— [427] or in the strict sense—by Jesus Christ through him.

How little natural brotherhood is to be expected between us men, i.e., how little proclamation of it as a universal, ethical truth, is shown by the story of Cain and Abel, Gen. 4³⁶, of which there are warning reminders in Mt. 23³⁵ and 1 Jn. 3¹²ᶠ. The story also has the significance of a promise. According to Heb. 11⁴, by faith Abel offered a better sacrifice, by which, even though he is dead, he still speaks on behalf of the murderer. But this is because Abel and Cain were, brothers, as the sons of Adam and Eve. It is because of the new brotherhood based on the fact that his sacrifice is prophetic of Jesus Christ and His sacrifice. The first-born among many actual brethren, the true and proper brother is, therefore, Jesus Christ (Rom. 8²⁹). It is only in Him and through Him that there can and shall be others. They are ἀδελφοὶ ἐν Χριστῷ ᴱᴺ¹⁴¹ (Col. 1²), because He is not ashamed to call them brethren (Heb. 2¹¹) and as such to be equal to them in all things (Heb. 2¹⁷). He speaks of them as His brethren (Mk. 3³⁴, Mt. 28¹⁰, Jn. 20¹⁷). He it is who gives this name to their mutual relationship (Mt.23⁸, Lk. 22³²). They are brethren as "brethren beloved of God" (1 Thess. 1⁴); and the word ἀγαπητοί ᴱᴺ¹⁴² must always be understood in this sense.

It must be observed that this qualified description of the neighbour as a brother is not noticeably applied in Holy Scripture to any but those who have already recognised each other as companions in the faith, and members of the Church. This does not exclude, but includes the fact that in every man we have

---

ᴱᴺ¹⁴¹ brothers in Christ
ᴱᴺ¹⁴² beloved

to expect a brother (for that only means a neighbour in the full sense of the word). What man is there who might not one day meet us as a messenger of the Word of God, a witness to the resurrection? At this meeting we would, of course, be reverting to the qualified usage of the New Testament in calling him brother. If in his humanity he reminds me of the humanity of Christ, irrespective of whether or not he shares my faith in Christ, and summons me to the proper praise of God in that way, that in itself is not the encounter which justifies this name. But how can it help but point beyond itself to that encounter? We will have to return to this point when we come to speak of love to the neighbour.

And now, in the christological context, we can at last understand why not consistently but very often in Holy Scripture the neighbour is represented as a fellow-man in great suffering and therefore in need of help, a fellow-man whom we have to love by bringing the help which he needs. If we are to keep strictly to the biblical witness to revelation we cannot answer this question with a doctrine which is roughly as follows: That suffering fellow-man in need of help directs the children of God to the task which God has appointed for them. God does not will the many griefs and sufferings and burdens under which we men have to sigh. He wills their removal. He wills a better world. Therefore we, too, should will this better world, and a true worship of God consists in our co-operation in the removal of these sufferings. Therefore our neighbour in his distress is a reminder to us and the occasion and object of our proper worship of God.

[428]   This kind of ("religio-social") teaching overlooks too many things and arbitrarily introduces too many things for us to be able to accept it. That God does not will the evil under which we men have to suffer is true to the extent, but only to the extent, that as His revelation shows, He does not will its cause, the alienation of man from Himself, and the world as fashioned by this alienation, which as such is necessarily a world full of evil. On the contrary, in drawing man to Himself in Jesus Christ, He inaugurates a new world and causes it to break through. This work of reconciliation, in the consummation to which Jesus Christ pointed and which He is to fulfil, is the divine removing of the things under which we now see both ourselves and others suffer. We are not told that we have to co-operate in this removing as such. We are not told that we have to undertake the amelioration of the world in fulfilment of a divine programme of amelioration. We are not told that we shall find a neighbour in our fellow-man because his pitiable condition stirs us to do something along these lines. What we are told is that we should love our neighbour by proclaiming to him—not only in word, of course, but in deed—the true amelioration and therefore Jesus Christ.

Our neighbour in the sense of that doctrine of world-amelioration would again mean Law (instead of Gospel first and then as such Law). This is the very perversion which our previous discussion has shown to be untenable. Even our suffering fellow-man in need of help does not primarily confront us with a task. On the contrary, he has something to impart, to give, to present; the most important thing in life and the most indispensable. For revealed in that way he is to us primarily and decisively the compassionate neighbour. Only then and as such does he confront us with a task, and the task must be understood only from the standpoint that he has already been of benefit to us. And his benefaction to us as a suffering fellow-creature in need of help consists in the fact that even in his misery he shows us the true humanity of Jesus Christ, that humanity which was not triumphant but submissive, not healthy and strong, but characterised by the bearing of our sins, which was therefore flesh of our flesh—the flesh abandoned to punishment, suffering and death. Our fellow-man in his oppression, shame and torment confronts us with the poverty, the homelessness, the scars, the corpse, at the grave of Jesus Christ. The indigence and helplessness of our fellow-man need not be particularly crying. It need not always be what we, in our human way of thinking and speaking, call trouble and need. The plight of man does not begin or consist only in what we can see. It may just as well be hidden behind an aspect of soundness, strength and victory, as revealed in sickness, weakness and defeat. It is enough that it should be there, crying or merely complaining, openly revealed or hiding under the appearance of its opposite. If we tried rashly and self-confidently to find the straits and helplessness of our fellow-men in what we see, we might easily overlook his actual misery and not recognise in him our neighbour. We say his actual misery, for our fellow-man is actually in misery and he can be recognised as a neighbour only in his actual misery. It is not necessary that when we recognise him as such we should feel pity. We may feel surprise and awe at his human greatness, or terror at his fate, or horror at his nature or lack of it, or [429] resignation at his character and conduct, whatever they are. His actual misery consists in the fact that he wills, wills to live, and yet—with or without mask, openly or secretly, perhaps indeed without knowing it himself—he cannot, cannot live, and is therefore caught in an always hopeless and hopelessly repeated and varied attempt to do so. If I recognise him in this, if with whatever feelings I see this as his oppression, shame and torment, I recognise in him my neighbour. And it is in this actual misery of his that there consists his actual similarity to the crucified Christ. We repeat, his actual similarity, for it is there, quite independently of his belief or unbelief. It is there without his having to give any account of his attitude to Christ. He resembles Him, even though he is His enemy. For it is this actual misery of man, the curse of an attempt to live which is foredoomed to failure, that Christ has taken upon Himself and carried, in that He became man, in that the eternal Word became flesh. For the sake of this misery, in His faithful actualisation, He became poor and homeless, tormented, dead and buried. What Is. 53 says of the suffering Servant of God is true at any level of any man so far as it simply speaks of his suffering. In the reflection of the prophecy about Christ there is a reflection of my neighbour, if I have the grace to recognise him in my fellow-man. And in recognising my neighbour in my fellow-man, I am actually placed before Christ. We repeat—actually. It does not make any difference to the actuality whether or not we recognise in our fellow-man the poverty and homelessness, the scars, the sufferings and the grave of Christ. Indeed, we shall certainly not recognise Christ in him in the first instance.

In what Jesus says about the last judgment in Mt. 25¹ᶠ·, both those on the right hand and those on the left declare quite definitely that they did not know that they had or had not given Jesus to eat and drink and sheltered and clothed and visited Him. This must be a warning to us that it is not a question of seeing Jesus in our fellow-man. The text does not say that He is to be seen in these "least" as His brethren, but that He actually declares Himself to us in solidarity, indeed in identity with them. And of the recognition of this solidarity and identity it says that it is only transmitted later by the saying of Jesus the Judge both to those on the right hand and those on the left, and to the great surprise of both. Therefore the encounter with the neighbour and the decision in relation to him precede this recognition. For the significance of the encounter and decision consists in the content of this recognition, i.e., in the fact that Jesus actually encounters us in our neighbour, and that we decide for or against Him in making this decision in relation to our neighbour.

The afflicted fellow-man offers himself to us as such. And as such he is actually the representative of Jesus Christ. As such he is actually the bearer and representative of the divine compassion. As such he actually directs us to the right praise of God. For him to be and do this, we do not need to know anything about his mission, about the sacramental character of his existence. At first we will not be able to know anything about it. We need to take him simply [430] as what he actually is: as the neighbour who is near us *propinquissimus*EN143 in his misery. That is how the purpose is fulfilled which God has with him and for us. That is how we have to do with Jesus Christ Himself in this world, in the time of waiting and watching. For that reason we need to have to do only with our fellow-man. In a purely secular, profane and human way, this fellow-man confirms to the children of God the Word of God, by which they are begotten: the Word of their reconciliation by Him who although He knew no sin, was made to be sin. How can it be confirmed to them more powerfully and clearly than by their recognising in their fellow-man the afflicted one, the sinner, the one who is punished for his sin?

3. We go on to ask what is meant by "Thou shalt *love* thy neighbour." In view of all that we have said about "shalt" and "neighbour " we can only reply that in the sense of the second commandment to love means to enter into the future which God has posited for us in and with the existence of our neighbour. Therefore to love means to subject ourselves to the order instituted in the form of our neighbour. To love means to accept the benefit which God has shown by not leaving us alone but having given us the neighbour. To love means, therefore, to reconcile ourselves to the existence of the neighbour, to find ourselves in the fact that God wills us to exist as His children in this way and this alone: in co-existence with this neighbour, under the direction which we have to receive from him, in the limitation and determination which his existence actually means for ours, in the respecting and acceptance of the mission which he actually has in relation to us. Would we rather have it otherwise? Is there a kind of secret unwillingness in us, that this is how it is intended and ordained, that we are not really alone, that even in the world we are not

---

EN143 most nearly

left to ourselves, that necessarily, inescapably and indispensably we have to have the neighbour? In relation to what we have just said, there might well be a reason for this unwillingness. Our fellow-man reveals himself to us as a neighbour in the sense of the second commandment when he stands before us, and we know him, as a man who is actually wretched, when the futility and the powerlessness of his attempt to live is manifest to us. It is our fellow-man who is sinful and punished for his sin who is our neighbour. So long as that is not clear, the possibility of that unwillingness will not be any problem to us. Why should we not be on relatively quiet and comfortable terms with our fellow-man so long as we do not see his actual misery and are therefore in a position, either to rejoice and find strength in what we regard as his strength and health and victoriousness, or in his tragic greatness, in relation to what we regard as his plight and need of help, to use our own surplus energies to improve his position and in that way, in the enjoyment of the superior position which we thereby adopt, to do ourselves a real kindness and perhaps more? The fellow-man who is unaware of his actual plight, the fellow-man to whom we can look and about whom we can concern ourselves, above all the fellow-man who helps   [431] to confirm and enhance us in the role of benefactor, mentor and ameliorator: this fellow-man does not constitute any serious problem, and any headaches which he may incidentally cause will not be mortal. But this in the last resort not at all disconcerting fellow-man is not our neighbour in the sense of the second commandment. He is not the one who, sent and authorised by God, shows mercy upon us. He is lacking in the most important quality, in which alone he could do so, an actual similarity to the crucified Jesus Christ. At least, he is so in our eyes and in his relation to us. That is why he is not at all disconcerting. That is why we do not experience any serious unwillingness in relation to him. But that is also why he cannot help us seriously. This fellow-man will not summon us to the praise of God. Only afflicted, sinful fellow-man can do that. Only this man is my neighbour in the sense of the second commandment. But this neighbour will cause me a really mortal headache. I mean, he will seriously give me cause involuntarily to repudiate his existence and in that way to put myself in serious danger. In face of this neighbour I certainly have to admit to myself that I would really prefer to exist in some other way than in this co-existence. I would prefer this because from this neighbour a shadow falls inexorably and devastatingly upon myself. The wretched fellow-man beside me simply reveals to me in his existence my own misery. For can I see him in the futility and impotence of his attempt to live, without at once *mutatis mutandis*EN144 recognising myself? If I really see him, if as *propinquissimus*EN145 he is brought into such close contact with me that, unconfused by any intersecting feelings which may influence me, I can only see his misery, how can it

---

EN144 in different circumstances
EN145 most near

be otherwise? This is the criterion: if it is otherwise, if I can still see him without seeing myself, then for all the direct sympathy I may have for him, for all the zeal and sacrifice I may perhaps offer him, I have not really seen him. He remains at root that in no way disconcerting fellow-man. He is still not my neighbour. The neighbour shows me that I myself am a sinner. How can it be otherwise, seeing he stands in Christ's stead, seeing he must always remind me of Him as the Crucified? How can he help but show me, as the reflection of myself, what Christ has taken upon Himself for my sake? The divine mission and authority which the neighbour has in relation to me, the mercy which he shows me, is not to be separated from this revelation. But for that very reason it is a question whether I will accept this neighbour. The whole nature of the time and world for which the redemptive order of the second commandment is instituted and obtains is revealed in the fact that this question is put to us. The children of God themselves in this time and world are still afflicted men, sinners. They not only participate in the divine justification; they also stand in need of it. They stand in need of it just because they participate in it. No virtue,

[432] sanctity or beauty can permit them to live by anything else but grace and in any other way than in faith in the righteousness of Jesus Christ. What we have is a human life and activity which, apart from the light of grace which falls on it from above, is completely covered by the same darkness as that which lies over all the world which now is and passes. Here and now the children of God are caught in the futile and impotent attempt to live which constitutes the plight of man. As sinners, therefore, they must be helped, or there will be no help. And for that very reason in this present passing world they are helped by the afflicted neighbour, answering to the fact that in relation to the world which comes and abides they are helped only by the crucified Jesus Christ. But for that reason their neighbour always and necessarily means a question. If they are to be helped by him, he must touch them at the very point where they really are: in their status as members of this world, as children of Adam. The accommodating fellow-man with whom they come to terms without any unwillingness is in his very harmlessness no real bearer and representative of the divine compassion. He is not the surgeon's knife which, by bringing them pain, is here and now their true blessing. It is, therefore, quite natural for us to confess that we would rather not accept the service of our neighbour. When it is a question of the indispensable praise of God in the life of the children of God, it seems as though there is an attempt to repeat the crisis of our abandonment and our redemption by the revelation of God in Jesus Christ. As those who are already redeemed in faith, we may easily prefer to be left to ourselves, to praise God according to our own fancy and free choice, bringing forth, and offering of ourselves, in a splendid isolation with the invisible God, what we think to be the work of thankfulness appropriate to His glory. Have not the Word of God and the Holy Spirit, which as the children of God we think we have received, put us into a position to do this? In faith, are we not free and good and quite capable of doing it? And now it again proves to be the case that

everything is quite different. Even for the children of God, even for the pardoned, there is no freedom outside the divine order. God wills from them, from them particularly, not an arbitrary but an obedient praise. Their neighbour is put before them for that very reason, that their praise may be obedience. And their neighbour is the afflicted neighbour. But the afflicted neighbour reveals that they are themselves afflicted, are sinners, as he is. And the fact that they are, even as the children of God, is nowhere more clearly seen than in their unwillingness as the children of God to be revealed and recognised as such. It seems as though the age-old revolt of Adam, all the wickedness of idolatry and self-righteousness, is again trying to become an event. There is a new and we might almost say a more frightful danger: that even as those who are saved, we might still be lost. That is the surgeon's knife. That is how God's mercy comes to His children. That is how He holds and bears and guides them. The neighbour is indeed and necessarily a problem—not to their   [433] perdition but to their salvation. For we have to continue that their meeting with the neighbour cannot be an insoluble problem, a problem in face of which they are helpless, a danger to life. It comes to them from the God whose children they are, from whom they come, who has loved them, and whom they love in return. It is a matter of the terrible seriousness of confirmation. If they are not God's children at all, if their love to God is a lie, then the seriousness of this encounter is the mortal seriousness of non-confirmation. How, then, can it be otherwise than that the confirmation of the children of God is also accomplished in the shadow of this dark possibility? But however near to the brink of this abyss their way may actually lead them, we can no more expect a fulfilment of this possibility in the life of the children of God than that their love to God should cease. If they cannot cease to testify that God has found them, they cannot finally and ultimately want to withdraw from the order in which God wills to be praised, from the neighbour that He has appointed, however difficult it may be to find themselves in co-existence with him, and even though they might prefer a thousand times to have it otherwise. They will, therefore, accept the fact—and this is where love to the neighbour really begins—that as the man he is, and therefore as a sinful, afflicted fellow-man, he is what they themselves are, and holds up to them a mirror in which they would rather not look. In face of this mirror they naturally have the greatest desire to revolt as Adam did. And that fact is a confirmation how much the mirror is needed. It will compel them to trust again and this time absolutely in grace, and not to entertain any illusions about the fact that, without their new birth by the Word and Spirit of God, they would be lost like everyone else. For that reason they can only repeat what they know already, but never know too well. For that reason they can only thankfully confirm their existence as the children of God. There cannot actually be a new outbreak of the revolt of Adam. Forgiven sin can, of course, still continue in all its guilt and corruption, but it cannot again become sin unforgiven and triumphant. The crucified Jesus Christ does not contract out of the mediatorial position which He

235

adopted in His resurrection and ascension. He does not, therefore, contract out of that solidarity and identity with sinful and afflicted fellow-man, in which as neighbour He crosses the path of His own. If it is He who meets them as the neighbour, this meeting can again reveal to them all their peril, again remind them of the lostness from which they are redeemed—but it cannot lead them to a new catastrophe, a new lostness. The neighbour can be to them avenging Law only in the framework of the Gospel, only as the bearer and representative of the mercy of God, which always involves chastisement. Therefore the meeting with Him will be to their salvation. They will praise God, according to the will of God. They will therefore love their neighbour. And this will begin with the fact that, however unwillingly, they accept his existence: and indeed in the last resort, beyond all unwillingness, they accept it willingly.

[434]

In concrete terms, this will mean, negatively, that faced with the problem of the neighbour whom they must love they will not take refuge in any form of religiosity under the title of love to God. In his well-known and familiar way, A. Ritschl sponsored the statement that "love to God has no free play for action apart from love to the brethren" (*Unterricht i.d. chr. Religion*, 1875, § 6, note *a*). And unfortunately R. Bultmann repeated that "there is ... no obedience apart from the concrete situation in which I stand as a man among men, no obedience directed straight to God ... so I can love God only by willing what He wills, by really loving my neighbour" (*Jesus*, 1927, 106). But that cannot be true, since for the community no less than for the individual it would exclude not only the practice of meditation, contemplation and oblation, but in the last resort prayer as well and Sunday worship and Sunday itself as the Lord's Day. The relationship between love to God and love to the neighbour is not that love to the neighbour is the only possible form of love to God and as such, as it were, absorbs the latter, or makes it invisible. In fact, the two relationships in which the children of God exist, the one to the invisible God and the other to the visible brother, come together in certain concrete activities, which do not coincide completely and of which we must not deny the one in favour of the other. It is, of course, true that all the activity of the children of God in the world which now is and passes is subject to the law of obedience and therefore to the law of neighbourly love. This is no less true of prayer than of work, of Sunday than week-day, of the solitariness than the fellowship of our existence. There is, therefore, no action of which we cannot also be asked concerning its relation to the neighbour posited for us (just as there is nothing of which it is irrelevant to ask whether it takes place in love to God). There cannot, therefore, be any question of using love to God as a refuge from the problem of the neighbour whom we must love. Meditation, contemplation, even theological activity and the like, cannot be advanced as an excuse for failure towards our neighbour, or as a mitigation or evasion of the embarrassment which he causes us. This is impossible because we cannot do anything meaningful or serious in these other spheres without at once being reminded of what we are trying to escape. If we really can find refuge in a safe sphere of religiosity, devotional edification and theology, quite apart from the plight and task created by our neighbour, then this is only a sign that we cannot do anything serious or meaningful in this sphere, that it has already become for us a heathen temple which can only be destroyed. We come under the saying in Hos. 6[6]: "I will have mercy and not sacrifice," as expounded in Mt. 9[13], 12[7]. Not that we are called away from true sacrifice, from a genuine religiosity, devotional edification and theology—as is often rashly concluded—but we are called back from that heathen temple to a real obedience to the twofold commandment in its unity and therefore to true sacrifice. There may, of course, be an equally arbitrary and impossible flight from love to God to a wrongly understood love to the neighbour. The children of God

236

renounce all movements of flight. The life of the children of God is fulfilled in a rhythm of this twofold love, and there is nothing more senseless and impossible than to play off the one against the other. The children of God "abide" in love: and this applies to both, because they know that, once they have fled to God, there is no other place to which they can flee.

But that they accept the existence of the neighbour, and willingly so, can never be the last word on the subject. To accept my neighbour necessarily means to accept his service. As we have seen, if I really recognise him as my [435] neighbour, he serves me by showing me in his own person my sin and misery, and in that way the condescension of God and the humanity of Jesus Christ the Crucified. We had to lay all the emphasis upon the fact that this is the actual content of my meeting with the neighbour as such. Of course, Jesus Christ is always concealed in the neighbour. The neighbour is not a second revelation of Jesus Christ side by side with the first. When he meets me, the neighbour is not in any sense a second Christ. He is only my neighbour. And it is only as such and in his difference from Christ, only as a sign instituted by Christ, that we can speak of his solidarity and identity with Christ. Therefore once again to love the neighbour necessarily means that we actually allow him, just as he is, and as we see him, to do the service which he has to do us. But again that means that we allow him to call us to order, to remind us of our place. Our place is not that of those who boast of a possession and have therefore to substantiate a claim. It is only by forgiveness that the children are saved from the judgment of God. That they have received forgiveness is their new birth, the work of the divine Word and Spirit within them. That they ought to live by forgiveness is the new life which is given them with all the gifts of faith, knowledge, holiness, joy, humility and also love, which are included in this life. The neighbour cannot bring us to this place. How could he? If we are not forgiven, our neighbour has nothing at all to say to us when he exemplifies our sin and misery. Our meeting with him can only lead to another act in the great revolt of Adam. We certainly will not let him say what he has to say to us. We certainly will not love him for fear he might try to say it. But if we are forgiven, if we find it necessary to remain in this place, if we know how pressing is the temptation secretly to leave it for an apparently nobler one, if we see the precariousness of our existence as the children of God and know that it is not in our power to maintain ourselves in an existence which we have not even founded for ourselves, then we shall obviously be grateful for every factual reminder that this and this alone is our place, and for every barrier which prevents us from leaving it. And this factual reminder and barrier is the neighbour. The neighbour cannot forgive me my sin. But if my sin is forgiven, my neighbour can say to me that I need this forgiveness, that I cannot choose between a life of forgiveness and some other life which will perhaps illumine me better. The neighbour can keep me to the fact that a choice and decision has already been made concerning me in this respect. The neighbour can speak to me about my own confession of sin. He can ask me whether I am still resolved and ready to stand by it. He can ask me whether I am still resolved and ready actually to live as the one I have confessed before God to be. He can ask me whether my confession is a real confession, i.e., a decision which cannot be withdrawn. He asks me this as he holds before me that mirror. I will not let this question be put without resistance, but I will be grateful that it is put. I will say to myself that I cannot be questioned too much or too seriously and stringently on this matter. I so easily forget the thing I am questioned about. And if I really did forget it, it would mean the collapse of my existence as a child of God. I will therefore willingly and joyfully accept what the neighbour has to show me, because I am actually in need of it. Whether willingly and wittingly or not, in showing it, my neighbour acquires for me a sacramental significance. In this capacity he becomes and is a visible sign of invisible grace, a proof that I, too, am not left alone in this world, but am borne and directed by God. But this fact alone means that I am actually bound to this neighbour. He does me the service of reminding me of my place. He reveals my lostness, and in that way he tells me indirectly but quite definitely that I can only live by grace. And in so doing he comes right into my existence. His co-existence with me loses its external, incidental and unnecessary character. Because I exist, therefore, and in the same way, he exists. How can I help loving him when he does me this service? And we get exactly the same result from the particular content of his service. He tells me what I am and where I belong by what he himself is. He calls me to order by calling me into line, and in the first instance into line with himself. He tells me that I am such a one as himself. Therefore at any rate in personal relation to himself, he takes me right out of the private existence which I perhaps thought I could achieve for myself. He shows me that there is a fellowship of sin and misery: a place where it is concretely true between us men that we cannot accuse each other; that we cannot claim any advantages, any superiority or superior position; that we all have to proclaim our common bankruptcy.

This is not in itself the fellowship of grace and forgiveness. But when I see myself placed with a fellow-man in this fellowship, the fellowship of sin and misery, I can hardly help understanding it as at least a pointer to the fellowship of grace and forgiveness and so taking it quite seriously for that reason. The reality of the common need in which I see us both would be no less even if it were an open question whether it is matched by the reality of a common aid. The fact that I myself know the reality of a help in need cannot divide me from the man who does not seem to know it, who seems only to know his need, and even that not properly. If I know my own need and see another in the same need, that is enough to drive and bind and engage me to him. Because I know the help of God, I shall also know that the need in which God helps is the judgment of God. And under the judgment of God I shall not be separated from the other, but see myself bound to him, even if I do not know whether he knows with me the help of God. How can I help loving him when I see him placed with me under the judgment of God? This reality on which I have stumbled with him is it not of itself strong enough to create a strong fellowship between him and me? Certainly we cannot say that this fellowship has any

[436]

[437]

ultimate and real strength, any autonomous strength, if we consider it purely as such. Its true and abiding strength is only in the strength of the fellowship to which it points. Fellowship in sin and misery is not usually true and abiding as such, and therefore in the last analysis it is not usually strong, but where it is, it quickly and distinctly dissolves into its opposite. The judgment of God certainly places men in a common need. But considered purely as such it would necessarily tear them apart and set them against one another, thus increasing their need. And the fact that they are torn apart and set against one another, the totality of isolation and dissension, is far more characteristic of the world which stands under the judgment of God than is the solidarity of folly and wickedness, sorrow and anguish, which is not wanting in the picture, and in the promotion of which it is thought that not a little help can be found. The neighbour puts the child of God in all seriousness and without any reserve into this fellowship, the fellowship of sin and misery. When he sees himself put there, when he loves his neighbour even in this fellowship, the fellowship has already secretly ceased to be *only* this. If it is a child of God who loves, even in this fellowship of sin and misery love to the neighbour cannot possibly mean that he can be satisfied and content to be characterised by the other as "such a one himself," or to recognise in him "such an one as himself." But this result of his meeting with the neighbour will inevitably have the consequence that he knows himself to be summoned afresh to the love of God, the God who first loved him in his sin and his misery. The encounter has certainly done him the service of pointing him afresh to the grace of God by reminding him of his lostness. It will therefore cause him to seek anew the one without whom he can be nothing. But it was the neighbour who mediated this reminder. It was the neighbour who came into his life with this benefit. He cannot therefore make this movement of new love to the gracious God by himself. He cannot dispense with the neighbour. For him, the child of God, the dissolution of his private existence by the known solidarity of need cannot be reversed. He cannot forget the one with whom he has seen himself in the same condemnation. He cannot leave him to his own devices.

For the one who not only knows the need, but also the help in need, a very definite obligation to his neighbour arises out of the fellowship which he has with him in need. Note that only now, even from the standpoint of Law, can we speak meaningfully and seriously about the claim of our neighbour and our responsibility to him. His claim and our responsibility are a direct result of the fact that he has done us a service and benefit as a living sign of the grace of God. In relation to our neighbour, then, the road does not lead, as we are often told, from Law to Gospel—there is no road that way—but from Gospel to [438] Law. We shall, of course, have to speak very definitely of our neighbour as a sign of the Law, of his claim and our responsibility to him. There can be no question of our being content simply with the fact that we ourselves are summoned afresh to the love of God. If we are, then the meeting with the neighbour has not really taken place at all. We have not really participated in his service and benefit. A solidarity of need has not really been established between him and me. But if this has really taken place, if I have entered into an indestructible relationship with him, then the moment I draw the conclusion that I must love God afresh and this time truly, the bond between us will inevitably turn into a question: What is to become of him, the other? And now the fact that the fellowship of sin and of misery is not as such the fellowship of grace and forgiveness becomes a difficulty. I do not know whether the neighbour who has shown me my need with his need, and in that way has done me service, also knows about the help in need. If I did, if I could assume without more ado that I also stand with him in the fellowship of grace and forgiveness, I could leave him to himself without concern. He would have no claim on me, and I would have no responsibility to him. I would know in advance that without any effort on my part, he has the same comfort as I have and will therefore do as I do. I would know that he, too, is summoned afresh and this time truly to the love of God, and this knowledge would exclude any concern about him.

We might almost hazard the conjecture that the angels know each other in this fellowship which is ultimately and finally freed from the Law. They do not, therefore, have any concern for one another. For that reason they live and move before God in the truest possible unity. And before us too, in the coming world of eternal life, there is a similar relationship one to another, a relationship which is absolutely free and therefore indissoluble.

But it belongs to the conditions of the present, passing world, of which we are members even as the children of God, that here and now we do not know each other in this way. We cannot, therefore, achieve this unconcern. We know our own redemption in need only as we look to God in Jesus Christ, only as we listen to His Word, and not as we look to our own being and activity as such. And we know of ourselves that this looking and listening is always necessary. As the children of God we know that this looking and listening can never be left behind as unnecessary. It is always before us as something which we have to do afresh. The fact that in our need we look to God in Jesus Christ and listen to His Word and then love God afresh and this time truly, is something which, if it happens, we can only accept as grace. And that is how we stand here and now towards our neighbour, with the difference that while we can, of course, accept grace for ourselves, we cannot accept it for him. We can know that God loves him, and that His Word is for him. But we cannot know that in his need he [439] looks to God and listens to His Word and is comforted. We cannot know that we also stand with him in the fellowship of grace and forgiveness. Even the closest personal acquaintance will not allow us any unconcern in this respect. Even the strongest conjectures we have of him in respect of this fellowship will not reduce the definite assumption that he is always just as much in new need of this looking and listening as we are. And for that reason, I cannot discharge my duty to him simply by summoning him to love God with me.

It was Augustine who (e.g., *De doctr. chr.* I, 22; *De civ. Dei* X, 3, 2) deduced from the *diliges proximum sicut te ipsum*[EN146] that the *diligere*[EN147] must consist in moving the neighbour (*hoc cum lo debet agere ... ut ei quantum potest commendet ...* [EN148]) to love God. If we cannot make any use of the doctrine of self-love presupposed by Augustine, we can hardly give this content to love for our neighbour.

I myself do not love God either of my own volition or because someone has told me that I should do so. I myself cannot suppose that I shall find help in my need by loving God. If I love God in my need, I do so because I must. But I must do so, because God has already helped me in that need by His love. If it is not true of my neighbour that he loves God because he must love Him—and I cannot know whether this is true of him: I must therefore reckon with the fact that it might not be true of him—then the summons to love God might only mislead him. It would lead him to assume that I can do something that he cannot do, as though a child of God were a kind of technician, whose hands he has only to watch closely to become the same. It would be to him a law whose fulfilment could not take him any further than to a love of the most terrible gods and idols. It would awaken the false hope of having found a means to help himself in his need. I cannot, therefore, satisfy the claim which my neighbour has upon me by this summons. Any attempt to do so would be an attempt to evade the claim, a clear token that at bottom I have no real concern for him. By summoning him to do something which, as I well know, can only happen when something has already been done for him, I repudiate any responsibility for the latter being done. I break off fellowship with him at the decisive point of answering the question: how can he ever come to love God? how does it help him to say that he must love God, as I myself must love Him? And if I can break off fellowship with him at this point, how does it stand with myself? How little thankful I evidently am for the service and benefit which the neighbour has done me. How superficially I am related to him in the depth of need. And how dark is my own way before me. How doubtful is my own love to God if I dare to enforce it upon my neighbour as a demand to make it a law.

We must be very clear that much well-meant and even Christian concern for the neighbour is actually in this forbidden direction of Law. What we have and intend to offer to our neighbour in alleged fulfilment of our duty towards him is an open or concealed "thou shalt," a counter-claim which is made upon him. It need not be only a moral claim. Even as a religious and Christian claim it may still be Law: the belief that the other man ought to [440] believe, to examine himself, to be converted, to subject himself to God, and therefore to love God in his need. And when this belief does not find any or any adequate justification, how quickly it is followed by the conclusion that the other will not let himself be helped, or helped in the right way. We have not really begun to help him at all. We have probably not noticed at all that he wanted to help us and has helped us, and that all that we have to do is therefore to respond: to realise the fellowship which his service has created between himself and us. We are probably completely deceived about ourselves, thinking that we can help

---

[EN146] command to 'love your neighbour as yourself'
[EN147] loving
[EN148] he must do this in relation to him ... such that he commends to him as much as he is able ...

ourselves, in the way which we so confidently think we should commend to him. This commendation—of which we ourselves know very well that it does not work out in practice—can, in fact, only mean that we want to be rid of our neighbour, while apparently doing the best we can for him. Is it surprising, then, if so much apparent love to the neighbour does not attain its object in spite of all the enthusiasm put into it, but only meets with misconception, ingratitude and hostility? If it were genuine love, that could and would not happen. Genuine love would desist even in the smallest and minutest things from putting the neighbour under the Law.

If this way cannot be considered, that does not mean that I will seek refuge in the excuse that I am not God, and therefore that I am not in a position to let the grace of the Word and Spirit be imparted to my neighbour, and in that way to stir up in him the love to God which is irresistible where this help is a reality. Indeed, I am not God, but only a man. Indeed, I cannot help another with what alone deserves to be called help. But does that mean that I am discharged from my responsibility to that other? Discharged from responsibility that this real help should be imparted to him? Because I am only a man, have I to choose between "Am I my brother's keeper" and the way of the Law? On the contrary, there is another alternative—and it is this which I owe to my neighbour—not as a God I am not, but as the man I am—and which gives him the most definite claim upon me. But this alternative consists in the fact that I praise God, i.e., bear witness to my neighbour of the love with which God in Jesus Christ has loved me and him. To love the neighbour, therefore, is plainly and simply to be to him a witness of Jesus Christ. That the duty of love is the duty of witness results from the fact that I am summoned by my encounter with the neighbour to expect to find in him a brother of Jesus Christ and therefore my own brother. I do not know this. I cannot perceive it in my neighbour. All the more reason, therefore, why I should definitely believe it of him when he actually proclaims to me the grace of God, when he acts towards me as a servant of God, when he has acquired for me this sacramental significance. If he has reminded me that I live by forgiveness, how can I not be summoned to assume the same of him? How can I believe that he will have a different future from myself? How can I not think of him that as one who is loved by God he will love God in return? It is this faith in respect of him that I now have to live out. And the living out of this faith is the witness to which he has a claim and [441] which I owe him. It will be as well—just because it is a question of helping the neighbour—not to connect the concept of witness with the idea of an end or purpose. Witness in the Christian sense of the concept is the greeting with which, if and when I believe, I have to greet my neighbour, the declaration of my fellowship with one in whom I expect to find a brother of Jesus Christ and therefore my own brother. I do not will anything and I may not will anything in rendering this witness. I simply live the life of my faith in the concrete encounter with the neighbour. The strength of the Christian witness stands or falls with the fact that with all its urgency this restraint is peculiar to it. Neither to myself nor to anyone else can I contrive that help will actually be given in need.

Therefore in my testimony I cannot follow out the plan of trying to invade and alter the life of my neighbour. A witness is neither a guardian nor a teacher. A witness will not intrude on his neighbour. He will not "handle" him. He will not make him the object of his activity, even with the best intention. Witness can be given only when there is respect for the freedom of the grace of God, and therefore respect for the other man who can expect nothing from me but everything from God. It is in serious acknowledgment of his claim and our responsibility that we do not infringe this twofold respect. I only declare to the other that in relation to him I believe in Jesus Christ, that I do not therefore meet him as a stranger but as my brother, even though I do not know that he is. I do not withhold from him the praise which I owe to God. In that way I fulfil my responsibility to my neighbour.

Now there are three decisive forms of this witness. We cannot draw up any general order of precedence or define the relationship between them. We can only say that if I really love the other—without withdrawing from, but also without intruding on him—all three are equally complete and adequate in themselves and yet all three are equally indispensable. Therefore my love and witness are basically fulfilled in each of the three forms, but basically they must always assume all the three forms.

(*a*) The first form of witness is that I do not grudge my neighbour the word as a word of help in his and my need. If I have really been helped myself and I now find myself in the company of another in that fellowship of sin and misery, then I shall have something to say to him and must say something to him about the other side which this need has for me. I would not be the man I am, if I wanted to withhold this knowledge. The only word of real witness is indeed that which is a declaration of this knowledge. How uncertain we really are of this knowledge (even if we think we are ever so certain of it), we only experience perhaps at the moment when we know that we are summoned to such a word of real witness. If the heart were full of the knowledge of the grace of Jesus Christ, the mouth would speak out of itself. But if neither is the case, then there is a pressing temptation to avoid what ought to be said, and merely for the sake of saying something to talk of things which are irrelevant.   [442]

There are two ways especially in which we may fail to bear true witness. The first is by talking about our own sin and need as such. It cannot, of course, be contested that when we bear witness we have to speak about our sin and need, for if we have to speak about the hope of a fellowship in help we cannot omit to speak about a fellowship in need. But while we have to speak about this, the witness itself does not begin there. We have to speak about it, but it must not become too prominent, it must not become the main theme. When I speak about it, I am not really praising God. It is not in any way helpful to my neighbour, indeed it is nothing new, to tell him how bad I have been and to what extent I am just such an one as himself. The story of my misery which I can tell him will at best be an interesting story. And it is more than probable that as the narrator of the story I will indulge my vanity, and evoke a corresponding vanity in the other in relation to the story of his misery. I cannot, of course, suppress the knowledge of my misery. I ought not to suppress it. But so long as I dwell on it, I do not express the knowledge of my salvation. There is, therefore, no witness. The second way in which there is no true witness is when I talk about those experiences, states and events in my life, in which I apparently think that I can see an alleviation or even a removal of my need. Here, too, we must say: how can it be otherwise than that we should also speak of our experience of help in need, when we want to speak about the help itself? How can we suppress this note, or why should we? But even this note as such is not itself the note of that witness which we owe to the neighbour. What I give him with the story of my positive experiences will only be relatively new, because he himself may not be entirely devoid of such experiences in his own way. And if I still make an impression on him, it is more than likely that this impression will be a legal one, which will lead him into error instead of helping him. Thus, while I can and must say that I know from my own experience the help which I have to attest, this experience of mine must not be put in the centre, it must not be the autonomous theme of what I say, if my word is not to lose the character of true witness. Either way, the temptation is strong, because it has to do with elements of our knowledge about which we cannot and must not omit to speak. But it is also strong because we are never at a loss for words when we come to speak of our sin and our positive experiences. Either way, that is, we seem to have a rich and certain knowledge. How easy to confuse this knowledge of ourselves with the much less intimate and tangible knowledge of the help itself. How easy, therefore, to speak of these things in and with the witness which is required of us. All the more urgent the need to distinguish and separate. To that end, we

[443] must remember that if I am a genuine sinner and have a real experience of God's help, then that is true, and in its simple truth it will speak for itself, and it will have the power of a sign pointing to the help itself: just as another man may by the very fact of his existence be to me a sign of the grace of God. In the witness required of me, a right to speak cannot be denied to my knowledge of these two things. But this self-knowledge is not important in proportion to what I say about it, but in proportion to the fact that it *is* as I say, and is *seen* to be so, irrespective of what I say. But it *is* as I say, and is *seen* to be so, when knowing myself—and we may grant occasionally speaking about myself—I am not really concerned to speak at all about myself and my sin and my experiences as an independent theme, but only about the help itself and as such.

When it is a matter of bearing testimony, there can be only one theme and centre of what I say. And that is the indication of the name of Jesus Christ as the essence and existence of the loving kindness in which God has taken to Himself sinful man, in order that he should not be lost but saved by Him. This name, and in the strict sense only this name, the name of the Helper, is what we know about help in need, and therefore can and must speak. This name is the word which we do not grudge our neighbour, but with which we have to greet him as a future brother. Where there is genuine love for the neighbour this name cannot and must not be withheld. The only word which is praise of God and a witness to the neighbour is a word which is praise of Jesus Christ and witness about Him. Every word which is that is true praise of God and a true witness to the neighbour. Such a declaration of the name of Jesus Christ will be a full recognition of what Jesus Christ is and of what has been done by Him. It will be a critical word, unsettling, pointing away, excluding the claims of all other names in which we might seek refuge. It will always be a word of thankful adoration before the majesty of free grace revealed in this name. But necessarily it will also be a word of confession, i.e., a word in which our recognition of this name as the name of the Lord is irrevocably revealed. But it will depend upon and maintain that assertion of the name which the name has created for itself among men. That means that it will be a churchly word, i.e., a word proceeding from the Church and calling to the Church. And its churchly character will consist concretely in the fact that it is basically an expository word, the explaining and applying of Holy Scripture as the primal witness to Jesus Christ which underlies and sustains all the rest. It is when I speak a word like this to my neighbour that I fulfil my responsibility to him. I tell him what I know of the other side of my and, as I hope, his need. This other side of the need, if indeed there is this other side, i.e., if God is manifest to man, is simply Jesus Christ. That God should be manifest to the neighbour in his need, that his need should have this other side, is something which I cannot control or foresee. But God can make use of my service to make it true. I have to show [444] myself prepared and ready for this service by not refusing to the neighbour my word of witness. I refuse it if I am silent or if I speak of things which are irrelevant. In the latter case my words are just words: I do not love my neighbour in deed and in truth. If my witness is a witness to the name of Jesus Christ, it is not just a word, but as a word it is the most concrete act, in the strictly literal sense it is the "expression" of praise of God and love to the neighbour. That it is not in my power to give this work the efficacy by which it is to the neighbour the fulfilment of revelation, the imparting of the Word and Spirit of God, by which therefore his need takes on that other side—this limitation belongs to its very nature as witness. We cannot try to transcend the limitation without destroying its nature as witness. We have to respect the limitation, especially if we do not want to cease loving our neighbour. But within this limitation there can be no doubt that we not only say the right thing but in doing so do the right thing to our neighbour when, because we are really concerned about him, we speak to him freely about the name of Jesus Christ.

(*b*) The second form of the witness consists in the fact that I give assistance to my neighbour as a sign of the promised help of God. At this point we touch the sphere in which love to the neighbour or the active expression of that love is particularly or even exclusively to be sought, according to a widespread view. But there is no place here for an emphasising or exclusive emphasising of this sphere. Certainly there can be no question of my duty to speak to my neighbour being limited or replaced by my duty to assist him, as though this were a different duty. The question could only arise—and also the notion that the witness of deed only begins here—if I did not properly comply with my duty to speak to my neighbour. But in that case it would already be decided that I do not properly comply with my duty to assist my neighbour, and that even my supposed actions in this new sphere are not at all in order. In point of fact it is simply a question of another, if necessary, form of the same duty. The need of my fellow-man, the need of his impotent attempt to live, the revelation of which makes him my neighbour, expresses itself like my own need in specific sicknesses, derangements and confusions of his psycho-physical existence. It expresses itself in the fact that his attempt to live is foredoomed to failure and confronted with death. I cannot really arrest this process either in its inner necessity or in its manifestations. I cannot help my neighbour to the extent that I can as little save him from death as I can myself. It is in the helplessness, in which we confront ourselves, that there consists the fellowship of sin and misery into which I see myself placed by him and with him. And for that very reason I shall not speak to him of myself but of Jesus Christ: of Jesus Christ as the Helper who is the end of this process, of Jesus Christ as life in death and

[445] beyond death. But how can I speak my word of witness without substantiating it, making it my own word, by showing that I participate in the sicknesses, derangements and confusions of his psycho-physical existence: participate not only as a fellow-sufferer—the concept sympathy is inadequate, as many in the world have more truly found than many in the Church—but as one who knows where help is to be found: knows, because I have already been actually helped in Jesus Christ in respect of my own sufferings. I can as little help my neighbour as myself. But I cannot be helped, as I am helped, without being laid under an obligation to tell my neighbour what help there might be. The help will be alien (as compared with the sin and misery of his attempt to live in his own strength). It will be help from without, the help of a brother. But it is a help which he needs and can use, and that help does exist. I myself am not the alien, the one who comes from without, the brother who can really help him. Christ alone is this brother; I can be so only by His commission. But how can I have this commission? How can I speak to my neighbour about Jesus Christ, without also witnessing to this real and helpful brother by my attitude to the psycho-physical manifestation of his need? My word of witness is a lie if I do not substantiate it in such a way that my attitude is a declaring of the brother, Jesus Christ. If my attitude is not a confirmation of what I say, if in my existence I fall short, as it were, of my word, I speak but I do not believe, I do not actually affirm what I say. And what kind of praise of God is that? If I believe, if I affirm what I say, if I affirm Jesus Christ to be the real, helpful brother of my needy neighbour, then I must act towards this neighbour as a brother. Certainly as a brother only by commission. Certainly as a brother who is incapable of any help on his own account. But all the same a brother who is summoned to a definite action. This brotherliness, this action, can only be an indication. But because and in so far as I have to say this word to him, it is always an action, and

246

a brotherly action at that. To substantiate this word to the neighbour necessarily means that I assist him as one brother assists another, that my action is an action for him. The limit within which I can act for him is clear: I can do nothing for him, which as my doing is identical with the only truly helpful assistance which God gives in Jesus Christ. By my assistance, I can only set up a sign of that assistance. But even in this limited sense I can and should and must act for him. And for the neighbour the sign of this real assistance can be all that may show and remind him that the vital need, in which he cannot help himself and no other man can help him, has nevertheless a limit. We cannot set the limit to this need. But we—who ourselves know its limitation by Jesus Christ—can and must act in such a way that it becomes clear to the neighbour in his life that there is this Nevertheless, this limit. How can that become clear to him? Obviously because he is granted certain, even if only temporary and partial, reliefs and mitigations of his evident need, when a halt is called to that [446] need at some definite point and in some definite measure. And I can purposefully see that this happens, i.e., with a view to this result. If I do so, this is the assistance, the brotherly action, the action on his behalf which within the clear limit of my commission and capacity is required of me. If I fail to give him this assistance I make the word which I may perhaps try to speak to him a lie. And I cannot excuse myself by saying that I was required to do the impossible. If I give him this assistance, I still owe him the real help which he needs. I cannot therefore pride myself on my action. But within this obligation I have fulfilled my responsibility to this extent: I have set up a sign of real help. I have done what I am required to do, and what I actually can do, in terms of my obligation. The fact that I have done so, that my efforts in this direction have been accepted as the required setting up of a sign, I cannot, of course, ascribe to myself. It is grace, and as such I can only receive and believe it. And that I have done what I have done successfully, i.e., that the sign has really shown him what it is supposed to show him in his need, is not in my power, nor in the last resort is it in the sphere of my knowledge. In this respect, too, I can only be ready for service with my brotherliness, to be used by the true brother Jesus Christ as and when He wills. These are two further considerations which will keep us humble even in the most zealous and sincere activity for others. But they cannot destroy the clear necessity and possibility of that activity.

Supposing we take the most obvious and illuminating case of possible assistance which one man can give another in this sphere. By sacrificing himself he can save, the physical life of another. (This is the case which is, of course, emphasised in 1 Jn. 3[16], cf. Jn. 15[13], as a confirmation of love for the brother.) Can he really help him by doing this? No, he has not saved him from death; for sooner or later death will overtake the one who is saved. Can he give his act the character of a sign of real help in face of death? No, for even the purest intention which he may have in this expressive act cannot create for it this character if it does not have it already, whatever may be his intention. Can he give to this expressive act the effect that the one who is saved does, in fact, recognise the sign of real help in face of death, the witness to Jesus Christ which is given him by it? Again: No, he cannot do that. Many a person has been saved from death by another without receiving and accepting in that event the witness of the one who saves him. He cannot really make the one who is saved see what there is to see in the act. Even, then, in this simplest and clearest instance of one man assisting or acting for another there has to be at least a threefold divine miracle if witness is to be borne by the service of the one to the other and if that witness is to be real assistance. Even the one who saves life cannot escape humility: for what has he done, if this threefold miracle does not occur? But how can it be disputed that the saving of physical life, which the one can do for the other, can actually mean for this other a knowledge of the limit of his need, a redemption in the light of which he learns to believe in the redemption, a comfort which will not fail, when the death which has for the moment been averted comes? Why should we not be summoned, in specific instances, at least to offer our neighbour this prom-ising service? Why should we not trust in its efficacy, when it is plainly demanded of us in

[447] certain cases? We shall have to be clear that our action does not give us control of the decisive miracle. But we act rightly, and therefore with the promise that it will be a brotherly action, only when we count on the decisive miracle as a miracle of God. All this can be meaningfully applied to other less obvious and illuminating possibilities, when it is "only" a matter of helping the sick life of another to rather better health, of lightening a little the burden he has to carry, of comforting him a bit in his trouble, of bringing a bit of joy into his sadness, of helping him in one way or another in the fight with inward difficulty or the outward hindrances to which he is subject. "Only?" There are no quantitative distinctions here. Love can be small or non-existent in the greatest act for another, and it can be real and strong in the smallest. As we are told in 1 Cor. 13³, I may give all my goods to the poor and let my body be burned, without it being any use to me, because in spite of it all I have not love. But "whosoever shall give to drink unto one of these little ones a cup of cold water only, in the name of a disciple, verily I say unto you, he shall in no wise lose his reward" (Mt. 10⁴²). And "pure religion and undefiled before our God and Father is this, to visit the fatherless and widows in their affliction ... " (Jas. 1²⁷). Love to the neighbour is weighed, not meas-ured. We are nowhere dispensed either from the great thing, if it is a matter of the great, or from the small, if a matter of being faithful in that which is the least. Everything must be done by us at the right time and in the right place: everything with the clear knowledge that we are unable even to give the sign, let alone to make it effective, to bring the help which it attests; but everything with the even clearer knowledge that we are required to give the sign, and to give it in deed as well as in word, that from the one motive of real obedience we will be content with the promise; and that therefore as far as we understand and are able there must be this helping, lightening, comforting, and bringing of joy, and it is our task. If it does take place, and, quite apart from any claim, if we are in a position to cause it to happen, why should we not be confident to bear witness of Jesus Christ to our neighbour in this second form, the form of our little assistance, and therefore be obedient to the commandment to love him? It is unnecessary to say that both the obedience in which alone this can happen and the spontaneity in which alone we can obey are possible and actual only in faith.

(*c*) The third form of witness consists in this: that I substantiate to my neigh-bour by my attitude what I have to say to him by word and deed. Here again it is not a question of a third thing, which has to be added to a first and second. If it had still to be added, then the first two, even my word and deed, would not be the witness which I owe to my neighbour. Again there can be no witness by an attitude apart from the word and deed. The witness in question is that of an attitude in the word and deed, of the word and deed as they become event in a definite attitude. By attitude as opposed to word and deed we have to under-stand the disposition and mood in which I meet my neighbour, the impression of myself which I make on him in speaking to him and acting on his behalf. The only attitude which we can regard as consistent with witness is the evangelical attitude. If my words and acts are real witness to Jesus Christ, then in, with and under them there is an additional and decisive something of my own subjection to the lordship of Jesus Christ, of the comfort of forgiveness, by which I myself live, of the liberty of the children of God in which I myself move. It is additional, i.e., it too speaks to my neighbour in my words and deeds as such. It [448] is an atmosphere which touches and surrounds him. The neighbour hears my few words and enjoys my little assistance. But he also notices that I myself look and listen where my words and deeds seem to invite him to look and listen. What I have to say to him is perhaps in itself very clear and true, a very clear and firm indication of the one thing necessary. And at the same time my practical attitude is perhaps one which has in itself the whole nature and possibilities of sincere illuminating assistance. But supposing the picture which the other gains of me does not harmonise with these expressions in the sense of witness? Supposing with my person I say something quite other than with my word and deed? In speaking and acting, have I also considered that these two can only be witness to the extent that they are the witness of my person? Naturally my person cannot claim to replace to the other man the only convincing and helpful person of Jesus Christ. And it is not in my power even to be a witness of Jesus Christ with my person. And especially I have no power to make an impression by the witness of my person. But that does not alter the fact that I am summoned to give my neighbour the witness which is the witness of my person and attitude. And if this is not done, again there is no witness at all. It is no witness if the picture which I present in my words and deeds is in the last resort that of someone who is indifferent, who is busied with his own sufferings and joys, who is enmeshed in his own activity. Where, then, is the indication of the lordship of Jesus Christ? If this is the picture I present—and my most earnest words and sympathetic deeds will not of themselves prevent me offering it—how can I praise God and love my neighbour, when my attitude is ultimately heathen? It will be surprising if in these circumstances my sacrifice, however great, is either accepted by God or respected by men. Again, my witness is not witness if I come to the other in a movement which is strong and apparently quite selfless, yet not in the patience which sees him in the hand of God, but in an impatience which would take him into my own hand; not in faith in the forgiveness which is prepared for him by God, but in a false belief that I am the man who has to forgive him (which will certainly lead finally to a knowledge that I cannot forgive him); not in the hope on Christ, in which I can freely give to him, but in a false confidence in what I have to say to him and he has to be told by me, in what I have to do for him and he has to receive from me. If this is my attitude, then with the best will in the world the picture I present is not a sign of the reconciliation which took place in Jesus Christ, but only a sign of the law which is not the Law of Christ. It is not, therefore, witness to Christ. It is not the praise of God. It is not the love of my neighbour, however clear and true my word may be and however helpful in itself my action.

[449]   For sure, a consideration of this third form of the witness required of us again throws doubt on the whole possibility of loving our neighbour, by witnessing to him of Jesus Christ. To speak to our neighbour about Jesus Christ and to show him brotherly assistance both appear at first sight to be realisable possibilities. But what can I do to ensure that the picture which I offer in my person is evangelical and not heathen or legal? What can I do about the disposition and mood and atmosphere which I spread? "The redeemed must look redeemed." But can we do anything to make this so? Now it cannot be denied that at bottom this is not a question of things right outside the realm of human possibility and decision. If it is required of us that we should be ready for the service to which we are appointed not only in word and deed but also in attitude, too much is not required of us. The limits of our responsibility do not, of course, coincide with the limits of our consciousness of responsibility, to which we might perhaps appeal. Once our attention is drawn to it, there is much we can do in relation to our inward and outward attitude; not everything, but one thing at least and perhaps the most important thing of all. The redeemed can very well look a little like redeemed. But it is true that here in this question of attitude, more clearly than in that of word or deed, we are reminded that the task appointed us in this time and world, to praise God and love our neighbour, demands more than an isolated doing and not doing—it demands the whole life. Here more clearly—and that is why it is so important that especially this third question should be put—we are reminded that we, who should love our neighbour, are the same who should love God with all our heart, and soul, and mind, and strength. The question of our attitude, of the picture we present, of the impression we make, is not, of course, identical with the question of the totality of our obedience. What is required of us cannot really be reduced to the concepts of sentiment, mood, atmosphere, personality, etc. And we cannot understand the tasks of word and deed without it becoming plain that what is involved is the task of staking our existence, without which neither our word nor our deed can be a witness to Jesus Christ. Yet obviously with the question of our attitude we touch particularly upon the comprehensive question of our existence as such. If in this third sphere there are possibilities, freedom, decision, if we cannot deny that we may be just as conscious of our attitude as of our words and deeds, that we can speak about it and knowingly and willingly alter and amend it, then from this point more nearly than from that of our doing we look out and back to the presupposition of it in our existence before God. Of course, we can and must differentiate between our petty attitude, as well as our petty word and deed, and our existence before God: for the one is only our activity as the children of God in this present, passing world, whereas our being before God is our being in Jesus Christ and in membership of the age which comes and remains. But this differ-

entiation can be made only within the unity of our existence as the children of [450]
God. It is we who are involved either way. And the question of our attitude
reminds us of this identity in word and deed and to that extent of our existence before God. Who are we—we, who for the praise of God, for the love of
neighbour, are summoned to stake our existence in its totality? What is it that
we have to stake and offer? What is it that we can give our neighbour in word
and deed and ultimately and decisively in attitude? What if this giving is obviously not exhausted when we bear a witness which is apart from ourselves?
What if it is the case rather that we ourselves, the witnesses, must be the witness
in word and deed and attitude? Now we have already indicated that the reality,
the work and the effectiveness of our witness can never be in our own power
and disposal, but that if there is to be a real praise of God and love of our
neighbour in our activity, there has to take place an activity of God which we
with our activity can only serve, and which from the standpoint of our activity
can only have the character of a miracle. In a few concluding sentences we
must now try to clear up this relation between God and us, between His activity
and ours, in the service to which we are summoned by the commandment to
love our neighbour.

4. We will do this in our survey of the final part of the text of Mk. 12, which
so far we have not discussed. What does it mean when it says: "Thou shalt love
thy neighbour *as thyself.*" One explanation is that by these words, alongside the
commandments to love God and the neighbour, a third commandment is set
up, that of love to self, and that this love to self is the measure and principle of
love to the neighbour. But this explanation we have already rejected. It is true,
of course, that we do love ourselves. And in the second commandment—but
only here, notice—this is presupposed to be true. But we are not commanded
to love ourselves. And this self-love is not mentioned as though it were, so to
speak, the normal type and pattern of love to the neighbour. Self-love means,
and must mean, to be alone with ourselves, to seek ourselves, to serve ourselves, to think of ourselves. Now it is true that we do this. It is true that we do it
even when we love our neighbour. It is true that this self-love is the visible and
tangible reality of the one who loves his neighbour. The commandment itself
recognises and establishes it to be true. But the commandment: Thou shalt
love thy neighbour, is not a legitimation but a limitation of this reality. If I love
my neighbour, that is the judgment on my self-love and not its indirect justification. When I love my neighbour I do not apply to him the same good thing
as I do to myself when I love myself. Far from it. When I love my neighbour I
confess that my self-love is not a good thing, that it is not love at all. I begin to
love at all only when I love my neighbour. The only positive meaning of "as
thyself" is, then, that we are commanded to love our neighbour as those who
love themselves, i.e., as those who in reality do not love, as the sinners that we
are. It is as those who in fact and absolutely and constantly seek themselves and [451]
serve themselves and think of themselves, in this reality that we are addressed

and claimed by the revelation and commandment of God and therefore concretely by the commandment to love our neighbour. This reality of self-love and therefore of sin is the reality of the life of the children of God in this present, passing world and therefore in relation to this activity. We have already asked who are we who are summoned to love our neighbour? and what have we to stake and offer who have not only to bear witness but to be witnesses in word and deed and attitude? We are now given the answer—by the commandment itself—that we can stake and offer ourselves only as sinners. Even as we love our neighbour, it will always be true that we love ourselves, that there is, therefore, no love in us. Our existence is that of those who absolutely and constantly withdraw from love. That, and the fact that we stand under the judgment of the commandment, is the answer which we must give to the question which is made particularly urgent by the problem of our attitude.

Now we must not overlook the fact that even in this final turn the commandment is full of the Gospel. It stamps us as the people we are, and it claims us as such. And in so doing it tells us that we are not to give way to boasting, when we dare to meet our neighbour not only as partners of his need but as those who know of help in his and our need. We are not to take anything to ourselves which does not belong to us, when we dare to do this. The commandment itself states that we are sinners, that there is no love in us. The one who commands us accepts this, as it were, on his own responsibility. In this present passing world he wants us for obedience to his commandment. He wants us as the people we are, i.e., in and with our self-love and therefore our lack of love. The commandment passes judgment on us, but in so doing it does not exclude, but includes us. It seriously accepts us as the children of God, as those who know of help in need, as those who can acquire and execute a divine commission. It summons us to love as those who are without love. It gives us the status of witnesses. And in so doing it cuts us off from all those enervating reflections on the worthiness of our own words and deeds and attitude which might hold us back or call us away from the venture of obedience. It sets us completely free. We are already judged. Even as we are told to love it is decided that we love ourselves and are therefore without love. God knows our existence, and indeed better and more radically than we can ever do even with the most profound of our reflections. When we think about this venture of meeting our neighbour as witnesses—as witnesses of that which is greater than his and our need—all that we can do is to recall that which is told us by the divine commandment itself. No reflections of ours could put it better or more strongly or radically than this critical "as thyself." It is rather to be feared that [452] our reflections would end optimistically, which would poison our supposed obedience to the commandment at the very root, because we would then rely on ourselves rather than wholly and absolutely on the promise. Or else they would end pessimistically, and we would regard ourselves as dispensed from all further attempts to be obedient because too much is required of us in word and deed and attitude. The "as thyself" tells us that *a priori*^{EN149} our obedience is thought of only as the obedience of sinners, and in that way it cuts off both these false paths. For this annihilating "as thyself" invites us to put our trust simply in the fact that the commandment is given us. That we have the commandment is our true being, with which we can and should be satisfied, leaving it to God to decide what will come of our doing and fulfilling of the commandment in view of that other fact which is simultaneously revealed to us, that it is a being of sinners. We have no foreknowledge of it except in Jesus Christ. The justification of our activity, the acceptability of the little praise we offer to God, the truth of the love we give our neighbour, we really have to leave to God. That we can do so, that as we are commanded to love we are invited to cast upon God all our care in respect of the fulfilling of the commandment is again, in this context, the Gospel within the commandment. But if this is the case, it is unequivocally clear that the reality, the work and the effectiveness of our witness—if we do bear witness, if we are witnesses—are not at our own power and disposing. There is, in fact, a risk in which we have no assurance apart from our faith in Jesus Christ. Apart from our faith in Jesus Christ we simply have to accept that risk when we dare to meet the neighbour of whom we know only that he is in need, in the same need as ourselves, meet him in word and deed and attitude as those who have something to say, to show, to give to him, who can be something to him. For what can we be to him? We can only love him as ourselves, i.e., as those who love themselves and are therefore without love. We have in fact no guarantee—but the one—that all that we say and do and are to him will not betray our self-love and lack of love. Can we believe or hope that in a kindly illusion the other will not be aware of this? Ought we perhaps to try to support the illusion? Unfortunately there can be no doubt that very much so-called concern about the neighbour is at bottom only the concern to hide from each other the judgment under which we all stand. However wholesome and good may be our intentions, we do not really love our neighbour. Our words and deeds and attitude cannot in these circumstances be real witness. This hardly needs to be proved. We have only to subject ourselves to the judgment of God. We have to see that we can obey the commandment only as those who are judged by the commandment, that it is the Gospel within the commandment that we should obey as those who are judged by the commandment. When we do, we shall cease trying to hide from each other. There is nothing to hide: we can and should love our neighbour only as the people we are, and therefore "as ourselves." We cannot meet him in [453] a self-invented mask of love. We can only venture, as the men we are, to do what we are commanded in word and deed and attitude, relying entirely on the fact that the one who commands that we—who are without love—should love, will see to it that what we do will be real loving. There can be no question about it—this fidelity to the Gospel in the commandment belongs to our

---

^{EN149} at the outset

obedience to the commandment as such—we have to rely on the miracle, the free grace of God, to make good what we with our own foresight can only bungle. We have to trust in the fact that Jesus Christ will be present in this meeting with my neighbour. It will be His business, not mine, and however badly I play my part, He will conduct His business successfully and well. We have to rely on the fact that it is Jesus Christ who has given me a part in His business; that He has not done so in vain; that He will make use of my service, and in that way make it real service, even though I do not see how my service can be real service. We have to rely on the fact that Jesus Christ is the Lord, in whose hand the other is the neighbour; that He became man and died for him; that my lack of love cannot and will not prevent Him calling the other to Him by me. These are not guarantees. They can only be an assurance. But this assurance is required of us when we are commanded: Thou shalt love thy neighbour as thyself. It is only in this assurance that obedience is possible. We can define it in two ways.

(*a*) The courage with which in obedience to the commandment, without foresight, indeed against all foresight, a man turns to his neighbour to fulfil the commandment by what he does, to be to him a witness in word and deed and attitude—this courage can only be the courage of humility, in which he puts himself at the disposal of the ministry and mission and commission of the Church. The commission to testify is in fact the commission of the Church. And the promise of this commission—the presence of Jesus Christ, His control in the midst of man's perversity, the power of the forgiveness of sin which He pronounces, the power of an action in His name—this promise is the promise which is given to the Church. In holy baptism I am placed by the Church under the promise of the Holy Ghost. I am instructed and comforted and led by the Church. In the Lord's Supper I am nourished by the Church on the true body and blood of Christ to eternal life. And it is in this sacramental positing and ordering of my existence that I lay hold of that assurance and put it into action. It is as I accept this sacramental determination of my existence in all its concreteness that I have the concrete courage for that assurance, and therefore for the obedience whose result I cannot foresee, and therefore for the love of my neighbour. We know, in fact, that the life of the children of God is simply the life of the Church of God.

(*b*) To lay hold of that assurance and to put it into action means calling upon [454] God in prayer. The promise given to the Church has still to be received again and again by each of its members. The Church with its commission and promise lives in its sinful members. And as the Church for its own sake cannot wish to crowd out and replace the Lord and the free grace in which He speaks individually to each individual, again for its own sake it cannot take away from the individual the calling on this Lord, the direct appeal to His free grace. Prayer is the subjective determination of the assurance in which we can love our neighbour, just as the Church and baptism and the Supper are its objective determination. Praying is the decisive thing, which makes this assurance possible for us: the casting of our care upon God: our care about ourselves—how it is with our loving; and our care about the other—whether our love will reach him. In the last resort we can only love the neighbour by praying for ourselves and for him: for ourselves, that we may love him rightly, and for him, that he may let himself be loved; which means that either way prayer can have only one content and purpose: that according to His promise Jesus Christ may let His work be done for and to ourselves and to our neighbour. Praying, asking of God, can consist only in receiving what God has already prepared for us, before and apart from our stretching out our hands for it. It is in this praise of God that the children of God live, who love God, because He first loved them.

INDEX OF SCRIPTURE REFERENCES

INDEX OF SUBJECTS

predestination 185
pre-Lapsarian religion 89
pride 59
primal knowledge 91
primal revelation 110
prophets
  New Testament contrast of 5–6
  Old Testament existence and activity
    of 25
Protestantism
  Christian 146
  Japanese 145–6
  Modernist 26, 27
  Neo- 6, 52, 90, 94, 95, 170
  real catastrophe of 97
Protestant orthodoxy 52
Pyrrhic victories 140

Radicals 52
rationalism 38, 93
reconciliation 113, 162, 229
  contradiction related to 70
redemption 5, 29, 46, 54, 66, 83,
    136, 144, 145, 169, 190, 204, 234,
    240, 248
  eternal 113, 168
Reformation 6, 30, 51–4, 140
regeneration 21, 143, 171
religion *see also* true religion
  Church as 81–2
  Church as contradiction to 105–27
  Church coordinated with 97
  condition of 119
  conflict of different 101
  as creature of grace 128, 142
  death of one leading to victory of
    another 125–6
  divine revelation on same level as
    human 98
  false 89
  God hidden in human 83
  God present in human 100
  human 82–4
  as idolatry 113–17
  illegal 135
  judgement in 128
  mysticism relating to 121–7
  natural 91, 92, 93
  nature of 100–1
  non-necessity of 119–21
  as outpouring of Holy Spirit 147

as possession of man 118
real crisis of 126–7
revelation as contradiction of 105–27
revelation of God as abolition of 81–163
as right worship of God 87
science of 98
as self-contradictory 117
theology in 81–100
true 87–101, 127–63
as unbelief 100–27, 128
weakness of all 119–21
religionism 94, 98, 100, 101
religious poetry 54–5
renunciation 45
repression 138
resurrection 71, 216
revelation *see also* signs
  acknowledgement of 34
  believing 98–9
  contradicting human religion 105–27
  development of God and 11–12
  as event reaching man 2
  expectations of 98
  faith activity corresponding to 104
  freedom of man to reach God's 47–57
  of God as abolition of religion 81–163
  God coming to us as truth of 104
  God's humanity conditioned by grace
    of 167
  grace and 110–27, 167
  Holy Spirit as subjective possibility
    of 42–127
  Holy Spirit as subjective reality of 1–43
  human beings receiving God's 7–11, 33
  Jesus Christ as objective reality of 39
  leap of thought of 33–4
  from man's side 35
  miracle of 69
  objective side of 30, 35–9, 45, 47–8
  primal 110
  reality of 3, 36
  as religion 81–2
  religion as contradiction of 105–27
  religion coordinated with 97
  sign-giving attesting to 26
  significance of Church 9–11
  signs of objective reality of 22–38
  subjective reality of 2, 20, 35–9
  theology based on 81–100
  true 93
  of Western Church 50

INDEX OF NAMES